The
Permanent
Government

The Permanent Government

Who Really Rules New York?

Jack Newfield
and
Paul Du Brul

The Pilgrim Press
New York

Library of Congress Cataloging in Publication Data

Newfield, Jack.
  The permanent government.

  Published in 1978 under title: The abuse of power.
  Includes index.
  1. New York (N.Y.)—Politics and government—
1951-
2. Finance, Public—New York (N.Y.)
3. Municipal services—New York (N.Y.)
I. Du Brul, Paul.   II. Title.
JS1230 1981.N48   320.8'09747'1   81-10572
ISBN 0-8298-0466-8 (pbk.)   AACR2

Grateful acknowledgment is made to the following for permission to reprint:

Fortune Magazine: From an article by Wyndham Robertson, August 1975, and from an article by Sanford Rose, December 1975.

David Muchnick: From his article that appeared in the Winter 1976 issue of *Dissent*.

The Village Voice: From an article by Adam Walinsky, March 1, 1973. Copyright © The Village Voice, Inc., 1973. Reprinted by permission.

The Wall Street Journal: From "New York City's Fiscal Ills . . . ," October 21, 1970. Copyright © Dow Jones & Company, Inc., 1970. All rights reserved. Reprinted by permission.

Second printing, October 1983

The Pilgrim Press, 132 West 31 Street, New York, New York 10001

For Janie, Sascha and Rebecca

Contents

Authors' Note

We began work on this book in February 1973. In the course of research and writing, we interviewed more than 250 people. We have also relied on our own personal experiences for anecdotes and observations.

This book was written as an act of gratitude and loyalty to New York City by two native sons. The only bias we admit to is a love for this city, and particularly for its neighborhoods. We were born here. We grew up in working-class families in neighborhoods called Bedford Stuyvesant and Elmhurst. The only reason we both have college educations is that the City University was free in 1956. We come from a tradition that believes in paying your debts. Our way of repaying New York City for our free college education is to try and tell the truth about what is happening now to our city.

This book was born, eight years ago, in our mutual recognition that something was profoundly wrong with New York and that the condition was worsening, despite decades of talk about "reform." The knowledge and the anger in these pages were nourished by day-to-day involvement with the city's small agonies. Welfare mothers with lead-poisoned children. Working-class Polish and Italian families losing their homes of a lifetime for someone else's profit. The unspeakable suffering, and the unspeakable corruption, in the nursing-home industry. People who have responded to arson by landlords with sweat equity projects that restore burnt-out tenements.

These are the people for whom we wrote this book, although many of them will perhaps never read it. We hope, though, that by describing the reality, by naming the names, and by proposing some remedies, we are offering a tool for others to use in liberating New York City in the future. This is the repayment of our debt.

JACK NEWFIELD
PAUL A. DU BRUL

Acknowledgments

We wish to thank: Nicholas Pileggi, for letting us pick his brains and use his files; Alexander Cockburn, for his economic insights and for finding us the perfect quotation from Marx; Pete Hamill, for being so generous with his ideas and so infectious with his passion for New York; Ron Shiffman, for sharing his planning and housing expertise with us; Jack Bigel, for giving us access to his storeroom of data and charts even though he disagreed with us most of the time; Wayne Barrett, for getting us the day-care leases and other documents; and Robert Caro, for the debt we owe to his book *The Power Broker*.

Introduction

Representative government in New York City, as Jack Newfield and Paul Du Brul demonstrate, has been turned upside down. The perpetrators are the ones represented by the City's politicians, not the victims—because the perpetrators are the selectors and electors of those figureheads. The few exceptions who are elected with their convictions about democratic process intact soon become overwhelmed or co-opted because they lack an organized constituency of citizens whose interests more nearly approximate the public interest.

At bottom, this is a book about urban oligarchy. The permanent government of banks, insurance companies, public authorities, lawyers, realtors, and associated power brokers is skimming off the substantial cream from an urban area lurching from crises to worsening crises. The crises, not their causes, then become the focus of attention. Politicians do not anymore campaign against the misuse of power but choose to display concern over the multiple crises without explaining how they came to be. This book does not deviate from its root analysis of who makes the decisions for New York and who reaps the profits. The authors introduce you to the rulers of New York who escape the civics books and the educated notice of the City's schools and colleges. And, by escaping as a subject for study by New York City's students, generations of young New Yorkers continue to be governed by anonymous private men working through depersonalized forces ensconced in tall buildings and plush offices. The schools, the courts and the media—the three sectors that could nourish accountability for the powerholders—have been inadequate to the challenge and, for the most part, very seriously so. The authors document this abdication in enormous detail.

Can the resurgence of democratic power come from anywhere other than the victimized populace itself? The rebuilding of New York City and other urban centers can only originate with the dispossessed, those without power or property. Such groups are large, and now include the middle class, whose quality of life has been declining in New York. There are glimmers of this civic assertiveness in the neighborhood and block associations and among citizen efforts such as the New York Public Interest Research Group, the People's Firehouse in Brooklyn, tenants, subway riders. Sprinkled throughout the City are models of community spirit—to prevent budget cutbacks that injure service, to improve police protection, to stop rent increases and co-op evictions, to stop redlining by savings banks, to keep hospitals and libraries open. There needs to be a mechanism to spread these models more widely, to promote a contagion of goodness and creativity that has broad, quantitative significance.

Certainly, the human material is there. What other city can marshall such skill, diversity and determination? But the self-realization is not yet into any momentum. "I love New York" is an advertising slogan for a product to be sold to visitors. A unifying vision of what the City can become is needed to motivate a critical mass of citizens into strategic thinking and commitment. It begins with a controlled moral indignation and is followed by a dedication of regular time to the process of citizenship. First a few individuals and then, through discussion and persuasion, more people join the civic culture for change, for justice, for recovering the City for its people from the parasitic or myopic forces that have it within their grip.

Social forces start with individual resolve. A teacher uses this book in class to inspire field projects on one or more of the City's problems; a member of the clergy prepares a sermon on secular injustice; members of a bar association start a project on citizen access to public decision-making; students organize new civic efforts as part of their education; neighbors begin to use old ideas and new technology to start cooperative ventures to solve their common problems; minorities organize to build power within their communities around patterns of abuses; professors begin articulating alternative qualities of urban life, media managers open their pages and airwaves to programs which mobilize as well as inform; retired people find roles to help reallocate resources and power for the citizenry; consumers come together to combine their negotiating power with private and public sellers. Private citizens need to become public citizens, entering with time and talent the arena where the qualities of societies are shaped. As "representative government" has been taken away from the people, direct democratic initiatives must rise to fill the vacuum if the direction of deterioration is to be reversed. This is clearly the philosophy behind most of the remedies the authors recommend.

Democracy is the underlying message of this book. But, exhortation to greater civic commitment is not only urging a major cultural change; it is recommending a recovery of nerve, a renewed sense of community patriotism, that breeds a dynamic of action fueled by an enduring metabolism. After all, democracy is never easy; but it is easier than what is in store for those who forsake its responsibility.

Newfield and Du Brul, writing in the noble tradition of Lincoln Steffens, have composed a textbook for community patriotism, as the remedy to invisible oligarchy.

RALPH NADER
Washington, D.C.

The
Permanent
Government

How Does a City Die?

How does a city die?

What does its death-rattle sound like? What are the terminal symptoms?

Almost a million citizens on welfare, 600,000 of them children. A decline in population of more than 800,000 in ten years. The loss of 450,000 manufacturing jobs in six years. The loss of four congressional seats as a result of the disputed 1980 Census.

How does a city die?

More than 10 per cent unemployment—40 per cent among black and Hispanic teenagers. Default under another name. The loss of democratic sovereignty to an unelected consortium of bankers, brokers, and business-men. An upsurge in drug use, alcoholism, and gambling—all escapes from an unbearable reality.

What is killing New York City?

Pretty red opium poppies in Iran, Afghanistan and Pakistan—"The Golden Crescent," feeding a Mafia Pipeline. Ribbons of highways, strangling the city and making gigantic suburbs possible. The Vietnam war, and the billions of our national treasure squandered there. A private group decision in March 1975 made by wealthy and privileged bankers and bond underwriters—with little-known names like Labrecque, Kezer, Smeal, Palmer, Brittain, Page, Berkeley, and Butcher—not to sell any more notes or bonds for the city of New York. A secret decision made by New York bankers even earlier to dump billions of dollars of city securities.

A century of racism in the American South that exiled hundreds of thousands of rural, uneducated blacks to New York on buses from Meridian in Mississippi, Waycross in Georgia, Jacksonville in Florida, and Bessemer in Alabama.

What else is killing New York City?

National priorities that diverted our tax dollars to defense contractors, interstate highways, and agribusiness in the "Sunbelt" from Atlanta to San Diego, and threatened to make the whole Northeast quadrant a slum belt.

Moral obligation bonds, a paper scam that John Mitchell huckstered to Nelson Rockefeller.

A man with a .22 caliber gun in a dirty kitchen pantry in the Ambassador Hotel in Los Angeles.

A national plague of unemployment, inflation and high interest rates.

A generation of municipal politicians who could not tell the truth.

A popular Mayor cutting services and getting away with it by convincing people it is inevitable or the fault of municipal unions and minorities and past mayors.

A walker in New York today can see many symbols and omens of its doom.

In a single police precinct in Brooklyn—the 77th—seven people are murdered during one hot summer weekend. At the South Bronx Neighborhood Youth Corps Center, a thousand teenagers line up by midnight for a chance at fifty summer jobs when the doors open the next morning at 7:30.

In East Harlem, a fourteen-year-old boy is dead of a heroin overdose. It doesn't even make the papers; in 1970, a twelve-year-old named Walter Vandermeer died of an OD, so it is not "news" any more.

Garment sweatshops filled with illegal aliens dot the City, in Chinatown, in the South Bronx, in Queens. Women are paid $5 a day without overtime, and labor in fear of deportation. Perhaps 50,000 aliens work in these sweatshops at wages $20 a day below the federal minimum wage of $3.35 an hour. Each month new sweatshops open, and swallow up more of the City's 1 million new illegal immigrants into a system of semi-slavery.

The Yankee Stadium was rehabilitated at a cost of $100 million to the taxpayers. Three years later, a consultant, who was paid $375,000 has reported there are dangerous cracks in the stadium that will cost $1 million more to repair.

On June 27 of 1980, two firefighters—Lawrence Fitzpatrick and Gerald Frisby—died in a Harlem fire because their nylon rescue rope broke. Six months later it was revealed that the Fire Department knew that the cheap half inch ropes were not safe before the two men died—and did nothing about it.

The City has suffered two total power blackouts since 1965. The 1977 blackout, caused by Con Edison's own mismanagement and negligence, led to rioting, burning and looting, especially in Bushwick, where some stores have never re-opened.

In the Bronx, 435 families, mostly working-class Italian, have been evicted to make way for a "new Fordham Hospital." The city has spent $6 million on site acquisition and relocation, and another $1.5 million for architectural design, but the money has run out. No new hospital has been built. The money has been wasted. The families have been evicted for nothing. Where their homes once stood, there are today three blocks of rubble, garbage, beer cans, broken bottles, and dead trees.

In Times Square, a blind man is mugged and his seeing-eye dog stolen by junkies. On Fox Street, a nine-year-old girl is raped and thrown off a rooftop. On 111th Street, parents are begging money on the street to pay for the funeral of their baby, who fell out of a tenement window. In Harlem, two men freeze to death in a slum building owned by a landlord named Gold, who lives in Miami.

In the Bronx, Hans Kabel, seventy-eight years old, and his wife Emma, seventy-six, commit suicide together after being robbed and terrorized in their own small apartment. They leave a suicide note behind that says, "We don't want to live in fear any more."

The slums of the Mott Haven community in the Bronx have bred a new strain of "super-rat" that is immune to poison. Super-rats eat warfarin and other "anticoagulants" with no ill effect. The new rat mutations, often sixteen or eighteen inches long, have survived the Bureau of Pest Control's costly extermination campaigns. When the city fired more and more sanitation workers, more and more garbage accumulated in the South Bronx, and more and more super-rats bred and passed immunity on to their offspring. By the summer of 1976 the Bureau of Pest Control had discovered that almost 15 per cent of the city's estimated 9 million rats could eat ten times the normally lethal dose of poison without dying. The Bureau of Pest Control has had to fire almost 500 employees during the last two years, as part of a budget cutback. But this will mean more children bitten by rats, and more disease spread by rats and rat droppings.

At 116th Street and Eighth Avenue, there is an open, outdoor heroin supermarket. At any time on any day at least a hundred buyers and sellers are milling around on the corner. This awful street, called the Pit, with the Royal Flush Bar, the Shelton Hotel, and a candy store, is the end of the heroin trail that begins in the Golden Crescent of Southwest Asia. The dealers sell their heroin under brand names like "Jaws," "Malcolm's Gold," "Good Pussy," and "Death Wish." On the same crowded street, other men and women sell rubber hoses and syringes. The dealers use fourteen-year-olds as messengers and money carriers. If they are arrested, they are under Family Court jurisdiction and likely to receive only a few months in a juvenile facility. These fourteen-year-old money carriers have been shooting baskets for $100 a hoop in a schoolyard two blocks from the Pit. Lieutenant Stephen Herrer, district commander of the Harlem narcotics division, says of the heroin supermarket, "It's there because it always was."

Almost six years ago, newspaper stories publicized the heroin supermarket.

Films were shown on television news programs. A few "buy and bust" arrests were made. But the main effect, according to Sterling Johnson, the city's special narcotics prosecutor, was that "the dealers moved from one side of the street to the other, that's all." Meanwhile, budget cuts have destroyed Johnson's effectiveness. His office budget was slashed from $2.4 million in fiscal 1974-75 to $1.1 million for 1976-77, and in one year his staff was reduced from 122 to 76. The Police Department's narcotics squad has been cut by 33 per cent since 1975.

All over Harlem, people ask: If a twelve-year-old kid can find a pusher, why can't the police? And some of us remember the campaign promises of 1977, repeated from a hundred platforms, that Ed Koch if elected mayor would add policemen to the force.

By the early 1970s, the South Bronx was perhaps the most wretched urban slum in America—its only rival Brooklyn's Brownsville. The infant mortality rate there was 29 per 1000 births. In 1970, the average median family income in the South Bronx was $5,200, compared to the city-wide average of $9,682. The South Bronx has a quarter of all New York's reported cases of malnutrition and 16 percent of all its cases of venereal disease. In 1972 less than 6 per cent of the public-school pupils could read at grade level. Three out of every four housing units were below standard and in violation of housing and health codes. There were 6000 abandoned buildings. Residents ran wires from an abandoned building with electricity to an inhabited one with none. Street gangs were armed with automatic weapons, and packs of wild dogs lived in the abandoned buildings.

Engine Company 82—immortalized in the book by Dennis Smith—responded to twenty alarms a night. The firemen were often ambushed and pelted with bricks and glass by teenagers.

Starting in the summer of 1975 a new factor began to make the South Bronx an even worse hell, an even more grotesque symbol for the fall of New York. Arson. Organized, systematic burning. Thirteen thousand fires broke out in the 12 square miles of the South Bronx in 1975. Forty people were killed, including three firemen. More than half the fires were reported as "cause unknown." Block after block today is in ruins, with only occasional charred halves of tenements standing.

An assistant district attorney in the Bronx told us that many of the fires were set by "teams of teenagers working very professionally. One kid would hack slits into the baseboards to free the way for the air and flames to come up from the floor below. A second kid would spread the gasoline all over the place. A third kid would actually toss the match in. And then a couple more would begin stripping the plumbing fixtures and metals before the ashes got cold. And it's hard to prove that any of the separate acts is a crime. And since the kids are thirteen or fourteen, even if they were caught and prosecuted they wouldn't do any time. It's a smart system. Somebody is paying the kids $100 a night." Bronx District Attorney Mario Merola believes that most of the torching is instigated by landlords in order to collect fire insurance. Insurance on a four story tenement can be more than $10,000. One landlord who was indicted for arson in the South Bronx owned six buildings and had filed $125,000 in insurance claims. A landlord named Joe Bald was convicted of arson in 1980. He was a "fire broker," who fire marshals believe helped arrange the arson of more than 200 buildings.

It is estimated that about 75,000 of the city's poorest people have been made homeless refugees by these arson-for-insurance fires. Families have been burned-out three and four times. Many of the victims now have to live in welfare hotels around the city, and large families have been broken up. In 1980, there were 10,000 arson fires—6,000 of them in Brooklyn because there was nothing left to torch in the South Bronx.

How does a city die? How many ways can it die? Can a city commit suicide?

In Vietnam, an army commander said of the village of Ben Tre: "We had to destroy it in order to save it." That same deranged logic was applied to New York City. In 1976, under a three-year financial plan and debt moratorium, the banks were saved and the city was condemned. Under pressure from "fiscal monitors," Mayors Koch and Beame cut the budget in self-defeating ways. Cops were fired or jobs not filled through attrition; crime increased; fear increased; more middle class families fled to the suburbs.

The strength of New York City's police force shrunk from 31,000 in 1972 to 22,000 in 1980. During the summer of 1980, gold chains were ripped off the throats of women at high noon on Fifth Avenue. More heroin was available than ever before during 1980. During 1980 murders, robberies, and burglaries increased in New York City, subway crime increased, crime in public housing developments increased. During 1980, New York City had more murders than in any year in all its history—1,790—even though the population continued to decline. In 1980, the number of felonies increased by 16 per cent—but **the number of felony arrests actually declined by 5.5 per cent.**

Sydenham Hospital was closed, even though Harlem suffered from one of the highest disease and death rates in the country.

The transit fare was increased to 60 cents during 1980 even as service, safety, and maintenance collapsed. Mayor Koch's clear campaign pledge to trade-in Westway's highway money for mass transit funds was broken.

In the middle of 1980, by the City's own evaluation, only 51 per cent of all city streets were acceptably clean. More than 60 per cent of Brooklyn's streets were filthy. The reason for this unsanitary city was obvious: the actual street-cleaning force had been cut from 2,700 in 1975, to 500 workers in 1980.

And after 129 years, the policy of free higher education in New York City died on June 1, 1976. The passage of upward mobility out of the slums—the dream that sustained each immigrant generation—was annulled in the bicentennial year.

There are many reasons for New York City to exist and endure as an entity in history. We are a great port and center of transport. We are an incubator of ideas and culture. We are a mecca for tourists. One reason for our existence should be the quality of life in this busy metropolis. Free higher education, adequate police protection, and good health care are among the many reasons for people to live in New York City. But families and businesses have moved out of New York because of crime, bad schools, lack of housing, loss of amenities. Each senseless, selfish budget cut has insured more crime, worse schools, less housing, fewer amenities. And more white flight. And a smaller tax base.

Those in power have tried to blur and conceal accountability for these suicidal decisions. When the subway fare was raised by 43 per cent in 1975 without a public hearing, the directors of the Municipal Assistance Corporation (MAC) blamed Mayor Beame. Mayor Beame blamed the federal government and the appointed members of the Metropolitan Transportation Authority (MTA). The MTA directors, who were appointed by Governor Nelson Rockefeller, blamed Governor Hugh Carey. Governor Carey blamed "the bond market" in public and Mayor Beame in private.

The same cynical ping-ponging of responsibility occurred over the death of free tuition at the City University. Mayor Beame and Governor Carey had pledged their commitment to the principle that all students, of all classes, should receive free, public higher education if their high-school grades were good enough. But Beame and Carey, and the city's new money managers, wanted free tuition ended to balance the budget. Yet they didn't want to be held accountable by history. So they tried to force the appointed, almost anonymous members of the Board of Higher Education to accept quietly public responsibility for the dirty deed, shielding those really making the decision. The BHE's chairman, Alfred Giardino, quit in protest rather than needlessly end the policy that had permitted him, like so many others, to rise out of the working class, gain a college education, and become a lawyer. Four of his colleagues on the BHE also resigned rather than be stooges for the bankers and politicians.

The next day, Mayor Beame appointed a new chairman and three new members, certain that they would vote to terminate free higher education. The new BHE chairman appointed by Beame was Harold Jacobs, sixty-three, an affable, respected, and rich man. Ignoring the formal screening committee for the first time in history, Beame also appointed Albert Maniscalco, a politician and director of several banks; Loretta Conway, a lawyer; and

Nicholas Figueroa, a former prosecutor in the Bronx DA's office. After studying the problem for seventy-two hours, the three new members voted, almost without asking any questions, to end a policy and a tradition that had begun 129 years earlier, to end it at the moment New York City became 40 per cent black and Hispanic.

Each day, as we compose our book, this wounded Paris, this hemorrhaging Athens, dies a block at a time, a family at a time.

In Queens, an alcoholism-treatment program closes and an old man goes to the bars again. A forty-five-year-old firemen has a fatal heart attack trying to fight a fire on his second overtime shift in two days. An after-school tutoring program closes in Bedford-Stuyvesant, and a chance for college dies. A mugger goes free because the cop who arrested him has since been laid off, and doesn't show up in criminal court to testify. A day-care center is "defunded" and an eighteen-year-old mother has to quit high school and go on welfare.

At the same time, the elite, the media opinion-makers, are more than satisfied. They believe New York is having a great economic revival. They speak of a miracle renaissance. But they only know a fragment of New York—a wealthy, white fragment between Wall Street and 96th Street in one borough called Manhattan.

In the middle of Manhattan there is definitely a renaissance going on. There is an influx of foreign investment; spectacular co-ops available to those with equity; lavish restaurants for those with expense accounts. Lavish luxury hotels like the Grand Hyatt and the Portman are being built and financed by the UDC, which was created in 1968 to build rental housing for the poor. In Manhattan, the UDC, with its $500 million bonding authority, is financing a new $400 million convention center, the South Street Seaport renovation for $120 million, and Theatre Row on West 42nd Street for $1 million. Tax abatements and incentives have gone to build new corporate Manhattan headquarters for AT&T, Philip Morris, and the New York Telephone Company. Twenty-six out of 27 landlords in Manhattan who petitioned the Industrial and Commercial Incentives Board (ICIB) for tax abatements have gotten them. More than $150 million of the ICIB's $200 million in tax abatements for the whole city, have been awarded to Manhattan projects. Manhattan also hosts the $1.7 billion Westway boondoggle.

The diamond iceberg of Manhattan is thriving. The white fortress behind the moat is prospering because it is being subsidized.

But New York has become a modern tale of two cities. While Manhattan becomes a luxury fantasyland, the residential neighborhoods of the outer boroughs—Flatbush, Coney Island, Astoria, East Tremont, Borough Park, Crown Heights, Bensonhurst, South Jamaica, Williamsbridge, Williamsburg—they are all bleeding from declining services, blockbusting, arson, crime, housing abandonment, redlining, and a rotting infrastructure of bridges, roads and subways.

The opinion makers, the tourists, don't see this alternative reality—this worst of times, this season of darkness, in the other New York.

When Robert Kennedy spoke against the Vietnam War, he often quoted what Tacitus said of Rome: "They made a desert, and called it peace." In our city, they are making a desert and calling it a balanced budget.

The True History of the Fiscal Crisis

The indebtedness of the state was in the direct interest of that fraction of the bourgeoisie which ruled and legislated in parliament. The state deficit was, in fact, the actual object of its speculation and its main source of enrichment. At the end of each new year a new deficit. After four or five years a new loan. And every new loan gave the financial aristocracy a fresh opportunity to swindle the state, which was artificially kept hovering on the edge of bankruptcy and was forced to do business with the bankers on the most unfavorable terms. Every new loan provided yet another opportunity to plunder that section of the public which invested its money in government securities by means of maneuvers on the Bourse [the Paris stock exchange], into the secrets of which the government and the parliamentary majority were initiated.

In general, the uncertain position of government bonds and the bankers' possession of state secrets put them and their associates in parliament and on the throne in a position to create sudden, unusual fluctuations in the price of government securities, which invariably resulted in the ruin of a mass of smaller capitalists and in the fabulously speedy enrichment of the big gamblers. The fact that the state deficit served the direct interest of the ruling fraction of the bourgeoisie explains why the extraordinary state expenditure in the last years of Louis Philippe's reign was more than double the extraordinary state expenditure under Napoleon. The enormous sums of money which thus flowed through the hands of the state gave rise, moreover, to crooked delivery contracts, bribery, embezzlement and roguery of all kinds. The wholesale swindling of the state through loans was repeated on a retail basis in public works. The relationship between parliament and government was reproduced in the relationship between individual administrative departments and individual entrepreneurs. . . .

. . . The July monarchy was nothing more than a joint-stock company for the exploitation of France's national wealth.

—KARL MARX
The Class Struggles in France: 1848 to 1850

The depression of 1974-75, the worst worldwide economic collapse since the Great Depression, hit rock bottom in March 1975. Ten million American workers were officially "unemployed" while millions of others, especially young blacks, weren't even counted in the statistics since they had never been able to hold *any* job. While every other economic indicator was plummeting, the cost-of-living index pushed to record levels. The inflation rate for the whole year of 1974 was 12 per cent and food prices pelted ahead at an even faster pace. Real wages for those lucky enough to have jobs dropped below those of 1973. Pollsters found the people angry and depressed, distrustful of government, business, and the banks.

This was the last month that New York City was allowed to borrow "normally" in the nation's credit markets. A month before, Nelson Rockefeller's favorite erector set, the New York State Urban Development Corporation, had defaulted on its short-term debt to investors. (The agency, in deep trouble since 1972, was actually scheduled to default five months earlier, at the height of the state election campaign, but it was bailed out by the major banks in a last-ditch attempt to aid the faltering attempts of Republican Governor Malcolm Wilson to fend off his Democratic challenger, Hugh Carey. The bankers lent $150 million of their depositors' money to an agency which they knew was losing $1 million a day.)

Vast subterranean economic pressures, built up over decades, were shaking the foundations of the postwar economy and threatened to topple the nation's biggest banks, the securities markets, giant corporations, and government agencies that stood at the pinnacle of an almost incalculable base of debt. The tremors had been felt since Richard Nixon's sudden devaluation of the dollar in 1971, and now they broke through at the system's most vulnerable point, New York City, the financial capital of the world.

Since then the city, and all of urban America, has been wracked by a series of aftershocks. In San Francisco and New York municipal workers have struck in impotent rage against massive layoffs. Unemployment, despite a fragile economic "recovery," remains at heartbreaking levels. Urban crime has reached a new peak and the overcrowded prisons are in open revolt. Bands of young Nazis roam the fringes of Chicago's white neighborhoods preaching racial Armaggedon. Detroit has been forced to rehire hundreds of laid-off policemen to impose a state of martial law. The nightmares forecast for our cities in the 1960s became the day-to-day realities of the 1970s.

Millions of words have already been written about New York City's fiscal collapse. For months it dominated the news, and the spasms of other major cities were treated as a footnote to the story. The agony of the cities has now emerged into the permanent scenery of the American spectacle. Like floods, hurricanes, and other natural disasters, it is taken for granted. As it continues to unfold on our front pages and television screens, the majority of the nation sits back, saddened for the victims, but relieved that this unavoidable disaster is happening to someone else.

We reject this fatalism about the cities. What happened to New York was neither inevitable nor inescapable. New York and the rest of our cities *can* be saved, but we must first understand how the current crisis emerged. In this and the next chapter we shall counterpose what we call "the true history of the fiscal crisis" to what has become the "official" history written by the press and academic commentators. It is the official history which has become the greatest barrier to achieving the many fundamental changes necessary to rescue our cities.

Abe Beame was wrong when he said, in late 1975, that "the dilemma of our city really has no villains, only victims." There *are* villains in New York's collapse, men who saw what was happening, could have prevented it, and profited from the agony of millions. But few of these villains are to be found in the ranks of journalists who reported on the fall of New York. Their sins were for the most part sins of omission. Reporters failed to dig deep enough, trusted sources who lied to protect themselves, allowed the "tunnel vision" that afflicts any reporter on a story to block out the simple truth that New York's problems had deep-rooted causes outside the city and its government. In the rush to judgment that is the bane of writing for daily deadlines, they accepted the "easy" villains they were fed: a bookkeeper-mayor and his acolytes who had financed with mirrors; municipal unions that had used their putative political muscle to extract massive pension settlements from an impoverished government; politicos who had a lust for cutting ribbons on new programs without caring where the money came from to finance them.

Inevitably the idea of these surface villains, and this deadline punditry about the urban crisis, created a myth: New York was different from other cities; it had tried to do too much for its citizens; now it must be punished. The hero in this trite little morality play then became that small band of professional money-men who had supposedly unmasked the city's Ponzi scheme at the last moment, before it destroyed the widows and orphans who had bought its worthless paper in innocent trust. A short term in the fiscal slammer would reform the culprit and everybody could then go on about their business as before.

An excellent synopsis of this "official" version of the New York crisis was given by Wyndham Robertson in the August 1975 issue of *Fortune:*

> As the nation's largest city struggles to extricate itself from the financial quicksand that has been threatening to drag it under, Americans watching the suspenseful spectacle have begun to wonder whether other large cities are headed for the same kind of trouble. The answer is fairly reassuring: New York is a special case.
>
> New York is different because it has had a credit card that enabled it to live beyond its means. For years its elected officials have had the sort of license that politicians dream about, but that only those at the Federal level were presumed to enjoy—namely the opportunity to spend without the concomitant necessity to tax. . . .

With that credit card available, city politicians seldom had to bring themselves to say no to anybody—whether union leaders making extravagant demands at contract time or citizens seeking benefits for themselves or others. If the city government had been forced to match expenditures more closely with cash revenues, hard choices would have been unavoidable. But the borrowing power, coupled with enormous political pressures from a citizenry both accustomed to costly services and suffering from some of the highest taxes in the U.S., led city officials to ignore fiscal realities. As a result, New York got committed to do more things than it could afford.

It was this concept of New York as a "special case" which eventually did the most harm. No longer just a sleazy con man hiding behind a fancy front, New York became the Typhoid Mary of cities, as the crisis deepened and threatened to spread to the nation's financial structure. If New York alone was the victim of this fiscal malady, it must be quarantined.

Few people did more to legitimize the idea that the only responsible solution to the fiscal crisis was massive layoffs and service cuts than Steven R. Weisman, who reported the crisis on a daily basis for *The New York Times*. Subtly, and often merely by omission, Weisman slanted his "objective" reporting to echo the latest thinking of the bankers and Felix Rohatyn, the critically important member of all the emergency committees set up to rescue New York. Weisman used the imagery of the city as a fiscal "junkie" whose only possible cure was to kick the habit "cold turkey." He made few comments about the profits, motives, or obligations of the pushers who addicted the junkie, however.

Weisman later became notorious among colleagues in the press for the "victory" jig he danced with Rohatyn, chairman of MAC, to celebrate the fact that the United Federation of Teachers' chief, Albert Shanker, had been forced to capitulate and buy additional MAC bonds for his union's pension fund. As one reporter from another daily paper recounted the event to us: "I've never seen anything like it on any other story I've covered. I started to take a punch at him but somebody grabbed my arm. No wonder anybody who reads the *Times* doesn't know what's really going on."*

*When Alexander Cockburn reported in his "Press Clips" column in *The Village Voice* that Rohatyn and Weisman had been seen "embracing and tickling each other after Shanker gave in," an indignant Weisman protested what he felt were homosexual innuendoes in the piece. That was hardly the implication, or the point, of what Cockburn had written. He was doubting Weisman's objectivity, not his manliness.
Weisman did something far worse in October 1976. On behalf of Chase Manhattan, he undercut an investigative piece by his colleague Martin Tolchin which confirmed for the first time that the big New York banks, led by Chase, had "dumped" billions in city securities, thereby causing a panic, and New York's exclusion from the bond market. A Chase vice-president crowed to us that "the Bank" had gotten Tolchin's piece buried, literally, on the obituary page. When we pursued this claim, we found that Weisman had challenged the Tolchin story with the desk and managed to get it rewritten and buried. For more details see our article in the November 22, 1976, *Village Voice*.

Timothy Crouse, whose *The Boys on the Bus* is the best modern book on the American press, has a marvelous scene in which he describes our top political reporters comparing the leads they have written on presidential campaign stories to detemine the consensus view that they will send to their editors. This kind of "pack journalism" now afflicted New York; the cardinal sin was to say something different from what everyone else was saying.

And so the myth grew, nourished by repetition. As a result, those who actually provoked the city's crisis—the banks—were effectively absolved of all guilt until subsequent investigations bared their machinations. An easily frightened national money market in desperate need of reform became the hero, not the villain, of the piece. A national administration that had heaped responsibility after responsibility on the tottering city not only escaped its share of blame for the crisis, but had a field day flagellating New York for collapsing under this unfair burden. All this was bad enough, but the greatest irony of all was that the city was cut off from the only thing that could solve its real problems: massive infusions of new money to restore its dwindling economy and provide stable jobs for the growing ranks of the welfare poor.

As with all myths, of course, the myth about New York City grew around a kernel of truth. As we will show, the city's finances *were* in an incredible mess; its debt *had* accelerated at an unsustainable pace; bookkeeping gimmicks *were* used to mask actual budget deficits. Some of the pensions won by municipal labor unions *were* excessive; some fringe benefits (such as giving cops two days off every time they donated a pint of blood) *were* bizarre and unnecessary. But none of these things, alone or together, caused the fall of New York. If we were to abolish all of them, lay off thousands more in addition to the tens of thousands of city workers already fired, close every city hospital, and destroy even more programs, we could never restore the city to fiscal health.

In fact, the current "recovery" program has significantly accelerated the city's decline. In the meantime, more businesses and jobs leave the city as police and fire protection are cut back, the mass transit system becomes unworkable, and the banks refuse capital for expansion. The city itself has been forced to abandon the construction of piers, markets, industrial parks, and shopping centers that would have created 22,000 private jobs.

It is important, therefore, to understand what really happened in those years and months before the banks slammed the credit windows shut on the city's outstretched fingers; to see why the federal administration jubilantly sought to "cut the city off and float it out to sea"; and to discern the larger implications behind the financial community's eagerness to force all the cities and states of America to reduce their demands on the nation's capital supply—and how it used New York's battered corpse to accomplish this goal. This is the "real history" we shall now seek to unravel.

The headline on the *Wall Street Journal* story was:

NEW YORK CITY'S FISCAL ILLS BOOST ITS COST
BY $7.4 MILLION AT $233.8 MILLION BOND SALE

NEW YORK—This city's shaky budget condition resulted in a sharply higher interest cost on $233.8 million of various purpose bonds it auctioned yesterday, market analysts said.

The article then explained how an 0.3701 increase in the interest rate would actually mean an added cost to taxpayers of $7.4 million over the eight-and-a-half-year life of the bonds.

The city's steeper cost was linked primarily to its well-publicized financial crisis. . . . [The mayor] recently estimated that New York's annual revenue had declined between $100 million and $150 million as a result of the nationwide economic slowdown, and he warned that city employees could be subjected to "payless paydays, pay cuts and layoffs."

The city's controller described the city's budgetary woes as only "one of several factors" responsible for yesterday's higher rate. He also cited a current supply logjam in the tax-exempt market, which is attempting to absorb a staggering $568 million of new state and city bonds this week alone.

The date on that story was October 21, 1970.

Anyone dipping into New York City's history in the last decade can find dozens of almost identical reports. We chose this one simply because it exemplifies so perfectly the coverage that preceded the city's fiscal collapse in the spring of 1975. All the elements of the final downfall are there: maximum interest being extorted from a city already in economic trouble, a national economic decline reducing tax revenues while at the same time forcing greater expenditures on a shaky municipal budget, a credit market unable to absorb the growing demands placed on it. And the two leading city officials trying to outdo each other in explaining away the mess. (For those with short memories, the mayor's name was John Lindsay and the controller was Abraham Beame.)

The deepest historical roots of New York City's fiscal crisis go back to Robert Moses and the creation of public authorities in 1934. The authorities meant the end of accountability. Moses and his successors, like Edward Logue and William Ronan, were able to spend money and make mistakes without democratic restraint. As Robert Caro has pointed out in *The Power Broker*, during a fifteen-year period Robert Moses was able to spend $4.5 billion on public works, while the mayors and members of the Board of Estimate spent a total of less than $3.8 billion on public works. The authorities also became the device used to destroy neighborhoods and dispossess tens of thousands of families. Caro quotes one study that says between 1946 and 1956 alone Moses evicted 320,000 people from their homes.

So the people of the city began to lose control over their democratic destiny in 1934; but a dangerous new element was added to this anti-democratic drift in 1960: moral obligation bonds. A series of historic meetings were occurring in New York City between two men who were to play significant roles in New York's history and in the history of the nation: Nelson Rockefeller and John Mitchell.

Nelson Rockefeller became governor of New York State in January 1959. One of the first problems to gain his attention was the increasing deterioration of the state's major cities, especially New York City. At the core of this problem was the flight of white, middle-class families to the burgeoning suburbs. The postwar suburban housing boom, fueled by Veterans Administration and Federal Housing Authority mortgages and by federal and state funding for a vast new highway program that provided automobile access to jobs in the downtown business districts was in full swing. While the feds were busily subsidizing these new communities of single-family homes, however, they were doing nothing to provide new housing at moderate rentals in the cities. As young families grew, therefore, the only suitable housing offered them was outside the neighborhoods and cities where they had grown up and married.

New York had recognized this problem in 1955 when it adopted the Mitchell-Lama middle-income housing program. But not much new urban housing had actually been constructed because of the requirement imposed by the state constitution that all new debt be approved by the voters at a general referendum. There was little enthusiasm among upstate and suburban voters for housing debt, which was seen primarily as a benefit for New York City. Besides, property values in these areas would continue to rise only as long as the suburbs grew and more home buyers could be attracted from the big cities. Small housing bond issues passed, but by narrower and narrower margins. As the population balance between city and suburb continued to tip, they were fated for defeat.

Rockefeller now looked to the financing mechanisms pioneered by the state's public authorities. These agencies issued bonds outside the state's publicly approved debt limit. They were "revenue" bonds, paid off through the collection of user fees, e.g., bridge tolls or admission charges at state parks, as opposed to the "full faith and credit" bonds of the state, which were backed by state tax collections. The projects financed by "revenue" bonds were said to be "self-liquidating" or "self-sufficient."

He therefore had the legislature create a Housing Finance Agency (HFA) which, using the state's superior credit rating and the lure of tax-exempt income, would issue bonds and then lend low-interest funds to private developers for the construction of middle-income housing. The bonds would be liquidated over their term by rental payments.

James Gaynor, Rockefeller's Commissioner of Housing, had called in John Mitchell, one of the nation's leading bond lawyers and later Nixon's attorney general, to help draft the HFA legislation. Mitchell questioned the revenue bond approach. As he later testified to the state commission investigating the collapse of the Urban Development Corporation, he told Rockefeller that issuers of mortgage-participation certificates and other real-estate obligations had defaulted in great numbers during the 1930s and the "investment community was pretty sour on that type of obligation." Investors would therefore exact a very high interest rate on the new bonds, which in turn would significantly raise rents and discourage tenacy.

Mitchell then proposed that "something more" be added to sweeten the pot: He suggested that the bonds include a "legislative intent" to provide appropriations from general revenues to back any shortfalls in the rentals necessary to pay off the bonds. This meant that the state would have a "moral obligation" to back its paper; but since the bonds were the debt of the agency and not the state and there would be no "legal" obligation for the legislature to appropriate money to assure repayment, the requirement for a public referendum was avoided.

While Mitchell went around peddling the new concept to the private rating agencies that appraise public offerings and the underwriters who buy bonds and resell them to institutions and wealthy investors, Rockefeller did his characteristic hard sell with the reluctant legislature, hammering away at the "self-liquidating" nature of the new debt. Robert Moses had long ago taught the legislators that public authorities could be a major patronage trough. The concept was adopted.

The reception accorded the first issue of HFA bonds in 1961 exceeded even Mitchell's enthusiastic projections. They received a high rating from Standard and Poor's, a leading rating agency, and as a result were sold at a low interest rate. Of equal importance, the U.S. Controller of the Currency ruled that the "moral obligation" allowed the bonds to be considered as general obligations of the state, and therefore suitable for investment by the nation's commercial banks. The banks, anxious to reduce federal and state tax obligations, gobbled up the new tax-exempt securities. The only cloud on the horizon was the negative reaction of the state's Democratic Comptroller, Arthur Levitt, who objected to circumventing the constitutional limits on borrowing and warned major bankers in several meetings in the early 1960s that the state's credit was being "distorted" by the new form of debt.

John Mitchell had given Nelson Rockefeller another Aladdin's lamp when he created "moral obligation" financing for the authorities. All the governor had to do was rub it and out poured even more massive building projects, jobs, and profits for banks, builders, architects, lawyers, developers, and dozens of related professionals. Running for re-election in 1962, Rockefeller promised to turn a handful of seedy teachers colleges into a full-fledged State University. The State University Construction Fund was established under the aegis of HFA and subsequently spent $1.7 billion planting campuses across the state—as much to meet the needs of local Republican politicians as to meet those of higher education. The bonds were to be repaid with the tuition fees of students—which is one of the reasons why Rockefeller perennially attempted to impose tuition on the separate and free City University system, whose tuition-free competition made him look bad and created pressure to keep the lid on tuition at the state schools.

Four years later, another election year, HFA was assigned the task of providing funds for a massive nursing-home program for the elderly. Eventually the agency would provide financing for public and private hospitals, neighborhood clinics, mental-health facilities, housing for the elderly, offices, and libraries. Its total debt in October 1975 equaled $5.29 billion.

HFA was only one, albeit the largest, of the 230-odd authorities which flourished under Rockefeller. Admittedly, a vast authority superstructure had long been in existence in New York State as the private empire of Robert Moses. But Rockefeller proved an incredibly eager pupil. During his term of office, the number of authorities was doubled. While Moses had actually created a shadow government standing separate and apart, Nelson Rockefeller extended that shadow until it overwhelmed and engulfed the formal state government apparatus. The authorities ultimately encompassed the universe of public concerns, stretching alphabetically from the Atomic and Space Development Authority to the United Nations' Development Corporation. Unnoticed by most, Nelson Rockefeller had created his own U.S. government in miniature. (New York even has its own Navy.) But then he had always warned us that he was practicing to be President.

Even this pyramid of vast wealth and power did not circumscribe Rockefeller's experiments with "creative financing." He also developed a series of complicated lease-purchase agreements involving the credit of the state's cities and counties. The most notorious of these was the development of the gargantuan Albany Mall (officially the Empire State Plaza) office-construction project, initially estimated to cost $250 million but ultimately consuming almost $1 billion in construction funding. Rockefeller induced Albany County to undertake the project by committing the state to lease office space on a flexible schedule that covers debt service and allows for all inflationary costs in building. In effect, this means that the state's taxpayers will absorb the entire cost of the project through annual rent payments in the state's operating budget for decades to come.

This private empire of authorities, always yoked with his own vast personal wealth, became the real foundation of Rockefeller's political power. He had learned well the lesson taught by another Hudson River Valley patrician, Franklin D. Roosevelt: "Spend, spend, spend; elect, elect, elect." The steady generation of construction jobs allowed him to buy the fealty of the powerful and nominally Democratic building trade unions, with at least 200,000 members in the state. (At the same time, he was successfully buying the support of state and city civil servants, especially the police and firemen, first by making pension agreements a subject for collective bargaining and then by consistently increasing the percentage of pension contributions to be paid by the state. This forced the city into a costly game of leapfrog with public employee pensions.) The constant flow of new bonds and new projects also guaranteed him a constant source of munificent campaign contributions from grateful bankers, builders, and developers; these supplemented the vast resources of his own family. Few commentators grasped the full irony of their own words when they wrote of Rockefeller's ability to "cement" together disparate coalitions.

The men he appointed to run these satrapies were generally skilled but low-key administrators, and he assured their loyalty with personal gifts and loans to supplement their lavish public salaries. Primary among them was William J. Ronan, ironically a trenchant critic of the independent power of the authorities when he directed a study for the legislature in 1956 as dean of the New York University School of Public Administration. Ronan became a rapid convert to the benefits of authorities, first as Rockefeller's secretary and subsequently as chairman of the Metropolitan Transportation Authority, which runs all public transit in New York City and the region's crucial commuter railroads.

Disclosures extracted during Rockefeller's confirmation hearings for the vice-presidency showed that he showered Ronan with $625,000 in gifts and loans, money which Ronan used, among other things, to speculate in suburban real estate.

But even the best administrators that money could buy couldn't keep Rockefeller's financial bubble from bursting eventually. Paul Bellica was Ronan's counterpart at the HFA. A self-effacing Swiss, Bellica ran his growing agency with all the conservative care befitting a Zurich banker. He took the concept of "self-sufficiency" seriously and took great pains to choose, in consultation with his colleagues at the Department of Housing and Community Renewal, only those projects that would produce revenues adequate to pay back the bondholders, first and foremost, and then meet their own operating costs. These studies took a great deal of time. Moreover, Bellica applied the same standards as the banks that bought his bonds. He refused to invest in changing neighborhoods; not only did the banks redline vast areas of the state, but so did the state's major housing agency. As he complained in a memo to Department of Housing and Community Renewal

Commissioner Charles Urstadt, "The program [HFA] has never been intended to satisfy the need of the lowest income group and to supplement the public housing system."

But there was no longer a growing public housing system. Federal appropriations had been reduced to a trickle during the escalation of the Vietnam War, and Richard Nixon soon shut off the faucet entirely. Between 1962 and 1965, five propositions for state-financed public housing had been soundly defeated at the polls. Yet the overwhelming demand of the cities was for decent housing to replace almost a million units of decaying, dilapidated apartments in low-income neighborhoods. The immense revenues that HFA was originally given the power to raise for housing had been diverted to other, politically more sexy projects.

Now the galloping inflation produced by the seemingly endless war in Southeast Asia meant that even those limited funds invested in housing built less and less at a higher and higher price. Ghetto riots over slum conditions were erupting with alarming frequency. Rockefeller was again gearing up for another shot at the presidency in 1968, having been so bitterly denied the nomination by the suicidal Goldwater legions in 1964. John Lindsay, New York's matinee-idol mayor, challenged him for the title of the nation's leading Republican liberal, and Lindsay was capturing the limelight as the man who had effectively "cooled" the most explosive ghettoes in America. The governor felt boxed in.

Rockefeller's answer to any problem had become reflexive; he would create yet another authority—bigger, more daring, almost all-inclusive—a super-authority. Actually he now combined two new authorities that his staff had designed, one to provide jobs for the urban unemployed, the other to provide housing in areas abandoned by private investment and the HFA, and he called the new entity the Urban Development Corporation.

On January 17, 1968, Rockefeller asked Edward J. Logue to review the proposal he was preparing to send to the legislature. Logue was at the peak of his career as a "master builder," a man with a national reputation for erecting large-scale projects without being stymied by the political squabbles or community resistance that condemned so many other urban-renewal projects to remain elegant cardboard models on display in the anterooms of mayors and governors. He had started by rebuilding downtown New Haven and then moved on to the Boston Redevelopment Authority. John Lindsay had gotten Logue to make the plans for New York City's Housing and Development Administration, but Logue had refused to take the top job in this agency because the powers he sought over planning, design, and development had been whittled down by city officials, concerned that he wanted not only the title of "housing czar" but the powers that such a title implied. He and the multimillionaire governor shared the view that opposition constituted obstruction. But many city housing and planning officials and community groups saw him as a "young Robert Moses," and they hadn't recovered from the old one yet.

Logue submitted a long memorandum on the draft proposal to Rockefeller on February 21, and the bill that was actually submitted to the legislature on February 27 contained his basic recommendations. The new agency would have the powers to override local zoning laws and often outdated and unnecessarily expensive building codes. It would be allowed to use the "fast track" method of construction—that is, to carry on through the primary stages of site selection, design, and the preparation of final plans and specifications before having a final mortgage commitment. The bonds and notes that would finance the agency would be based on "the full faith and credit of the corporation"; in other words, rather than being amortized by the income of specific projects, the basis of HFA financing, bonds would be repaid from the total income stream of UDC from all its projects.

The state legislature hesitated, perhaps fearing that UDC's mandate to build in "substandard, blighted areas" might finally put to the test their willingness to back up the "moral obligation" with hard tax dollars if the agency experienced a series of project difficulties. Suburban legislators were fearful of the provision that allowed UDC to override local zoning; they saw it as an opening wedge for building low-income (read minority) projects in previously middle-class (read white) areas. (Most planners by now accepted the premise that "white flight" from the central cities was inevitable; they now simply held that it was necessary to provide blacks with the option of leaving the cities as well, thereby providing them access to suburban job opportunities and slowing the trend toward black-majority cities surrounded by a "white noose" of suburbs.)

For a while the bill languished in Albany; then history intervened. Martin Luther King, Jr., probably the most important black leader in American history, was assassinated in Memphis on April 4, 1968. Black outrage exploded in devastating riots all over America's cities. The following morning Rockefeller, never a man to miss an opportunity, sent a "message of necessity" to the legislature reducing the amount of time permitted to elapse before a vote could be taken on the UDC bill. On April 8, he flew to Atlanta to attend Dr. King's funeral with the rest of the nation's elite. The bill was rushed through the state Senate as King's funeral was in progress, but the Assembly voted it down that same afternoon, a minority rejecting the governor's move as "opportunistic" and "cynical"; the opposition to the zoning-override provision held firm, and a handful of liberals presciently charged that the proposed new authority would not provide meaningful housing aid for the poor.

Rockefeller quickly flew back from Atlanta and pulled out all the stops. His top aides and housing officials went scurrying down the corridors of the legislature—issuing threats, calling in old debts, and making promises. Early the next morning, the pummeled Assembly, terrified as much by radio reports of growing black violence as by Rockefeller's ham-handed lobbying, reconvened and passed the bill by the same margin by which it had defeated it the previous afternoon.

George Woods, former head of the World Bank and a director and former chairman of the First Boston Corporation, a major investment banking firm, was Rockefeller's first choice as chief executive officer of UDC. Someone who could reassure the banking fraternity—in addition to Rockefeller himself, of course—was needed to raise massive amounts of cash for the new agency. Woods explained that he had no experience in real-estate financing or development, and declined. But Rockefeller continued to press, and Woods finally agreed to become chairman of the board on the condition that First Boston would become the senior managing underwriter for all UDC offerings. (The senior underwriter receives the lion's share of the profits in the syndicates formed to buy public offerings and then resell them to the public. The profits derive from the spread between the interest rate that government must pay, say 8½ per cent, and the rate that is paid to secondary purchasers such as banks or wealthy individuals, say 7½ per cent. Comptroller Levitt subsequently revealed that the seven underwriters, among them Citibank, Chase Manhattan, Morgan Guaranty, and Salomon Brothers, had earned profits of $3.9 million on the initial UDC offering of $250 million.)

The writer Mary Perot Nichols subsequently revealed in *The New Republic* that Woods also demanded protection from any charges of conflict of interest. He received a secret letter from State Attorney General Louis Lefkowitz, always a willing Rockefeller ally, absolving him of any conflict as long as he refrained from voting at board meetings on matters affecting the business of First Boston. (Lefkowitz's son Stephen would become general counsel for UDC.) This was a complete charade, since Woods remained the dominant financial voice at UDC, and the other members of the board subsequently testified to the state commission that they had no expertise in the bond markets and "depended on Woods's judgment in these matters." Woods's role in these financial decisions did not become a public issue until after the UDC collapse, however.

On April 27, 1968, Logue was appointed president and chief executive officer of the new corporation (he received $200,000 in "gifts and loans" from Rockefeller during his tenure) and began to carry out what he later called "a directive to go out and build, build, build." And he did. By December 31, 1970, UDC had in construction or planning 45,438 units of housing with an estimated cost of $1.9 billion, as well as commercial and industrial developments around the state. (He actually completed less than 30,000 housing units.) For a brief time, Logue became the right man in the right place at the right time.

Shortly after the creation of the UDC, Congress had passed the capstone of the Great Society, the Housing and Urban Development Act of 1968, which contained direct subsidies (Section 236 monies, they were called) that reduced the interest charges on approved projects to only 1 per cent. On paper, at least, these subsidies made many projects viable that would otherwise be unrentable. Logue had really the only agency in the nation geared up to absorb the new subsidies on a large scale, and the Rockefeller-Logue combination had an open door with the new Republican administration which came to office in 1969. As a result, Logue snatched 66 per cent of all Section 236 monies available for the entire country before Nixon impounded the program in January 1973.

Logue had been so sure of federal funding that he had 58 projects in process that required Section 236 subsidy when Nixon dropped his bombshell—but he had never bothered to ask for formal federal commitments. UDC would have collapsed on the spot then and there, but Nelson Rockefeller scuttled to Washington and got Nixon's domestic chief, John Ehrlichman, to suspend the moratorium for Logue's projects.

The overwhelming irony is that Logue finally built very little housing for the poor in either the cities or the suburbs. Despite the legislation's clear mandate that the new housing should be for "persons or families of low income," the UDC unilaterally established its own formula, which stipulated that 70 per cent of the housing on any site would be for middle- and moderate-income families, 20 per cent for low-income families, and 10 per cent for the aged.

The concept of publicly subsidized "moderate"-income housing was actually a UDC creation. In effect, it meant, after applying the complex formulas of various state housing programs, that families earning up to $65,000 a year fell into this category. "Middle-income," originally defined by statute to mean those earning between $8,000 and $12,000 a year, in practice came to mean those earning between $18,000 and $25,000 a year. The rents in Logue's projects came in so high that they never effectively competed with the better deal which most families could still get by moving to the federally subsidized suburbs.

When Comptroller Levitt released a report on the "Financial Viability of Completed Projects" on October 29, 1974, he disclosed that an apartment then renting at $159 in Coney Island required an 84.9 per cent rent increase simply to meet its mortgage costs, exclusive of escalating operating costs. A Yonkers apartment renting for $190 would have to be raised to $365, a 92.1 per cent increase. The smallest rent increase projected by Levitt was 29 per cent.

Logue actually tried to introduce a very modest housing program for the minority poor into the suburbs, but Rockefeller caved in to the demands of

Republican legislators from suburban Westchester County (this was known as the Nine Towns controversy), and the provision allowing UDC to override local restrictions was repealed on June 5, 1973. Logue received an additional $500 million in bonding authority as a consolation.

As a result of the fantastic escalation in building costs and the failure to fill existing projects, the money kept going out faster than it could be repaid. Attempts were made to get Logue to cap the building program or at least to slow it down until income and outgo achieved some sort of balance. A typical Logue response was given in an internal memorandum in late 1971: "We are going to build as much as we can. . . . When, having prudently managed our affairs, we have gone as far as we can go, and we can't borrow any more, that is another day." That day would not come for another two years and only after UDC had borrowed $2 billion.

UDC was hit with a series of body blows in 1973. Nixon's moratorium was the first. Then the UDC accountant refused to certify its 1972 financial statement, provoking uncomfortable disclosures, and on October 5, Moody's lowered the UDC's bond rating to Baa, the lowest possible level at which many banks and institutions could still invest in its bonds. Then, on December 12, Nelson Rockefeller resigned as governor in order to allow Lieutenant-Governor Malcolm Wilson, his perennial second fiddle and enforcer in the party's conservative wing, to accede to the top post in preparation for a run at a full four-year term the following November.

During his fifteen-year reign, Rockefeller had increased the state's debt from $1.97 billion in 1961 to $13.37 billion in his final budget year—a seven-fold increase. With the imposition of "moral obligation" debt, he had radically altered the shape of the nation's credit markets (many other states had followed in New York's footsteps), had provided a bonanza in profits and tax-exempt income for banks and wealthy individuals, and had actively stoked the forced-draught economic expansion that a few months later would collapse, plunging the nation into its second worst depression in history. As Hugh Carey, his successor, who always showed restraint when dealing with Rockefeller's excesses, later blurted out: ". . . in New York State, we haven't found only back-door financing. We got side-door financing and New York's borrowing over the years—through the state government, its authorities and agencies and UDC and MTA—we got money going out the doors, the windows, and the portholes."

It was UDC that finally caused this multi-billion-dollar house of cards to collapse. Morgan Guaranty pulled out as an underwriter soon after Rockefeller's departure. In May 1974, UDC had to withdraw a $100-million short-term note sale because the interest rates asked by the nervous banks were prohibitive. By the end of the summer, the major underwriters, led by the Chase Manhattan Bank, were in fact running the agency and provided funds adequate to keep UDC from collapsing under Wilson's election campaign.

After Wilson's defeat in the fall of 1974, the credit dried up. Carey attempted to win a $178-million appropriation from the state legislature to cover UDC's immediate cash needs, but he failed, and on February 25, 1975, UDC defaulted on $104.5 million in short-term notes that had fallen due. It was the biggest collapse of a government agency since the Depression. The state investigating commission subsequently estimated that it would require "a total of $240 to $320 million of State funds" to complete UDC projects in construction when the collapse came, and much much more "if projects don't meet the required level of income"—almost an inevitability. The bubble had burst.

Two months later, New York City found itself facing the specter of default for the first time.

Whatever else one may say about Nelson Rockefeller, he was magnanimous with his opponents. As Democratic Mayor Robert Ferdinand Wagner, Jr. came to the end of his twelve years in office in 1965, he had a problem. His budget didn't balance, and he needed $255.8 million. He proposed to borrow the money needed to cover the deficit, and he needed the approval of the state legislature to do so. While Republican legislators responded to this proposal with cries of outrage, Nelson Rockefeller shrugged and said "Why not?" After all, "creative financing" had worked for him; maybe the city deserved a taste of the good life.

The two master politicians then went about constructing a complicated compromise. Rockefeller received the Democratic votes he needed to institute a state sales tax, and Wagner received the Republican votes he needed for an increase in the city sales tax and a new borrowing formula that allowed the city for the first time to borrow against *estimated* revenues. In the past the city had been allowed to issue "Revenue Anticipation Notes" (RANs) against state and federal aid and uncollected taxes and fees, but there were strict limitations: All the uncollected funds had to be due in the same fiscal year in which the loan was made, and the amount of state and federal aid borrowed against could not exceed the amount that had actually been received in the prior fiscal year. Under the new formula the mayor would be limited no longer to prior-year collections but to what he said the collections should be. The taxes and fees owed need no longer be payable in the fiscal year in which the loan was made—minor changes actually, but then so is a pin-sized hole in a dike.

John Lindsay, then the Republican-Liberal candidate for mayor, denounced Wagner's "credit-card" budgeting. Abraham Beame, Wagner's controller and the Democratic mayoral aspirant, squeaked that the Wagner plan was an "unsound proposal, which threatens the credit and financial standing of the city." Wagner, a man who genuinely despises conflict, answered with one of his classic evasions: ". . . a good loan is better than a bad tax." Since any tax is a bad tax to politicians, who never know whose support they may someday have to seek, this aphorism hardly closed the debate.

Almost invariably, the "official" commentators have named Wagner's borrowing scheme as the "original sin" in New York City's long decline to perdition. Frankly, this is unfair. Wagner was certainly no great problem-solver, but he kept a fairly tight rein on city finances and worked hard and competently to increase the city's niggardly share of state and federal aid. Many of the real innovations of the subsequent federal War on Poverty were pioneered in New York. Wagner granted the unions collective-bargaining rights, a long-overdue inevitability, but he proved a masterful and tightfisted bargainer and frequently gave labor little more than his ready smile. It was John Lindsay, with his anti-union bluster and Ivy League aides, who ended up granting a succession of union benefits which the city treasury simply couldn't support. Lindsay was the one who avidly joined the pension competition with Rockefeller, and went along with larcenous gimmicks such as using outdated mortality tables to understate the actual costs of the pension settlements he had negotiated.

Yes, Wagner opened the door to the astronomical increases in city borrowing that took place under his successors, but he didn't push them through it; they went of their own accord.

In reality the major effect of that Wagner-Rockefeller deal lay not so much in the fact that it allowed city borrowing to increase, as in the fact that it removed pressures on city officials to collect the funds necessary to support that borrowing. The point may seem subtle, but it was crucial in setting the city's budget adrift on the churning currents of urban politics. It is part of the hidden history of the fiscal crisis that we would now like to examine in detail.

For many years we have heard the refrain that New York has been doing "too much" for its citizens, that its taxes were too high and its tax base was shrinking as a result, that only massive retrenchment—layoffs, salary freezes, program slashes—would restore a balanced budget. The rhetoric has recently become more hyperbolic; the writer Ken Auletta has even suggested that the basic flaw lay in the city's attempt under Lindsay to create "local socialism," a perception of urban policy that would no doubt come as a profound shock to the residents of Harlem and the brokers of Wall Street.

And while there may be differences of opinion among editorial writers and politicians as to where cuts should be made, or how many layoffs would actually do the job, only one set of "solutions" has ever received serious consideration: to reduce expenditures. One of the many problems with this prescription is that it ignores a basic lesson taught to all freshmen accounting students: that there are two sides to every budget—income and expenditures. If you have exhausted all sources of income, then obviously you limit expenditures to achieve a balanced budget. But only then.

Astoundingly, New York City hasn't done this. In 1976 alone, more than $1 billion in taxes, fees, and fines went uncollected. If the amounts uncollected just since 1970 were added to this sum, a figure between $2 and $3 billion would accumulate—a substantial portion of the short-term debt that the city found itself incapable of "rolling over." In addition, New York City has been systematically bilked, through welfare and Medicaid frauds, of hundreds of millions of dollars. Another serious drain has resulted from borrowing costs occasioned by the painfully slow transmittal of aid funds owed by the state and federal governments. Put these figures together, and a radically altered picture of the city budget emerges; in fact, it almost balances—without meat-ax layoffs, without transit-fare increases and service reductions that simply create greater future deficits, without the destruction of a free university, without elimination of those services to the poor which offered the only meaningful hope of trading a welfare check for a payroll check.

What were the sources of this fantastic money hemmorrhage?

First and foremost were cumulative unpaid arrears in city real-estate taxes amounting to $570.8 million as of June 30, 1976. (Interestingly, the nonpayment of real-estate taxes, and Tammany's nonchalant response to it, was a major factor in the first bankers' "take-over" of city government during the 1930s Depression.) The issue has been a political hot potato for at least a decade. A handful of liberals have fought to change the state law governing the collection of these taxes, but they have never received the support of city administrators, who would have benefited most from up-to-date collections. In 1976, the City Council reduced the delinquency period to one year. Unfortunately, the Koch administration refuses to apply the law and fails to foreclose on tens of thousands of tax cheats. We present the real-estate tax delinquencies as an interesting case study of how one special interest has been protected by a succession of city administrations, which in turn depended heavily on campaign contributions from the same group of people.

Landlords in New York City were not required to pay real-estate taxes for three years. (Until a few years ago, it was four.) While they must pay interest charges on arrears, the interest has always been lower than that charged for loans by commercial banks. In effect, then, the city has been making low-interest loans to property owners, among them some of the largest commercial landlords in New York, during a period when it was forced to borrow at extortionate rates in the municipal market.

After the one-year period has expired, the city may move in court to take the property "in rem" (in place of) the taxes it is owed. Several studies have shown that at this point three out of four landlords will make a payment sufficient to forestall foreclosure, although never the full amount owed. And then the cycle begins all over again. (Those buildings actually seized by the city—buildings now freed of excessive mortgage payments—can provide operating profits equal to the previous taxes.)

The landlords have always successfully argued that they are unable to keep current with their taxes because of the strictures of New York City's rent-control system. But 43 per cent of the arrearages occur in tax payments for uncontrolled commercial properties (office buildings, hotels, and stores) and 23 per cent for single-family homes. The remaining third are arrears in tax payments for multiple dwellings, where rent controls have been seriously relaxed in recent years. As rent rolls have risen, however, so have tax delinquencies. One dead-beat landlord candidly admitted that the taxes weren't paid simply because they were "the cheapest loan in town."

New York City is not the only culprit in the tax-evasion boondoggle. In recent years the state has become responsible for collecting the city sales tax. According to one source, the city is losing $200 million a year in taxes collected by merchants but never turned over to the tax collector. The state itself loses $300 million a year from uncollected sales taxes; combined, this is a cool half-billion dollars. The sales-tax collection system is a fantastic giveaway for retailers even if they don't cheat. The taxes, collected with each purchase, are required to be turned in only every three months. The bank interest earned by the retailer in this period is his "reward" for serving as a tax agent. In the meantime, the state and city must borrow to cover their own weekly operating costs. Out-of-state merchants collect city and state sales taxes but rarely turn back anywhere near the amount collected. They are never audited.

In May 1976, City Controller Harrison Goldin privately distributed to the top officers of the city an audit of one tiny part of the city's sales-tax collection system for an eight-month period that ended on February 29, 1976. This audit showed that "the city's sales tax collecting unit issued assessments of $7.5 million, while incurring operating costs of $359,000." This works out to $20 of sales-tax assessments for every $1 the city spends to fund the unit. A 20-to-1 ratio would seem a wise investment for a bankrupt city. But the collection unit has not been expanded.

Withholding taxes, taken from the wages of employees to cover state and city income taxes, also have a strange habit of disappearing before they ever enter the public treasury. Comptroller Levitt found in a 1972 audit (not published until 1975) that employers simply kept $36 million in these taxes owed to the state. It may be assumed that these companies did the same with the smaller wage taxes owed the city, for a combined amount of $50 million. There have been no audits published for succeeding years, but it should be remembered that 1972 was an artificial "boom" year, created with a massive increase in the money supply by a friendly Federal Reserve Bank to insure Nixon's re-election. In the following recession years, it can be conservatively assumed that this amount doubled—a loss somewhere in the range of $400 million to both levels of government. Levitt found that little of this money was ever recovered because the statute of limitations for prosecution frequently ran out before state tax auditors discovered the delinquency.

The list goes on. Of the twenty-two separate taxes levied by New York City, not one can be certified as fully collected. The state, with more than twice the number of residents, has an equally depressing record. The problem is hardly restricted to New York, however. One congressional staffer estimated in an article in *Washington Monthly* that as much as half of all state taxes go unpaid. Two years ago, officials of the Multistate Tax Commission, a confederation of state tax agencies trying to stem the problem, told us off the record that the annual state tax shortfall, exclusive of property taxes, was then $12 billion, But New York, unlike California (an effective tax collector), has never even bothered to join the MTC in order to benefit from jointly conducted sales tax audits of the biggest national companies.

Medicaid frauds cost New York City at least $300 million a year, according to a U.S. Senate study. As Robert Sternberg, chief auditor for medical payments of the city Department of Social Services, told *The New York Times:* "We don't have enough help to process the paper, let alone audit the providers." He said that a staff of only three auditors, working with a computer, had detected duplicate payments of $2.5 million to Medicaid "mills" in 1975. "If we had six people, we would have collected $5 million."

Nine per cent of the city's million welfare recipients were "ineligible" in 1976. If they had been expunged from the rolls, the city would have saved an additional $100 million.

Landlords who received city loans to rehabilitate vacant buildings through the scandal-plagued municipal loan program owed $107 million.

An audit of the Parks Department revealed that $2 million was owed by concessionaires, including Good Humor ice cream and the Circle Line Sightseeing Boats (whose chairman, Francis Barry, is a Bronx Democratic wheelhorse and a member of the Municipal Assistance Corporation set up to issue city debt and supervise the revision of the city's accounting practices.)

Obviously not every last cent owed to New York City was collectible, but a good part of it was. No one tried—and billions were irretrievably lost. The master managers who were swept into power with the formation of MAC and the Emergency Financial Control Board in 1975 have shown no more interest in collecting delinquent revenues than the hacks they replaced, who could always shrug off a tax shortfall with another loan. Apparently stringent collection policies don't fit in with the new "pro-business" image that is being cultivated by both City Hall and Albany. It is now more than seven years since the fiscal crisis became official; an army of auditors has been poring over the city's books and issuing one damning report after another. But there should be another army of auditors poring over the books of landlords, department stores, manufacturers, proprietary and voluntary hospitals, Medicaid mills, and the dozens of other institutions that have been milking the city for at least a decade. That army doesn't exist, and there is little likelihood it will be formed. In fact, some of the city and state auditing personnel have been cut back in the budget crunch—to "save money," of course.

As we found when we were both involved in investigating the putrid nursing-home scandals in 1974, auditors are the key to efficient management of all government programs. Any auditor is worth at least ten times his annual salary in the money he will recover. Just the knowledge that someone is looking over their shoulders is enough to deter many of the predators who have made large fortunes ripping-off government programs. In the long run, it is the legitimate businessman and the honest taxpayer who are the victims of the tax deadbeats and thieves. They must carry a larger burden when the unscrupulous are allowed to run free without paying.

The list still goes on and on: $4 million owed in mortgage payments by private landlords, $3.5 million in uncollected water bills (for several years the city had been sending the water bill for a luxury high-rise apartment house to a neighboring city park). It is a portrait of almost mind-boggling incompetence and mismanagement. Yet consistently, the politicians who run the city have been excoriated by the press and the business community for borrowing too much, rarely for collecting too little. Why?

The answer is inescapable. There is an unspoken, conservative bias in the efforts to restructure the city government, which holds that the poor and the powerless must now pay the price for decades of economic and political misgovernment.

The city's crisis is a reflection of a much larger national and international crisis affecting the entire capitalist system. And while New York is always *sui generis*, it is important to recognize that the "solutions" imposed nationwide by the Republican administration—massive unemployment, reduction in government services, a general decline in the standard of living—are the same as those being prescribed for the city. At the center of this strategy is a vast, complex struggle over who will control the limited capital resources of mankind in the decades to come.

In the next chapter, we shall analyze in greater detail this struggle between corporate priorities and democratic priorities, the conflict between investing for profit and investing for the needs of people. An awareness of this struggle is critical to any understanding of the city's turbulent present and its uncertain, ominous future.

Right now it is important to keep that broader perspective in mind as we consider another crucial element in the real history of New York's fiscal collapse: the role of the banks in the final withdrawal of credit. There is no element of New York's recent history that has been so poorly reported or badly misunderstood. As we shall show, the generally accepted perception that the banks were hoodwinked by the city's politicians is pure myth.

Instead it was the bankers who did the hoodwinking—lying to thousands of hapless investors, to the press, and even to the City Hall sharpies who were left holding the bag after a fullfledged market panic had commenced. The true story took almost three years to emerge: New York didn't jump; it was pushed.

In early 1973, UDC was already deep in trouble and First Boston and the other underwriters, including Chase, Citibank, and Morgan Guaranty, knew it. Logue, in his usual blunt fashion, told them that UDC "would not be self-supporting" for some time and proposed that they continue selling bonds so that he might "roll over" current debts as they came due—borrowing to pay off earlier borrowing. They acceded, but as the state investigating commission reported: "They also realized that UDC would probably at some future date be the first test of the state's legislative intent to honor its 'moral obligation' to make up a deficiency in a debt service reserve fund." And if the legislature reneged—down would come the whole house of cards.

The report continued:

It was clear to the underwriters that, at best, the Legislature was not aware of UDC's financial condition and, at worst, as a result of the Nine Towns controversy, was antagonistic to UDC. Significantly, the uncertainty over future legislative backing for UDC did not depreciate the viability of the moral obligation in the eyes of the managers, because they were assured that UDC had an excellent relationship with the Governor. Given Mr. Rockefeller's preeminent position in the political power structure of the State, this was no small assurance.

And there you have it. The banks didn't give a damn about the soundness of paper that the state, or the city for that matter, had been churning out, for as long as Nelson Rockefeller held the reins of power, they felt protected. It was Nelson's "moral obligation" that motivated them, not the legislature's, and his assurance that he would always place their interests first in any subsequent crisis. He would keep the legislature in line, as he had so often in the past, using his personal wealth, the patronage powers of his office, and his entrée at the White House to see that whatever happened the banks would be protected.

And then Rockefeller resigned. It was a thunderclap for the banks. As the state investigators noted in their classicly understated prose, "His long tenure in Albany had created expectations on the part of the financial community, and Malcolm Wilson's succession cast doubt on those expectations."

The banks were already being buffeted on all sides. Defaults on real estate investment trusts, the Yom Kippur war, and the Arab oil boycott had all occurred only a few months before, throwing money markets into chaos and auguring a major change in international power relationships. There was talk of war coming from Henry Kissinger and the White House, and this was not simply an attempt to get Richard Nixon off the Watergate hook. Even without the unsettled oil situation, the United States had begun its slide into the recession long forecast for 1974. With inflation raging as never before, it was clear that not even the Chairman of the Federal Reserve, Arthur Burns, could bail the banks out as he had after the 1970-71 nightmare. And now Rockefeller was gone, perhaps to await the call to lead the nation that had never come in more stable times, but perhaps not.

The time had come for the bankers to take a careful look at all that New York state and city paper with which their vaults were stuffed. They didn't like what they found. If the state was in trouble, then the city faced a calamity. The city is totally dependent on the state for taxing power and a significant part of its revenue. It was at this point, in February 1974, that Morgan Guaranty dropped out as an underwriter for UDC. This should have served as a signal—to the legislature, the financial press, the editorial writers, the financial markets, even the bevy of Rockefeller watchers, always sensitive to even the slightest movements around the throne. With everything else in such a state of flux, however, the Morgan action passed almost unnoticed.

While the banks kept a stiff upper lip in public, a note of panic was seeping into internal memorandums. Consider this statement from hitherto secret minutes of Chase Manhattan's municipal credit portfolio review committee in mid-March 1974—exactly a year before the banks shut off the city's credit:

New York City is a different problem. In terms of the credit quality the City's rating has been wobbling between a– and baa + for over a decade. In recent months the City's financial situation has deteriorated, partly because reality began to catch up with past budget gimmickry and partly because of the re-emergence of a growing gap between receipts and expenditures. Although New York City's economic base is enormous and a financial collapse is difficult to imagine, we view the City as being saddled with fundamentally adverse financial trends. . . .

New York City obligations present a special problem because of the City's disappointing financial performance. Although a final assessment of the City's credit should await completion of the new study currently in progress, our present impression is that the market's evaluation of the New York City name once again could begin to slip. In view of this assessment, our judgment is that the portfolio's New York City bond holdings are somewhat heavier than desirable, particularly since sizeable additional New York City obligations are held in the short-term note account.

Within the framework of overall Bank objectives regarding loss taking, holdings of New York City bonds should be reduced while New York State and energy-related issues should not be increased.

By August 1, the minutes of Chase's portfolio strategy committee listed as its first priority in tax-exempt bonds: "Look for opportunity to sell about $50 M [million] of intermediate New York City's [bonds] taking small loss if possible." By November 20, the bank's dealer strategy committee noted that it was "continuing to sell NYC obligations at every opportunity." The panic was on.

As subsequent investigations by the federal Securities and Exchange Commission and the state's Office of Legislative Oversight and Analysis would show, the big New York City banks, as well as other major banks across the nation, quietly dumped approximately $2.3 billion in New York City securities on the market between the summer of 1974 and March 1975 when that market finally collapsed. Many of these sales were made without charging commissions, a symbol of the extent of the banks' panic. During the same period, many of these same banks were underwriters for the billions in new debt issues which New York required to meet its daily needs and stave off default.

This pattern of using "inside" information as a basis for dumping doubtful securities was chillingly familiar to those who knew how the big banks had bailed out just before the Penn Central collapse in 1970. History was repeating itself.

In private meetings, the bankers who were members of Controller Goldin's technical debt committee—Thomas G. Labrecque, the 39-year-old executive vice-president of Chase Manhattan; Richard F. Kezer, senior vice-president of Citibank; and Frank P. Smeal, executive vice-president of Morgan Guaranty—meantime warned that the interest rates which Beame and Goldin had jointly denounced as "unfair, unwarranted and outrageously high" would be going even higher in order to attract buyers in a "glutted" market. Goldin had clear indications that the banks might be "bailing out," because his staff had presented him with Federal Reserve reports early in 1975 which showed that the banks were heavy sellers of municipal obligations for their own accounts. These figures did not reflect what the bank trust departments, which manage large aggregations of money left in their care by institutions and wealthy individuals, were selling, but as the Penn Central situation showed, the "Chinese Wall" which is supposed to exist between separate divisions of a bank is often full of gaping holes.

In an interview with us in September 1976, Goldin, with a mournful bust of Abraham Lincoln peering over his shoulder in his cavernous office in the Municipal Building, admitted that he had "suspicions" as early as the summer of 1974. He muted his statements to the press, however, because the information presented him was not "dispositive," a lawyer's word for conclusive. "I don't know to this day that they did" dump the city's obligations, he said.

Goldin, however, did present his suspicions to the Board of Estimate, in some of the "crisis" meetings that were to become an almost daily occurrence as the situation worsened. The Board is a unique feature of New York government, a hangover from the days when each county Democratic machine wanted to make sure it was getting its fair slice of the pie. On it sit the mayor, comptroller, City Council president, and the borough presidents of each of the five boroughs, or counties, that make up the city. In the past, the borough presidents sat as surrogates for their county leaders. This situation has changed only slightly in recent years, with the minor inroads of the city's reform Democrats. Until the Emergency Financial Control Board (EFCB) was created by the state, the Board of Estimate had vast powers, far greater than the almost irrelevant City Council, and it still must pass on all major city contracts as well as the capital budget submitted by the mayor. It was the real locus of power in city government until September 1975, although in effect a creature of the mayor since most of its members are allied with the mayor through the county Democratic organizations. (The Board of Estimate was a bone in Lindsay's throat until he made peaee with the Democratic machines after his re-election in 1969.) If there was to be a counterattack against the banks' undermining of the securities markets, this was where it must be generated. City Council President Paul O'Dwyer, a perennial candidate for higher office even though he was then in his late sixties, at least tried. On several occasions he denounced the banks for attempting to decide the city's social priorities. A few other Board members mumbled similar populist sentiments and were quickly jumped on by the establishment.

No one dared to mention that it was the banks themselves that had overloaded the market. So as everyone rushed for the exits, the city's leading politicians sat with their hands folded and said nothing, lest they cause a "panic." This left the banks in an awkward position. After they had decided to stop peddling the now worthless city paper, it was important to let everyone know that the panic had already taken place. To solve this problem, Jac Friedgut, a vice-president of Citibank, held a session in Washington with the city's congressional delegation in mid-March 1975, and told them that his bank would no longer buy city notes because the city had lost the confidence of the market. Beame was in Washington the same day and rejoined, "If he made that statement it's outrageous. The top officials of that bank owe the city an explanation." Poor Abe. No one had told him the show was over because the theater had burned down.

William Haddad, an award-winning investigative reporter who had been one of the first to notice that Robert Moses had clay feet back in the 1950s, was one of the first people poking around in the ashes. After more than a decade in private business, Haddad had returned to public service as director of the Office of Legislative Oversight and Analysis in the state Assembly, a sort of inspector-general for the Democratic majority in the lower house. He intuitively figured out what the banks had been up to, although he at first thought it an elaborate scam to drive up interest rates when in fact the banks were more than grateful simply to escape with a whole skin.

Haddad wanted the Assembly to hold hearings immediately, but he was shot down by his nervous employers. (When he asked for crucial documents, the banks threatened that his investigation might cripple the state's delicate refinancing arrangements with them; similar threats were made to SEC staffers during the initial stages of their investigation.) He kept on plugging away, as can be seen by the following confidential memorandum he sent to George Cincotta, chairman of the Assembly Banking Committee on July 7, 1976:

> . . . As you may recall, the premise of our inquiry was based on the following chronology.
>
> (1) The political changes in Albany (Rockefeller's departure and Wilson's inability to win the election) caused the banks to review their portfolios. The UDC crisis was on the horizon already and with their protection in Albany removed, they were exposed.
>
> (2) They began to rapidly and quietly (and, perhaps improperly and illegally) unload their New York City bonds *and thus saturated the market*[italics in original]. You recall, they claim the market was saturated and hence they could not sell their bonds. This seems to be untrue. In fact, it appears that Chase unloaded two billion dollars' worth of bonds in a very short time!
>
> . . . Here is where the situation gets sticky for the banks. They had knowledge of the problems ahead, but they kept this knowledge to themselves while unloading their portfolios to others. They created the panic by their heavy sales. There are many examples of poor, little people being crushed by this fraud (one a blind woman, several who had moved to Florida for a year while testing out the climate there and investing their money in "safe" municipal bonds, etc.).
>
> In short, Chase alone unloaded two billion dollars of paper they knew was going bad without telling their customers. They not only created the panic, but profited from it.
>
> (3) When the banks saturated the market with their own paper [i.e. city bonds originally purchased for their own accounts], they turned to the State and the City and shouted "Help." The market was flooded and they could not sell their bonds. This, in turn, led to us bailing them out, and to higher interest rates for every municipality in the country. It led to the EFCB and a substantial portion of the enormous debt service we are now carrying.
>
> If I do nothing else with this office, this is a case we need to prove. We now have the SEC as our ally, at least at the team level here (top-flight lawyers). And we were right last year when we said all this and everyone smiled at us.

By the time this was written, no one was smiling—least of all the banks. The City of New York brought suit in August 1976 to stop the SEC investigation, claiming the agency lacked jurisdiction over municipal securities sales.

There can be little doubt that had the press reported, and the public fully understood, how the New York City crisis had been artificially fostered by the bank panic, New York's immediate history would have been quite different.

Even someone as obtuse as Gerald Ford or wearing the ideological blinders of an Arthur Burns or a William Simon would have been hard pressed to pillory the city for a crisis for which it was only partly responsible. The impact on the banks, already reeling under the disclosure of failing loans to the real-estate investment trusts, to builders of giant oil tankers that would never be used, to overextended corporations and shaky foreign dictators, would have been profound. As it was, eleven insolvent banks were forced to close their doors in 1975, the highest number since the country emerged from the Depression in 1942. Disclosure of bank manipulation of the municipal-securities markets might have doomed some of the biggest on the list of almost 300 "trouble" banks maintained by the Federal Deposit Insurance Corporation—and Chase Manhattan would have been among the first to go.

When Tom Labrecque approved the order to sell the more than $1 billion Chase held in city securities, he entered the ranks of the nation's all-time high rollers. He wasn't playing only for the solvency of his own institution; the stability of the international banking community rode on his decision. And he won, because no one—city officials, the state legislature, federal banking regulators, or the City Hall press corps, which at least heard rumors about what was going on—bothered to tell the people.* The big loser of course was the city and its people. But everyone in the nation lost as well. Michael C. Jensen, writing in *The New York Times* of October 19, 1975, estimated that *all* states and municipalities ended up paying an additional $3 billion in inflated borrowing costs as a result of the New York crisis. Jensen figured, "That amounts to $14 for each man, woman, and child in the United States." A high price to pay for protecting the good name of the banks.

A week before the Democratic primary in 1977, the SEC released its anxiously awaited report on the fiscal crisis. It was harshly critical of Mayor Beame and Controller Goldin accusing them of having "misled public investors in the offer, sale and distribution of billions of dollars of the city's

---

*Fred Ferretti, another City Hall reporter for *The New York Times* during the fiscal crisis, subsequently wrote a book called *The Year the Big Apple Went Bust*. In it Ferretti treats the banks "bailout" as a throwaway line in his first chapter. Writing of the summer before the crisis year, he says: "During this period too the banks began to toy with unloading their own stacks of city notes, and later they were to sell off great chunks." That's all.

Reviewing Ferretti's book in the June 21, 1976, *Village Voice*, the political writer Geoffrey Stokes quoted a line in the book, "What is the purpose of a government—to care for its citizens or make heroes of its accountants?" and went on shrewdly to observe: "New Yorkers have asked that question in a dozen different languages and one hundred different accents over the past eighteen months. For us—and for Ferretti—the answer is obvious: The real question is why it wasn't equally obvious to the powers in Washington and on Wall Street. One reason is that they'd been reading *The New York Times*, in which the passion that informs Ferretti's book has been conspicuously lacking. Indeed, the tone of his book is an implied indictment of Ferretti's own daily reporting. . . . Ferretti, who concludes his book with an impassioned defense of the city's efforts to make life as decent as possible for its inhabitants, has been systematically turning out daily reporting that counteracts the book's angry thrust."

municipal securities." It is also charged that six of the city's leading banks and the nation's largest brokerage house had been unloading their own holdings of city notes while touting them as good investments to the public. The six banks were: Citibank, Morgan Guaranty Trust, Bankers Trust, Chase Manhattan, Manufacturers Hanover Trust, and Chemical Bank. Merrill Lynch was the brokerage house. Standard and Poor's and Moody's were criticized for failing to independently verify the city's financial claims as were the four bond counsels: Hawkins, Delafield and Wood; Sykes, Galloway and Dikeman; Wood, Dawson, Love and Sabbatine; and White and Case.

Everything in the report verified a story we had written almost a year before in *The Village Voice,* but which the rest of the New York press had refused to follow up. The only real casualty of the report was Abe Beame, who lost his re-election bid on September 8, 1977. Despite talk of criminal prosecutions for the banks, the whole matter was quietly interred by Robert Fiske, the U.S. Attorney for the Southern District on a quiet Friday afternoon in August, two years later, with a four sentence press release. Prior to assuming the U.S. Attorney's job, Fiske had been a partner in Davis, Polk, the lead lawyers for Morgan Guaranty. He himself was an attorney for the bank. Fiske resigned in early 1980 and has returned to his law practice.

Before we move on to a consideration of the federal government's participation in the city's crisis, there is one final item, also obscured or ignored by the "official" chroniclers of the crisis, that demands our attention. This is the long-term breakdown of the municipal credit markets—no small contributor to the current mess. After all, New York City accounted for only 5 per cent of the country's total municipal debt before it collapsed, although it issued 29 per cent of the short-term debt.

As Sanford Rose noted in the December 1975 issue of *Fortune:*

> The effects of New York's troubles have cast a pall over the entire municipal market. Yet it would be a gross overstatement to say that the current crisis in the market is solely, or even primarily, a consequence of New York's situation. Actually, the crisis started before that city's difficulties became well known in the market place, and is likely to continue long after its problems are resolved. . . .
>   . . . The municipal market is going through a crisis—one of the worst in its history. It is a crisis that could well lead to a thorough revamping of the market's structure.

The reasons for that crisis aren't hard to find. As Rose explains, "State and local governments are expanding borrowings at a rapid pace just when traditional holders of tax-exempt bonds are cutting back on their purchases."

The municipal bond market caters exclusively to banks, corporations, and wealthy individuals seeking to protect their income from federal, state, and local taxes. Constitutionally, one level of government is banned from taxing the financial instruments of another. This means that the federal government cannot tax the income from a New York State bond, for instance. New York State and the city also treat income on their bonds as tax exempt. For individuals and corporations in high tax brackets this is a major boon. For someone in the 50 per cent tax bracket, an interest rate of 8 per cent on a tax-free bond is equal to an interest rate of 16 per cent on a taxable corporate bond. Since taxable bonds rarely pay such high rates, at least not bonds from corporations with any prospect of remaining in business long enough to pay back the original investment in the bond, municipals have been good deals for the wealthy and even the not-so-wealthy. With municipals today paying interest that is about 80 per cent of that paid by corporates, even people in the 30 per cent bracket—$15-$20,000 a year—can make a tidy profit from the offerings of government agencies. The same goes for smaller corporations.

Tax-free institutions (a major portion of the national capital pool) such as pension funds, foundations, churches, colleges, and mutual savings banks gain no benefits from this tax exemption, however, and when they buy municipal bonds it is only as a safety hedge against the mercurial nature of the stock market.

Until recently, the largest purchasers of municipals have been commercial banks and, to a lesser degree, the casualty insurance companies. Wealthy individuals constitute the third largest component of the market. But in the last few years the banks have developed so many other tax loopholes that they have significantly cut back on new purchases of municipals. They still account, however, for about half of municipal-bond holdings.

Banks pay almost no federal taxes and minuscule state taxes. For instance, in 1974, the ten largest bank holding companies in America paid an average of only 2 per cent in federal taxes on worldwide earnings of $2 billion.* All of the large banks, those with $500 million or more in deposits, paid only 11 per cent in taxes, while medium-sized banks, those with deposits between $100 million and $500 million, paid only 12 per cent. In contrast, a worker earning $8,000 in 1974 paid 20 per cent in federal taxes.

Aside from the purchase of municipals, the banks' tax writeoffs have come from two gaping loopholes. In recent years, almost half the profits of the big banks are coming from operations in foreign countries. But the taxes paid to those countries—a cost of doing business abroad—are treated as if they were paid to the U.S. Treasury. That is, the banks can deduct foreign taxes from U.S. tax liabilities on a dollar-for-dollar basis. Besides seriously depleting the

---

*The ten were: BankAmerica, Citicorp, Chase Manhattan, J. P. Morgan, Manufacturers Hanover, Chemical New York, Bankers Trust New York, Continental Illinois, Security Pacific and Wells Fargo. Chase Manhattan, with profits worldwide of $235.5 million, and Chemical, with $97 million, actually shared tax rebates from the federal government amounting to $21.6 million because of the laxity of the tax laws. The statutory tax rate for all corporations is 48 per cent, and after standard deductions and investment credits, the average effective corporate tax is 30 per cent.

Treasury and shifting the tax burden to those least able to pay, this loophole constitutes a major inducement to export American wealth and jobs abroad, frequently to dictatorships like Chile, Brazil, and Korea, where the rate of profits is high because workers can be shot for striking for higher wages.

The second loophole is a product of the bank holding company laws first passed in the 1960s. This allows banks to use their capital to buy other businesses. As a result, banks have taken to leasing high-cost machinery like computers to industry and taking the depreciation and investment tax credits allowed by Congress as an inducement for capital spending. The banks are in fact only middlemen, but they take the lion's share of these benefits.

Purely and simply, the banks have found these new writeoffs more profitable than municipal bonds. In addition, the banks are beginning to worry that the public may be waking up to the full amounts of tax ripoffs they are allowed. In order to keep things quiet, they must pay at least token taxes, and, with the embarrassment of options now available to them, municipals are losing their allure.

As for the casualty insurers, also major purchasers of municipals, they have had no profits to protect from taxes since they took such a bad bath in the stock market in 1975 and since the costs of replacement parts for cars, for instance, have been driven through the roof by the giant auto monopolies. This situation is now changing because lax state insurance regulators have allowed astronomical rate increases for drivers, and insurance company profits are due for a sharp rebound; but this hardly spells salvation for the municipal market.

In fact, it is interesting to note that the market is particularly hard hit by the roller-coaster ride the economy has been taking. Demand for municipals falls at the very time when economic decline places the greatest pressure on state and local spending. The market is increasingly dependent, therefore, on wealthy individuals. This entails a number of problems. First, the rich have other more profitable income-protection schemes available, despite all the blather about tax reform. Second, to avoid the ravages of inflation, a lot of their wealth is increasingly invested in property rather than paper. Third, the rich lie a lot, and put their money in Swiss banks.

All of this leaves too narrow a market to support government borrowing needs, and it leads to constantly increasing interest rates. The fastest way to expand the market would be to offer municipal bonds to the many moderate- and middle-income investors who would jump at the chance to buy them. However, these bonds are offered exclusively in such large denominations ($25,000, $10,000, and occasionally $5,000) that ordinary people can't invest; one bond might equal their total savings. There have been continued demands from city officials to reduce these amounts—offering, for example, $100, $500, or $1,000 bonds. But even at the height of New York's crisis, this alternative was rejected by the banks and other municipal sellers, who claimed it would increase administrative costs for the city. But since this increase would be balanced by lower interest costs from a broader market, the argument doesn't hold water. The real reason for the hostility is much simpler: Financial institutions don't want to lose the vast amounts they now hold in small savings accounts at federally prescribed low interest rates. This is especially true of the savings banks that systematically ship large amounts of capital from the Northeast to other parts of the country—a drain that is responsible for a severe capital shortage in the very areas that generate most of America's capital.

(Small investors have been given a break in the Tax Reform Act of 1976, which allows mutual funds to invest in municipals for the first time. Now an investor can buy a share in a block of high-priced bonds and still receive the tax exemption on his portion of the interest.)

In addition, the municipal market has been overwhelmed by a glut of spurious new "municipals" that are in fact simply private borrowings hiding behind a government fig leaf. These are the "pollution-control" and "industrial-development" bonds. Many localities also issue general-obligation bonds to subsidize everything from private colleges and hospitals to commercial baseball and football teams.

As *The Wall Street Journal* revealed on July 21, 1976, the basic problem with industrial-development bonds is that they often go sour. For instance, Burns Flats, Oklahoma, issued industrial-development bonds to build a factory for the Western States Plastics Company. The company, not the town, was liable for repayment of both the face value of the bonds and the interest; it quickly went under and investors were left holding the bag. The SEC and the Oklahoma Securities Commission have been investigating the case for fraud—a frequent charge in many of these issues. As the *Journal* noted: "In many cases, government investigators' preliminary findings on suspected fraudulent issues seem to implicate not only the recipients of the bond money but also the sponsors who helped bring the issues to the public."

Similarly, in the case of "pollution-control" bonds, everyone seems to lose but the company that is having its equipment financed. As Rose explained in *Fortune:*

Federal law permits state and local agencies to issue tax-exempt bonds in order to finance pollution-control equipment for the benefit of private corporations. Typically, the equipment is leased to the corporations, with the lease payments structured to meet the debt service on the bonds.

The pollution-control bond gives the corporations a triple or, in some cases, a quadruple subsidy. The company gets the benefit of the state's lower borrowing costs. It can also treat the pollution facility as its own property, and so depreciate it on an accelerated basis, and, under certain conditions, it may even be able to deduct a part of the lease payments as business expenses. As if that were not enough, in most states, pollution-control facilities are exempt from local property taxes.

Rose cites one federal source as estimating that $4-$7 billion is now tied up in this kind of financing.

Many solutions to these problems have been bandied about for years. Rose and others, among them Senator Edward Kennedy, favor the issuance of taxable municipals underwritten by direct federal interest subsidies. Since the federal government now loses about $1.40 in taxes for every $1 saved by municipal borrowers, they feel that the subsidy would save money for both the Treasury and lower levels of government. While taxable bonds would have to pay higher yields, they would open the market to the tax-free institutions, and this significantly increased demand should keep a reasonable lid on yields. At the same time, by reducing the supply of tax-exempt bonds, yields for those exclusively interested in the tax exemption would fall and prices would rise. This would both stabilize and broaden the market, they argue.

Opposition to these proposals comes primarily from municipalities who fear dependency on a federal subsidy that might be withdrawn by some future Congress. The investment bankers are also opposed, because a simpler market might put them out of business.

Many large cities are hesitant about the taxable bonds, but they certainly want to see Congress act to restrict the proliferation of new types of bonds, such as the industrial-development and pollution-control issues. They think the feds should subsidize these activities through direct investment tax credits.

We'll have more to say about this when we make some recommendations for salvaging the cities at the end of the book. Right now we would simply observe that it is fascinating that an administration which went berserk dreaming up tax writeoffs for utilities, defense contractors, and giant corporations left the municipalities and a major securities market to twist in the wind. Treasury Secretary Simon was at great pains to reassure Congress that no reforms in the municipal markets were necessary—after New York had been excluded. Almost every other observer feels that our outdated, inadequate municipal markets are long overdue for a complete restructuring.

Nixon Was The One | 3

In early 1973, Robert Lekachman, the most incisive of our popular economists, wrote, "President Nixon . . . is celebrating his second term with the most coherent conservative program of redistribution of income, wealth, public services and political power from poor to rich that has been offered by any major American politician in living memory." The major victim of the Nixon counter-revolution was America's cities, especially the aging cities of the Northeast and Midwest.

Only a few short years after the trauma of Watergate, it is hard to remember just how powerful Richard Nixon was in the wake of his landslide victory over George McGovern. It was the height of the Imperial Presidency. Congress was impotent, despite its overwhelming Democratic majority. If it passed legislation that Nixon disapproved, Nixon would veto it. If it overrode his vetoes, he would impound the monies it appropriated. If it sued to set aside his impoundments, the issue would wend its way through the courts, even to a Supreme Court whose conservative majority he had shaped. To all intents and purposes, Richard Nixon was *the* American government.

Yet Nixon seemed immune to the nourishing mystique of the presidency. Although a cunning politician, as a president he was lacking in self-confidence and driven by insecurities, paranoia, and petty venality. He probably did not burn the White House tapes out of fear of losing certain tax advantages. He seemed to doubt his own legitimacy to rule. As JFK once said, he "had no class." He brooded over minor resentments and past slights. In the twisted mire of the Nixon mind, he resented—among so many things—America's large cities, with all their unruly minorities and nonconformists.

He signaled his intentions in a now-famous postelection interview with *The Washington Star* when he vowed to stop "throwing dollars at problems' Whether carefully rehearsed or spontaneous, this was a brilliant phrase, and its echoes can still be heard—not only from Republicans but from a whole new generation of Democrats with their admonitions to "lower our expectations." Nixon captured in that one phrase all the frustrations of the many hardworking, tax-paying Americans who saw government—all government—as an alien bureaucracy demanding an ever greater share of their paychecks in order to lavish new benefits on blacks and other minority groups; pot-smoking, foulmouthed college students; and insolent, "unproductive" public employees.

The reality of course was quite different. The Great Society had never been even minimally financed to deal with the true scope of the problems it vowed to eradicate. Seventy per cent of the increase in social spending during the late 1960s and early 1970s had been for Social Security and Medicare, and the rest was mostly window dressing. Meanwhile, progressive taxes on businesses and wealthy individuals had been cut by $25 billion between 1969 and 1974 while regressive payroll taxes on workers had been raised by $20 billion.

No matter, at the heart of Nixon's re-election campaign had been a promise to punish all of the groups in our society that had raised their voices against exclusion and oppression. Now Nixon read the election returns as a mandate to repeal not only the modest social experiments of the Great Society years but the profound accomplishments of the New Deal as well. His first postelection budget was a blueprint for vengeance, an "enemies list" that included the majority of the American people.

Nixon proposed to eliminate or sharply reduce no less than 101 programs that had developed over almost four decades. Lekachman has cited a few of the outstanding examples:

> The Nixon body count includes reductions in housing for lower-income families, rural electrification, public service employment, special programs in mental health, model cities, urban renewal, manpower training, some aids for education, student loans, support for libraries, improvements and extensions in the national parks, research and development on mass transportation, and training programs in medical and biological research. Just for good measure, the White House has also impounded half the money Congress appropriated for pollution control, disbanded the Office of Economic Opportunity and placed in limbo its generally acclaimed legal services program, and interred the Family Assistance Plan, a year or two ago hailed by the President as the center-piece of his New American Revolution.

A quick glance shows that most of these programs had as their principal purpose the improvement of conditions in the large cities.

All of this would be done in the holy name of fighting inflation and reining in the "runaway" federal budget. Not that Nixon actually intended to reduce spending: Even while slashing social and antipollution programs by $14 billion, he projected an $18-billion overall increase to cover increased debt service costs, Social Security hikes necessitated by inflation, and a $5 billion expansion of the Pentagon budget for new weapons and old wars—including the continuing conflict in Vietnam. He skillfully danced around the fact that 54 cents of every dollar in the national budget would go for military spending. It still does.

In Nixon's view, a view shared by conservatives in both parties, gorging the Pentagon was "necessary spending"; spending for education, housing, health care, or clean rivers and lakes was "wasteful spending."

Actually, the Congressional liberals lent Nixon a great deal of unwitting support in his program against social spending and the cities. This was the year when the long crusade for "revenue sharing" finally bore fruit—and revenue sharing was predominantly a liberal program. Although first introduced by Republican Congressman (later Defense Secretary) Melvin R. Laird in 1958, the idea had been rapidly adopted by John Kennedy's staff, especially by Walter Heller, his chairman of the Council of Economic Advisers. As Milwaukee Democratic Congressman Henry Reuss described the idea in his 1970 book, *Revenue Sharing:*

In the main, state and local governments must still look after our great domestic needs—education, public safety, public health, the environment, welfare, the future of our cities. But demands for public services are fast outstripping local financial resources.

The problem is exacerbated because state and local governments rely mainly on property and sales taxes that fall especially hard on the person of modest income. The Federal government relies heavily on the progressive income tax, based generally on ability to pay. Moreover, Federal revenues grow with the economy much more rapidly than do state-local revenues. Increasingly, therefore, the federal government will have the revenues, and state and local governments will have the problems.

Reuss and other liberals supporting revenue sharing foresaw a massive "peace dividend" at the end of the Vietnam war. They wanted to take these monies and share them with state and local governments to redress the imbalance in the tax bases. At the same time, they felt that the Washington bureaucracy was too rigid in its administration of social programs, and too remote from the groups being served.

Behind these arguments lay another purpose, however. The proliferation of categorical grant programs, especially the War on Poverty designed under Kennedy and enacted by Johnson, tended to weaken the power of state and local Democratic machines. More and more, the feds were dealing directly with new neighborhood groups and nonprofit agencies, and even the funds flowing through elected administrations or establishment institutions required "citizen participation" and oversight by local community people. This reduced the potential for old-fashioned patronage and weakened the power bases of incumbents, who wanted to be able to go to Washington with the assurance that everything would remain quiet on the home front. Revenue sharing with local governments would return the control over social spending to the traditional machines.

When revenue sharing was finally enacted, the Vietnam war still was dragging on. (As usual the liberals had underestimated the power of the military-industrial complex: even after the war ended, there was no "peace dividend." Instead, the money went into the maw of the Pentagon to develop new weapons, to reassure our frightened allies that we had not gone "soft" in the face of defeat, and to finance that other brainchild of misguided liberals—a volunteer army.) Instead of surplus revenue in 1973, Congress was faced with a budget where the cost of everything had been driven up by war-induced inflation. In Nixon's hands, revenue sharing therefore became a tool for severely cutting, not increasing, social spending.

Let's take a look at just one area to get some idea of the program's effects. The Community Development Revenue Sharing program, introduced by Nixon in March 1973 and signed by Ford thirteen days after he came into office, lumps together a series of pre-existing programs such as model cities, rehabilitation, code enforcement, and demolition; and it establishes a yearly funding that the cities can then allocate to their needs as they see fit.

The federal Office of Management and Budget and Department of Housing and Urban Development arbitrarily established a first-year funding level of $2.3 billion—as opposed to a real need estimated by the U. S. Conference of Mayors and by an independent survey of 200 cities at $5.5 billion. New York would receive an allocation of $101 million against a spending need of $240 million.

In addition to serious underfunding for the major cities, the program, through a bureaucratically established national formula, actually shifted money away from the areas of greatest need to the suburbs and growing cities of the Sunbelt. New York and Chicago, for example, remain frozen to prior spending levels, while other major cities fare even worse, as David Muchnick explained in the Winter 1976 issue of *Dissent:*

The next seventeen biggest central cities in the North and the East eventually will lose an estimated $168 million yearly, compared to their combined average yearly receipts between 1968 and 1972 under previous programs. From a five-year average of $378 million, their funding will be sliced almost in half, to $210 million yearly in fiscal 1980. Philadelphia, Detroit, Baltimore, Washington, D.C., Boston, and Cincinnati will lose over $97 million annually among them. By contrast, Houston, Dallas, Memphis, New Orleans, Phoenix, Jacksonville, Fort Worth, Miami, El Paso, and Birmingham will gain over $71 million annually. . . .

To finish the illustration, Massachusetts' 14 central cities will lose $6 million annually by fiscal 1980, while aid for its suburbs and rural areas will increase by $15 million and $1 million respectively—a net annual statewide loss of $30 million. Alabama's 18 central cities will gain $5.4 million annually, while funding for its suburbs and rural areas will increase by $23 million and $6 million respectively—a net annual statewide increase of $34 million. Nationwide, central cities will lose $276 million annually by 1980, while Federal investment in suburbs and rural areas will increase by $757 million and $291 million respectively. . . .

Local officials of these older central cities argue that the consequences of universal entitlement on the basis of population results in the loss of dollars by cities with declining populations, in the provision of scarce funds to wealthy communities with no poor and no overcrowding, and in the financial, administrative, and political reinforcement of those suburbs that deny residential and occupational opportunities to low-income workers, poor people, and minorities.

In other words, the federal government takes from the poor and gives to the rich, a Nixon-Ford twist on the old Robin Hood legend.

The revenue-sharing fiasco was only one of the nasty surprises that Nixon had in store for American cities. As we have noted, he suspended the subsidized housing programs in January 1973, even before he was sworn in for a second term. Now he enunciated a new program that concentrated almost all federal housing dollars in the Sunbelt and left the cities with a "trickle-down" rent subsidy program that virtually ended the production of new housing for the poor and middle classes.

Traditionally, American housing policy has overwhelmingly favored the construction of single-family private homes. The federal government does this in a number of ways: Mortgage interest payments are exempt from taxation; FHA and VA insurance is structured to induce builders to construct this type of housing; and the government often underwrites the capital costs of providing the sewage treatment plants and street networks needed for new subdivisions. Private-home subsidies accounted for two-thirds of the $15.3 billion in federal housing support and tax preferences in 1972. Nixon vowed to intensify this approach.

In that same year, two out of every three new private homes in the country were already being built in the South and the West, and the South and Southwest accounted for more than half of all federally insured mortgages on new homes, according to Muchnick's figures. "The southern and southwestern real estate industry's contribution to GNP reached more than $41.6 billion in 1971, providing nearly 2 million jobs in the nonagricultural sector," he notes.

In the rest of the nation, new construction and building employment remained at a standstill:

In the North and East [Muchnick continues], this policy will continue to provide subsidies for suburban homeowners and secure transfers of ownership in the existing stock of private homes. More than nine out of ten federally insured mortgages in the Northeast in 1972 covered such transactions, compared to 75% nationally. In that year, New England, New York, New Jersey and Pennsylvania accounted for only 5% of the FHA new homes. Only on the fringes of metropolitan areas are new federally insured units likely to be built. Elsewhere in the metropolis, the higher costs of land, construction and financing have pushed prices of new single-family dwellings to the limits of federal insurance ceilings, and, more important, beyond the financial reach of more than four out of five American families.

Since the Depression, the federal government had recognized the refusal of the private market to finance housing for the urban poor. Although public housing began as a program to put unemployed construction workers back on the job, a variant of WPA, it continued as the only way in which decent housing could be created at reasonable rents for the many city-dwellers whose only other option was festering slums. As we have seen, private housing construction for anyone except the very rich would have been at a standstill in New York had it not been for city, state, and federal housing construction programs in the 1960s and early 1970s. Much the same was true in other older northern cities.

Now Nixon brought new construction in the cities to a wrenching halt. As a substitute he offered rent subsidies to the poor, especially the aged poor, under a program known as the Section 8 program. Instead of providing for the construction of new housing, Section 8 forced the eligible poor to shop on the *free market* for available housing. If government housing agencies approved the new dwelling, a subsidy would be paid to the landlord, in addition to a quarter of the tenants' income, to meet the rent cost. The logic was that with these new dollars floating around, private landlords would independently build new housing to attract subsidized tenants.

In most aging cities, that plan is a cruel hoax. First of all, banks won't invest in new urban construction, preferring instead to meet the highly profitable demands for their scarce funds coming from the booming, federally subsidized Sunbelt. One part of the federal program therefore cancels out the other. Second, the plan ignores racial segregation, a fundamental component of the urban housing problem. Landlords in all-white areas are afraid to rent to nonwhites lest they set off a panic that the neighborhood is "going" and thereby reduce the resale value of their buildings. Speculators might in fact participate in the Section 8 program, but this is a prescription for rapid housing decline, not improvement. Besides, most speculators operate only in minority neighborhoods; they lack the capital to buy buildings in stable, white neighborhoods. Third, landlords traditionally seek maximum occupancy in existing buildings. It would be counterproductive for them to construct new housing, even in tight rental markets like New York's. When a housing shortage occurs, they will subdivide existing apartments rather than build new ones. This, of course, means a further decline in the quality of the housing stock. This Nixon program, like so many others, is built on the rhetoric of the free market, not the reality of the existing capitalist system.

Realistically, the Section 8 subsidy will only achieve a further inflation of rents in existing low-income neighborhoods. While some families will perhaps move into marginally better housing, the net effect will be negative, the more so because the program provides the illusion of hope where none exists. It is a program for slumlords, not tenants.

In one after another problem area, the pattern is the same. In the 1960s, cities, and especially New York, had rushed to establish programs that would be eligible for federal support. They often created job opportunities for unemployed or underemployed minority group members. (Mayor Beame told a congressional committee that employees in federally aided programs in New York had increased 37 per cent while cops, firemen, etc. had declined 4 per cent in the last decade.) People became dependent on the services—such as welfare mothers who could find jobs because of the availability of day care for their children. Then the federal government sharply reduced its support or ended it entirely. The problems didn't disappear, nor did the demand for the services, which had so obviously improved people's lives. The cities attempted to absorb the costs and continue the programs, and stumbled deeper into debt.

Here are just two brief examples: Head Start was one of the clear, identifiable successes of the Great Society. It confirmed the long-held belief of educators that children's learning capacities should be engaged at a much earlier age than the customary kindergarten or first-grade starting time for public school. Middle-class parents now deem preschool education a must for their children. When the poor were given an opportunity for the same advantage, thanks to Head Start, their children matched the achievement levels of other children in the first few years of formal schooling. Then the glaring inadequacies of ghetto schools began to take their toll, and the children fell behind again as they grew older. The obvious solution was to continue improving and enriching the higher grades in these schools; but the Nixon-Ford response was to freeze funding for Head Start so that it could not be expanded, and the cities were forced to absorb the costs of existing programs as the inflationary spiral continued.

As a result, the public-school system in our cities is deserted by parents who have the resources to send their children to private schools. The disastrous inadequacy of the public schools is often the determining factor in the decision of moderate-income families—both white and, increasingly, black—to move to the suburbs. Racial apartheid in the cities is the inevitable result.

Neighborhood health centers, first sponsored by the federal Office for Economic Opportunity, and subsequently by the Department of Health, Education and Welfare, were the replacement for the family doctors who deserted inner-city neighborhoods in droves during the 1950s and early 1960s. The centers provided good medical care for the sick and instituted screening programs, especially for children, to identify diseases in their early, curable stages. The major beneficiaries were families of the working poor who earned too much to qualify for welfare medical benefits but too little to pay the costs of traditional health care. When the Nixon-Ford administration suddenly ordered these centers to become "self-supporting," it was the working poor who were turned away. In New York, with its network of municipal hospitals, the burden of caring for these people was then dumped on an already seriously underfinanced system. The results were growing deficits for the city and a continuing deterioration in the quality of health care.

When aides to President Ford denounced the Great Society during the 1976 presidential campaign for having "raised the hopes of the poor and then dashed them," it was an exercise in political chicanery. Even Daniel Patrick Moynihan, now New York's junior senator, who provided Nixon and Ford with much of their more sophisticated rhetoric against the Great Society, admitted that it had been "underfinanced and oversold." The inescapable fact is that the anticity policies of Nixon and Ford "dashed the hopes of the poor" and hastened the bankruptcy of our cities in the process.

On Thursday, June 26, 1975, in Washington, D.C., promptly at 9:45 A.M. the Commerce, Consumer and Monetary Affairs Subcommittee of the House of Representatives convened in Room 2247 of the Rayburn House Office Building. Ben Rosenthal, a deceptively meek-looking congressman from a Jewish middle-class district in the heart of Queens, was in the chair. Sitting before him at the witness table, his hair so sleekly brilliantined that it reflected the overhead lights, was William Simon, erstwhile Wall Street bond peddler, currently the Secretary of the Treasury.

The subcommittee had scheduled three days of hearings to find out what help the federal government could provide to New York, as its inability to borrow in the open market brought it closer to default with each passing day. Rosenthal said he also wanted to examine the role of the banks in the collapse, and the performance of the three federal entities that are supposed to regulate them.

Mayor Beame had been the first witness when the hearing opened on June 23, and he mumbled his usual litany of excuses for the city's situation. He danced around the issue of whether or not the banks had dumped city securities, hinting broadly that he found the sudden cash boycott "puzzling." So much for Abe Beame as populist whistle-blower.

George Mitchell, vice-chairman of the Board of Governors of the Federal Reserve System, had appeared next, a stand-in for the sacrosanct Arthur Burns. Mitchell admitted that the Reserve system had the power to make loans to the city, but he denied that the city met its criteria. Primarily, he doubted New York's ability to solve its problems on a short-term basis, and he rejected the idea that its bankruptcy "would have a significant detrimental economic and financial impact on the surrounding area, the region, or the nation." Mitchell said, "Access to a source of temporary credit . . . may tend to defer or prevent the remedial actions that are necessary, difficult as they may be." In other words, we intend to hold your feet to the fire until you do exactly what we tell you. He did have other interesting things to say, too. Under sharp questioning by Rosenthal, he left the distinct impression that every large bank in New York except Morgan Guaranty was in a shaky position, but he was emphatic that their weaknesses didn't stem from the amount of New York City bonds they held—by now reduced to only $1.26 billion.

Now, on the second day of the hearings, Bill Simon appeared as a uniquely qualified "expert" witness. From January 1964 until December 1972 he had directed the municipal and government bond departments at Salomon Brothers, one of the biggest operations on Wall Street. He had been a key member of the small band of men—no more than twenty-five—who "make" the market for municipal bonds. And business had been good.

He had also served as a member of Controller Beame's technical debt management committee and had sat across the table from him at a meeting on April 20, 1971, when Beame ranted about a Virginia bank that had called New York "a potential Penn Central." Simon had sold more than $1 billion of the short-term loans floated in 1971 and 1972. If anybody knew New York's finances, it was Bill Simon.

Now, of course, he wore a different hat. *Business Week* had called him "Washington's No. 1 Capital Cap Crusader," a misnomer since the title actually belonged to Federal Reserve chairman Arthur Burns and Simon was simply Burns's front man. He was, instead, "Washington's No. 1 Capital Gap Salesman."

What is a "capital gap"? The phrase had begun to appear with amazing regularity. Chase Manhattan had been the primary popularizer of the concept, taking full-page ads in major publications with bold headlines like "OUCH!" and "SCREAM!" The basic message was simple: American corporations and individuals weren't saving enough of their incomes to provide for the massive investment in new sources of energy, industrial modernization, and foreign expansion that would be needed in the next decade. As a result, we would fall behind in competition with other nations and no longer be Number One among the world's powers.

The major villain in the Chase scenario was government. It collected too much in taxes (apparently Chase wasn't satisfied with the multimillion-dollar tax rebate it had gotten from the feds in 1974) and thereby blunted the profit incentive; it borrowed too much in the capital markets, "elbowing" out the corporations; it pumped too much money back into the economy and therefore caused "runaway" inflation. The answer to these evils was simple enough: The federal government should reduce taxes on corporations and wealthy individuals and underwrite risky new corporate investments. It should sharply reduce its costly social spending. It should balance its budget and reduce its finance market competition with industry for the savings of the nation. If these admittedly profound changes were accomplished, American capitalists could then go on to build the future for which they had already drafted blueprints: carpet the nation with nuclear power plants, develop a trillion-dollar synthetic fuel complex, fully automate basic industry, and accelerate the corporate penetration of developing Third World economies.

The realities behind this scare campaign were rather more complex. The rate of profit was inexorably falling in mature industries and advanced nations. Unemployment, which had always been used to cow labor's wage demands, could do so no longer since workers had fought for and won benefits that would sustain an acceptable standard of living even during layoffs. Capitalism had exhausted the profit potential in the radical changes in life-style, such as suburbs, superhighways and shopping centers, that had accompanied the growth and development of the automotive age. Natural resources were rapidly and tangibly disappearing. The specter of a static and therefore profitless economic system was haunting the boardrooms. It threatened to usher in an age of democratic planning and income redistribution such as the world had never seen. Government had been manipulated to create every Golden Age of profit in the past. Government funds had underwritten the construction of the canals and railroads, the permanent war economy, the leap into space, and America's expansion into war-torn Europe and the underdeveloped world. Now government must underwrite the costly investments necessary to pump new blood through the aged and cracking arteries of capitalism.

This was really just an echo of what Nixon had been saying all along. Inflation, not unemployment and poverty, was the nation's "real" enemy and inflation was caused by government spending, which in turn produced the dual evils of full employment and high wages. (The conservative economists around Nixon and Ford simply shrugged away the paradox that prices were rising at record rates during the second worst economic downturn in modern history. Democratic claims that monopoly control of the leading industries led to "administered prices," and that this was the real source of inflation, were dismissed as "anticorporate propaganda.")

So Simon would now appear to give the House subcommittee another lesson in "fighting inflation" and the evils of spending tax dollars on people rather than corporations. As is often the case in hearings of this sort, the chairman invited him to summarize his written statement, and Simon then gave the standard recitation of conservative plaints about the city: New York spent more per capita on its citizens than other American cities; its pensions were too generous; and it had more employees per thousand residents than other cities. (He happily noted that Baltimore, New York's close runner-up in this last category, had just been forced to lay off 20 per cent of its payroll.) It had a tuition-free university, too many ineligibles on welfare, too many municipal hospital beds. It had borrowed to meet deficits, and as its borrowings accelerated, the market got leery and finally closed down. He was at great pains to emphasize that the anonymous "market," not the all too identifiable banks, was the source of New York's calamity.

He then briefly ran through the decision-making process that had led the Ford administration six weeks before to reject aid to New York City after the by-now famous May 13 meeting between Beame and Carey and Ford/Rockefeller/Simon *et al.*; and he went on to say that the creation of the Municipal Assistance Corporation had made things better (this was soon to change precipitously, MAC debt becoming as suspect as the city's, and as unsalable) and to cite parallels between New York and the federal government itself. He concluded with the admonition, "Whether we can prevent the nation from falling into the same plight as our greatest city is now the central issue before us." He spent the rest of the morning in hostile but vague bantering with the subcommittee members for the benefit of the assembled press corps. He reiterated his view that New York's collapse would occasion a "moderate, short-lived disruption." He did let it slip that meetings between his staff and the city's fiscal people had uncovered the fact that New York had been shortchanged by $90 million in welfare reimbursement, but he dismissed this as petty cash. Otherwise, no one laid a glove on him.

The press and the committee ignored Simon's written statement. This should be a cardinal sin in Washington, as I. F. Stone has proved by decades of the best Washington journalism that has ever appeared. Stone, almost completely deaf for most of the years he spent digging out federal secrets, was forced to read written statements and reports instead of listening to the press-conference and official babble that suffices for most journalists, and he got some of his biggest scoops from these public documents. We bothered to read Simon's statement. It contains a chillingly frank dissection of President Ford's decision to refuse aid to New York City, and leaves the inescapable impression that this policy was based on the assumption that New York would default, and that this outcome was to be heartily applauded. New York's default had become crucial for Ford's economic plan to deal with inflation by putting the nation's cities through the wringer. It also provided him with a convenient blood sacrifice to offer up to the implacable gods of Republican conservatism in his bitter contest with Ronald Reagan for the party's nomination.

We quote this section of Simon's testimony in its entirety:

In the course of numerous meetings at all levels, we stressed this disturbing set of facts to City officials. And we were not alone. From *The New York Times,* from the New York Clearing House, from the Citizens Budget Commission, the same message was repeated again and again: get your spending into line with your ability to pay.

How did the City respond? Speaking bluntly, I think they thought we were all a bit naive. You could fight crime, you could fight pollution, you could fight poverty and ignorance, but—in New York—you could not underestimate the powerful forces for spending being brought to bear on the City's elected officials, driving the City into the slow and painful death of bankruptcy.

Now I know enough about New York to know that Mayor Beame and his colleagues would be in the fight of their lives the moment they touched their scalpel to the growing layer of fiscal fat which is strangling the City. One only has to look at that incredible pamphlet off-duty policemen, firemen and others were handing out to tourists earlier this month to appreciate the kind of problem the Mayor was dealing with. But we make a tragic mistake when we resolve questions solely on the basis of which side is more threatening or more unscrupulous.

But as of early May, when I, and then the President, met with the Mayor and the Governor, no resolution of the problem was in sight. The issue as then presented was plain and simple: give us the money to get us through the immediate crisis, then we'll begin to worry about a solution.

As I have indicated, it had become clear that the only real solution lay in a responsible program of fiscal reform. Such a program would reopen the market and avert the possibility of a default by New York City. But because no such program had even been suggested by City officials, it was our responsibility to evaluate the constant suggestions that a default by New York would have a devastating impact on the capital markets, the banking system and the national economy as a whole.

It was quickly apparent that the principal adverse effects would be based on psychological factors, not objective ones. To be sure, many parts of the economy— especially in New York City—would suffer severe harm. On the whole, however, our markets, our banking system and our economy are large and diversified enough to withstand the temporary inability of even an entity the size of New York City to meet its obligations.

But I have been around markets long enough to know that one ignores psychology at his own peril. Accordingly, before reaching a decision, we asked ourselves three more questions about the psychological effects of a default:

First, what impact would a default have on the securities markets, particularly the municipal markets?

Second, would a default influence the condition of the major banks?

And third, what impact would a default have on public confidence nationally?

With respect to impact on the market, it is fair to say that there were differences of opinion. Certain market professionals from the private sector did tell us the effect could be devastating. But my staff and the Federal Reserve Bank of New York, which as you know serves as the focal point for our public securities markets, advised me that whatever impact did occur would be temporary, and even so confined, would be negligible.

Three factors produced this judgment. First, it was uniformly believed that any default would be shortlived and that there was enough underlying value in New York City to assure that all holders would eventually be paid 100 cents on the dollar. Second, the municipal market had recently experienced the prospect of a major tax-exempt issuer default—New York State's U.D.C.—and had weathered it well. Third, New York's problems had been public knowledge since at least November and the market, at least in large part, had reflected this risk by discounting the prices of New York City and other weaker issues. This last judgment was confirmed by the strong rally in the municipal market when "Big Mac" was established.

We found the banking system even better equipped to handle whatever shock might occur. The New York City holdings of the major New York banks, while large in absolute terms, were only a fraction of one percent of the total assets of these institutions. The sophisticated investors, whose large deposits were in question, were aware of this fact, and were also aware that, upon a default, this portion of the banks' holding of New York securities would hardly become worthless.

This lack of a realistic basis for fearing large withdrawals was coupled with a recognition that the system was designed to handle such an event, if it did occur. A primary reason for establishing the Federal Reserve System was to correct temporary imbalances of liquidity in our banking structure. And the System clearly would have been able to handle any imbalance which might have occurred in these circumstances.

Finally, working with Chairman [Alan] Greenspan of the Council of Economic Advisers and senior economists at the Federal Reserve, we looked at potential consumer and business reaction. In view of the general knowledge of New York's situation and an awareness that at least many of the underlying problems were of the City's own making, we saw little risk that a default would be viewed as an indication of more widespread economic malaise.

Concluding that a default would not have precipitated an economic crisis did not mean that a default should not be avoided at virtually any cost. But when we reviewed our analysis of what other cities have done and are doing to meet the economic challenges of these times, another barrier to special treatment for New York became apparent. Many of our leading cities are having troubles these days, troubles largely attributable to the recession and unemployment levels, and to the impact of these phenomena on municipal revenues. But as I discussed earlier, and as confirmed by a recent Joint Economic Committee staff study, virtually all these jurisdictions have met their problems head on recognizing that meaningful cuts in spending levels were a critical part of any solution. As we in this town are altogether too aware, spending cuts do not come easy for any elected official, especially when a direct impact on one's own constituents can be identified. But throughout the country, brave local leaders have literally put their political futures on the line by insisting that all questions, however painful, be addressed and that the problems be solved in a responsible manner.

Under our system of government, it is not, and should not be, the job of the Federal government to manage the finances of State and Local government. That function must be handled locally, by government's duly elected leaders. But we do have a responsibility to those leaders not to undermine their efforts. And if we had provided funds to New York, what would we have said, for example, to the Mayor of Detroit or to the Mayor of Cleveland, each of whom has incurred the wrath of major political forces in his own city by taking steps to see that they pay their own way. No, if our system is to continue to function, it was clear we had to protect the credibility of local leaders. And aid to the one major city which had not taken action to meet its fiscal responsibilities would have destroyed that credibility overnight.

These were the elements of our decision-making process. As you can see, the decision was not made hastily, lightly, or without complete attention to all relevant considerations. It was not an easy decision, but I think events to date have shown it was the right one. With the Federal avenue closed off, so to speak, all parties could again turn their full attention to developing a solution at the appropriate government level.

About the only question that wasn't asked was: What would be the effect of default on the 7½ million Americans who lived in New York? The answer was, however, clearly understood.

Simon, although tightly wrapping himself in a cloak of "economic realism," had laid out a political, not an economic, plan. As he acknowledged, all of America's big cities were in serious trouble. In his own words, "by comparison to other cities, New York was not a particularly hard-hit victim of the recession or the so-called urban crisis." While that judgment is, of course, relative, it was accurate as far as it went. The rest of urban America was coming apart at the seams. And most cities had been forced to resort to suicidal layoffs of public employees that accelerated their decline. If New York were able to avoid drinking the hemlock pressed on it by the administration, they would all seek a reprieve.

Unwittingly, Simon was taking a page out of another country's history. Henri Christophe had the unfortunate habit of occasionally shooting the last of his soldiers to climb over a mountain. "Pour encourager les autres," he would explain. Now Simon, at the behest of Burns and Ford, was issuing a death warrant for New York—"to encourage the others."

As the situation worsened from month to month, and the financial community and Congress became more restive about the fallout from a federally induced default by New York City, the "capital gap" gang around the vacuous Gerald Ford drafted stronger and stronger denunciations for him to issue against the beleaguered city. In August, for instance, he went out of his way to berate New York to a puzzled Zivorad Kovacevic, mayor of Belgrade, who welcomed the president and his attendant phalanx of correspondents in Yugoslavia. Ford had managed to give New York a karate chop from 6000 miles across the globe. In mid-October, he vowed: "I can tell you—and tell you now—that I am prepared to veto any bill that has as its purpose a federal bailout of New York City to prevent default."

On October 29, he made a nationally televised speech to the National Press Club in Washington outlining his proposals for placing the city in bankruptcy after what then seemed its imminent default. Like a Mafia don, he would send the biggest wreath to his enemy's funeral.

From the beginning, Ford, Burns, Simon, and a frustration-poisoned Nelson Rockefeller had sought one goal. All the speeches, and leaks, and meaningless meetings with city and state officials had only one purpose. It was left to the inimitable *Daily News* headline writers to compose the perfect epitaph. When the early-bird edition hit the stands the evening of Ford's October 29 speech, the front page said it all:

FORD TO CITY:
DROP DEAD

In the end, though, it was Gerald Ford or, more accurately, Arthur Burns who "blinked" in this colossal but ridiculous staredown. On October 17, the city had almost gone down until Albert Shanker of the United Federation of

Teachers was finally bullied late in the afternoon into buying more MAC bonds with his union's pension funds. But this latest episode in the city's "perils of Pauline" had given a foretaste of what might have come from an actual default. The stock market had plummeted and the bond market, corporate and municipal, was motionless, seemingly frozen in terror. The international currency markets also held their breath; gold prices soared. (In August, *U.S. News and World Report* had estimated that holders of *all* municipal bonds had experienced a loss of $12 billion in the value of their holdings since the crisis began the previous March.) On October 18, the Holy Trinity of New York's big banks, Citibank's Wriston, Chase's Rockefeller, and Morgan Guaranty's Patterson, issued a joint statement to the Senate Banking Committee warning that "the recent decline in the value of the dollar, which followed a period of strength, is probably an indication of anxiety about New York City and the consequences of default." What a flair for understatement! The rest of the capitalist world thought Ford was crazy. Foreign bankers attending the American Bankers Association convention in New York in November said in unmistakable terms that if New York went under, there would be a massive run by foreign depositors on the city's banks, period.

Also in November, the Federal Reserve published a report showing that 546 banks in 26 states held $4.178 billion in New York City, state, and state agency bonds. (By now, everyone assumed that the three were so intertwined that they would all go down together.) It also showed that 179 banks in 24 states had at least half of their capital in New York bonds; 367 banks in 26 states had between 20 and 50 per cent in these obligations. The report was actually seriously understated, but it moved Arthur Burns to observe ponderously that while he still didn't believe the city merited federal assistance, "I am closer to such a conclusion than I have been in the past." The White House stated, "The President has not changed his position one iota."

Less than two months later, after the president had changed his position 180 degrees under pressure from the bankers and an increasingly nervous Arthur Burns, the Federal Reserve issued a second report with the real facts. This one, released on New Year's Eve so that few people would read it the next day, admitted that 954 banks in 33 states actually held $6.491 billion in paper issued by the city, the state, and its agencies. If they went under, 234 banks in 29 states might have seen half of their capital wiped out and 718 banks in 33 states would have lost between 20 and 50 per cent of their capital. Was this what Simon meant by "no more than a moderate and short-lived disruption"?

Early in November, Hugh Carey, who had said he would be "willing to have egg on my face, to have stones thrown at me, and to walk on nails in order to prevent a default," now proceeded to prove that he wasn't kidding. He called a special session of the state legislature. At his request, they voted additional taxes, appropriated funds to keep New York City's northern neighbor Yonkers from defaulting, put up the money to bail out the now-bankrupt state HFA, forced city workers to contribute more to their pensions, and, finally, gave Ford his last pound of flesh by enacting a moratorium on the payment of $1.6 billion in the city's outstanding notes. Noteholders would be paid interest, but not the principal, on their investment. They could exchange the notes for long-term higher-interest MAC bonds or hope that they could cash in the original short-term notes at the end of the city's three-year "recovery" period in 1978. Technically, New York had defaulted. In return, Ford agreed that the federal government would make "seasonal" loans of $2.3 billion to the city to finance its day-to-day needs until quarterly taxes and erratically spaced government aid payments were made. An interest rate 1 per cent higher than the rate paid by the federal government for these funds would be exacted. New York would be allowed to survive—crippled, degraded, perhaps mortally weakened—but it would live. Until the next crisis.

The "capital gap" crusaders had won a victory beyond their fondest hopes. Two months later, Brenton Harries, president of the Standard & Poor's bond rating agency, stated that "the bond market will remain closed to New York for the next 20 years" as a result of the federally enforced default. New York City accounted for about 5 per cent of total state and municipal indebtedness, but 29 per cent of the short-term loans. New York State and its agencies would also find themselves severely restricted in any future borrowings. Every city and state, even in the federally subsidized Sunbelt, would face higher rates and a constricted market for their obligations. This meant a shift of tens of billions of investment dollars to the corporate market and lower prices for the giant utilities, manufacturers, and multinationals seeking to expand with borrowed funds.

Perhaps even more importantly, the new repressive social policy that is a must for continued corporate profitability was imposed in the stronghold of liberalism—and there was no revolt. The municipal unions, a new force that was viewed by the conservative elite very much as the CIO had been in the late 1930s, had been emasculated. Wages were frozen, 30,000 workers were axed, future pension benefits were reduced, and the unions' pension funds themselves—not the banks—became the major source of emergency city financing. Hospitals were closed. Transit fares—a crucial cost-of-living item in a city where 89 per cent of the population uses trains and buses to get to work—were increased by 43 per cent. A free university education—the traditional passport between poverty and the middle class—would soon be abolished. If New Yorkers could be forced to accept these reductions in the quality of life, then they could be imposed anywhere. In many cities, they already have been.

In the face of these attacks, the cities and the unions proved politically powerless. The Democrats, with overwhelming majorities in both houses of

Congress, were gearing up to unseat an unelected Republican president who presided over the worst depression in forty years and was perceived by the average American as a simpleton. The Democrats were supposed to be the party of the cities and the unions. In the event, they proved helplessly divided, allowing the conservative rural and Southern tail to wag the urban-industrial dog. "After all," the conservatives said, "everyone hates New York. New York is different from Philadelphia, Detroit, Chicago, Cleveland, Baltimore, Milwaukee, St. Louis, Seattle, and San Francisco. New Yorkers are snotty, they talk too damn fast, they think they know it all. I'm not going out on a limb for those bastards." The traveling circus of liberal presidential hopefuls told New Yorkers what they thought we wanted to hear because they wanted New York votes and New York money. They did nothing in Congress. Candidates on the right openly abused the city. Jimmy Carter treated the city as if it had VD (until the general election, when New York became the key to his narrow victory). Henry Jackson said in a nationally televised debate that "the tenth floor of an apartment house is no place to live or try to raise a family."

Much more than an attitude was involved, however. There were very real sectional advantages at stake. In the midst of a depression, everyone, especially near neighbors like economically depressed New Jersey and Connecticut, wanted the industries that were fleeing New York. The large Chicago banks wouldn't mind pre-empting the big banks in New York. On a far larger scale, the Sunbelt had been sucking the blood of the Northeast for decades. First the southern and western states had lured away labor-intensive industries like textiles, clothing, and furniture with the promise of low wages and no unions. Now they were siphoning off hundreds of billions in federal taxes and investment dollars through the political power they had accumulated in both parties over the years. New York City became a pawn in this mammoth national struggle for economic primacy.

The economist Richard Morris has developed the most up-to-date figures on how this giant ripoff of the Northeast works. As he points out, New York is again the biggest single victim. "The fifteen states from Maine to Minnesota pay $44 billion more in Federal taxes than they receive in Federal aid and expenditures. Their fifteen counterparts reaching from Virginia to California along the southern rim get $32 billion more than they give. For every dollar the Northeast sends to Washington, it gets 78 cents back. For each dollar the South pays in taxes, it reaps $1.35 in federal spending," he calculates.

The Northeast loses 7.5 per cent of its personal income to Washington every year, while the Sunbelt states reap a bonus equivalent to 7.1 per cent of their personal income. New York State, the biggest dollar loser, pays $14 billion more to Washington each year than it gets back—a deficit greater than the *total* indebtedness of New York City.

The explanation for this disparity is simple and at least superficially rational. New Yorkers earn more on the average than their counterparts in other states and are therefore taxed at a higher rate. What the tax laws ignore, however, is that the cost of living here is much higher than anywhere else. A New Yorker must earn $25,470 to buy exactly as much as an Atlantan earning $18,825. Similar differentials exist for people living in other large cities in the North. If cost-of-living adjustments are made, then the ten largest metropolitan areas in the Northeast have a per-capita personal income 2.8 per cent lower than their opposite numbers in the Sunbelt, yet they pay 22 per cent more per capita in federal taxes. In other words, the government is bleeding 44 per cent of its population so that another 38 per cent can enjoy relative prosperity. In an earlier day, this situation would have provoked a second civil war.

The major instrument of this regressive form of wealth redistribution has been the military budget. Half of America's military expenditures in the continental U.S. are made in the Sunbelt. California alone gets 17 per cent of the total military budget, especially those fat research and development contracts. In many states—Georgia, Louisiana, Mississippi, Tennessee, and New Mexico, for example—the defense industry is the largest employer. Seymour Melman, chairman of the Columbia University department of industrial and management engineering, has explained how this allocation took place as the "permanent war economy" became the cornerstone of American capitalism in the last three decades:

> Members of Congress from the Southern States have sought out positions on the armed services committees in the House of Representatives and in the Senate and have obviously used their positions as points of leverage for funneling military installations (read *payrolls*) into their districts and states in a prodigal fashion. As this has proceeded, these states, in turn, became centers of support for military oriented policies of the United States around the world. Thus, the states of this region were the last hold-outs of major support for the Vietnam War.

Despite the experience of Vietnam and the constant fear that nuclear war is a very real possibility in an insanely over-armed world, the 1976-77 military budget was the largest in American history. It may be suicidal, but for the moment it's very good business for the most economically buoyant area in the nation.

New York City's plight is merely part of a much larger world economic crisis. Nations, as England's recent experiences have shown, as well as regions and cities are being torn apart in the scramble to rule in the new era of scarcity. Right now those who have always ruled—the rich, the powerful, and the ruthless—are successfully shaping the future that we and our children will have to endure. It is, by any measure, bleak and hostile. At the end of this

FEDERAL TAXES VS. FEDERAL EXPENDITURES, 1975
(in millions of dollars)

The Northeast

State	Taxes Paid	Expenditures Received
Maine	760	1,277
Vermont	319	641
New Hampshire	714	1,145
Massachusetts	7,622	8,474
Rhode Island	1,204	1,243
Connecticut	5,946	5,137
New York	39,007	24,269
New Jersey	11,083	8,395
Pennsylvania	17,697	14,462
Ohio	17,194	10,822
Indiana	6,860	5,412
Illinois	21,774	13,462
Michigan	14,778	9,095
Minnesota	6,150	4,497
Wisconsin	5,422	4,443
NORTHEAST TOTAL	156,530	112,774

NET OUTFLOW: $43,756

The Sunbelt

State	Taxes Paid	Expenditures Received
Virginia	5,035	8,906
North Carolina	5,996	6,100
South Carolina	1,875	3,485
Georgia	4,784	6,786
Florida	7,787	11,512
Tennessee	3,511	5,425
Alabama	2,684	4,816
Mississippi	1,167	3,740
Louisiana	3,287	4,596
Arkansas	1,241	2,544
Texas	16,048	15,806
Oklahoma	3,361	3,871
Arizona	1,789	3,646
New Mexico	708	2,264
California	28,510	35,838
SUNBELT TOTAL	87,783	119,335

NET INFLOW: $31,552

SOURCES FOR FEDERAL TAXES: 1975 Annual Report of Internal Revenue Service.

SOURCES FOR FEDERAL EXPENDITURES: *Federal Outlays In Summary*, Community Services Administration, December 1975, with the following adjustments: public debt interest, foreign aid payments, international organization subsidies, TVA bonds, and civil service life insurance deducted because geographic data was misleading.

book, we shall discuss some of the alternative solutions that we feel could improve New York's, and other cities' chances for survival. But narrow, local answers are inadequate in a world as concentrated and overcrowded as ours.

If any of us are to survive in dignity, all of us must. This will require a profound restructuring of political and economic power and the creation of a whole new set of democratic institutions. One of the basic theses of this book is that New York is ruled by a small group of unelected power brokers. We call them the permanent government. Yet there is a "permanent government" in Washington, as there is certainly a "permanent government" in Peking and Moscow; there is one in every major city and every small town in America. Perhaps the simplest way we can outline the political goal of this book is to say that it is our objective to make the rule of all these "permanent governments" as temporary as possible.

The Permanent Government

4

By the powerful we mean, of course, those who are able to realize their will, even if others resist it. No one, accordingly, can be truly powerful unless he has access to the command of major institutions, for it is over these institutional means of power that the truly powerful are, in the first instance, powerful.

—C. WRIGHT MILLS
The Power Elite

Ultimate power over public policy in New York is invisible and unelected. It is exercised by a loose confederation of bankers, bond underwriters, members of public authorities, the big insurance companies, political fund-raisers, publishers, law firms, builders, judges, backroom politicians, and some union leaders.

The power of this interlocking network of elites is based on the control of institutions, money, property, and the law-making process. It endures no matter who the voters elect as mayor, governor, or president. Its collective power, when organized, is greater than the elected, representative government.

This permanent government is not an invincible conspiracy. It is only the creative self-interest of the rich. It sometimes can be beaten, as when 50,000 residents of Co-op City waged a thirteen-month rent strike in 1975-76 that successfully conquered a rent increase. Or when neighborhood activists stopped the Lower Manhattan Expressway in 1967. Or when the Northside Community in Brooklyn forced the city to re-open a firehouse it had closed for austerity reasons.

The permanent government is not as monolithic now as it was a decade ago, when Nelson Rockefeller and the men around him controlled public and private power to a terrifying extent.

The balance of power within this elite group shifts. A few years ago the real-estate developers and construction unions had more influence than they

63

do now. But with the onset of the recession, foreclosures, and the fiscal crisis, the banks and financial institutions that control lines of credit, bonds, venture capital, and mortgages became much more important. But our point is this: Whenever an assemblyman casts a vote, or when a public-works project is begun, or when a developer gets a zoning variance to build a highrise, or when federal funds come into a district, or when a decision is made to raise the interest rates that the banks charge the city—in all these situations, the real decision-makers are usually off stage, and unknown to the public. This means the average citizen does not know who is controlling his or her life. This is, fundamentally, a book about the abuse of power.

A few more qualifying statements.

Power in New York is less centralized than in other places. There is no one political boss like the late Richard Daley of Chicago. There is no single controlling financial family, like the Mellons in Pittsburgh, or the Duponts in Delaware. New York is so big that even the Rockefellers have to share power with the Vanderbilts, Astors, Whitneys, Schiffs, Loebs, and Lehmans.

There are occasionally titanic conflicts within the power elite. One famous example was when the Rockefeller brothers finally ended the 44-year public career of Robert Moses in February 1968. Another was Mayor Wagner's turning against Carmine DeSapio, Charles Buckley, and the Democratic machine in 1961.

Elections can make a difference. They can change the balance of power between rival elites. If Richard Nixon had lost the presidency in 1968 it would have had a great beneficial effect on New York. If Herman Badillo had won the Democratic primary for mayor in 1973 it would have made a significant difference. Lindsay's defeat of Beame in 1965, Wagner's defeat of Levitt in 1961, and Rockefeller's defeat of Harriman in 1958 did alter various power alignments.

In 1974, a preponderance of the monied interests backed Howard Samuels for governor in the Democratic primary. But Hugh Carey had a millionaire brother and shrewd handlers in David Garth and Alex Rose, so Carey won. Yet today the banks have more power than ever. In November 1980, the banks were given the power to charge interest rates up to 25 per cent on loans and credit cards.

New York's permanent government has different components than the national power elite. The national elite is dominated by multinational corporations like ITT and conglomerates like Gulf and Western; giant oil companies like Mobil, Gulf and Exxon; the defense establishment, CIA, and military contractors like Lockheed and General Dynamics; agribusiness corporations like Tenneco; and, as ever, the banking industry. The shift of wealth and power within this structure to the Sunbelt has had a severe negative impact on New York and the entire Northeast region.

Not all the members of the permanent government represent inherited wealth. A few rose out of the working class during their own lifetimes, on their own talents: lawyer Harold Fisher, publicist Howard Rubenstein, union pension fund consultant Jack Bigel, and political boss Stanley Friedman.

But despite all these qualifying disclaimers, there is an unseen power establishment. New York is not like Dallas, where a dozen bankers and oilmen can assemble in one broad room and settle everything. But there are about 1500 or 2000 people in New York City who have pieces of a power that is decisive, concealed, and therefore unaccountable. And over the last fifteen years, this group, plus four mayors and two governors has been responsible for the policies and decisions that have swept New York to the lip of ruin. These 1500 or 2000 people all know each other and deal with each other as members of the same club.

At the start of 1981, the permanent government, at its upper reaches, contained not a single black, Hispanic, or woman who commanded authentic institutional power. There was no Dorothy Schiff, no Percy Sutton or J. Raymond Jones, no Herman Badillo. There was no academic or religious leader. There was no elder, no wise man of the tribe, no moral conscience in the tradition of Rabbi Stephen Wise, or Judge Sam Seabury, or Eleanor Roosevelt. There was mostly the fraternity of power in a selfish era of scarce capital and insecure status.

The apex of permanent institutional power is banking and finance. Manhattan is the home of six of America's ten biggest commercial banks, which together control more than **$350 billion** in assets—an unparalleled concentration of the world's wealth. These commercial banks have won every legislative battle they have waged, including ever higher interest rates.

- Walter Wriston, president of Citibank with assets of $106 billion, is the premier banker. He is tough, smart, successful, and at 61 has four more years at the top. Citicorp earned most of its $600 million in 1979 income from outside the United States.
- Chase Manhattan Bank ($65 billion in assets) is in transition. David Rockefeller is retiring, but his 558,000 shares of Chase stock will continue to make him a force within the bank that is an extension of his family. The new Chase president is Thomas Lebreque, 41, who was the bank's architect of its fiscal crisis policy that the SEC said "misled" investors, and dumped city securities on the market.
- John McGullicuddy is chairman of Manufacturers Hanover Bank and he lives in Rye, New York. Donald Platten is chairman of Chemical Bank and he lives in Darien, Connecticut. Alfred Brittain is chairman of Bankers Trust and he lives in Greenwich, Connecticut. Preston Lewis is

the chairman of the Morgan Guaranty Trust, and he lives in Mt. Kisco, New York.

- Other financial powers include: Felix Rohatyn, economic counselor to Governor Carey, the chairman of MAC, and a senior partner at the international investment banking firm of Larzad Freres; Roger Birk, the new chairman of Wall Street's biggest brokerage house—Merrill Lynch, and his predecessor, Donald Regan, now Secretary of the Treasury; Peter Peterson, the chairman of Lehman Brothers Kuhn Loeb, which earned more than $100 million before taxes in 1980; Robert Lindsay, the president of the Morgan bank and the brother of former mayor John Lindsay; George Ball, former Under-Secretary of State in the Kennedy and Johnson Administrations and now a senior partner at the 131 year old investment banking house of Lehman Brothers; and Robert Baldwin, former Navy Under-Secretary and now president of the investment banking company of Morgan Stanley, whose clients include Mobil Oil, General Motors, and the government of Venezuela. Baldwin is regarded as Wall Street's spokesman on the securities industry.

  Another financial force is Richard Shinn, the president of the Metropolitan Life Insurance Company who also sits on the board of the Chase Bank and the Allied Chemical Corporations.
- Among savings banks, there is the Dime Savings Bank and its president, Harry Albright. The Dime has $5 billion assets and has been accused of "unconscionable" redlining by the City Human Rights Commission. Albright is a former state superintendent of banking. The Dime is the third largest saving bank in the country.
- Vincent Quinn is the politically active president of the Brooklyn Savings Bank, and is the main lobbyist spokesman for the state's 117 savings banks. The Brooklyn Savings Bank has assets of **$1.5 billion,** and during all of 1975 according to a study by NYPIRG, this bank gave only $2 million worth of mortgages in all of Brooklyn. Quinn calls redlining "a myth," while 1 percent of his bank's total assets are invested in its home borough, where it draws most of its deposits.

The next level of permanent power are the owners of New York's most valuable resource—the major landlords and developers. The lords of the land need the most favors from government, tax abatement, zoning variances, approval to co-op, less regulations on rent—and they are the largest source of campaign funds for most candidates.

- Harry Helmsley owns $5 billion worth of property with at least 100,000 tenants. He owns seven hotels, 60 commercial buildings, and four large residential developments including Park West Village and Parkchester.

Bernard Gallagher, the publisher of the business newsletter—*The Gallagher Report*—began a crusade for commercial rent control after Helmsley tried to raise his rent by 300 per cent on his lease renewal. Helmsley also tried to raise rents retroactively in Park West Village by $1500 per household; the tenants went on rent strike, and Helmsley tried to evict 310 families for rent non-payment. Financial writer Dan Dorfman once asked Helmsley about building housing for the middle class, and Helmsley replied: "I can't think of anyone in that income bracket. There's always trailers down South and used houses . . . and this is what a lot of people are going to have to get used to." On another occasion when Helmsley testified before the city's Industrial and Commercial Incentives Board (ICIB), seeking a tax abatement, board member asked which public amenities he was thinking of building into his project. "I don't believe in providing amenities for the general public," Helmsley replied. Helmsley's luxury hotel—The Palace—at 451 Madison Avenue, received a $6.2 million tax abatement from the ICIB.

• Donald Trump, not yet 35, is the city's most aggressive and politically connected developer. Trump and his family have donated or loaned money to almost every important elected official in the city and state, including giving Governor Carey a total of $102,000 in his last two elections—plus co-signing a $300,000 bank loan. Trump has hired Carey's fund-raisier—Louise Sunshine—as his own lobbyist; he has hired Carey's friend and fat cat—lawyer Arthur Emil—as one of his lawyers; and he has hired the law firm of Roy Cohn and Stanley Friedman as his lead lawyers. He even donated $5,000 to Mayor Koch during 1979 and 1980—when there were no elections.

As a result, Trump managed to get the city to rescind the taxes on his new Grand Hyatt Hotel for 40 years; he managed to convince the city to spend $375 million to build a new convention center on land he held an option on; and he managed to get all the necessary zoning variances and municipal assistance in purchase of the Bonwit Teller building on Fifth Avenue, where Trump is building a 62-floor luxury tower, and where he admits: "The rents are so high that Americans can't afford to live there."

Trump also managed to receive a 20 year lease from the MTA for the operation of a tennis club in Grand Central Station, even though another competitor—former tennis champion Ham Richardson—made a substantially lower bid. Manhattan City Councilman Henry Stern called Trump's lease "a sweetheart deal." The total assets of the Trump Organization—founded by father Fred Trump—are now about $1.4 billion, including Trump Village in Brooklyn with 4,000 units.

• Rudin Management was founded in 1924 by Samuel Rudin to collect rents from a couple of Manhattan and Bronx tenements. Today, his sons,

Lewis and Jack, control property worth $750 million, including 4,000 apartment units in Manhattan, and 5.5 million square feet of office space. Lewis Rudin is the founder of the booster group—the Association for a Better New York—and he did round up other landlords to pre-pay $600 million in real estate taxes at the nadir of the fiscal crisis. But the Rudins are not in the charity business. They have gotten numerous reduced real estate assessments from the city, and a $3 million tax abatement from the ICIB on their new building at 560 Lexington Avenue. Lewis Rudin contributed $52,000 to Hugh Carey in 1978, and $11,000 to Ed Koch in 1977.

● Other super-landlords include: Crude, colorful Sam Lefrak with 55,000 residential units; Larry and Zachary Fisher with estimated assets of $1 billion including the CBS building, and the 50-story Burlington House on Sixth Avenue; Seymour Durst with almost 100 parcels of property in mid-Manhattan; Sylvan Lawrence and Seymour Cohn, who own 130 commercial properties, including the Bank of Tokyo Building and 95 Wall Street; the Tishman Brothers, who control assets of about $500 million and contributed $40,000 to Hugh Carey in 1978; and the reclusive Reichmann family of Toronto, which owns Olympia and York.

The Reichmanns now control 10.5 million square feet of prime Manhattan office space. They hired lawyer John Zuccotti, who got them an $11 million tax abatement from the ICIB for 466 Lexington Avenue. And Olympia and York has won the preliminary contract to develop $1 billion worth of commercial space in Battery Park City. Before winning the bid, Olympia and York hired away two of the Battery Park City Authority's executives—Thomas Galvin, the general manager, and Harold Frazee, the authority's comptroller.

With Ronald Reagan in the White House, three Republican national eminences have even more municipal influence than they had before, which was never insignificant.

● Maxwell Rabb, 69, was the Cabinet secretary under Eisenhower. Now he is senior partner in the Wall Street law firm of Strook, Strook, and Levan, and president of Temple Emanu-El, the city's most prestigious synagogue. He's known as "Reagan's man in New York."

● William Rogers, former Secretary of State to Richard Nixon, is senior partner in the law firm of Rogers and Wells. His clients include Dow Chemical, Shell Oil, and United Airlines. The Rogers firm was paid over $700,000 in its successful lobbying efforts for Air France and its Concorde Supersonic plane. The firm gets paid $750,000 as bond counsel to New York City. Rogers is a director of Merrill Lynch, which last year also paid Rogers' firm $1.8 million in fees. Rogers is also a director of 20th Century Fox, which paid his firm $1.3 million in fees.

- Henry Kissinger is producing millions of dollars in new business for the investment banking firm of Goldman, Sachs, which pays him $100,000 a year for a very part-time job. Kissinger is also paid $1 million as a consultant to NBC, and serves as a consultant to the Chase Manhattan Bank, where he chairs the international advisory committee. Kissinger also enjoys vast silent influence on finance, politics, and the media through dinner parties and luncheons at private clubs. Kissinger has armed body guards authorized by the Attorney General to make arrests.
- Roy Cohn, chief counsel to Joe McCarthy during the witch-hunts of the 1950s, has re-emerged as a sinister, and mysterious force in New York's affairs. His clients have included the Catholic Church, Mafia godfather Carmine Galante, FBI officials, landlord Sam Lefrak, real estate developer Donald Trump, and city contractors and franchise-seekers. He can manipulate judges and the making of judges, he can manipulate the press, he can manipulate political nominations in three political parties. He can raise tens of thousands of dollars for political campaigns, and he personally was a gaurantor of a $100,000 loan to Stanley Simon, the Bronx borough president.

Cohn, now 54, has been acquitted in three separate criminal trials; he owes the federal government $800,000 in back taxes; and in 1976 he was accused by a Florida probate judge of tricking an elderly and sick client into making a change in his will that would have given Cohn partial control over the $75 million Schenley estate. Cohn's law firm—Saxe, Bacon and Bolan—has two partners who amplify Cohn's clout. One is Thomas Bolan, who is a founder of New York's Conservative Party and is chairman of Senator Alfonso D'Amato's screening committee that will recommend federal judges and United States attorneys. The other partner is Stanley Friedman, the Bronx county Democratic Party leader, who controls judgeships and hundreds of city jobs. Friedman was recently paid a $15,000 fee by three groups of taxi owners to lobby against a proposed 8 per cent tax on taxi medallion sales. Friedman got the tax reduced to 5 per cent, thus saving his clients $3 million annually.

Many of Cohn's criminal clients have lost their cases, including mob loanshark Tony Salerno, disco owner Steve Rubell, and Adela Holzer, the Broadway producer. Many of his publicized divorce and corporate cases have ended ambiguously. But Cohn's invisible power to manipulate and intimidate has grown inexorably, and will continue to grow with Reagan and D'Amato in office.

- Authorities are the notoriously unaccountable and self-perpetuating fourth branch of government. The MTA is the conglomerate authority with jurisdiction over subways, buses, bridges, tunnels, and the LIRR. Since the days of William Ronan it has been chronically mismanaged by power brokers. In the late 1970s, the MTA chairman was Harold Fisher, who was primarily an election law expert and political fund-raiser. The present MTA chairman is Richard Ravitch, a landlord and real estate developer by profession. Under Ravitch's leadership, New York's subways have collapsed to the cusp of chaos, despite a fare increase to 60 cents. During 1980, the subways suffered record levels of delays, cancelled trains, long lines to buy tokens, subway cars without lights, broken doors, track fires, and violent crime, including an all-time record number of homicides. But one reason the MTA exists is to deflect responsibility for these things from the Mayor and Governor, who have to run for re-election.

Ravitch, although responsible for improving mass transit, refused to apply for the mass transit trade-in of Westway's $1.7 billion. More than a dozen other cities traded highway funds for public transportation funds, but Ravitch's loyalties to the permanent government prevented him from acting in the self-interest for the institution he was administering.

- Richard Kahan is the secretive, 34 year old chairman of both the Battery Park City Authority and the Urban Development Corporation (UDC). The UDC was created April of 1968, as an alleged memorial to the memory of Martin Luther King. It was given drastic powers to condemn property, issue bonds, and ignore zoning laws. Its original function, mandated in the legislation that created the authority, was to build rental housing for the poor. But it has abandoned its function. It is not building a single unit of low income housing this year. Under Kahan's leadership, the UDC has increased its bonding authority to $500 million, and it has built and financed $1 billion worth of projects, including luxury hotels, convention centers, sports arenas, shopping centers, and even a new office building for Hooker Chemical Company—the polluter of Love Canal.

Since Kahan became the UDC president, on June 29, 1978, more than $6 million has been paid out to politically connected law firms in legal fees, while staff lawyers complain they are not given enough work to do. UDC has virtually become a private bank for permanent government insiders. One lawyer—Charles Goldstein, of Weil, Gotshal—has been paid more than $1.5 million in fees. And UDC's extravagant patronage to lawyers has never been audited by any state comptroller.

On November 20, 1980, the UDC quietly altered its by-laws so that board meetings could take place in private by conference telephone call, instead of in a public forum. Robert Freedman, the executive director of the State's Committee on Public Access, said this change was a violation of the state's open meetings law.

- The bi-state Port Authority was founded in 1921 to bring regional coherence to marine terminal and transit policy. It is now the biggest and richest public authority in the country with $4.5 billion in assets and annual profit of about $500 million. But its primary purpose long ago became returning money to its bondholders. It runs 26 tax-exempt facilities, including JFK Airport, the World Trade Center, and the new midtown Bus Terminal. The Port Authority's executive director is 40 year-old Peter Goldmark, the former state budget director. Goldmark has cleaned up a petty expense account scandal and stopped some of the luxury living by officials, but he has not yet converted the PA into the regional mass transit planner that critics like lawyer Theodore Kheel have been urging for 20 years. And secrecy remains an obsession of the authority's 12 commissioners and top staff. The PA is still more responsive to the bond market than to the public.

● In the press, power is in a few conservative hands. Arthur Ochs Sulzberger, the publisher of *The New York Times*, and A.M. Rosenthal, the executive editor, dominate that formidable institution. Michael O'Neill is the editor and executive vice president of *The Daily News*. It was O'Neill who fired popular columnist Pete Hamill in 1979 for being too liberal. Rupert Murdoch owns *The New York Post* and more than 100 other publications around the world. In February of 1980, Murdoch met with President Carter, and five days later one of his companies got a $290 million loan, at 8.1 per cent interest, from the Export-Import Bank. And a few days after that, *The Post* endorsed Carter over Ted Kennedy in a series of rabid editorials. Murdoch also played politics in the 1977 City election. After the election, 50 *Post* reporters signed a petition protesting the *Post's* biased coverage in its news pages favoring Ed Koch and Carol Bellamy.

● Television has replaced much of the traditional electoral authority of political machines. Politicians with big money can now appeal directly to the voters by saturating the airwaves with commercials. This development has made media campaign consultant David Garth more influential than any party leader in electing candidates to public office.

There is no question that Garth is the most creative and the most tactically adroit of the media consultants. He is also the most ruthless. Garth's temper tantrums can bully reporters. And he does intimidate some competitors by having no sense of limits; he will say or do almost anything to win an election. In 1977, he exploited the death penalty to elect Ed Koch, and in 1978, he used Hugh Carey's opposition to the death penalty as proof of Carey's humanity. Garth also works for foreign governments (Bermuda, Venezuela) and has commercial clients like oilman Leon Hess and Warner Communications that often turn out to be contributors to the politicians who employ Garth. In 1980, Garth helped

Jay Rockefeller spend a pornographic $12 million—most of it his own money—to get re-elected Governor of West Virginia. It came out to $29 per vote.

● Publicist Howard Rubenstein has inherited the mantle, from the much less savory Sydney Baron, as the proprietor of the most powerful public relations company in the city. Rubenstein's client list of more than 100 includes: 11 voluntary hospitals, NYU, McDonald's, Dillon Read, UDC at $40,000 a year, the Equitable Life Insurance Company, several civil service unions, Rupert Murdoch, and almost every major landlord including Trump, Rudin, Helmsley, Tishman, and the Real Estate Board. He usually counsels compromise rather than confrontation to his clients when dealing with community groups or the press. His high credibility stems from the fact he tells the truth, even if it is not flattering to his clients. He has, in the past, generated simultaneous, favorable editorials for his clients in all three daily newspapers.

● Backroom clubhouse power, once dominated by Carmine DeSapio, is now dispersed among Democrats Meade Esposito, Stanley Friedman and Donald Manes, and Republicans George Clark and John Calandra.

And just as in DeSapio's time, some of the county leaders have business interests that profit from their political influence. Meade Esposito is part-owner of an insurance brokerage company—Serres, Visone and Rice—and until recently was a paid director of a mortgage brokerage company named Mortgage Affiliates. Stanley Friedman has law clients who do business with the city, most notably Ed Arrogoni, who owns the highly lucrative express bus franchise. John Calandra has insurance interests and a reputation as the lawyer to hire if you want a liquor license from the SLA. Calandra is a former deputy commissioner of the SLA.

While the political bosses have lost much of their electing influence to the Garths and Murdochs, they still have the institutional stamina to bend elected governments. The bosses still control patronage jobs, and influence funding, vendor, franchise, zoning, construction, and contract decisions. If you want to become a judge, or get a parking lot contract, or kill a controller's audit, or take-over a community planning board, you still have to go see a clubhouse boss.

● Union leaders with power include: Albert Shanker of the UFT, who has 200,000 state-wide members, and uses phone banks and a disciplined organization to produce votes for the candidates the union endorses. The union also controls most of the city's 32 elected community school boards. Victor Gotbaum is the president of District Council 37, the largest municipal employee union. Ex-radical Jack Bigel is the advisor and pension fund consultant to most of the public employee unions, including the firefighters, the sanitation workers and Teamsters Local 237, which has 14,000 members. The credibility of Local 237's president, Barry Feinstein, may have been injured by the disclosure that his union's welfare fund had paid almost $3 million in phony excess fees and commissions to an insurance broker who was also a relative of Feinstein's.

• Among private sector unions, ILGWU president **Sol Chaiken**, is influential, and his union contributed $69,000 to Hugh Carey's 1978 campaign for Governor. Anthony Scotto, former president of Local 1814 of the ILA, was enormously powerful until his federal conviction for bribery and racketeering. Scotto's clout extended from port projects, to workmen's compensation policies, to government appointments, to financing candidates.

The volatile internal politics of the police, fire, and transit unions have prevented those leaders from acquiring the stability necessary for serious power.

• Some national and international corporate executives are based in New York, and want things from local government. Steve Ross is the president of Warner Communications. He contributed $48,000 to Hugh Carey in 1978 and flies Carey around in his corporate jet. Ross wants cable television franchises, and is interested in casino gambling. Saul Steinberg, "the Howard Hughes of Brooklyn", according to his estranged wife, is the 42 year old president of the $3 billion conglomerate, Reliance Group, Inc. In 1978, Steinberg gave $40,000 to Carey's campaign, and $8,000 to a legislative campaign fund controlled by State Senator Manfred Ohrenstein. Steinberg also discussed making a $25,000 donation to the campaign of Democrat Harrison Goldin. All Steinberg wanted was the exclusive franchise to build bus shelters in New York City. He had it for a while, but then lost it in a bid-rigging scandal that led to the conviction of powerbroker lawyer Jack Bronston and to Steinberg taking the Fifth Ammendment before a Grand Jury.

• David Margolis is the $574,000 a year chairman of Colt Industries which controls 15 per cent of America's handgun market. Margolis is Mayor Koch's most intimate adviser from the corporate world. Margolis is irrationally anti-union, and his inflexibility helped push the city into the 1980 transit strike. Margolis, a CCNY graduate, also played a key role, as an EFCB member, in killing free tuition at the City University.

Margolis is one of the leaders of the New York Partnership, a big business lobby wearing the mask of public interest. Chief corporate officers active in the Partnership include: James Robinson, chairman of American Express; George Weissman, chairman of Philip Morris; Rexford Tompkins, president of the Dry Dock Savings Bank and chairman of the Citizens Budget Commission; and Donald Smiley, chairman of Macy's department store. They all enjoy privileged access to Mayor Koch, and have input on public policy decisions ranging from street crime to rent controls.

Finally, there are the lawyers, the lawyers who know all the judges, the lawyers who used to work in the government before they wanted to become rich, the lawyers who drafted the laws so they know how to find the loopholes for their clients.

● Harold Fisher, now 68, thinks for the permanent government. He was counsel to the Speaker of the Assembly, he was chairman of the MTA; he is still the president of the Dime Savings Bank of Williamsburg. He is a fund-raiser for Mayor Koch and Governor Carey; he is the personal lawyer to Meade Esposito; he is the quiet adviser to Council President Carol Bellamy. In 1978, he was hired by Comptroller Harrison Goldin to knock Steve Berger off the ballot. And Fisher was successful in proving that Berger violated a few technicalities of the election law that Fisher helped write. Fisher also defended Representative John Rooney after Rooney's pals had stolen an election from Allard Lowenstein in 1972. Fisher's small Brooklyn firm represents UDC, Teamster Local 237, and dozens of companies seeking city and state contracts. Fisher also has a silent say in who becomes an appellate or administrative judge.

● William Shea is the senior name partner in Shea Gould, the 131 member law firm, and is the man for whom Shea Stadium is named. Shea is a director of five companies, a former member of the MTA, counsel to two savings banks, and a fund-raiser for many politicians. In 1976, Shea's law firm was paid a then record lobbying fee of $80,000 by the Securities Industry Association to lobby for repeal of the stock transfer tax. The stock transfer tax was repealed by the 1976 session of the state legislature.

In 1980, Shea's firm registered as lobbyists for 13 organizations, including: Telepromter cable television company, Salamon Brothers, Aetna Life Insurance Company, the Tobacco Tax Council, the Pharmautical Manufacturers Association, New York University, and the Securities Industry Association.

Shea's power has recently declined somewhat, as the power of the Catholic Archdiocese—which he represents—has declined, as its parishioners move to the suburbs.

● Other permanent government lawyers with exceptional clout and contacts are: former deputy Mayor John Zuccotti, who specializes in Section 8 housing subsidies and tax shelter syndication; Charles Goldstein, who has been paid more than $3 million by three public authorities; labor mediator and mass transit expert Theodore Kheel, whose law partner is now HUD Secretary; former city Transportation Administrator Mike Lazar, who practices more influence than law;

former Buildings Commissioner Charles Moedler, who represents the Sanitation Workers Union and several major landlords; former Mayor Robert Wagner; and former City Planning Commission chairman Donald Elliot.

This is the permanent power structure. With individual exceptions, these are the institutions that controlled the decisions which helped New York City decline and go broke: to invest billions of dollars in a World's Fair and a World Trade Center; to bulldoze and redline neighborhoods in New York City; to build highrise luxury housing rather than to restore and renovate existing housing for moderate-income families; to make planning decisions that favored the automobile over subways; to make large profits on selling the city's notes and bonds and then close the market; to accept the concept of moral obligation bonds and create an Urban Development Corporation that would go bankrupt; to keep the Port Authority's surplus funds from being used to subsidize mass transit; to loot and ruin the Mitchell-Lama housing program that should have kept the middle class in New York City.

The permanent government is essentially bipartisan. Above a certain level of wealth, above a certain level of power, there are no Democrats and there are no Republicans. Except perhaps on Election Day.

Alton Marshall, the Republican president of Rockefeller Center, sits on the board of directors of the City Title Insurance Company with Stanley Steingut, the former Democratic Speaker of the Assembly. Democratic Speaker of the Assembly, Stanley Fink, joined the committee to raise legal defense funds for Nassau County Republican political boss, Joe Margiotta, following Margiotta's federal indictment for extortion. When asked to explain his decision, Speaker Fink told *Newsday*: "He's a member of my profession, and, of course I feel *sympatico* toward him."

Liberal Party boss Ray Harding is a partner in the law firm of Democratic Party fund raiser and power broker, Bill Shea. John Klein, the former Republican county executive in Suffolk County is now law partners with Jack English, the former Democratic Party chairman of Nassau County. And as previously noted, Roy Cohn's law firm includes as partners Thomas Bolan the Conservative Party leader, and Stanley Friedman the Democratic Party leader.

When the influential Republican party leader Perry Duryea was indicted for violation of the state election law, Harold Fisher was his lawyer—although Fisher had helped rewrite the law. Fisher also was appointed to the MTA by Nelson Rockefeller, and then, with his son, contributed $45,000 to Hugh Carey's 1974 campaign. One of Fisher's law partners was Syracuse Republican power broker, Gary Axenfeld.

In 1973, the Republican Rockefeller and the Liberal Alex Rose tried to draft Democrat Wagner to run again for mayor, this time as a "fusion" candidate. In

1973, David Rockefeller contributed $5000 to Democrat Beame. Among the names on the original charter for Century National Bank are Vincent Albano, the Republican boss of Manhattan, and Bernard Ruggieri, then an aide to Democratic Mayor Wagner, now a partner in the Shea, Gould law firm.

In a city as large and complex as New York, the permanent government takes great pains to control philanthropic and cultural institutions. They sit on the boards of hospitals, universities, museums. And whether Catholic, Jewish, or Protestant, they become the fund raisers, the voluntary counsels, the go-betweens with government. The same is true for the vast network of ethnic organizations in this most ethnic of cities. And, in the greatest irony of all, it is these men, frequently from the wealthiest levels of society, who control the institutions serving the poor: the settlement houses, the Community Service Society, Legal Aid, Catholic Charities, the Federation of Jewish Philanthropies. Once this was a logical arrangement since they in fact provided the lion's share of financing for such undertakings. This is no longer true. Almost all of these agencies today are dependent on government grants or broad support from the general public. But the power remains concentrated in self-perpetuating boards of the very rich.

The cornerstone of the permanent government is the Golden Triangle of politics-real estate-banking. New York has no natural resources, like oil in Texas, or tobacco in North Carolina, or coal in West Virginia. It became the nation's greatest city and center of commerce because it was the nation's pre-eminent port. Its great fortunes were built on the crazily escalating value of its land. Much of the Wall Street financial district at the tip of Manhattan was once swamp, but landfill operations to expand the amount of real estate in this choice location began before the Revolution and continues to this day. And just as the squatters' hovels of nineteenth-century "river rats" were razed to make way for expanding commerce, it remains the dream of banks and realtors to drive out the poor who cling to neighborhoods surrounding the financial district (like the Lower East Side, Little Italy and Chinatown) in order to construct a walk-to-work "golden ghetto" for the financial community. Banker Rexford Tompkins, a former chairman of the Real Estate Board who once said, "Every wealthy person in the world should live on the Island of Manhattan," told the City Council in 1970: "Easier evictions is our only hope for reviving the sagging construction industry."

It was natural, then, that political life in New York more than in any other American city came to revolve around issues of land: who owns it, what can be built on it, how much tax it will pay. Real estate is the primary generator of wealth, of jobs, of the quality of life. The value of the land, in many cases its scarcity, has shaped the life style of the city and its people. For instance, because of high land costs the vast majority of New Yorkers live in apartment houses as opposed to the private homes that predominate in most other cities.

Less than 10 per cent of the city's residents own their own homes. New Yorkers aren't immune to the American dream of a "home of one's own," as the suburban exodus of white middle-class families in the postwar years clearly showed. It is simply that home ownership today, except in certain ghetto neighborhoods, is becoming less and less possible for all but the very rich.

So the vast majority of New Yorkers, some 2 million families, live under roofs that someone else owns. It is a misnomer to speak of a "housing" industry in New York, however, since this implies that the purpose and profitability of the industry lie in providing people with a fundamental necessity—a place to live. In fact, profitability in the industry involves the ability to buy and sell buildings and maximize gains despite the tangled skein of local, state and federal tax laws affecting real estate; "housing" and the people who live in "houses" are at best secondary considerations. Similar observations can be made about the commercial rental market. (Even the largest corporations rarely own their headquarters buildings, although many buildings are named, and renamed, after the largest tenants; e.g. the Uniroyal Building has just become the Simon and Schuster Building.)

The current investment in land and buildings in New York is astronomical, more than $100 billion. Almost all of this capital has come from banks, which of course make money by investing the money of their depositors. This means that the most powerful realtors and America's largest banks are perpetually trying to figure out ways to increase their profits on investments in New York real estate—a realization that might cost the average New Yorker a lot of sleep if he bothered to think about it at all.

The primary way in which the banker and real-estate magnates can accomplish this goal, next to their unstinting attempts to rape the Internal Revenue Code, is to manipulate the politics of New York city and state. They've been at it for a long time, and the relationship has proven fruitful for everyone but the people.

An amazing number of individuals can become involved in any building project in New York City: the seller of the site, the builder of the project, architects, dozens of separate construction trades, title-search insurance brokers, contractors, property insurance brokers, truckers, building inspectors, bankers (to finance the sale of the land, the cost of construction and ultimately a long-term mortgage)—and almost all of them will be accompanied by legions of lawyers, accountants, and tax experts. Real estate remains the nation's most irrational, fragmented, and arcane industry, something to make the medieval guilds blink in admiration. It is New York's $100 billion cottage industry. In turn each of these groups has its own lobbyists, string-pullers, and political godfathers operating at City Hall and the State Capitol, and each is a source of campaign contributions, favors, and political foot-soldiers for "sympathetic" politicians.

Whenever a major building project is under consideration at the Board of Estimate, City Hall looks as if it were under assault from an army of pinstripe-suited ants. The most outraged and organized community defending itself from such a project is no match for this onslaught. Ordinary people who must give up a day's pay to attend a public hearing are unlikely to do so; zoning lawyers who earn $100 an hour are more patient, and have a longer span of attention. Even the most honest politicians, even the ones who refuse the massive campaign contributions, the jobs for supporters (private patronage is as important, if not more important, than jobs on the public payroll for the city's thriving political machines), the implied promise of lucrative employment after public office—even they find the permanent government irresistible in these situations. For in the forefront of this phalanx march the "experts," the good-government representatives who never tire of speaking of the "trickle-down" benefits to the city's poor from each new building project. Then come the city's own architects and planners—responsible only to the mayor—who praise the brilliance of yet another new scheme to evade the zoning laws; followed by the private engineers and architects, who gently tell the elected officials that while *they* may not understand all of the intricacies of the proposal, it has all been worked out by computer. (Some members of the Board of Estimate, seriously burned by two recent projects—Yankee Stadium and the Bronx Terminal Market, where former city officials were quoted in the *Times* as bragging about how effectively they had lied to them—contemplated putting city officials under oath and making them subject to perjury penalties, but they discarded the idea when the public outcry abated.)

In the last analysis, the permanent government simply overwhelms the temporary elected government. Those officials whom it can't buy are bludgeoned into submission, for they lack the cadre of professionals, public-relations men, and political operatives throughout the infrastructure of government which banks, developers, and realtors can command. The permanent government, representing an alliance of special interests, is more powerful than the elected government, which theoretically represents the interests of all the people.

During a period when government at all levels is in low esteem, is this arrangement necessarily a bad thing? After all, we live in a nation where private profit is officially perceived as the maximum good—the engine of all progress. The permanent government is hardly unique to New York. It has its analogue at the national level where giant oil companies, defense contractors, and multinational corporations have effectively defined the nation's priorities and allocated its resources through a long series of administrations that have unswervingly agreed with Calvin Coolidge's observation that "the business of America is business." In the early 1960s, John Kennedy quickly learned that a president, no matter how popular, who confronts the combined interests of corporate America is walking into a meat grinder. Faced with the choice between massive public works and social spending, or the "trickle-down" economics of business to cure the Eisenhower recession, he found it expedient, in the face of a carefully orchestrated corporate propaganda campaign, to opt for investment credits for industry and tax cuts that aided the wealthiest segments of society. In dealing with the nation's balance-of-payments problems, he encountered the same wall of opposition and finally observed: "It's a ridiculous situation for us to be squeezing down essential public activities in order not to touch private investment and tourist spending—but apparently that's life."

"Life" hasn't changed much in Washington, New York, or hundreds of other cities across the land as we begin the nation's third century. Corporate power still dominates public need.

There are many ways in which the permanent government is bringing about the downfall of New York. We have seen that it was the driving force behind the city's borrowing binge. It has held the large amounts of federal revenue available for basic public services hostage to its own private master plan for the city's future. It has systematically wasted the tax revenues necessary to maintain vital services like police, fire protection, schools, and health care. The irony, of course, is that the visible clowns of the elected government have been held responsible for these disasters by the press and the public, while the permanent government has been given even greater control over the life-support system of the city.

What we have outlined, and shall develop in greater detail, is simply "business as usual" in the nation's largest and most important city. Power fattens on the tragedies of the powerless. The operations of most members of the permanent government are not illegal, although as we shall suggest in Chapter 10 organized crime is an active, if silent, partner in some of the areas of city life under the hegemony of the permanent government.

Why break the law when it was drafted to serve your purposes? As long as the rich and powerful are the only source of the vast amounts of money needed to wage a successful campaign for public office, elected officials from the mayor and governor on down will court their favor and do their bidding. Why bribe a commissioner or regulator when it is perfectly legal to offer him a high-paying job instead? The example to young, honest idealists is that government service can be a profitable audition for a career with the permanent government.

Elliot Vestner, for example, was the state's regulator of banking until he quit in 1975, at the age of thirty-nine, to become senior vice-president and general counsel to Irving Trust, New York City's seventh largest commercial bank.

Vestner's predecessor as state banking superintendent was Harry W. Albright. Albright had resigned his job to become president of the Dime Savings Bank.

During the Lindsay administration there was constant traffic from that "reform" government to the executive offices of the real-estate industry. Jacquelin Robertson, a member of the City Planning Commission, quit to become vice-president of Arlen Realty and Development Corporation. Robert Rosenberg, a deputy Housing and Development administrator became general manager of Starrett City, a vast housing development owned by a subsidiary of the Kinney Corporation. Joseph Stein, Lindsay's Buildings Commissioner, resigned to become a vice-president of Tishman Realty. Albert Walsh, the city Housing and Development administrator, quit to take a $75,000-a-year job as head of the National Realty Board, an organization of landlords and real-estate investors. Kenneth Patton, Lindsay's Economic Development administrator, resigned to become president of the Real Estate Board of New York, also at $75,000 a year. Lester Schulklapper, the city's housing lobbyist in Albany, took a job with the Citizens Tax Council, a landlord lobbying group. He was interviewed for the job by two of the city's biggest landlords—Harry Helmsley and Charles Benenson. Donald Elliot, once the chairman of the City Planning Commission, is the lawyer for some of the biggest landlords and developers in the city.

And then there is the case of Edgar Fabber, the city's deputy commissioner for Economic Development. At EDA, Fabber negotiated a ninety-nine-year lease with the United States Lines for 187 acres on Staten Island, and the city then agreed to spend $71 million to build a containerport for the shipping company. The deal was severely criticized as a give-away, and a law suit was filed to stop it on the grounds that there was no competitive bidding. State Supreme Court Justice Morris Spector threw out the suit, but admitted in his decision that there was no competitive bidding. On January 31, 1976, Edgar Fabber left his $38,771-a-year job with the city and went to work at a much higher salary for Walter Kidde & Company, the congolomerate that happens to own U.S. Lines.

Almost all of the elected legislators at City Hall or in Albany are lawyers who spend a few days, or in many cases a few hours, a week doing the public's business and the rest of the time conducting their own. Public office for at least one of the partners in a law firm is considered a great draw for business. Lawyer-legislators who determine the budgets of public agencies then go on to represent clients with cases before those agencies. They propose bills that can aid a client and fight to kill those that might harm his interests—without any requirement even to show their own financial interest in the legislation before them.

(Few scandals in New York have shocked the public more than the disclosure of massive frauds perpetrated by owners of nursing homes, who maintained the sick and the elderly in concentration-camp misery while milking the federal, state, and city treasuries. Yet in the face of uniform public outrage, the Albany lawmakers steadfastly refused to ban their members from representing nursing homes, or any other private business client, before state agencies attempting to protect the public's health and tax dollars.)

The lawyer-legislators would obviously prefer to risk the public's wrath than to alter a system whose rewards are so lucrative. The oldest law of politics is "The public has a short memory"; the second oldest is that the powerful pay only for "value received."

Why would any power broker bother with the classic "little brown envelope" filled with cash, when he can "buy" the vote of key legislators, committee chairmen, and even the top leaders of the legislature with a legal retainer or an insurance contract? Influence peddling in New York is a carefully codified business where everyone knows the rules, and anyone willing and able to pay the price can play.

There is no better single example of the overwhelming power of the permanent government than the way it has implemented its private master plan for the development of Lower Manhattan—with massive subsidies from public tax dollars.

The brainchild of David Rockefeller, this monumental twenty-year undertaking set off a speculative building boom from which the city may take decades to recover. It has undermined the financial viability of existing office buildings, not to mention their tax value; overwhelmed the human services in the downtown area, especially the mass transit network; and for almost a decade threatened to bulldoze some of the city's most stable ethnic neighborhoods in order to build yet another expressway. Hundreds of thriving small businesses have been destroyed. Ninety acres of landfill have been dumped into the already polluted Hudson River. Public revenues desperately needed for transmit improvements in two states have been sequestered to pay off bond-holders in the biggest white-elephant construction project in history—the twin towers of the World Trade Center.

For two decades, the balanced growth of the rest of the city, indeed of the entire metropolitan region, has been sacrificed to the demands of the downtown financial elite. Even after these plans were exposed by events as ludicrous pipe dreams, hundreds of millions in public monies are still tied up in projects that will never be built. More than $1 billion in federal transit funds remain earmarked for Westway a four-mile super-highway to serve Wall Street and the minuscule 3 per cent of daily commuters who would use the road, while the subway system, which serves 89 per cent of the city's workers and desperately needs these monies, is allowed literally to crumble away.

Debating which Rockefeller brother, Nelson or David, actually has the most power long ago became a parlor game at New York cocktail parties. By the mid-1950s, both were clearly on the way to the top. David had entered the family business, the Chase Manhattan Bank, and while still a vice-president was a crucial decision maker in what was then America's, and perhaps the world's, leading financial institution. From the bank's aging headquarters at 18 Pine Street, David looked out at a financial community that was stagnating. The major corporations that made their headquarters in New York seemed to be moving uptown en masse to the midtown area where new office buildings were springing up in one of the city's periodic building booms. Chase itself was planning to consolidate its various functions, which were sprinkled in a number of downtown office buildings. If Chase followed the exodus to midtown, there was a widespread fear that the other major financial institutions would follow suit, sounding the death knell for the old financial district. David decided to stay, and to reshape the Wall Street area into a citadel befitting what one of his aides called "the heart pump of the capital blood that sustains the free world."

There is still a dispute about the magnanimity of this gesture. Perhaps David had merely been infected by the "edifice complex" that afflicted his father and brother. Others suspect that he was more interested in protecting the bank's $40-million investment in downtown real estate. Whatever the real motivation, he took the plunge in classic Rockefeller style.

In 1956, he called together fifty-five of Wall Street's most powerful leaders and established the Committee for Lower Manhattan, which emerged two years later as the Downtown-Lower Manhattan Association with himself as chairman. From that time on, he called the shots in a multi-billion-dollar reconstruction of the financial district. The DLMA quickly issued a plan calling for an initial investment of $1 billion in public and private monies to be spent for office buildings, housing developments, parks, highways, and transit improvements.

David's master plan envisioned the expansion of the Wall Street district into a sort of "golden ghetto" where financial executives and junior staff would live, work, and play in a carefully controlled environment. The whole of Lower Manhattan would be cut off by a Chinese Wall expressway running across Broome Street from the Holland Tunnel to the Williamsburg and Manhattan bridges—a long-time dream of master builder Robert Moses. The area south of the expressway, encompassing the traditional communities of Little Italy, Chinatown, and the Lower East Side—economically healthy and self-regenerating—would be incorporated into the new city of finance. When David looked at these communities, he saw only an area "largely occupied by commercial slums, right next to the greatest concentration of real estate value in the city." He chose to ignore the fact that some 50,000 people had considered it their home for generations. "I don't know of any other area in the city where there's as good an opportunity to expand inexpensively," he stated.

Chase put some of its money where David's mouth was, and began construction of a $120-million headquarters building. Characteristically, the centuries-old street names adjoining the building were erased, and the new structure became 1 Chase Manhattan Plaza. But the cornerstone of the downtown renaissance was to be another Rockefeller brainstorm—a mammoth World Trade Center that would attract and consolidate a major hunk of the city's commercial renters in 9 million square feet of office space in two 110-story towers surrounded by six smaller buildings and acres of retail space, plazas, and a 2000-car garage.

The World Trade Center was to fill a totally unperceived need. New York had stumbled along as a leader of world shipping and commerce for 200 years without any demand being raised for this kind of super-concentration under one roof. As the small businessmen and residents on the World Trade Center site charged in court, the whole concept was simply a gimmick to give the New York-New Jersey Port Authority an excuse to undertake the project as a "public benefit" for the district.

David Rockefeller could not have found a more willing partner for his enterprise. Established by New York and New Jersey in 1921 to establish order in the chaotic transfer of cargo between ships and the region's rapacious railroads, the Port Authority had slipped the reins and become an institution in search of a purpose. Perhaps because of its early failures, those who ran the public agency had developed a violent dislike for anything that ran on rails. During the Depression it had built the Holland Tunnel and the George Washington Bridge to facilitate auto travel between the two states. It subsequently took over operation of the two city-constructed air-fields, La Guardia and Kennedy (then Idlewild). In the late 1950s and early 1960s, there was a growing public demand that it return to its original purpose and coordinate the collapsing rail transport system between New York and New Jersey. But the suggestion was anathema to the long-time guiding hand of the Authority, Austin Tobin, who had managed to play the two states off against one another and ran his vast empire as he saw fit.

In 1960, David asked the governors of the two states (his brother Nelson had become governor of New York in 1959) and the mayor of New York to have the Port Authority undertake a feasibility study for constructing an international trade center. By 1962, both state legislatures had given go-aheads; New Jersey exacted a promise that the PA would continue to operate the now bankrupt Hudson and Manhattan railroad, the only remaining rail link for the many Jerseyites working in New York City. The Port Authority agreed to this compromise, but in turn demanded that it be absolved of any other rail involvements; it incorporated this provision in the bonds it sold for the joint project, bonds that will not be paid off until well into the twenty-first century.

The involvement of the huge Port Authority was crucial: It could sell tax-exempt bonds for the project, bonds that were backed by its vast flow of revenue and would be snapped up by investors. (As an underwriter for the bond sale, Chase of course made a bundle.) In addition, it had the power to condemn land, avoiding both the delay and escalation of price involved in a negotiated sale by a private party.

The site tenants, small commercial businesses who had done business happily and profitably at the same location for decades, resisted bitterly, but they were attacking a dinosaur with snowballs. After being moved from the site, many didn't even both to reopen, since their customers, accustomed to coming to the same location over the years, would never know where to find them. Another problem emerged when it became obvious that the new towers would destroy television reception in a broad swath reaching into Westchester County, since signals transmitted from the top of the Empire State Building, until then the highest point in the city, would bounce off the new aluminum-sheathed monsters. The Port Authority's imperious answer: "Move your aerials."

Although still uncompleted, the Trade Center opened for tenants in the early 1970s. Long before, however, it had become apparent that the buildings could not attract enough occupants to be self-sustaining. The bright young men of Mayor Lindsay's City Planning Commission had been busily devising loopholes in the zoning law that sparked an artificial office-building boom. Manhattan was glutted with vacant office space. In the first ten years of the Downtown-Lower Manhattan Association, 14 million square feet of new offices were built in the financial district alone, compared with only 3 million in the previous decade. By the end of 1972, another 28 million had been completed. When the Trade Center was looking for tenants in early 1971, 15 million sqare feet of prime office space elsewhere in Manhattan was vacant, about 12 percent of all the space that had been constructed since World War II.

When your brother is the governor of the richest state in the nation, however, being stuck with a few million feet of vacant space in your favorite project need only be a brief embarrassment. In 1969, the state's Office of Government Services had begun a crash effort to consolidate its various New York City offices under one roof. Strangely enough, that roof was the World Trade Center, where it signed forty-year leases for about a quarter of the total floor space.

Once the World Trade Center construction was assured in the mid-1960s, additional schemes for Xanadu on the Hudson could be unleashed. And new players were clamoring to join the game.

An imposing foundation is required for a project the size of the World Trade Center. Miles of earth must be excavated and, in the normal course of events, dumped someplace else. In 1966, the Port Authority and the city signed an agreement requiring that the rock and dirt excavated for the Trade Center be dumped into the Hudson River in a giant landfill adjacent to the site.

Nelson Rockefeller, running for re-election as governor, then unveiled a proposal sure to stir the lust of the politically potent construction trades. He would build 14,000 apartments, a 2200-room hotel, and two 67-story office towers on the landfill site. The brothers Rockefeller seemed intent on erecting a new Stonehenge at the mouth of the Hudson. Nelson called his segment Battery Park City.

The announcement of plans for Battery Park City set off a decade of bitter in-fighting between the city and state, the city's minority communities and the powerful building trade unions, and ultimately within the permanent government itself. The harsh street noises of the city were beginning to disrupt the placid dreamers in Wall Street's executive suites.

(David got a brief glimpse of the handwriting on the wall when the Lower Manhattan Expressway was killed by Mayor Lindsay after several vacillations in 1967. A united community, and a public increasingly disenchanted with New York's gagging air pollution, had won a stunning upset in the last round of a twenty-year fight. Most importantly, a whole new attitude about preserving and strengthening existing neighborhoods had taken root in the public consciousness—this largely through the work of Jane Jacobs, a brilliant writer and urban-planning critic who had been an important leader in the fight against the expressway and in the successful effort to preserve the adjacent West Village community from Robert Moses's bulldozers.)

Lindsay countered Rockefeller's plan for Battery Park City with a more modest version of his own. A final plan emerged in 1968, close to the Rockefeller original. Having already milked the Port Authority for the World Trade Center, the governor established a new authority to build his city within a city. The chairman of the new authority was Charles Urstadt, formerly Rockefeller's state housing commissioner. Urstadt had been the principle owner of a major real estate management firm, Douglas Elliman Co. He is best remembered for his successful gutting of New York City's rent control law in 1971 and the introduction of vacancy decontrol, which removed rent controls on apartments as their tenants moved out. This stroke of genius led to rents doubling and tripling in the city's stable middle-class communities, and managed to drive untold thousands of young white families to the suburbs at a time when the city most needed them to provide tax dollars and racial balance in its schools.

Battery Park City was conceived not only as a big office-building scheme but as a community for executives and their families. It was one of a number of ephemeral ideas for attracting back corporate staff who had fled to suburban tax havens in New Jersey and Connecticut, where large backyards and good schools were plentiful. The unstated logic was that a separate community—white, affluent, and well serviced—could be insulated from the general problem of New York City while offering all of its advantages, such as proximity to the theater, cultural institutions, and fine restaurants. The site also offered spectacular views of New York Harbor, still one of the most exciting vistas in the world.

But construction costs were escalating dizzily because of the building boom, and it soon became evident that even this community for the moderately wealthy would have to be subsidized with public monies. This threw the issue before the Board of Estimate and into the turbulence of racial politics in the late 1960s. Compromise was inevitable and, after a bitter series of public hearings and private meetings among city officials, finally emerged in 1969. The office towers, 7 million square feet of office space for Lower Manhattan, would be constructed first. The housing would be divided equally among moderate income—$100 a room per month; middle—$70; and low—$30, which would be traditional and separate brick public housing.

The Battery Park City Authority accepted the compromise grudgingly, and warned that renting would be difficult. They particularly protested a requirement that the office space be forced to subsidize the housing component. But the project moved ahead, at least on paper. In 1972, the Authority sold $200 million in "moral obligation" bonds through the Wall Street firm of Goldman, Sachs (whose president was the late Gustave Levy, a Rockefeller confidant and appointee to the board of the Port Authority). The proceeds of the bond sale were deposited with Chase Manhattan. (In 1976, the proceeds that had not been spent for administrative overhead—$110 million—were still in the hands of Chase.) The only benefit that New York City has thus far derived from Battery Park City is that its vacant expanse served as an ideal viewing stand for the Operation Sail extravaganza staged by the city on July 4, 1976, in celebration of the Bicentennial.

While Battery Park City limped forward, David Rockefeller was preparing another pyramid to optimism on lower Manhattan's eastern flank. In 1972, he and John Lindsay announced a mammoth $1.2 billion project, developed by the city government's Office of Lower Manhattan Planning, which they called Manhattan Landing. This included plans for 6 million square feet of office space; 9500 units of exclusively luxury housing; a new building for the New York Stock Exchange; a 400-room hotel; and a permanent home for the sailing ships and restored blockfronts of the South Street Seaport; as well as a marina, an indoor sports complex, and a 1000-car garage. Lindsay—who was then in the midst of his abortive campaign for president, generously financed by builders and developers who had cashed in on his Planning Commission's largesse—called the proposal "a strong affirmation of faith in the city's future by the planners who conceived it, the financial community who will back it, and the developers who will build it."

In fact, the sponsors for the various Manhattan Landing projects were a roster of the permanent government. Twenty commercial and savings banks were to finance the private share of the construction to arise on the 113-acre landfill site. Major builders—Uris, Trump, DeMateis, Tishman, and Arlen Realty and Development—all laid claim to parts of the package. Prominent architectural firms like Edward Barnes; Davis, Brody; and the ubiquitous Skidmore, Owings & Merrill were already busily at work.

There were a few hitches, however. First, Manhattan Landing made Battery Park City unworkable. Urstadt was willing, even anxious, to tell any listener that he couldn't rent high-income apartments in a mixed-income project if he had to compete with an all-luxury project with greater amenities only a mile away. This problem had one obvious solution—and the Lindsay planners jumped at it. They simply tore up the 1969 compromise and severely reduced the proportion of low- and middle-income housing in Battery Park City. Despite opposition from Manhattan Borough President Percy Sutton, the city's highest black elected official, and Bronx Borough President Robert Abrams, this new plan for Battery Park breezed through the Board of Estimate.

Other problems were less easily resolved. To make it marketable even for tenants earning $65,000 a year, Manhattan Landing would require massive public subsidy, including an 80 per cent tax abatement and a minimum direct investment of $100 million in public funds for construction. The city had nearly exhausted its middle-income housing funds (many public middle-income projects had already defaulted on their mortgages), and it had created yet another bonding mechanism, called the Housing Construction Fund, to pump money into programs that had been largely vitiated by the rapidly inflating building costs stimulated by the Vietnam war. Since two-thirds of the HCF monies were reserved directly for hardcore slum areas, Manhattan Landing alone would absorb the lion's share of the remaining housing-construction monies available for most of the city's neighborhoods.

As chief executive of the city's poorest and most troubled borough, Bronx Borough President Robert Abrams led the opposition to Manhattan Landing. He had been a consistent critic of concentrating city housing subsidies in Manhattan, its wealthiest borough:

There is something inherently immoral in creating artificial land on the fringe of Manhattan's financial district at a cost of $40 a square foot [he wrote], while hundreds of acres of existing land stand vacant or undeveloped in other parts of the city and a once thriving community like Brownsville is a square mile of rubble. . . . New construction of low-income and middle-income housing in the boroughs outside Manhattan has fallen to a trickle, and we continue to lose more housing units each year than we build. There is obviously something desperately wrong with our housing and planning priorities. . . . Manhattan Landing is a luxury we simply cannot afford in the face of spreading neighborhood decay throughout the city. Could there by any conceivable benefit to either the business community or the community at large if this pleasure dome were left standing resplendently in the midst of a city in ruins?

When the project was brought before the Board of Estimate for a public hearing, Abrams continued his attack, this time revealing an internal Planning Commission report that questioned the rentability of the proposed office space. "One unanticipated result of past office construction is a substantial oversupply of office space," the report said. "This oversupply is not a result of the recession but a miscalculation of the total demand and a breakdown of the financial controls on office buildings." In other words, so many new offices and luxury housing projects would not have been approved all at once if the Planning Commission itself had not provided gimmicks and incentives for the builders.

One of these gimmicks is the sale of air rights over existing buildings, which allowed builders to add floor space that an adherence to the zoning laws would have forbidden. Another is the granting of several additional floors in a building, if a plaza is provided at ground level. Caught up in the spirit of the times, one midtown apartment-house builder, for example, had simply gone ahead and added three extra floors to a building he was constructing, and was outraged when a chairman of the neighborhood planning board happened by and counted the number of floors. This small detail had eluded city inspectors on the job. "Creative zoning," like "creative accounting," obviously has its moment of truth.

Since office space under construction in 1972 might not be fully absorbed into the market before 1978, the report went on to warn of a cut-throat price war in the rental market: "Any narrowing of the rent differential between old and new office buildings will weaken the competitive advantage of old structures. If the current surplus of office space (particularly in lower Manhattan) causes a general reduction in rental level in 'middle-aged' buildings, unmodernized pre-1920 structures will lose tenants and may go under.

Confronted with this analysis by his own staff, the Planning Commission chairman, Donald Elliott, stared at Abrams for a moment and then blithely replied, "Well, you just have to have faith in the city's future." With that bit of gallows humor ringing in its ears, the Board of Estimate proceeded to vote acceptance of Manhattan Landing.

Today there isn't even a peeling signboard left to mark the Manhattan Landing site.

On February 29, 1976, state Comptroller Arthur Levitt, suggested that the governor consider dissolving the Battery Park City Authority and making some arrangement to pay off the $200 million in bonds that were borrowed for the project. Levitt noted that the Authority was paying its own salaries and current interest on the bonds with interest on the capital funds it has invested. He estimated that all of the money would be dissipated by 1984 unless revenue-producing facilities could be built on the site, but said there was "no indication of an early disposition" of the obstacles that had kept both housing and offices from construction.

David Rockefeller can look down from his office at Chase Manhattan Plaza at a radically altered financial district, and, if he cranes his neck a bit, he can see three of the four boroughs that were experiencing a slow death while he and his cohorts in both the elected and permanent governments concentrated the diminishing resources of the city on tinkering with "the heart pump of the capital blood that sustains the free world."

If the permanent government has any claim to legitimacy, it is that it uses its wealth, power, and prestige for what it defines as the "best interests" of New York City and its eight million people. Echoing Charles Wilson's famous dictum, "What's good for G.M. is good for the country," members of the permanent government lay claim to the support, if not the affection, of the rest of us because their various projects and businesses provide jobs for everyone from construction workers to waitresses. The facts—that no one but the very wealthy can pay the rents in even publicly subsidized new housing, and that the whole infrastructure of the city, from its subways to its sewers, is collapsing because public revenues are inadequate—are conveniently ignored.

As the city teeters on the edge of ruin, the sophisticated boosterism of the permanent government has developed a hollow ring. There can be little doubt that the David Rockefellers, the Urises, and the Urstadts sincerely believe that they have done well for the people whose lives they dominate. Their problem is that the people are beginning to understand that in fact they have merely done well for themselves.

More than any other group in the permanent government, the banks are now encountering a crisis of confidence from a once unquestioning public. The word "redlining" is slowly entering the average New Yorker's vocabulary. And with it comes the growing sense of outrage and victimization that must befall someone who has just been robbed with his own gun.

Redlining has become the one-word definition for the growing pattern of urban disinvestment practiced not only by banks, but by insurance companies, pension funds, and other financial intermediaries. It is derived from the way mortgage officers once drew a red line around a section on a map and refused to make any further investments in the proscribed neighborhood. Today, whole counties, some would even claim the entire city of New York, has been redlined. But no bank officer would be foolish enough to commit his bias to paper. After all, this is the age of the "equal opportunity lender."

Redlining first emerged as a national urban problem in ghetto areas; then it rapidly spread to so-called "transitional" neighborhoods undergoing racial change. Today, any urban area that might someday undergo racial change is liable to be redlined—in other words all parts of our cities except gilt-edged communities like Manhattan's Sutton Place or Chicago's Lake Shore Drive. But resistance to the bank's redlining habits has grown rapidly, especially in white ethnic homeowner areas in industrial cities like Chicago, Cleveland, and Buffalo. "Anti-redlining" coalitions, often consisting of white working people and middle-class blacks, have been formed to demand disclosure of bank lending policies by state legislatures and Congress and, more recently, to confront local banks and savings-and-loan associations directly and to withdraw savings en masse from those that refuse to plough back investment into the neighborhoods.

In New York City, the redlining issue has been slow to take hold. Embattled tenants in most neighborhoods, facing declining services and rising rents, directed their protests at landlords—not realizing that many landlords only begin seriously to "milk" a building in preparation for abandonment after they have discovered that the banks have already given up the neighborhood as lost.

As noted earlier, the only true value of a property to a landlord is its resale value. Without bank financing, resale becomes almost impossible and landlords can extract their capital only by literally destroying the building. In recent years, more and more landlords in redlined areas have put the torch to unsalable properties so as to gain the insurance money. The epidemic of arson in areas like the South Bronx is directly traceable to redlining, while no less heinous for that reason.

The bitter irony in all this is that the victims of disinvestment are the only source of deposits for the savings banks and savings-and-loan associations. The same observance can be made about the insurance companies and certainly about union pension funds. It's *our* money, but *they* spend it.

Since savings banks are the principal source of mortgage investment in the city, we shall concentrate on their role in redlining. A brief excursion into banking history is required.

Savings banks have always been the poor relations among the nation's financial institutions. In the early days of banking, the large commercial bankers dealt exclusively with business firms. They spurned the nickels and dimes of immigrant workers and small farmers, and by the time they realized that enough nickels and dimes together can be big business, a separate system of banking had grown up beneath their feet.

Many savings banks actually started as burial societies, with several employers in one area or industry getting together to accept the small deposits of their workers and then reinvesting them to provide enough incentive to keep the workers saving for a decent funeral. In 1834, a group of employers in the old Bowery meat market established the first savings bank and called it, logically enough, the Bowery Savings Bank. They kept deposits in a small leather-bound wooden chest fourteen inches wide and seven inches deep. The Bowery still preserves the chest to remind it of its humble beginnings.

The most logical, and safest, form of investment in those early days was mortgages on the homes and small businesses being erected in the rapidly growing city. Mortgages are still the safest investment next to federal bonds. In the 1974-75 economic collapse, only five mortgages in every 10,000 defaulted.

Savings banks initially were neighborhood institutions. They found it too risky to invest in areas that their officers and directors didn't know personally. Because they were local institutions, the savings banks developed a high degree of loyalty among depositors, who also were their major borrowers; this loyalty persisted long after the banks had changed their size, character, and function. But when the savings banks tried to move further afield, the commercial banks were quick to induce legislators to pass laws restricting the geographic scope of savings-bank activities and the type of services they could offer.

So the first crucial lesson that the commercial banks taught their fledgling competitors was that banking and politics go hand in hand. Savings banks soon made it a point to add prominent local politicians to their boards of directors and to court friends in Albany and at City Hall. It was a lesson that began paying big dividends. Today in New York City the boards of saving banks read like a *Who's Who* of the permanent government: William Ellinghaus, a former member of the EFCB and vice-chairman of AT&T, is a trustee of the Union Dime Savings Bank. Alton Marshall, former secretary to Governor Rockefeller and now president of Rockefeller Center, is a trustee of the Lincoln Savings Bank. Former Governor Malcolm Wilson is a trustee of the Manhattan Savings Bank.

E. Virgil Conway, a director of Con Edison, is president of the Seamen's Bank for Savings. Charles Urstadt, whom we met as chairman of the Battery Park City Authority, is a trustee of the New York Bank for Savings. Eugene Keogh, the former Brooklyn congressman, a director of City Title Insurance Company and of Mortgage Affiliates, is a trustee of the East New York Savings Bank. Former depty Mayor John Zuccotti is a trustee of the Central Savings Bank.

Paul Screvane, the former chairman of the Off-Track Betting Corporation, is a director of the Jamaica Savings Bank. Former Mayor Robert Wagner is a trustee of the Metropolitan Savings Bank, and so is William Shea. Harold

Fisher, the peripatetic lawyer and ex-MTA chairman, is chairman of the Dime Savings Bank of Williamsburgh. David Yunich, former chairman of the Metropolitan Transportation Authority, is a trustee of the East River Savings Bank. Donald Elliott, former chairman of the City Planning Commission, is a trustee of Independence Savings Bank. William Ronan, ex-chairman of the Port Authority, is a trustee of the Metropolitan Savings Bank.

Federal housing insurance, instituted in 1934, then supplemented by veterans' insurance in 1945, made a big difference for the savings banks, for it meant that they could invest in mortgages outside their immediate areas without fear of being sandbagged by local speculators out to bilk the city boys. But state laws regarding uninsured commercial loans were still highly restrictive. So were branching regulations, which allowed savings banks to open only one additional branch a year.

The savings banks conducted a war of attrition. First, they had their friends in government pass a bill allowing branching in other counties, mostly in Manhattan's central business district and later in the proliferating suburbs in Nassau and Westchester counties. Next, they won the right to make commercial loans in neighboring states. Finally, the big breakthrough came in 1966, when they won the right to make commercial loans anywhere in the United States. Predictably, the banks' investments in New York City plunged as they began pouring their money into the burgeoning Sunbelt states of the south and west. These states were experiencing a historic housing boom but had little capital of their own to finance mortgages. The sky was the limit on mortgage rates.

A study conducted by New York University showed that multifamily properties in New York City secured by conventional savings-bank mortgages fell by 20-25 per cent in the years 1967-72. It is no accident that the number of housing units abandoned in the city leaped during the same period. The study also showed that disinvestment by savings-and-loan associations and insurance companies was increasing at an even faster rate. (The banks refuse to issue separate figures for New York City but admit that 65 per cent of their mortgages were in the state in 1955, only 41 per cent in 1967.)

The banks immediately countered that they were simply seeking more security for their depositors' money—a euphemism for their anxiety about ghetto unrest in the 1960s. But the NYU researchers found that there was no significant upward trend in either the delinquency rate (late payments) of mortgages or the foreclosure rate experienced by New York City savings banks. The banks were simply out to make more money. This is hardly a crime in the American economy—except for one crucial fact. Savings banks are mutual banks, theoretically owned by their depositors; they issue no stock, or bonds for that matter. They are, by law, *nonprofit* institutions. In other words, their only responsibility is to earn enough to pay the legally prescribed rate of interest to depositors and to cover overhead. In the depression-inflation year of 1974, when banks were offering premium interest rates of 8 per cent for monies left on deposit a minimum of six years, the actual costs of depositors' accounts was only 5.7 per cent while the banks earned a net return of 6.8 per cent, leaving them a comfortable 1.1 per cent, or approximately $600 million, to meet overhead. (In 1975, New York State savings banks had assets of $66 *billion;* about $44 billion was invested in mortgages—a little less than half of which, $21 billion, was invested out-of-state.)

In December 1976, the New York Public Interest Research Group, a Nader spinoff, published a study of bank mortgage practices in Brooklyn. One startling disclosure in this study came from data amassed by the Finance Administration, revealed by NYPIRG for the first time. Three of the biggest Brooklyn banks had admitted to the city that while the bulk of their deposits came from city residents, only a minuscule proportion of their mortgages was still given within the city limits. Dime Savings Bank had 73 per cent of its deposits from city residents, but only 17 percent of its mortgages were on city properties. The ratio for the Greater New York Bank for Savings was 98 per cent in deposits, 15 per cent in mortgages. The Williamsburgh Savings Bank showed 81 per cent in deposits, 15 per cent in mortgages. Only the medium-sized Greenpoint Savings Bank was doing a creditable job, with 93 per cent of its deposits from city dwellers and 61 per cent of its mortgages held in the city. In calendar 1975, Greenpoint invested $25 million in Brooklyn. The Dime (four times it size) invested only $5.3 million. Five other banks in the survey invested amounts ranging from only $1 million to $3 million.

Despite New Yorkers' growing alarm at the increasing disinvestment in both the city and state, the savings banks continued to avoid effective regulation by the state superintendent of banks and began a major drive in the state legislature for greater power. In 1975, they won a bill that allowed them to open a limitless number of mini-branches with computer terminals in such locations as shopping centers, train stations, etc. In return, they bought a paltry $180 million in state securities to help bail out state agencies caught in the spinoff effects of New York City's fiscal crisis. And then they made their biggest power grab.

The key commercial banking preserve that had been denied to the savings banks was the right to offer checking accounts. In partial compensation, savings banks are allowed by federal law to pay a slightly higher interest rate on savings accounts, currently ¼ of 1 per cent more, than the commercials do. In several New England states the savings institutions are allowed to offer checking accounts, however, and the New York banks, which account for about half of all savings-bank deposits in the entire country, wanted the same power. They had consistently lost this battle in the state legislature as a result of heavy commercial-bank lobbying.

After another defeat in the state legislature in 1974, Harry W. Albright, Rockefeller's superintendent of banking, dredged up an ambiguous section of a banking law passed in 1965, and unilaterally granted savings banks the right to offer "payment order" accounts—checking accounts in all but name. While the commercial banks ran to court, the savings banks offered free checking and quickly signed up 176,000 customers for their new service. The courts uniformly ruled against Albright but refused to dissolve the new accounts and in effect threw the issue back to legislature. (When Albright resigned he became president of Dime Savings Bank, the second largest in the state and third largest in the nation.)

The legislature refused to resolve the issue in its 1975 session because the Democrats had amended the checking-account bill to require the savings banks to establish a $3-billion mortgage pool over a ten-year period; anyone denied a mortgage by a savings bank could turn to the pool, which would have a publicly appointed board of directors, as a lender of last resort. It was hoped that this mechanism would limit the effects of redlining and encourage the banks to make more loans, since they would ultimately have to bear the risks of the same mortgages through the pool.

When insurance companies had begun redlining ghetto areas in the 1960s, the banks had supported the pool concept to provide fire insurance for all landlords. (In New York State, the mortgagee, usually a bank, receives the proceeds of any fire-insurance policy first; the landlord gets whatever is left. There is no requirement that the insurance be used to restore a partially damaged property. This arrangement actually serves as an inducement to arson.) But when the pooled-risk concept was applied to them, the savings banks fought it like a cornered tiger. They preferred to let the checking-account bill die than to be told where to spend their money—correction, *our* money.

Although originally slated as a sleeper, the checking-account bill became one of the most bitter issues of the 1976 legislative session in Albany. Urban liberal Democrats, spurred by a decision in the Court of Appeals that would force the banks to dissolve the illegal checking accounts by April 1 unless the legislature legitimated them, prepared to mount a drive for the mortgage pool. They were in for a rude shock.

First Governor Carey announced an agreement drafted by his superintendent of banking, John Heimann, and agreed to by the banks. Under this plan, the banks would publish their loans by census districts, theoretically allowing local groups to monitor bank lending policies and to publicize redliners. After reading the fine print, however, activists rejected the plan as too weak. Besides, they countered, a federal district court in Ohio had held that redlining was a crime. Would the superintendent negotiate an agreement with embezzlers, or would he put an end to their criminal behavior? Heimann then announced that he supported a "naked" checking-account bill—without the mortgage-pool requirement—a complete reversal of the position he had taken in the previous legislative session. When questioned by angry legislators, he simply announced that he had been "new," i.e., inexperienced, the previous year.

Heimann's sudden change of heart wasn't the last urban legislators would encounter. The mortgage-pool concept had been the official Democratic position throughout the prior legislative session. Now the Democrats learned from Assembly Speaker Stanley Steingut that this was no longer so. As a matter of fact, Steingut called the "antiredliners" into an angry late-night session and frankly told them that he had made a deal with Warren Anderson, Republican leader of the state Senate; the checking-account bill would pass both houses as long as the Democratic reformers in the Assembly did nothing "duplicitous," like adding the mortgage-pool amendment. George Cincotta, a wheelhorse of the Brooklyn Democratic machine and chairman of the Assembly Banking Committee, was the sponsor of this "naked" bill. Cincotta had close ties with the savings banks in Brooklyn. ("George can get anyone a mortgage in an hour," one Assembly Democrat told us.) His son is a vice-president of Citibank.

The savings banks were, of course, carrying on an unprecedented lobbying campaign. Huge billboards urging passage of a checking-account bill assaulted the legislators as they drove into Albany on the State Thruway. Full-page ads appeared in newspapers across the state, especially in New York City. As the debate heated up, the ads took on a harsher tone. The savings banks ignored the redlining issue and posed as a populist force seeking to give the people free checking accounts. (There had been no specification that the accounts would be free in Cincotta's original bill; an amendment to require this was added by the antiredliners in the floor debate.) At one point, opponents of the "naked" bill were accused of being tools of the commercial banks. Meanwhile the savings banks stimulated thousands of letters from depositors who wanted the convenience of doing all of their banking under one roof and saving a few extra bucks on their checking accounts in the bargain. Most depositors seemed oblivious to the likelihood that if the savings banks weren't forced to provide more mortgages in their neighborhoods, the banks might be the only roof left standing.

At one point, an angry group of state senators, led by Manhattan's Franz Leichter, probably the most anti-bank legislator in Albany, confronted Governor Carey on the issue. Carey said he would try to get the banks to negotiate a bill containing the mortgage pool. The anti-redliners were jubilant, but the governor's commitment evaporated like the Irish morning mist. The banks went on to offer minority legislators secret mortgage commitments for a handful of their constituents if they would vote against the mortgage-pool clause. The anti-redlining coalition was slowly reduced to a corporal's guard, which voted against the final bill. The Democratic leadership praised the bill as a victory for consumers.

As a result, things have never looked better for the savings banks. With the passage of the checking-account bill, they have become small commercial banks. The next logical step seems to be the transformation of the larger ones into stockholder-owned institutions, which will give the commercial banks a chance to acquire them on the open market or through negotiated mergers. This kind of "bank consolidation" was proposed by a special federal study group appointed by Richard Nixon, and it seems the most lucrative road for the industry. Savings banks are rapidly diversifying their investments and drawing back from their mortgage commitments, not only in the cities but throughout the entire Northeast.

Things have never looked worse for New York City housing. Savings banks not only provide the capital to maintain a market in buildings but are the source of the mortgage refinancing that allows landlords to renovate buildings. As the banks have accelerated their withdrawal from the city housing market, they have required faster repayments of financing at higher rates of interest, making it difficult for even the best landlords to upgrade profitably.

New York City, which supplies three-quarters of all the savings-bank deposits in the state, is America's largest single capital exporter—at a time when its own housing stock is literally crumbling before our eyes for lack of capital. The banks themselves have created this abandonment problem, which they then point to as the rationale for reducing investment in the city. For the sake of profit and institutional aggrandizement, they are willing to see the city die. Yet the permanent government, which controls not only many of these institutions but also the state apparatus that could force them to change lending policies overnight, allows the hemorrhage to continue unabated.

Some housing activists suspect that a Machiavellian game plan to destroy rent control lies behind these disinvestment policies. Certainly the banks have always hated rent control, but this is largely because it symbolizes the threat of adoption of controls in other communities—not because of any real economic impact in New York, where rents are actually rising faster than in the rest of America. The banks are sophisticated enough to know that rents in New York have reached their upper limits and are already absorbing an extraordinarily high degree of disposable income (often more than 35 per cent)—a much higher expenditure for housing than is found, for instance, in home-owner communities (where it may be as low as 10 per cent).

The poor pay the highest rates, both as a proportion of their income and in absolute terms, since for decades rent increases of 15 per cent every two years were allowed for new tenants, and the least desirable slum apartments had a high turnover rate. Slum buildings are abandoned for only two reasons: The tenants are in revolt and refuse to pay rent because of lack of services; or some major system, such as the heat or plumbing, has completely broken down and requires a significant capital outlay for replacement or repair. No slum building was ever abandoned because its cash flow from rents was inadequate for ordinary upkeep.

If rent control is abandoned, there will be no upsurge in institutional mortgage lending, although more private speculators might be attracted to the market. When vacancy decontrol went into effect in 1971, there was no change in the pattern of disinvestment, although rent rolls skyrocketed.

The only conclusion that we can draw is that the permanent government is unwilling to use its vast power over financial institutions to rebuild the city—at the very moment in history when they are so vociferously demanding sacrifice from everyone else in order to "save" New York. More than anything else, it is this double standard—applied to *people*, but not to *capital*—that is destroying New York City's future as a living environment.

Throughout this analysis we have shown how the permanent government operates to shape key decisions affecting all of our lives: invisibly, through its political operatives or controlled institutions, desperately anxious to conceal the hand that pulls the strings. Occasionally, however, something goes wrong and the permanent government is forced into a raw display of its power. For a brief but instructive moment, the public has a glimpse of how things really operate.

Such a moment occurred in the closing hours of the 1976 legislative session in Albany.

The Museum of Modern Art is one of the capstones of New York's cultural life and has been a favored charity of the elite, especially the Rockefellers, the Paleys, and the Whitneys. (Nelson Rockefeller was until his death the most important collector of modern art in the world.) While its permanent exhibition is one of the true wonders of the world, its cellars are crammed with significant masterpieces which are never seen except by those anointed by its powerful board. MOMA itself is a second-rate, perhaps even a third-rate, building shoe-horned into a side-street plot on 53rd Street off Fifth Avenue. While many museums, especially the Metropolitan, have made efforts to decentralize and reach out to the general public in recent years, MOMA has remained remote, still charges a stiff admission fee, and retains the aura of a rich man's gallery rather than a cultural repository for all the people.

In recent years, problems have set in. Lavish private contributions have been falling off, as they have in many other areas of the city's cultural life. The very wealthy—men like board chairman William Paley of CBS—control the museum but are increasingly reluctant to pay the bills for their expensive hobby.

Expansion, more room for the collection, and greater reliance on revenues from commercial activities like the book store and restaurant suggest one way out of this dilemma. The museum owns several adjoining small buildings and can double its size by tearing them down and building an extension. Here again, however, the private fund raisers were unwilling to raise $17 million in expansion costs, although gifts to the museum are tax-deductible.

Richard Weinstein, formerly director of the City Planning Commission's Office for Lower Manhattan and a participant in the development of the Battery Park City and Manhattan Landing schemes, left city employment to become an executive of the Arlen Realty and Development Corp. Weinstein was one of the "bright young men" under Donald Elliott who fostered the 1960s building boom at the Planning Commission. In 1975 Weinstein proposed another of his innovative schemes: This one would allow the Museum of Modern Art to expand and at the same time provide Arlen with one of the choice sites for a mid-Manhattan luxury building. (Elliot, one of the few Lindsay officials to ascend to membership in the permanent government, is now counsel to MOMA as a partner—with Lindsay—in the white-shoe law firm of Webster, Sheffield.) Between them they hatched the following plan:

The museum would demolish the extra buildings it owns on 53rd Street and build a ten-story expansion to its building; above it would rise a 40-story condominium whose units would sell in the $250,000-per-apartment range. This expansion would be financed by tax-exempt bonds to be issued by a public development corporation specifically established for this purpose. The bondholders would be repaid by diverting the real-estate taxes that would normally flow to the city from a project of this size to the development corporation instead.

A bill to accomplish this complex undertaking was duly filed with the legislature, brought out in the last-minute rush to adjournment when special-interest bills are customarily passed with the speed of light. At another time it might have breezed through and been praised as another example of the "creative financing" that kept New York afloat on a sea of red ink for decades. This year, however, the legislators balked. Given the spector of unfinished school buildings, apartment houses, and health centers stopped in midconstruction throughout New York City, they refused to vote for funds to build a bigger museum and a luxury apartment house that should be the responsibility of private philanthropy. The bill was defeated in the Democratic-controlled Assembly on Monday, June 28, 1976, by a vote of 72-53. (It passed easily in the Republican-dominated state Senate.)

Then, in the early morning hours of June 30, the legislature's final day, the bill *passed* the Assembly by a new vote of 86-40. In the interim, the permanent government had gotten on the phone. Mayor Beame; his deputy and former Planning Commission Chairman John Zuccotti; former Mayor Lindsay; William Paley; Richard Rosenbaum, state Republican chairman and a long-time trusted Rockfeller aide; Alex Rose, chairman of the Liberal Party; and several county Democratic chairmen made it clear to the runaway legislators that this bill was to pass. It did. Elliott explained to the *Times:* "We can no longer go to the big contributors because the money isn't there." He failed to mention where it had gone.

In a few years, the Museum of Modern Art will have a bright new building, Arlen Realty will have another luxury apartment house, the taxpayers who subsidized the project will continue to pay for entry into the museum, and it is likely that schools and new apartments in East Harlem will remain uncompleted.

And the permanent government will continue to preach "sacrifice" as the road to fiscal stability for New York City.

Legal Graft 5

Everybody is talkin' these days about Tammany men growin' rich on graft, but nobody thinks of drawin' the distinction between honest graft and dishonest graft. . . . Yes, many of our men have grown rich in politics. I have myself. I've made a big fortune out of the game, and I'm gettin' richer every day. But I've not gone in for dishonest graft—blackmailin' gamblers, saloon-keepers, disorderly people, etc.—and neither has any of the men who have made big fortunes in politics.

There's an honest graft, and I'm an example of how it works. I might sum up the whole thing by sayin': I seen my opportunities and I took 'em.

—GEORGE WASHINGTON PLUNKETT

Politics is business. And legal graft is the currency of the permanent government.

Legal graft is finder's fees, title insurance, city contracts. It can be interest-free deposits of government funds, zoning variances, insurance premiums, or condemnation awards. It can be campaign contributions, bond sale commissions, public relations retainers. It can be real estate leases, mortgage closings, or, most often, legal fees.

As Al Smith said one day strolling through a law school library and noticing a student absorbed in a book: "There's a young man studying how to take a bribe and call it a fee."

Legal graft is the disguised quid pro quo. I'll get you a nursing home license, and you hire my law firm. I'll get you a ninety-nine-year lease from the city, and you give my friend some insurance. I'll make you a judge, but your two brothers each have to contribute $7500 to the party by purchasing tables at our dinners. If your union contributes to my campaign, you can name the next chairman of the workman's compensation board.

Legal graft is no stranger to residents of Chicago, Boston, Cleveland, Philadelphia, Maryland, New Jersey, or the sunwashed new communities of Arizona. But in New York City it is bigger, more sophisticated, and all-pervasive.

100

Legal graft built the $2-billion Albany Mall. Legal graft was the oxygen of the Robert Moses empire in New York City.

The National Commercial Bank and Trust Company of Albany was chosen by Governor Nelson Rockefeller as the depository for cash proceeds of bond sales on the Albany Mall, his gigantic building program in the state capital. About $1 billion flowed through the bank as a consequence. Democratic Mayor Erastus Corning of Albany is a director of National Commercial Bank and Trust, a member of its executive committee, and a substantial stockholder.

Two other bank accounts were set up in the State Bank of Albany: one to process the state's rentals to the county, and the other to redeem the revenue bonds. Mayor Corning and his mother and father were also directors of the State Bank of Albany.

During construction of the mall, Mayor Corning was also president of Albany Associates, Inc., an insurance agency and brokerage firm which sold construction insurance policies to M. Kramer and Sons, a contractor with $12.8 million's worth of heating and plumbing jobs on the mall. The policies sold by the mayor's company covered bodily injury up to $5 million, and property damage up to the same amount.

In April 1976, state Comptroller Arthur Levitt estimated that the final total cost of the Albany Mall—including debt service—would be $2 billion. His auditors estimate the actual final cost of construction will be $985 million. When Nelson Rockefeller had first announced the mall project, he had predicted that the construction cost would be $200 million.

In his remarkable *Moby Dick* of urban biography, *The Power Broker: Robert Moses and the Fall of New York*,* Robert Caro describes how three powerhouse Democratic politicans shared in the insurance business from the Triborough Bridge and Tunnel Authority—business worth $500,000 a year in premiums and $100,000 per year in commissions. The three—Carmine DeSapio, Stanley Steingut, and James Roe—even made sure that one Republican politician, a man named John Crews, the Brooklyn county leader, received some of the premiums, since he too was in the insurance business. The public, of course, had no way to know their leaders were getting this private enrichment. Steingut flatly denied it. The distributor of this bipartisan legal graft was Robert Moses.

When he controlled the World's Fair Corporation in 1964, Moses was a Santa Claus of legal graft. Thomas Deegan, the politically well-connected press agent, told the media he would publicize the Fair without compensation—"without any fees or expenses of any kind." But Moses gave Deegan an annual fee of $100,000, plus expenses that included a

*From which many of the details in the following paragraphs come.

$1000-a-month suite at the Waldorf and a $572 monthly salary for a chauffeur. That was for Deegan individually. Thomas J. Deegan Co., Inc., received an additional $350,000 a year. All public funds. Today Deegan is on the payroll of the Battery Park City Authority at $3000 a month as a consultant.

Meanwhile, all the insurance on the World's Fair was steered to a company favored by Carmine DeSapio, the Campo & Roberts agency. The Fair's charter required all exhibitors to purchase their insurance from companies "approved by the Fair Corporation," and DeSapio and Moses made sure that Campo & Roberts was the only "approved" insurance agency. It came to $3 million in commissions. At the same time all the legal fees from the Fair Corporation went to the law firm of Samuel Rosenman, whose newest partner was Charles Preusse. Preusse had once been City Administrator, in which role he had helped to draft the legislation that exempted the Fair Corporation from the city's Code of Ethics.

Moses and Rockefeller were Pharaohs who built pyramids. They understood that "public works" was a license to legal graft.

Other politicans followed and built office towers, highways, bus terminals, sports stadiums, shopping centers, luxury housing, viaducts, hotels. Each project fed the construction complex of banks, unions, lawyers, insurance companies, architects, bond underwriters, press agents.

And it all helped to bankrupt and destroy New York City. We have seen how the World Trade Center—conceived by David and Nelson Rockefeller—cost $1 billion and killed the commercial real-estate market. Meantime, throughout the city, debt services grew. Priorities were distorted. Services deteriorated. Neighborhoods died. Housing decayed, since so little attention was paid to rehabilitation and restoration. The area south of Canal Street has lost 50,000 jobs since 1968, many in the printing industry, a distinctive New York business. And 30,000 construction workers found themselves unemployed—as a consequence of the insupportable orgy of overbuilding in earlier years.

But the construction complex became swollen and fat on all the "bribes called fees." The Moses empire—the public authorities—survives. The Rockefeller empire, anchored by the Chase bank, prospers. In 1975, the city lost 30,000 construction jobs. These flesh-and-blood workers were expendable. The institutions of wealth count, and they endure.

Legal graft is apolitical. It is important to understand that above a certain level of power, at the level of permanent power, there is no party politics. There are no Democrats and no Republicans. There are only class colleagues sharing profits.

Among the vessels of legal graft are various business enterprises that include important politicians from both parties as partners. Law firms, banks,

PR firms. Mortgage companies. Brokerage houses. Public-utility companies.

There is, for example, City Title Insurance Company. The board of directors includes: Stanley Steingut, the Democratic Speaker of the state Assembly; Willis Stephens, senior Republican on the Assembly Ways and Means committee; Eugene Keogh, a former Democratic congressman from Brooklyn; Alton Marshall, Nelson Rockefeller's former secretary and now president of Rockefeller Center; and Arthur Quinn, chairman of The New York Bank for Savings, and a Republican Party fund-raiser. City Title has insured the title on more than $50 million's worth of state-aided moderate-income housing projects.

The Brighton Houses is such a project in Brooklyn. City Title was awarded the bulk of its title insurance. The brokerage fees on other insurance went to Grand Brokerage, in which Steingut and Brooklyn Democratic boss Meade Esposito each owned a 25-per-cent interest. And the legal fees on the project went to the late Bunny Lindenbaum, the clubhouse zoning lawyer and fund raiser.

On the state-aided Brooklyn Jewish Hospital staff residence, City Title got the insurance. The firm of Alfred Lama, who drafted the state law providing subsidies for moderate-income housing, received $67,000 in architectural fees. And Steingut's law firm—Halperin, Shivitz, Scholer and Steingut—got $14,710 in legal fees.

The law firm of Shea, Gould is a factory of legal graft. Shoup Voting Machines, for instance, sold $8.5 million's worth of equipment to the city shortly after retaining William Shea's powerhouse firm. It was the first time in thirty-seven years that Shoup had been able to sell the city a single voting machine. TelePromTer Corporation got a cable television franchise from the city as soon as it retained Shea's firm in 1965.

A more complex Shea deal involved the Long Island Rail Road and First National City Bank. In 1965 Shea was designated by the state legislature to be its representative in negotiations with the Pennsylvania Railroad to buy its faltering subsidiary, the Long Island Rail Road. Shea was designated through the office of the Democratic leader in the Senate, Joseph Zaretski. (Zaretski's counsel at the time was Shea's law partner, Bernard Ruggieri.) Within seven weeks Shea and Governor Rockefeller's negotiator, William Ronan, recommended that the state pay Pennsylvania $65 million for the LIRR. According to a subsequent report by Arthur Levitt, $65 million was much too much for a line that had lost $2.5 million in 1965 and would require at least $200 million to improve its commuter service. Moreover, a Levitt audit showed that the Shea-Ronan formula would really cost the taxpayers $131 million, since they had also agreed to give up 65 acres of LIRR property, air rights over yards, and about $8.4 million in station concessions.

Several years after the dubious deal went through, Ralph Nader published a study of Citibank. Nader's study showed that $60 million of the $65 million in state funds paid for the LIRR went toward repayment of a Citibank loan for which the nearly bankrupt Pennsylvania was liable, and which probably would have been defaulted without the Shea-Ronan bailout. Nader's study also showed that Eben Pyne, senior vice-president of Citibank, had earlier been a member of a special state committee looking into the LIRR, representing the "creditor's interests," i.e., his own bank.

When the Metropolitan Transportation Authority (MTA) was created, Rockefeller's first appointments in 1968 were William Ronan as chairman, and William Shea and Eben Pyne as members.*

Legal graft can take the form of an honorary title that confers legitimacy on someone who needs it. On July 31, 1925, Bronx Democratic Party boss Ed Flynn appointed Arthur Flegenheimer an "honorary deputy sheriff of Bronx County." Flegenheimer is better known as Dutch Schultz, the efficient executioner for Legs Diamond.

Legal graft can take the form of a favor bestowed without any cash, a favor on which there is an invisible mortgage. For example, Frank Costello—the Mafia's Kissinger—used his influence to make Thomas Aurelio a State Supreme Court justice in 1943. We know this because there is a famous, legally wire-tapped exchange.

COSTELLO: "When I tell you something is in the bag, you can rest assured."
JUDGE AURELIO: "Right now I want to assure you of my loyalty for all you have done. It's undying."

Since no one could prove the commission of a crime, Aurelio became a judge despite the public release of this recording by Manhattan District Attorney Frank Hogan.

Legal graft can take the form of a job bartered for a favorable policy or decision of government.

In 1973, Paul Levine was a $32,000-a-year official in the city's Economic Development Administration. He participated in the decision to tear down two blocks of homes in a working-class, Polish section of Brooklyn called Northside. The homes must be torn down, Levine said, because the S&S Corrugated Paper Machinery Company wanted to expand. Ninety-two families were evicted and watched the bulldozer demolish their homes of a lifetime in front of their tear-filled eyes. Three months later, Paul Levine went to work for S&S. He admitted he had been negotiating with S&S for his new

*For all you need to know about Bill Shea, read Nicholas Pileggi's seminal article in *New York*, November 11, 1974.

job even as he participated in city meetings to plan the evictions. The city's Board of Ethics ruled Levine did nothing wrong.

Legal graft is a way to get around the law without breaking the law.

Let us examine some methodologies of legal graft in New York. We will start with the story of a real-estate developer named Christopher Boomis.

In January 1971, Luis Alimena, an official in Local 707 of the Teamsters Union, approached New York City's Economic Development Administration (EDA) with an idea to build a pier and refrigerated warehouse in the Hunts Point section of the South Bronx. Alimena was accorded easy access to the right city decision-maker, Edgar Fabber, soon to become the commissioner of Ports and Terminals. Both Alimena and Fabber were good friends of dock union boss Anthony Scotto.

Fabber's recollection of the meeting was: "Alimena said he had the right guy for the deal. A guy named Chris Boomis, a developer. I had never heard of Boomis. No one I knew ever heard of Boomis. So I checked him out with George Douris [City Hall reporter with the *Long Island Press*]. Douris was supposed to be the head Greek, and Boomis was supposed to be Greek. But Douris came up empty. He said no one knew anything about Boomis. He said Boomis must be a Turk, since no Greeks ever heard his name. . . . Mostly on Alimena's word, we gave Boomis the Hunts Point deal."

"The Hunts Point deal" was two linked leases for $37 million with no competitive bidding. For the pier project Boomis would be both builder and lessee. On the warehouse, he would be contractor and tenant.

Overnight, Boomis became a force in New York City. He had the prestige of a $37-million contract with the city. The Hunts Point project was announced in May 1972 at a City Hall press conference, with a beaming Boomis seated next to Mayor John Lindsay. The Board of Estimate approved the lease unanimously—and without debate—on April 12, 1973, and the Budget Bureau promised the Board that the city would make a profit on the lease. The mayor declared that the Boomis project would "capture 65 per cent of the total meat imports to the Northeast United States. . . . This facility will create 2000 new jobs." All this—the profit and the jobs—proved to be a fiction.

Suddenly Boomis began to acquire the discretionary favors of government. He went from mystery man to insider overnight. The city gave Boomis a two-year real-estate tax exemption to build a 31-floor luxury highrise at 96th Street and Broadway. Despite strong community opposition, Boomis had no trouble evicting the commercial-site tenants. Somehow he had clout at City Hall. *The New York Times* real-estate section published a favorable profile of Boomis by Carter B. Horsley on May 12, 1974. Boomis announced plans to build five more luxury buildings around Manhattan.

Kenneth Patton, the city's EDA Administrator, told other city commissioners that Boomis was "good for the city." State Assembly Democratic leader Albert Blumenthal assured journalist Phil Tracy that Boomis was honorable and community-oriented. Shea told bankers and mortgage companies that Boomis was a sound investment—and Boomis got $20 million in credit. Meade Esposito told cronies that "Boomis is my guy." Boomis gave a fund-raiser for Patrick Cunningham in his own lavish triplex apartment. On the hot air of word-of-mouth, Chris Boomis floated to the top of a very competitive real-estate market.

In the spring of 1975, we began to research the curious rise of Boomis. How did it happen? How could he build, when all the giants of the construction business in New York—Lefrak, Tishman—and the best professionals could not build? How did he get city contracts and tax abatements and quick evictions?

Here's how.

Boomis gave all his insurance business on $24 million worth of properties to Grand Brokerage, which as we have pointed out is owned by Stanley Steingut and Meade Esposito. In 1973, Boomis says, he contributed $23,000 to Abe Beame's campaign for mayor, under his own name and through four other people who were either relatives or employees. In 1974, he gave $40,000 to Hugh Carey's gubernatorial campaign, including $10,000 after Carey was elected. (To hedge all bets, Boomis also spread around $15,000 to the loser in the Democratic primary, Howard Samuels.) His wife Zaida donated $5,000 to Republican candidate Malcolm Wilson. Boomis also gave $5,000 to a legislative campaign fund under the control of Stanley Steingut.

And Boomis gave away a 25 per cent limited partnership interest in Chris Boomis Associates to Luis Alimena for a token $100. When asked to explain this sort of charity, Boomis said that Teamster leader Alimena had "promised to introduce me to an efficient trucking company."

But Boomis was not subtle. He was not patient. He was not smart.

The first person to catch on to Boomis, to begin his fall, was a career civil servant of twenty-five years named Walter Prawzinsky. Prawzinsky was the chief engineer in the office of the city's controller. His deputy, Mario Grauso, has worked for the city for twenty years. Together they figured out that Boomis was submitting padded bills to the city for $200,000.

Later Boomis was sued by his own contractors for not paying them more than $1 million. Later still the scaffolding and building skeleton on his 96th Street site collapsed from too many violations of the safe demolition code. And after that, construction stopped at Hunts Point because Boomis would not allow an inspector onto the site.

But Boomis was still a king when Walter Prawzinsky began to scrutinize his reimbursement vouchers and bills and compare them to the terms of the written lease for Hunts Point. Boomis had tried to get the city to reimburse him for such items as legal fees, accounting fees, property liability insurance, "preliminary engineering studies," and "preparation of master plan." They were not covered by the lease.

So the civil servant challenged the fat cat. "We had two face-to-face meetings with Boomis," recalls Prawzinsky. "He screamed and yelled a lot. He dropped a lot of names. He kept saying he had powerful friends. I had read in the paper that he was a big contributor, so I treated him with kid gloves. But I gave him nothing. He implied he had influence wih Cunningham and Esposito. He said he could go directly to the mayor. But we insisted he was over-billing the city by at least $200,000. Then he wrote a letter to my boss [Controller Harrison Goldin] calling me a bastard and a liar. But we had him on the facts."

After this, others began to see through Boomis. Other city agencies became wary. Boomis stopped paying his insurance premiums to Grand Brokerage, and Esposito began to pass the word that Boomis was "a nut." Investigations by law-enforcement agencies began. Banks began to foreclose on mortgages. Bill Shea began to deny he even knew Boomis.

The lesson of Boomis is in the process, not the result. He was too greedy. But for three years he played the game, and he was successful. He understood that government was really a vending machine. If you put enough coins in the right slots, the goodies came out the bottom. Boomis just tried to cheat the vending machine itself, and was dropped by the permanent government when he overreached. The city paid Boomis $2.1 million before his mask fell.

Unnecessary construction is another staple of legal graft.

Early in 1972, Mayor John Lindsay convinced the Board of Estimate to approve a $24-million "urban renewal expenditure" to renovate Yankee Stadium because the owners threatened to move the franchise out of New York. Skeptics, led by the *Daily News* editorial writers, questioned the reliability of the $24 million price-tag. But Lindsay insisted $24 million was all the job would cost, and he invoked "hard fiscal data based on the operations of Shea Stadium."

Lindsay also tossed in a "sweetener"—a promise of $2 million to rehabilitate the streets and shops around the stadium, a working-class residential neighborhood fighting not to become a slum.

By November 1973 the cost of the renovation had gone up to $49.9 million. The City Planning Commission approved additional funds, and so did the City Council by a vote of 27–9. Most of the negative votes were cast by conservatives of both parties like Matthew Troy, Frank Biondillio, Walter Ward, Thomas Manton and Edward Curry. (All the Bronx councilmen voted in the affirmative.) During the debate Troy vainly reminded his colleagues that a whole new stadium had just been built in Pittsburgh at a total cost of $45 million.

The Board of Estimate also approved the additional $15.9 million expenditure. Lindsay voted yes, and the then controller, Abe Beame, voted yes. The vote came after the EDA administrator promised (but not under oath) that the stadium renovation would benefit the city with $3.4 million in taxes, wages, and jobs. Deputy Mayor Edward Morrison said, "This is not a luxury. This is necessary."

On July 16, 1975, Mayor Beame disclosed that the cost of the renovation had escalated to $57 million. When questioned, Municipal Services Administrator John Carroll said the new money outlay was "still a bargain for the city" and a "marvelous engineering project." On October 10, he acknowledged that the cost had risen to $66 million, but quickly added, "The overall investment in the stadium is a bargain at this price."

In April 1976, the new stadium opened at a gala ceremony of pols. The total cost as of that date was $101 million and was still rising. By then the city was bankrupt. And the original $2 million for the community near the stadium was silently deleted from the 1976–77 budget. Yet in 1975, a brand-new 80,400-seat stadium had been completed in Pontiac, Michigan, for less than $60 million.

The $101 million included $22 million to Kinney Systems, Inc., to build two parking garages and remodel a third. From this arrangement Kinney also got rent, a management fee from the city, most of the fees paid for parking, and a $2-million tax exemption. The contract was awarded without competitive bidding. Steven Sallup—as counsel to EDA—negotiated the contract for the city, but by the time the stadium opened in 1976, he was working for Kinney Systems as a lawyer.

We might also mention that Kinney is a subsidiary of Warner Communications, a conglomerate that also owns the New York Cosmos soccer team.

The $101 million included $300,000 for "equipment" for the Yankees team, including plush carpeting and toilets in the VIP boxes.

In 1973, the Democratic Party boss in the Bronx, Patrick Cunningham, became the lawyer for the Yankees, on a retainer believed to be about $100,000 a year. Cunningham says he got the job through his friend Neil Walsh, who handles the Yankees' insurance. Walsh is also one of the city's deputy commissioners for public events. Cunningham, as Bronx Democratic county leader, helped Walsh get that job, which helps Walsh make contacts for his insurance business.

The owner of the Yankees' team franchise is George Steinbrenner. In 1974, Steinbrenner pleaded guilty to making illegal corporate contributions to Richard Nixon's 1972 campaign. He also pleaded guilty to the less commonplace felony of coercing his own employees to lie to the FBI and the grand jury, as part of a cover-up. His penalty for these crimes was a fine and an eighteen-montn suspension from baseball. During Steinbrenner's suspension, Patrick Cunningham was the designated owner of the Yankees, as well as their counsel.

In April 1976, when the stadium opened, Henry Gavan, the new counsel to EDA, admitted the original estimated cost of $24 million had been "picked out of the air" by the Lindsay people.

The general contractors on the stadium were Nab Construction and Tern Construction. At Cunningham's 1975 Bronx County dinner, Nab and Tern each had puchased a table for $1,000. Most of the construction unions that worked on the stadium job also bought $1,000 tables. One reason political machines have such dinners is to set up just such a turnstile for contractors.

Everyone profited, everyone skimmed the deal—everyone, that is, except the ordinary people who live in the Bronx. No one will ever call Yankee Stadium the House that Truth Built.

Another example of legal graft in the Bronx involves the same cast of characters. The Bronx Terminal Market, built in 1935, stands on thirty-one acres adjacent to Yankee Stadium. In 1971, the city was making $300,000 a year on this wholesale produce market, where it rented stall space to merchants doing business there. The merchants wanted to convert it into a cooperative, but the city administration, in the person of EDA administrator Kenneth Patton, decided instead to award a private real-estate developer named David Buntzman a ninety-nine-year lease to operate the market. The lease was given without competitive bidding and without payment by Buntzman; he had only to put up a bond.

The ninety-nine-year lease was amended in October 1973 to make it even more favorable to the landlord. The amendments gave the Yankees two of the market's thirty-one acres for a parking lot, and Buntzman received 4.2 additional acres that the city purchased from the Erie Lackawana Railroad for $790,000. In the amended lease, the city also agreed to assume more than $6.5 million of Buntzman's obligations to make improvements in the market. And Buntzman paid the city no rent at all for the first year.

The lawyer who renegotiated this lease for Buntzman was Patrick Cunningham. Altough Buntzman at first denied this, Cunningham admitted to us that he had been paid $60,000 in legal fees by Buntzman for one year.

Buntzman has raised rents in the market by an average of 80 per cent. He now charges the merchants an average of *$3 per square foot*, while he is paying the city an average of *61 cents per square foot*. In three years, he has evicted sixteen commercial wholesalers from the market in his campaign to raise rents, and this has driven 700 unskilled jobs out of the South Bronx. The evictions were approved by judges who got their judgeships from Cunningham. One—Joseph Brust—has been indicted for lying to a grand jury in response to questions about his disposition of a case based on an eviction at the Bronx market.

The city's 1975–76 budget included $9 million for the Bronx Terminal Market, and the city is also paying the debt service on the cost of construction of a $4.1 million warehouse the taxpayers built there for Buntzman. So far, Buntzman has collected $3 million in rents.

When John Hess, a reporter for *The New York Times,* asked Cunningham about this whole deal, Cunningham suggested that Hess go see John Scanlon; who had been press aide at the city's EDA when the lease was negotiated. Cunningham neglected to inform Hess that Scanlon, after leaving city employment, had become a paid public relations consultant to Buntzman. When Hess found out this salient fact, he published it, and Scanlon was forced to resign his job as public relations consultant to the Municipal Assistance Corporation. (Scanlon was also a paid flack for Anthony Scotto and the nursing-home builder Albert Schwartzberg, while working for MAC.)

In 1976, it was revealed that Buntzman had made a large, unreported cash contribution to John Lindsay's 1972 presidential campaign—six weeks before the market lease was signed, and while the negotiations were still going on.

A legend of legal graft in New York City was the Brooklyn attorney Abraham Lindenbaum, known as Bunny to everyone. Friendly, shrewd, and philanthropic, Lindenbaum was the model of the clubhouse lawyer elevated to civic statesman till he died in 1980.

Lindenbaum became an election captain in the Madison Club in Crown Heights at the same time Abe Beame was assistant budget director of the city and Stanley Steingut was a lawyer waiting to inherit his father's seat in the Assembly. In 1960, Lindenbaum was appointed to replace Robert Moses, who was resigning to go to the World's Fair, on the City Planning Commission. But in October 1971, Lindenbaum was forced to give up his position on the Planning Commission when he was caught soliciting campaign contributions for Mayor Wagner from builders who did business with the city. More than $25,000 had been raised from forty-three builders and landlords during a luncheon at Skakele's Restaurant on Montague Street in Brooklyn.

Since then Bunny had mastered most of the techniques of legal graft. He had received an estimated $150,000 in patronage fees from the Surrogates Court, including $25,000 in 1973 alone. Lindenbaum became the registered lobbyist for five landlord organizations, including the Real Estate Board of New York and the Rent Stabilization Association. His lobbying fees in 1976 were more than $20,000. Lindenbaum's specialty, however, was as a zoning and tax lawyer for the city's biggest property owners. Records on file with the Board of Standards and Appeals show that over a ten-year period Lindenbaum's clients had received more zoning variances, on a percentage ratio, than any other lawyer's clients in the city. Applications on file with the

Tax Commission also reveal an unmatched record of success in winning lower real-estate tax assessments. The legal justification for some of these reduced assessments was effectively questioned in a series of articles by Ralph Blumenthal in the *Times* in February and March 1973. Blumenthal reported how Jerome Minskoff was awarded a $4.5 million reduction in assessed valuation on a midtown skyscraper, even though Lindenbaum supplied the Tax Commission no income or expense data on the building.

Lindenbaum had also been the attorney on many state-subsidized housing developments, where his fees have been criticized as too high, or not warranted by the amount of legal work performed. In 1973, the city Controller's office refused to pay Lindenbaum a "consulting fee" of $36,164 for work with the city-funded West Side Convention Center Corporation. Lindenbaum as unable to provide time records and work sheets to justify his fee. The convention center's full-time counsel, John McGarrahan, said at the time that Lindenbaum had been hired to draft plans for a special zoning district. But this work was actually done by the City Planning Commission.

In July 1976, Lindenbaum was awarded a mysterious $35,500 "brokerage fee" by the city in connection with the sale of Central Commercial High School to a real-estate developer named Charles Benenson, who is a client of Lindenbaum's. When asked by John Hess of *The New York Times* what service Lindenbaum performed, Benenson replied: "He arranged the deal. . . . He arranged a lower purchase price." The price for the 150-foot-wide strip of property extending from 42nd Street to 41st Street, east of Third Avenue, was $2 million. The original asking price had been $3 million, before Bunny began to peddle his influence.

Other incarnations of legal graft are patronage jobs bestowed on clubhouse and campaign cronies who would not qualify under standards of merit.

People volunteer for election campaigns generally for two reasons—commitment to issues, and hope of some personal reward. Most of the people who helped Abe Beame run for mayor wanted jobs. And after he won, they got them, regardless of qualifications.

Abe Beame saw his mission as the rebuilding of the clubhouse system—a system that nourished his whole career. The City Club, a group of businessmen, estimated in 1976 that "5000 to 7000 unnecessary patronage jobs" on the city payroll remained filled, even after 8000 cops, firemen and sanitation workers had been fired—a public subsidy of the clubhouse system which cost the taxpayers between $100 million and $150 million a year.

At the start of 1976, nineteen Bronx Democratic Party district leaders were on the public payroll, six of them as clerks at the Bronx courthouse. Seven Queens party district leaders had jobs with the Queens Borough President, Donald Manes. More than fifty members of one political clubhouse—the

Madison Club in Brooklyn—had city or state jobs, including Mayor Beame, Speaker Steingut, Comptroller Levitt, and seven judges.

In September 1975, Edwin Weisl resigned as New York City Parks Commissioner. A few days after he quit, we talked to Weisl, and he candidly explained to us how the patronage system works, and how it is subversive of the public interest.

When I was first hired as parks administrator I was too naive to ask whether I could choose my own staff. But soon it became clear I could not. I had to hire people based on political connections. And I had to fire the holdover people who had no clubhouse sponsorship or protection.

My first month on the job, Jerry Kay called me up. He was a personal friend of mine. Kay said he was seeking a judgeship, and it would help his chances if I would come to dinner with him and Meade Esposito. We had dinner in a private club on Macdougal Street. Esposito arrived with a typed list of existing jobs in my agency, and a typed list of the names of people he wanted me to hire. [Kay, who set up the dinner, subsequently received his judgeship.]

Meade told me to hire William Swain [an ex-football player] for a job that paid $29,000 a year.

Paul Screvane [the OTB chairman] also called me and told me to hire Swain. Cavanagh [then first deputy mayor] also called and asked me to fire Joe Davidson and give his job to Swain. Davidson was a great career professional, so I had to make a deal with Cavanagh. In order to keep Davidson as my recreation commissioner, I agreed to hire Swain as his deputy. He never did much work on the job.

Next I was told to hire Bob Fellner. Kevin McGrath [a partner in Shea's law firm] called me up and said hire Fellner because Fellner had been an advance man in Beame's campaign, and I should give him a job. I was forced to take him. Fellner was lazy and did no work. I tried to fire him, but Tom Roche [Mayor Beame's patronage dispenser] wouldn't let me fire Fellner.

Ernest Gluckman was another of those hacks I was ordered to employ. He was a friend of Irving Goldman [Beame's cultural affairs commissioner, who was later indicted]. I had to pay Gluckman, who is seventy years old, $35,000 a year as a consultant. He literally never did one day's work. After Goldman was indicted, I fired Gluckman, but the next day I was ordered to reinstate him.

There were some people I just refused to hire. That began to make me unpopular at City Hall, and they began to leak stories that I was an incompetent administrator.

One guy I refused to hire was Fred Baroni. He was a law secretary to a judge, and totally inept. Pat Cunningham called me up and asked me to hire Baroni at $40,000. I said no.

When Matty Troy was county leader of Queens he sent me the resume of Frank Mangino. Troy wanted Mangino to get a $40,000 job. Troy wanted Mangino to run the whole field force. But Mangino had no administrative experience. Cavanagh also asked me to hire Mangino, but I just would not.

By that time, the politicians began to get suspicious of me. Stanley Steingut called me up and said I should do what I was told. Then his son [Councilman Robert Steingut] came to visit me one day. Young Steingut said that I should play ball, and that I have a great future.

In March 1975, Beame himself came to see me. He told me I was being an obstructionist. He told me it was my duty to hire loyal Democratic Party workers.

Then in July 1975 came the issue of summer jobs. There are about 4500 summer jobs in the budget. They are intended for poor and minority kids. But City Hall wanted to control 800 of these jobs for the clubhouses.

Stanley Friedman [another deputy mayor] went around me. He called my payroll department directly and put relatives of politicians on the summer job payroll, including Troy's son.

By the end of the summer I was beaten. Beame and Cavanagh wanted me to cut $1 million by closing swimming pools in the South Bronx and Red Hook. They had no interest in pre-school programs for kids. They never talked to me about solving problems, or new ideas. All they ever called about was jobs for the clubhouses. They wanted useless projects. They blocked me on management reforms. I wanted to hire more foremen to improve productivity. I wanted to hire one guy to computerize the inventory. They said no. Who wouldn't be a lousy administrator with such restrictions?

Legal grafters also love do-good programs like Medicaid and day care. For years the nursing-home industry in New York has run on conflicts of interest and legal graft. Nursing-home operators like Bernard Bergman and Albert Schwartzberg hired political lawyers and political insurance companies, and in turn got favors and preferments from the government. They got licenses, they got favorable Medicaid reimbursement rates, they got personal access to the highest officials in the state. And both became multi-millionaires, philanthropists, and respected citizens.

Bergman gave his insurance business on the Towers nursing home and the Park Crescent home, to Steingut's and Esposito's Grand Brokerage. At various times, Bergman used as lawyers Stanley Lowell, a former deputy mayor; C. Daniel Chill, the legislative counsel to Stanley Steingut; Robert Douglas, former secretary to Governor Rockefeller; and John Marchi, Republican chairman of the Senate Finance Committee. (To his credit, Douglas withdrew as counsel after a few weeks when he realized Bergman was lying to him about many facts.) For example, Chill would write a letter to the State Health Department on Assembly stationery. A civil servant or health professional would assume the political clout of Steingut was behind the request. The civil servant could not know that Chill was getting paid a fee as a private lawyer for Bergman. Chill also made phone calls to and attended meetings on Bergman's behalf with both city and state health officials. His law firm even had a legal option to get a 14 per cent interest in one Bergman nursing home on Staten Island that he was pressuring the health department to approve.

Theodore Lucas, the director of the city's Bureau of Mental Retardation, testified under oath to a special Moreland Act commission created to investigate nursing-home abuses about the pressures brought upon him by Stanley Lowell in behalf of Bergman. Lowell, he said, in the course of a meeting over the conversion of a Bergman nursing home into a facility for the retarded, reminded him that he was personally close to Beame, former Mayor

Lindsay, the controller, and many city councilmen. The final Moreland commission report said that if Lucas's testimony was accurate, then Lowell's conduct was "improper" and an "attempt at a power play."

In addition to representing the Bergman family interests, Lowell was also the highly paid counsel of the New York Nursing Home Association and special counsel to the New York State Health Facilities Association. (In another case he went over the head of a dedicated city official who was doing her job. In 1971 Dr. Florence Kavaler was arranging unexpected night visits by inspectors to nursing homes to check on conditions. Lowell, instead of complaining to Dr. Kavaler or to her direct superior, Health Commissioner McLaughlin, went instead to the very political Deputy Mayor Richard Aurelio to try and get these valuable visits stopped.)

Through the influence of Steingut, Lowell, and businessman Samuel Hausman, Bergman was able to get private, face-to-face meetings with Governor Rockefeller, Governor Wilson, Mayor Beame, and other important politicians. Bergman's general, odious reputation for mistreating and neglecting his elderly patients did not seem to reach these elite decision makers. And they all professed shock when Bergman was indicted and pleaded guilty to cheating Medicaid of $2.5 million.

Albert Schwartzberg, the president of Di-Com Corporation, became New York State's biggest builder of nursing homes and remained a partner in the real estate or operations of at least twenty-five of the homes he built. Schwartzberg always seemed to get his way with government agencies. Like Bergman, he seemed to have unlimited access and invincible power.

He gave his insurance business to Youngs & Linfoot, Inc., a small company in upstate Geneseo, New York, from which Assemblyman James Emory receives about $20,000 a year in salary and commissions. Emory was assistant majority leader of the Assembly during the Wilson and Rockefeller administrations and is now deputy minority leader. Emory admits he brought in Di-Com as his insurance company's biggest client. Between 1966 and 1975, Schwartzberg and Di-Com paid Youngs & Linfoot more than $250,000 in premiums. Emory (like Chill) did not tell the civil servants of his personal financial interest whenever he called to lobby and pressure for Schwartzberg.

Martin Ginsberg, chairman of the state Assembly's Health Committee during the Rockefeller years, also pressured the state health department in Schwartzberg's behalf—and he too was acting as a private lawyer for Schwartzberg. When he tried to make a secret investment in one of Schwartzberg's nursing homes, however, it was discovered and disallowed by the health department. In 1972 Ginsberg ran for the Family Court and was elected. He reported $12,000 in campaign contributions, of which $4,000 came from Schwartzberg. (In December 1974 Judge Ginsberg was convicted of perjury in a case unrelated to nursing homes).

In 1975 and 1976, the state legislature refused to enact a law prohibiting members of the legislature from representing paying clients before state agencies like the health department. Insiders called this a "one-house bill": The Democrats had agreed to vote for it and pass it in the Assembly, based on the private assurance that the Republicans, who controlled the Senate, would kill it. This permitted the Democrats a public posture of rectitude, knowing it had no meaning. And it was reciprocated when the Republicans passed a bill in the Senate abolishing the city marshal system and the Democrats killed it in the Assembly by prearrangement.

The one-house bill is merely one of the many clever devices of the permanent government.

Day care is a good idea, a very good idea. It frees women to finish school, or to work, instead of going on welfare. It is beneficial to children, improving learning and ensuring that they are well fed during the day. It fosters class and ethnic integration. It offers working-class women a chance at a second life.

But New York City's day-care program has been a textbook model of how another positive government program became exploited by the parasites who see government as a business, and reform as a market.

In day care, the permanent government took its skim in leases. Between 1969 and 1971, the Lindsay administration gave 171 leases for day-care centers directy to private landlords, with no competitive bidding. This was done by Real Estate Commissioner Ira Duchan, and approved blindly by the Board of Estimate. About 275 other day-care programs operated under indirect leases, often at much less cost, in churches and schools. (The average direct-lease day-care center costs $20 per week, per child. All other centers cost an average of $6 per week, per child.) But the direct leases were especially desirable to landlords for several reasons. The city paid the rent money directly to them. The city—not the landlord—paid all the utility bills and real-estate taxes. And the leases were all uncommonly long—for fifteen or twenty years. So prized were the leases that landlords were able to show them to banks and get construction mortgages (in redlined neighborhoods) for more money than their renovations cost.

The day-care sites were selected in an ass-backwards fashion. Instead of first looking for community groups, parents' groups, or block associations, the city started the program by reaching out first for private landlords. The people who really cared about quality day care were excluded from the process. The ultimate result of this policy, of course, was that a few politically connected landlords, lawyer-politicians, and power brokers got rich off the program. And the children got screwed.

In 1976 we analyzed who got what out of the direct-lease system.

N. Hilton Rosen, the brother of Richard Rosen, a commissioner and assistant to the mayor in the Lindsay administration, got seven direct leases worth $886,000 in annual rents. His wife was a member of the state Labor Relations Board—at $35,250 a year. The legal fees on all seven leases went to Shea, Gould. The title insurance all went to City Title, which is one of the smaller title companies in the city.

Brooklyn Assemblyman Leonard Simon was only the second Democrat to endorse John Lindsay for mayor in 1969. In a dramatic City Hall press conference, Simon had said he was risking his career by "placing principle above party" and standing with the forces of light. Then, within eighteen months, one of Simon's law clients—Getz Construction Corporation—got 22 day-care leases from Lindsay's administration, worth $1.8 million in annual rents. Getz built the centers with fast, shoddy work, and as they began to leak, chip, flood, and attract rats, Getz sold all twenty-two to other speculators. Simon had made a windfall profit in legal fees by "placing principle above party."

Brooklyn City Councilman and district leader Samuel Wright got two day-care centers. One, the Samuel D. Wright Day Care Center, was opened in the building directly next door to his clubhouse, at 2071 Fulton Street in Brownsville. The architect was a member of Wright's political club. And Wright's wife Josephine was appointed executive director of the center. A second day-care lease was given to a company owned by the former president of Wright's political club. On this one, Wright also collected the legal fees. The annual rent is $100,000.

Stanley Lowell, who represented Bernard Bergman, was also the lawyer on two day-care leases (including one at 510 West 145th Street, one of the worst in the city, with so many structural deficiencies that the city stopped paying rent for several months).

If we look at the total number of direct leases, title insurance on 40 per cent was awarded to Steingut's City Title, while the Shea, Gould law firm collected legal fees on thirty-five leases and also received fees for arranging mortgage financing on a total of forty centers, through banks where Shea was either a director or counsel. Building permits disclosed that Colonial Sand & Stone was employed by fifty centers to supply cement for construction and remodeling. (Shea is a director of Colonial Sand & Stone and counsel to the $80-million-a-year construction company.)

Three day-care leases were in the name of the late Sidney Ungar. Ungar, who died in 1974, was a most notorious slumlord, first exposed by William Haddad in the *New York Post* in 1959, when Ungar was picked by Robert Moses to be a sponsor of a slum-clearance program. Ungar was also accused of discrimination against blacks in a report by the City Commission on Human Rights issued in 1971.

Ted Menas, a Queens landlord, got two day-care leases from the city. Records on file with the Board of Elections show that Menas is a campaign contributor to Queens Democratic district leader Ralph DeMarco and to former state Senator, now judge, Nicholas Ferraro. In February 1976, Menas wanted final appoval for his second direct-lease center (the Marine Terrace Day Care Center at 18–40 20th Avenue in Astoria); the lease was for twenty years, at $75,384 a year. An aide to Queens Borough President Donald Manes called the chief of the housing and real estate division of the City Law Department at least three times, trying to expedite the second Menas lease. But on August 5, Menas and his partner, Anthony Nastasi, were each indicted on six counts of trying to hide from a grand jury the books and records of several corporations they control.

Late in the 1976 legislative session, a bill was introduced that would have given the Emergency Financial Control Board authority to review all 171 direct leases and renegotiate all those found to be exorbitant. The bill passed the Senate, but was killed on the last day of the session in the Assembly, after Mayor Beame telephoned his opposition to Speaker Steingut.

In August 1976 Controller Goldin released an audit of the direct-lease program. Goldin said that twenty-six of the thirty-seven folders on individual lease negotiations that he had requested from Ira Duchan, the Commissioner of Real Estate, "were missing." These files contained correspondence about how the leases were given out and how various rentals per square foot were calculated. Nixon and ITT apparently did not have a monopoly on shredders.

Judgeships are not exempt from the subtleties of legal graft. An honest, independent judiciary is essential to democracy and the rule of law. But a political, beholden judiciary is essential to the clubhouse system, especially to disqualify opponents who want to run against the machine in primary elections, and to dispense fees and guardianships to the right lawyers.

Judicial nominating conventions and election of State Supreme Court justices are a farce. They offer the illusion of choice. State justices are chosen by party leaders in private brokered deals. Of the last 150 State Supreme Court judges elected in New York City, 126 ran with the endorsement of both the Democratic and Republican parties.

In most cases, judgeships are not bought directly with cash. That would be illegal graft. Occasionally a judgeship can be a reward to a politician for a valued vote in a legislative fight. For instance, in 1971 Manuel Ramos, a Bronx Democratic assemblyman, broke with his party to provide a decisive vote to the passage of Governor Rockefeller's tax package. The following year Rockefeller appointed Ramos to the Court of Claims. Or again, when John Walsh, a Manhattan assemblyman from 1959 to 1971, lost a tough primary to a reformer, he joined the Democrats for Nixon. Even his best friends admit that's how he became a judge the next year.

Some people get their black robes through family pull or cronyism. Three judges appointed to the Civil and Family Court in 1975 by Mayor Beame were John DeLury, James F. O'Donoghue, and Edith Hendon. DeLury is the son of the powerful leader of the Sanitation Workers Union. O'Donoghue is Pat Cunningham's brother-in-law. And Mrs. Hendon was appointed even though the Queens Bar Association found her "not qualified." She was Mary Beame's regular mahjong partner.

There is also a perfectly legal way to buy a judgeship: have a relative make a contribution to a political party, and then promise to buy a table for $1,000 every year at the party's county political dinner. A careful reading of old election records in New York City at 80 Varick Street will be instructive in this method. Let us take just one year, 1970.

In that year Irving Rader was nominated for the Civil Court bench in Brooklyn. Election records show that Rader's two sisters, Rose and Gertrude, together happened to contribute $7,500 to the Democratic Party of Kings County. Similarly Maria Tavorminia is listed as a $7,500 contributor to the Brooklyn Democrats—and her husband was nominated for the Civil Court in Brooklyn. John Monteleone ran for the Supreme Court in Brooklyn, although he had no need to campaign at all, since Meade Esposito had arranged for him to receive both the Democratic and Republican nominations. But the records show that the Brooklyn Democratic organization received $8,000 from a campaign committee organized for the election of Monteleone—who had no competition. (Monteleone has since made several rulings favorable to organized crime figures that have angered the Brooklyn district attorney.) The same transaction shows up with Frank Composto, who was elevated to the bench, the only difference being that his campaign committee, in an uncontested election, gave the county committee only $7,500.

And where do these prospective independent jurists get the money to contribute to the political party? From clubhouse lawyers, on whose cases they will pass judgment.

On the outside of the Brooklyn courthouse, inscribed in marble, are the words: EQUAL JUSTICE UNDER THE RULE OF LAW. Scrawled on the wall in the men's room is the more realistic motto: IT'S BETTER TO KNOW THE JUDGE THAN TO KNOW THE LAW.

Property owners in New York pay a tax rate of $8.17 for every $100 of assessed valuation. The City Tax Commission gives reduced real-estate tax assessments to landlords on the basis of proven "hardship." In 1975, for example, the tax commissioners overruled professional assessors and awarded 12,000 hardship reductions on buildings they never personally visited.

The problem is that there are no precise or consistent standards or guidelines for making these judgments. It is discretionary, almost impressionistic. The seven members of the Tax Commission are all appointed by the mayor and traditionally have been highly political. John Lindsay appointed Norman Levy, his campaign fund-raiser, as chairman, and Beame named Philip Lagana, who later became a Brooklyn Supreme Court justice through the normal clubhouse channels.

Historically, landlords who have been campaign contributors to the "right" candidates and landlords who hire the "right" lawyers have found it much easier to make convincing hardship arguments before the Tax Commission. Claims of expenses which they submit are not investigated or verified. On hardship applications we have looked at, the landlord's claims of payments of real estate, water, and sewage taxes, do not conform to the city's own billing and payment records. But the Tax Commission does not even follow or apply basic rules of accountancy. We have read hardship applications where two sets of procedures—cash and accrual—are used on the same building. The commission makes no effort to reconcile these two different accounting methods.

In 1975, the city's Tax Commission granted 80 per cent more hardship tax reductions to property owners than it did in 1974, and 1975 was the year when New York City's fiscal gimmickry and deception became a full-fledged crisis. As a result of this generosity to a few large, influential landlords, the city collected $21 million less in real-estate taxes in 1976 than it should have. Among the recipients of "hardship" real-estate tax reductions in 1975 were: the New York Stock Exchange, the Prudential Insurance Company, Con Edison, Chemical Bank, American Shipping Company, the New York Telephone company, the Bank of New York, Citibank, and Rockefeller Center. And in 1976 the list included: Con Edison, Metropolitan Life Insurance, New York Telephone, Rockefeller Center, Bankers Trust, and Citibank; also Distrigas, which owns the liquified-natural-gas tanks on Staten Island, got a reduction in annual taxes worth $700,000. One of the lawyers for Distrigas is Patrick Cunningham.

In 1975 Local 371 of the Social Service Employees Union completed a painstaking, six-month research project into the patterns of reduced assessments by the Tax Commission. The study, whose facts have never been challenged or disproved, concentrated on the real-estate empire of the family of Lewis Rudin. Rudin is the well-publicized chairman of the Association for a Better New York, a mid-town Manhattan group of landlords that uses the rhetoric of civic boosterism as a figleaf for self-interest. Rudin and his immediate family contributed $15,000 to Mayor Beame's campaign in 1973, and $10,000 to Lindsay in 1969.

The Rudins owned thirty-three buildings in Manhattan in 1975. Lew

Rudin's net worth is more than $100 million. Between 1970 and 1975, Rudin Management made 209 requests for assessment reductions to the Tax Commission. Of that number 137—or 66 per cent— were granted, and the total reduced assessments given Rudin Management was $32.3 million. During that same 1970–75 time frame, people with less political clout, owning buildings on the very same blocks as Rudin's buildings, submitted a total of 1411 applications for hardship reductions, of which only 16 per cent were approved. (For example, 40 Park Avenue, owned by the Rudin family, received six consecutive tax reductions in six years; owners of other properties on the same block made sixty-four applications for tax relief, only seven of which were granted.)

The most apparent distinction between Lewis Rudin and his neighboring Park Avenue landlords, is that he is a big campaign contributor with social access to mayors and power brokers. Rudin once said to Jack Newfield during a discussion with the executive committee of the Association for a Better New York, "The trouble with you is that you don't understand power. You think I have power. You think David Rockefeller has power. You think Felix Rohatyn has power. Well, you're wrong! You know who has power in this city? I'll tell you! The crazy people who can stop a McDonald's. That's who have power in New York!"

In terms of nonpayment of real-estate taxes the champion seems to be Sol Goldman, the survivor of the notorious Goldman-DiLorenzo partnership in property holdings. Goldman is the largest private landlord in New York City. Operating behind a maze of shell and interlocking companies with names like Avon, Newport, and Wellington, Goldman owned more than four hundred buildings in 1976, a majority of them commercial properties. The records of the city's Finance Administration disclosed that Goldman owed the city $18.8 million in unpaid real-estate taxes on properties assessed at a total of $445 million. Yet the Goldman empire also profited from reduced assessments. Curiously, many Goldman properties declined in assessment over the years while adjacent buildings did not.*

---

*A building at 18–20 St. Nicholas Place, assessed at $98,000 in 1970–71, was reduced every year and assessed at $60,000 in 1976. A property at 116–124 East 124th Street, in an attractive, middle-class community, went from $375,000 in 1970 to $340,000 in 1976. Records show that nineteen of twenty-five Manhattan properties owned by Goldman's Newport Associates had lower assessments in 1976 than they did in 1970. One typical example of apparent favoritism: A Goldman building at 18–24 Clinton Street received six consecutive tax reductions between 1970 and 1975, during which time other landlords on the same block submitted fifty-one applications and had only seven granted. Another is Goldman's property at 310–318 Convent Avenue. This property won four of six requests for reduced assessments. Other property owners, on the same block, made fourteen requests, not one of which was granted, during the same five-year period. Goldman is the landlord at 4913-23 Broadway, where he received four lowered assessments in six years. The other property owners on the same block made thirty applications for reduced taxes, and only two were granted.

There is some reason to suspect that the New York City Tax Commission is a vending machine for legal graft.

Lawyers are the most frequent beneficiaries of legal graft, as wise old Al Smith understood.

Between 1963 and 1976, the controller's office of New York City awarded fifty-five mortgages to developers from the city employees' pension fund. On almost every one, the lawyer who collected the closing fee was politically influential. The attorneys were appointed by the controller. The fees, negotiated between the attorneys and the builders, usually came to thousands of dollars for a few hours' routine work that required no preparation, and could be as much as 1 per cent of the total mortgage.

Closing fees on city pension-fund mortgages are a wholly unnecessary form of patronage. The work could easily be performed by the city's own Corporation Counsel staff of thirty lawyers. But out of the 40,000 lawyers in New York City the ones chosen for this extravagant patronage plum are the elite of the permanent government.

Bill Shea's law firm handled three mortgage closings worth $4.6 million. The law firm of Brooklyn Congressman and Judge Abraham Multer was attorney for $6 million in pension-fund mortgages. Congressman Bert Podell's law firm closed two mortgages totaling $7.2 million—before he was convicted of bribery in 1975. Other favored lawyers included: Joseph Slavin, chairman of the Brooklyn Democratic organization's law committee, and now a judge; former presiding Justice Bernard Botein; former Bronx Assemblyman and current Judge Alexander Chananau; former Bronx Congressman and Judge Paul Fino; Bronx Congressman Mario Biaggi; John DeLury, son of the sanitation union leader, now a judge; Howard Goldfluss, now a judge; and Irving Berman, who is also now a judge. Also, two former controllers: Joseph McGoldrick closed a $1.6 million mortgage, and Lazarus Joseph closed one for $1.5 million.

In an interview with Sam Roberts of the *Daily News*, Mayor Beame defended the current system by saying only lawyers who have special expertise in closing bank mortgages are chosen, and having the Corporation Counsel's office do the job would waste the time of lawyers who work for the city. But as usual, scrutiny of documents suggests a pattern based more on political than legal expertise. In fact, even a geo-political pattern can be discerned from the records on file in the controller's office. When Mario Procaccino of the Bronx was controller, most of the fees went to Bronx lawyers like Biaggi, Chananau, and Goldfluss. When Abe Beame of Brooklyn was controller, most of the fees went to Brooklyn lawyers like Multer, Podell, and Slavin.

For years, the city's finance administrator was allowed custody over about $10 million in city funds. This was known as "political money" to be kept in non-interest-bearing accounts in a few favored banks, as a form of political patronage. It cost the public more than $1 million a year to keep these public funds in accounts that drew no interest. These deposits were like gold to the bank, which could make a 9 per cent profit on this public money.

The manipulation of interest-free accounts, it should be underscored, is hardly a mutant activity found exclusively in New York City. Jimmy Carter has recounted how the game was played by politicians in Georgia in his book *Why Not the Best?* *The Washington Star* has exposed interest-free deposits in Alabama, and *The Washington Post* has exposed the practice in Maryland. And five years ago, Sam Roberts revealed in the *Daily News* how it was done by Governor Rockefeller. Early in 1972, a man named James Hellmuth changed jobs, quitting as vice-president of Morgan Guaranty Trust and becoming vice-president of the Bankers Trust New York Corporation. Hellmuth was also the treasurer of the state Republican Party and a member of the Port Authority. A month later, an $11-million interest-free account—the stock transfer fund—followed Hellmuth from Morgan to Bankers Trust. The money had been deposited by the state with the Morgan bank for several years when it was suddenly switched.

During the Lindsay administration in New York City the two banks that profited most from these illogical interest-free deposits were Century National Bank and the Central State Bank, two of the least professional, most investigated, and most political small banks in the whole state.

Century National Bank received its charter from the federal Director of the Currency on June 24, 1963. Its original incorporators were predictably bipartisan and politically connected. One was Vincent Albano, the Republican county leader of Manhattan. Another was Joseph Ruggiero, then law chairman of Albano's county organization, and later to serve a prison term for perjury. A third was Bernard Ruggieri, a former aide to Mayor Wagner, counsel to state Senate Democartic leader Joseph Zaretski, and soon to become a partner in Shea, Gould. A fourth was Lawrence Marchni, who would become Mario Biaggi's campaign treasurer in his unsuccessful 1973 bid for mayor.

In May 1964, during the first quarter the bank was open, Mayor Wagner, Controller Beame, and City Treasurer (now Judge) Hilda Schwartz approved with uncommon alacrity the new Century Bank as a depository for city monies. Within a year Century Bank had $1.2 million in interest-free city deposits. Richard Lewisohn, who later reformed the interest-free swindle in 1973, said of the Century deposits, "It was very abnormal for a new bank to get so much so soon."

While Democrat Ruggieri's connections to Democrat Wagner helped in

1965, it was the Republican chairman of the bank, Vincent Albano, who helped when Republican John Lindsay became mayor on January 1, 1966. The interest-free accounts are under the control of the finance administrator, and Lindsay's first two finance administrators, Roy Goodman and Fred Perotta, both came out of the Manhattan Republican organization and owed their jobs to Albano. By early 1967, under the beneficence of Roy Goodman, Century Bank held $1.6 million in interest-free city deposits, more than twice what any other bank of equivalent assets, capital, and public depositors had.

Century was given all this public money even though a report filed by federal bank examiners criticized Century for sloppy and inadequate records. The federal report disclosed that the auditor for the bank was not even a legitimate CPA. Stephen McDonald, a former deputy finance administrator for the city during the Lindsay years, told us: "Century was not a good bank. The work they did for the city was poor. They would lose checks. They sometimes wouldn't send us stop-payment notices on lost checks. Their records were badly kept. And I think they had some problems with embezzlement. I once suggested we take some of our money out of the bank, but nothing was ever done."

In 1970, under Fred Perotta, Century was given a total of $1.9 million in city deposits, the absolute legal maximum permitted under the city charter, and thereby became the only bank that ever reached the legal limit. This meant an extra $100,000 profit in one year to the bank, which made loans, mortgages, and investments at high interest rates with the public money placed in its custody by the Lindsay administration.

A bank's records are private, so there is no way to tell what favors Albano did in return for these public deposits. But one favor did become public knowledge. In 1972 Albano's bank made a $9,000 unsecured loan to Sid Davidoff, who had been Mayor Lindsay's assistant, so that Davidoff could go into the restaurant business. The loan was at 7½ per cent, less than the going rate at the time. Davidoff was Lindsay's personal representative on the commission that approved and monitored the banks that got interest-free deposits. The restaurant eventually went bankrupt and Davidoff was indicted for nonpayment of taxes to the state.

Central State Bank was chartered in 1925 and taken over by a group led by the brothers Al and Nathan Kevelson in 1959. On February 28, 1962, the bank was approved by the city's banking commission as a depository of city funds. By 1966 the key directors of the bank were Alfred Lama, the ranking Democrat on the Assembly banking committee (a stunning conflict of interest by itself); the late Larry Pierez, a behind-the-scenes power in Queens Democratic politics, and James Farley, Jr., the son of FDR's postmaster general. Not one professional banker in the lot. The counsel to the bank was the ubiquitous Bernard Ruggieri, and Congressman Mario Biaggi was on the bank's payroll as a "business getter," even though he never showed up at the bank, and performed no apparent work.

During 1968, Finance Adminstrator Roy Goodman increased the amount of interest-free deposits in Central State Bank from $300,000 to $1 million. By 1970, the city had $1.5 million in the bank in accounts that accumulated no interest—despite the fact that the bank had a general reputation as shady. (In December 1967, a group of the bank's dissident stockholders had filed a lawsuit against the Kevelsons, Farley, and Lama, charging they had made "improvident loans to cronies that went into default." This suit was dismissed in the courts.)

In 1976, Al Kevelson, Central State's former chairman, and his brother Nathan were found guilty of seeking to cheat the federal government out of more than $900,000 in taxes on personal and corporate income. The brothers had used Central State Bank to cash checks and conceal some of the income they withheld from the government.

There is also the case of the American Bank and Trust Company, which collapsed in September 1976 and was taken over by the Bank Leumi of Israel.

American Bank and Trust was one of the most political banks in New York City. Abe Beame was a director of the bank and chairman of its finance committee between 1966 and 1969. The bank's chairman, Abraham Feinberg, had contributed more than $40,000 to both his mayoralty and Carey's gubernatorial campaigns. Patrick Cunningham was indicted for not telling a grand jury that he was paid $50,000 over two years by American Bank and Trust for legal work he never performed. But Cunningham *had* pressured city and state officials to deposit interest-free government accounts in American Bank and Trust, and Meade Esposito was also paid an undisclosed annual sum to help secure those precious government deposits.

And so, on the day American Bank finally collapsed, it had $20 million of city and state deposits—more than 10 per cent of its total, and a higher percentage than any other bank in the city. Among the causes of American Bank's failure were: the disappearance of $18 million; loans long in default kept on the books as interest-bearing; loans made in excess of the legal limit; and self-dealing with companies in which various directors of the bank had financial interests.

Campaign contributions, gifts, loans, favors, and support are another tender of legal graft. In 1980, Alfonso D'Amato raised almost $3 million and won the Senate seat from New York. The way he financed his campaign was using his influence as Presiding Supervisor of the town of Hempstead to raise money, to manipulate the discretionary decisions of incumbency to benefit once and future fat cats.

Officers and lawyers of Kravco, located in King of Prussia, Pennsylvania, contributed $5,000 to D'Amato's campaign. A few months earlier, the town of Hempstead, at D'Amato's suggestion, saved the out-of-state company more than $200,000 by ruling that an environmental impact statement was not required for a planned expansion of the Green Acres Shopping Center in Valley Stream. State guidelines had recommended an impact statement should be filed.

Three executives of the DeMatteis organization, including chairman Fred DeMatteis, each gave D'Amato $1,000. Earlier D'Amato had negotiated a sweetheart deal with DeMatteis to develop Mitchell Field. D'Amato agreed to rent the land to the developer for $10,000 a year—**6 percent of its value.** Consulting engineer Richard Pezenik and family gave D'Amato $2,300 after receiving $200,000 worth of county business, including a contract from D'Amato to study the cost of new Nassau Beach cabanas. Richard Hartmen is the labor negotiator for the Nassau County police; members of his family and firm donated $3,750 to D'Amato's campaign. In 1979, D'Amato agreed to binding arbitration with the Nassau police that resulted in a 24.5 per cent pay increase, making the Nassau cops the highest paid in America.

The Grumman Political Action Committee (PAC) gave D'Amato a $5,000 contribution. In January of 1980, the county board of supervisors—dominated by D'Amato—gave Grumman a $8.4 million property tax rebate, and a $4.4 million assessment reduction for future tax payments. Fortunoff's department store also was awarded a $1.2 million tax reduction and D'Amato received $10,000 in contributions from Fortunoff executives.

D'Amato's campaign received $100,000 in loans from the Bank of New York. These loans were unsecured by collateral or by guarantors other than D'Amato. And some of the loans were as much as **8 per cent** below the prime commercial lending rate. In 1979, a public Grand Jury report rebuked D'Amato for placing Hempstead's property tax revenues in interest free bank accounts, which cost the taxpayers $3 million in interest payments between 1976 and 1978. At the time of the Grand Jury's report, D'Amato had deposited **$8 million** in branches of the Bank of New York—the same bank that made the favorable loans to his campaign committees.

During his campaign D'Amato was given the use of a six passenger Cessna plane owned by the Folz Vending Machine Company of Hempstead. D'Amato used the plane 11 times for trips to Buffalo, Syracuse, Albany, and other upstate cities. He only had to pay about half of what the flights would have cost his campaign on commercial airlines. Experts say the flights were worth $5,000 to D'Amato and his campaign aides. Roger Folz conceeded to us that he saved D'Amato's campaign at least $3,000, and that that first flight was on January 7, 1980, and he did not bill the campaign until eight months later. The flights were not reported on D'Amato's first three campaign disclosure reports.

Moreover, the Folz Vending Machine Company received a $500,000 loan—at 8½ per cent interest—from the Hempstead town government in

1978, a few months after D'Amato became presiding supervisor. The loan enabled Folz to build a brand new $1 million plant. Folz Vending was also given a 50 per cent tax abatement as part of the loan package. Roger Folz told us that he believes the total value of the abatement is "between $50,000 and $100,000."

Finally, there is the story of the cable TV deal. Advances in satellite, electronic, and computer technology have made this the period in which fortunes can be made in cable television. All over America, corporate giants like Warner Communications, Time Inc., and Cox Communications are competing for franchises to wire homes. A 20 per cent return on investment is predicated for the companies that win the bidding.

On July 1, 1980, the Hempstead town board, chaired and controlled by D'Amato, held a routine meeting. During the meeting, a cable TV franchise for Hempstead—worth millions of dollars in projected profits was transferred to Cox Cable of New York, Inc., a subsidiary of Cox Communications of Atlanta—a $2 billion conglomerate.

There was no debate. There was no public hearing for citizen input. There was no advance public notice that the franchise was on the agenda. There was no competitive bidding procedure. The whole process took only a few minutes. In most cities it takes years. A resolution was unanimously approved that said it was "in the public interest" that D'Amato be authorized "to execute the assignment of the franchise" to Cox Cable of New York.

Cox Cable of New York is 16 per cent owned by the law firm of Joseph Margiotta, the Republican party boss of Nassau and D'Amato's main sponsor in politics. Only a few weeks before, Margiotta had used his muscle to assure the votes for D'Amato in the Republican state convention that gave D'Amato the 25 per cent he needed to enter the Republican primary against the incumbent Jacob Javits. Margiotta has not denied published accounts that he paid no compensation for his firm's 16 per cent share of the Cox stock. Margiotta also has a buy-out deal with Cox. Cox will buy back Margiotta's shares once the franchise is successfully snared through his influence.

D'Amato's fast shuffle, however, did not work. The state's cable television commission refused to approve the transfer of the franchise.

Our point is not that Shea, or Albano, or Steingut, or D'Amato are unique individual villains. The villain is the moral structure of the system itself. People like Steingut have mastered the rules of the game because they helped write the loopholes into the rules. As long as the line between legal and illegal graft is fuzzy, as long as the difference between a felony and a windfall is a nuance, then the Steinguts and Sheas of this world will see opportunities, and take'em.

Most people in politics have what David Burke, the former secretary to Governor Carey, calls "a hole in their retina." They can't see right from wrong. Millions of taxpayers' dollars are there to be skimmed in the grey area between what is generally unethical and what is precisely illegal. As long as legislators have law practices, as long as county leaders have insurance companies, as long as campaigns need contributors, there will be legal grafters.

The few insatiable ones will be caught at some crime. The vast majority will have stadiums named after them, or perhaps law schools. The Bergmans will come and go. But the permanent government's system of legal graft remains. And will continue to prosper from twenty-year leases, legal fees, title insurance, mortgage closings, interest-free leases, legal fees, mortgage closings, interest-free government bank deposits, reduced assessments, cable TV franchises, and all the other modern technologies of legal graft, barely imagined by George Washington Plunkett a century ago.

The Temporary Government: Wagner Lindsay Beame

6

There is nothing economically or socially inevitable about either the decay of old cities or the fresh-minted decadence of the new unurban urbanization. On the contrary, no other aspect of our economy or society has been more purposefully manipulated. . . . Extraordinary governmental financial incentives have been required to achieve this degree of monotony, sterility, and vulgarity.

—JANE JACOBS
The Death and Life of Great American Cities

In some ways Robert Ferdinand Wagner, Jr., mayor of New York City from January 1, 1954, until December 31, 1965, was not a bad mayor.

He was a decent, shy, reasonable man who did not personalize disagreements. As a result, he got along with the city's various establishments. There were no disruptive municipal-transit, teacher, or sanitation strikes under Wagner. More housing units were added to the city's stock during his twelve years than during the next twelve years of Lindsay and Beame. Except during his last year, his budgets were balanced, and free of gimmicks and fakery. He chose his police commissioners wisely—Stephen Kennedy and Francis W. H. Adams—and police corruption declined from its rampant peak during the O'Dwyer and Impellitteri administrations. Wagner was no Pericles, but he was also neither a Tweed nor a Caligula.

Wagner's fatal weaknesses were passivity and procrastination. He didn't like conflict. He thought chicken soup and schmoozing could make the problems go away. The motto he learned from his father, New York's popular senator in the 1930s and 1940s, was: "When in doubt, don't." As a result,

128

Wagner was cautious in dealing with the basic problems of the city then congealing just beyond the horizon of everyday life. This caution, this indecision, this passivity led him to abdicate much too much of his authority to two pure avatars of the permanent government—Robert Moses and Carmine DeSapio. Wagner created a vacuum, and they lived in it.

Wagner had a bad habit: Whenever a "problem" appeared, he would appoint a "committee" to "study" it. By the end of his second term in 1961 he had appointed more than 200 separate committees by directive. Some never met. Most had no effect at all, except to invent the illusion of action for reporters who believed press releases.

While Wagner shuffled paper committees, the two great migrations began. One million poor blacks and Hispanics moved into New York City and 800,000 white middle-class families moved out. In eight years, the city's welfare population doubled.

Meanwhile DeSapio's patronage appointees from the clubhouses greased the wheels of legal graft. And Robert Moses bulldozed sound neighborhoods that were the distinctive essence of the city. In East Tremont alone, for example, Moses evicted 1530 lower-middle-class Jewish families to make way for the Cross Bronx Expressway. And he squandered millions of dollars on what historians and journalists call the Title I scandal—since it involved federal Title I housing funds—and millions more on the 1964 World's Fair.

The downward spiral of New York City was under way.

DeSapio was Robert Wagner's principal sponsor and strategist when he ran for mayor in the Democratic primary of 1953. The Democratic bosses of Brooklyn, Queens, and Staten Island supported the incumbent, Vincent Impellitteri; Bronx boss Ed Flynn was for Wagner, but he died a month before the primary. On election day, DeSapio was the only boss standing with Wagner, and Wagner won by 169,000 votes. The next year, DeSapio arranged the Democratic nomination of Averell Harriman for governor, and Harriman was elected by a margin of 11,125 votes out of 5 million cast. As a result, DeSapio became the most powerful politician in the state. He was leader of Tammany Hall. Harriman appointed him secretary of state. He became a member of the National Democratic Committee. And he controlled most city and state patronage.

Humorless, courteous, immaculately dressed, and corrupt, DeSapio used his power selfishly. He filled the city government with clubhouse hacks. He picked bad judges. He steered business to the Broadway Maintenance Corporation, which got the valuable franchise for servicing the city's street lights, parking meters, and air raid sirens in Manhattan, the Bronx, and Staten Island. The State Investigation Commission reported that the company cheated the taxpayers out of $2 million through "extensive irregularities." (These included a billing to the city for $7.90 for changing one light bulb.) The

SIC report was released in the fall of 1960; on June 30, 1961, Wagner renewed the city's contract with Broadway Maintenance. (Some things never change. On August 24, 1976, Controller Harrison Goldin reported that Broadway Maintenance had over-billed the city by $195,023.86 for the first six months of 1976. Broadway Maintenance appears to have a permanent contract with the permanent government.)

In 1960, the City Club of New York issued an ambivalent assessment of Wagner's first two terms. Among other things, the thirty-five-page pamphlet observed: "Scandals, involving theft, collusion in the sale of city-owned property, excessive rentals paid by the city to favorite real estate concerns, relocation frauds and bill padding in connection with the maintenance and repair of city property, shook what used to be the Department of Real Estate."

In 1957, a taxi driver found an envelope containing $11,200 in hundred-dollar bills in his back seat, a few moments after DeSapio had left the cab to enter the Hotel Biltmore. DeSapio denied the cash was his, although only a few school children believed him. And when no other claimants appeared, the cabby kept the cash.

This episode failed to make Wagner any more skeptical of DeSapio. On May 14, 1959, he described DeSapio as "the best leader the Democratic Party has had in New York." Earlier (on April 26, 1957) Wagner said that he "had set an example of undivided allegiance to the principles of good government—of government devoted exclusively to the needs and the welfare of the people."

When Wagner finally broke with DeSapio it was over politics, not principle or issues or ethics. They disagreed over who should get the party's Senate nomination in 1958, and over the selection of a new Manhattan borough president in 1961. In September of the latter year Wagner defeated Arthur Levitt, the hand-picked candidate of DeSapio and the other party bosses, by 160,000 votes in a bitter primary that ended DeSapio's overt power. This was the campaign where Murray Kempton observed that Wagner ran against his own record and won. Nine years later DeSapio went to federal prison after being convicted of bribery. (He was the third modern Tammany boss to serve time, the others being William Marcy Tweed and Jimmy Hines.)

The only time Robert Moses ever tried democracy and ran for office, he lost by 808,000 votes, to Herbert Lehman in 1934. But by the time Wagner was sworn in as New York City's mayor twenty years later, Moses's empire of unelected power was at mature strength. Moses was chairman of the Triborough Bridge and Tunnel Authority. Moses was a member of the City Planning Commission. Moses was City Construction Coordinator. Moses was City Parks Commissioner. And Moses served on six state boards and commissions. Even though Moses had publicly supported Impellitteri in the Democratic primary, Wagner did not remove him from any of his three city jobs. Wagner wanted to fire him. Wagner talked about firing him. Wagner intended to fire him as Planning Commissioner. Here there was a clear conflict of interest. As Construction Coordinator Moses proposed public works projects and as Planning Commissioner he sat as judge of their merit.

In his 1967 book, *What Have You Done for Me Lately?*, Wagner's former aide Warren Moscow described how Moses bullied the new mayor:

[Moses] staged the scene differently in the crowded reception room of City Hall on January 1, 1954, as Mayor Robert F. Wagner and other members of the incoming administration were being sworn into office. Moses was a key participant because three of the many jobs he held at the moment required new oaths of office administered by a new Mayor. Wagner was willing, in fact happy, to reappoint Moses as Parks Commissioner and City Construction Coordinator, but he was listening to those in the Establishment who felt Moses should not be appointed to the City Planning Commission. . . .

When Moses asked Wagner where the third oath of office was, the latter, anxious as always to avoid a scene, stalled Moses by saying that the clerks had not yet prepared it. Moses acted with characteristic aplomb. He strode back into the clerk's office, seized a blank oath of office, sat down at a typewriter and filled in the blanks of his own reappointment to the planning post. He brought it back triumphantly to the new Mayor. Wagner, his bluff exposed, had no option but to swear Moses in for his third job.

Under the outgoing Mayor Impellitteri, Moses rather than the Mayor had dominated the administration. Wagner had been determined that would not happen in his. But at the facedown just narrated, Wagner lost his battle on the day he took office. Moses increased the dimensions of his victory by relating the story of his hand-typed oath to only 50 or so of his most intimate friends, all in city government.

Four days later Moses wrote to Wagner requesting authority to "represent" the city in negotiations with state and federal governments, as part of a redefinition of his role as City Construction Coordinator. "Certainly," Wagner wrote back. And so, for fifteen more years, Moses shaped the face of the city.

The 1950s was the decade of the bulldozer, of grand designs to end slums for all time. Experts and planners called this "urban renewal," but social workers called it "Negro removal." Federal Title I funds were available—but so was cynicism. In New York City the money and the plans for tearing down slums were under the custody of Robert Moses; among his many titles was chairman of the Slum Clearance Committee.

The Title I housing scandal was the result of the alliance between Moses and DeSapio.

The Title I scandal was peeled away like a rotten onion over several years by Fred Cook and Gene Gleason, writing in *The World Telegram*, and Bill Haddad and Joe Kahn, writing in the *New York Post*—four antiestablishment journalists who shared their information, although working for competing afternoon papers. When the revelations began on July 30, 1956, Moses was a natural target. DeSapio's friend Percy Gale was a member of the Slum

Clearance Committee, and the vice-chairman was Thomas Shanahan, chairman of the Federation Bank and Trust Company, a DeSapio man who was Tammany's fund raiser (and therefore Wagner's in 1953) and Moses's banker. In 1948, the Triborough Bridge and Tunnel Authority, on Moses's order, had deposited $15 million in Shanahan's bank, all in interest-free accounts; at the time, the *total* deposits of the bank were $35 million. On the board of directors of Shanahan's Federation Bank was George Spargo. Spargo was also secretary, at $40,000 a year, of the Triborough Bridge and Tunnel Authority, and personal assistant to Moses in Moses's capacity as chairman of the Slum Clearance Committee. Thus the interlocking power of Robert Moses and Carmine DeSapio was cemented by institutions—a bank, and a public authority—whose books and records were secret.

The Slum Clearance Committee evicted and relocated an estimated 170,000 tenants across New York City. Many of these powerless tenants were dumped into Brownsville, the Brooklyn neighborhood that had produced the generation of gangsters known as Murder, Inc. Sites were condemned, and then landlords called "sponsors" were chosen by Moses and DeSapio-through-Shanahan. (Shanahan was vice-chairman of the committee that picked the landlord/sponsors.) The sponsors all had clubhouse ties, and they were all customers of Shanahan's fast-growing little bank.

Each of the eleven sites were milked and skimmed by lawyers, architects, insurance companies, banks, sponsors, stockholders, contractors, rental and managing agents, and private relocation companies. There was little heat or hot water for the tenants. Some tenants were relocated two and three times. It was a textbook case of how to make slums with a committee called Slum Clearance. And enrich a few insiders in the process.

One of the eleven Title I sites was called Manhattantown, on the Upper West Side, and its sponsor was Sam Caspert, a DeSapio crony from the clubhouses. Moses turned over to Caspert 338 apartment houses and tenements. Earlier Caspert had been given title to six blocks of property, worth $15 million, for a fee of $1 million. And Caspert collected all the slum rentals he could from these tenements.

Moses appointed a landlord named Sidney Ungar as the lucrative sponsor of Riverside-Amsterdam urban renewal site in Manhattan. Post reporter Haddad then exposed Ungar's other properties as wretched slums where children suffered rat bites, and pointed out that Ungar was a campaign contributor to Wagner and other politicians.

Robert Caro has described how the insurance on one slum clearance site was handled by a Democratic district leader, Robert Blaikie, an Impellitteri loyalist. As soon as Wagner won the primary, "Blaikie lost the insurance account—to a broker associated with DeSapio."

Cook and Gleason disclosed in the *Telegram*, on April 24, 1956, that while favored sponsors and developers had made "fortunes" on the Title I properties, they had not even bothered to pay the required real-estate taxes to the city. "The city is holding the bag . . . to the tune of nearly $1 million in delinquent taxes and interest," they wrote. Haddad and Kahn revealed in the *Post* that DeSapio's personal publicist, Sydney J. Baron, was being paid $1500 a month by an "association" of Title I landlords. And Fred Cook documented how the Soundview project in the Bronx generated "a clear $500,000 windfall to political insiders."

While all this was going on, the *Times* was largely ignoring the unfolding scandal and still trying to depict Moses as a planning statesman above party politics. On June 25, 1959, a *Times* editorial commented: "Our confidence in Mr. Moses as an honest, incomparably able public servant is unshanken. His resignation from office would be an irreparable loss. Where is his equal?"

(The frequent misjudgments of the *Times* editorial board have been a major contribution to New York City's agony. In addition to treating Moses as a sacred cow, the *Times* also endorsed the villain of villains, Nelson Rockefeller, for re-election as governor in 1970, over Democrat-Liberal Arthur Goldberg. In a brilliant analysis of *Times* editorial policy, Christopher Norwood wrote in the November 3, 1975, issue of *New York:* "In both 1971 and 1973, the paper swallowed its own environmentalism to support transportation bond issues that still included massive highway money, on the basis of Nelson Rockefeller's debatable claim that otherwise the subway fare would immediately jump to 60 cents. The *Times* regularly quotes Lewis Mumford on 'humanizing' the city, but has backed a parade of massive undertakings that make urban humanists weep, including tracts of public housing, giant urban renewal projects, Lincoln Center, and the World Trade Center which it greeted as 'a miracle of organization and order.' . . . For saviors, the *Times* has served up Moses, Rockefeller and Lindsay. . . .")

No one will ever know for sure how many millions of dollars of public money were wasted and grafted out of the Title I program. No one will ever know how many low-rent apartments it knocked down, how many vital neighborhoods it spoiled, how many anonymous lives it broke and stunted.

What we do know is that, during the 1950s, the people and the institutions that launched the disintegration of New York City were Moses and his authorities; Shanahan and his bank; Baron and his PR firm; and DeSapio and his Democratic Party structure.

And Robert Wagner, a decent man, let them do it.

The 1964-65 World's Fair was one of those great big concepts that everyone with power likes. It was like the Albany Mall, or the World Trade Center, or the recurring plan to build a convention center in Manhattan. Everyone was behind the idea of a World's Fair in New York City—the banks, the Rockefellers, Wagner, Moses, the construction unions, the business elite, and all the political insiders who would collect fees, commissions, and retainers.

In the summer of 1960, Robert Moses resigned his jobs as Planning Commission member, Parks Commissioner, City Construction Coordinator, chairman of the Slum Clearance Committee, and member of the City Youth Board, to accept appointment as president of the World's Fair Corporation for seven years. (He retained his jobs as chairman of the Triborough Authority, chairman of the State Power Authority, and president of the Long Island State Park Commission—all state, not city, appointments.)

Further demonstrating that real power is usually invisible power, Moses arranged for his fawning disciple, Newbold Morris, to replace him as Parks Commissioner. Through the bumbling, deferential Morris, Moses kept control of the Parks Department payroll and budget, and actually made all major decisions himself.

According to Robert Caro's estimate, the total New York city expenditure to the private Fair Corporation was more than $60 million, although the exact figure is unknowable because of various budget deceits. In addition, New York State and the federal government each spent $12 million on the Fair. And that's just the public money. A consortium of banks held $23 million in notes from the Fair Corporation and made millions more in loans directly to individual pavilions.

The New York City Council and Board of Estimate voted for a $24 million appropriation to the Fair, on the promise the money would earn the city a profit on its investment. Mayor Wagner, Controller Beame, and City Council President Paul Screvane all voted for this $24-million "loan."

In the end, more than a billion dollars passed through the Fair's bank accounts. And in the end, the Fair lost money for the taxpayers. The Fair even defaulted on its notes to the banks, repaying only $10 million of $23 million. The city never got back its $24 million. When the Fair closed on October 17, 1965, it had a $10-million deficit.

Where did all the money go? Moses used the Fair, as he had used the Triborough Authority and the Slum Clearance Committee, to create a blue-ribbon pad for the permanent government of his day. The Moses pad was not like a grubby police pad with a $100 bill in an envelope. It was an imperial pad—legal, and in the millions of dollars. And it was the public's money, not some bookmaker's or madam's.

Allied Maintenance Corporation, well connected politically, got the Fair's exclusive contract for cleaning, disposal, and private garbage collection. In one year, this private carter with a monopoly franchise collected more than $10 million from exhibitors at the Fair. And the only insurance company approved by the Fair's corporation board was Campo & Roberts, DeSapio's favorite company (another sign of DeSapio's enduring covert power and relationship with Moses, even *after* his defeat in the 1961 primary election); its commissions on Fair insurance came to more than $3 million.

Further, the Fair hired the politically influential firm of Thomas J. Deegan to handle publicity. Deegan had told the press, "I . . . expect to continue to serve without any fees or expenses of any kind," but as we have seen, he received an annual fee of $100,000, plus an additional $350,000 for his company, plus a $1000-a-month suite at the Waldorf, plus a chauffeur. On top of this, the firm owned by William Donoghue, who had been Mayor William O'Dwyer's publicist, got a $400,000-a-year retainer from the Fair. The Fair also hired dozens of popular former newspapermen to make the old city-room network sympathetic: offiial expenses for "public relations" for the Fair's first year were $2,772,542.49.

The Fair's vast legal fees went to the firm of Moses's favorite lawyer, Samuel Rosenman, who had been close to FDR. One of the engineering contracts went to Blauvelt Engineering, a company with a new partner—George Spargo, who had been an aide to Moses for thirty-five years. And the contract for the Fair's souvenir program went to Henry Luce's Time, Inc. Both *Time* and *Life* magazines, owned by Luce, published favorable cover stories on the World's Fair and Moses; the *Life* story was called, "Everything Coming Up Moses." None of these contracts involved competitive bidding.

In retrospect, one can only imagine what might have happened if the estimated $60 million of public treasure which the city poured into the Fair had gone instead to renovate existing housing, or upgrade the public schools, or restore the docks and port facilities; in some way to improve the quality of life, create jobs, and thus keep the middle class living in New York City. But Moses's genius as an empire builder, and Wagner's passive nature, unfortunately set other priorities.

John Lindsay gave good intentions a bad name.

John Lindsay was a vessel for a lot of expectations and a lot of dreams. He wanted to do good, but he didn't know how.

His reform campaign in 1965, as the Fusion and Republican candidate against Democrat Abraham Beame, was an exciting echo of John Kennedy's 1960 bid for the presidency. The campaign poster on every subway platform in the city showed a smiling, long-striding, lean Lindsay in shirtsleeves on a city street, and over it a quotation from the columnist Murray Kempton: HE IS FRESH AND EVERYONE ELSE IS TIRED.

Lindsay's campaign attracted 10,000 volunteers and was able to open up one hundred twenty storefronts to battle the clubhouses across the city. We both voted for Lindsay.

On election night, in November 1965, the grand ballroom of the Hotel Roosevelt was rush-hour jammed with 6000 campaign workers—mostly the Yale-Princeton young and fashionably dressed, but also more than a few blacks. A band played swing and Dixieland jazz as the seesaw vote totals came in all evening. Finally, at 2 A.M., Lindsay sprinted 100,000 votes ahead on the ballots of middle-class Jews from districts reporting from Flatbush in Brooklyn. Someone tossed from a balcony copies of the last edition of the *Herald Tribune*, the front page declaring Lindsay the winner. The campaign workers ripped up the papers and joyfully tossed the instant confetti into the electrified, smoky air.

Suddenly, a deep-throated animal roar went up, starting at the entrance on the right, and sweeping across the mass in the ballroom. John Lindsay was coming to the podium behind a wedge of cops to claim his victory. He was forty-three and movie-idol handsome. The people in the ballroom embraced, screamed, and a few wept for joy. John Kennedy was dead. But they had a new liberal hope.

Lindsay turned out to be a disappointment, almost a tragedy, as mayor, given his potential and the hopes invested in him.

He had been a superb advocate as a congressman, and he would have made a fine senator or Ambassador to the United Nations. But he had few talents as an executive. Lindsay dramatized the role of mayor, but he couldn't *do* it. He was the mayor of America, but not of Queens. From St. Paul's School and Yale, he lived in the bubble of Manhattan culture. He was a WASP running the greatest ethnic city on earth, and he did not understand the ordinary lives of ordinary people in the four other boroughs. Lindsay was an activist with poor judgment. Lindsay was an actor with no self-knowledge.

Lindsay's weaknesses fed each other. A poor judge of character, he was malleable in the hands of a few people. Like Augie March, his character was his fate. He always seemed to be pushed by others into his major political decisions. His brother David got him to join the Manhattan Republican Club in 1949. Former Attorney General Herbert Brownell convinced him to run for Congress in 1958. Robert Price, the clever, cynical man who managed his congressional campaigns, took him on a walk through the city in the spring of 1965 and badgered him into running for mayor. And late in 1971, Deputy Mayor Richard Aurelio and chief of staff Jay Kriegel convinced him to run in the primaries for president only a few months after he had joined the Democratic Party. Lindsay seemed to lack an inner originality about his own life.

Lindsay was always preoccupied with the appearance rather than the reality of things. As late as the summer of 1976 he could say to one of his former assistants: "You know, Beame still doesn't understand that this whole fiscal crisis is really just a PR problem, a question of restoring public confidence." And as mayor, Lindsay saw most things as a "PR problem." He made sanitation the highest priority of his second administration because it was the most visible of city services. If garbage wasn't collected or snow removed, everyone noticed. As a result, diminishing resources were directed away from more fundamental problems—housing, heroin, jobs, education—because actual progress in those areas was not so easy to dramatize to the media.

Lindsay often asked his aides, when making a decision, how will it be played by the *Times?* How will it look on the six o'clock news? The image of things dominated Lindsay's mind to a fault. He was a successful candidate because he understood the power of television, but he was a failure as mayor because he could not see the limits of television as a surrogate for reality.

Lindsay frequently named the popular mayor of New York, Fiorello La Guardia, as his hero, and he once told Newfield that was the reason he had originally registered as a Republican. But in some respects Lindsay as mayor was more like La Guardia's opposite, Jimmy Walker. Like Walker, Lindsay was a great actor who was star-struck and loved show biz. Like Walker, he was a sexy celebrity, a *Zeitgeist,* a devastating campaigner. And like Walker, Lindsay had terrible judgment in choosing his deputies and lacked the attention span to be an efficient administrator.

Lindsay's objectives were sound. Let us examine several ways he gave good intentions a bad name. He wanted to decentralize the city's bureaucratic school system. But he foolishly chose three black and Hispanic neighborhoods for the locations of the three experimental decentralized school districts. (The main influence on Lindsay's decision was McGeorge Bundy, president of the Ford Foundation.) A shrewder executive would have picked at least two white, middle-class areas, to defuse fear and criticism. A consequence was that the teachers' union president, Albert Shanker, was able to convert the decentralization debate into a bitter racial issue—black parents versus Jewish teachers. The two basic liberal constituencies of New York City were put at each other's throat by this stupidity.

Lindsay had deep and genuine empathy with the city's blacks. But he felt little empathy with the city's ethnic middle and working classes. He went on highly visible walking tours of Harlem and Bed-Stuy, but the citizens of Howard Beach, Corona, Woodside, Bay Ridge, Greenpoint, Inwood, and Belmont never saw him on their streets, although they did see Lindsay's regular visits to the black sections on television every summer. The result was a feeling of alienation in white working- and middle-class neighborhoods, already hurting from inflation and crime. They didn't vote for Lindsay. And so Lindsay resented them even more.

In 1966, Lindsay's rigidity and inability to negotiate forced a city-wide referendum on the creation of a civilian complaint review board to monitor allegations of police brutality. The concept was useful although too symbolic to justify a costly, polarizing referendum.

Manhattan liberals and civil libertarians loved the idea of a review board. But Lindsay appeared to be handcuffing the police at the very moment crime and street violence were increasing. The review board lost, 63 per cent to 37 per cent. It went down to defeat even in some black neighborhoods, where the fear of street crime was the biggest concern of all, although Lindsay did not recognize it at the time.

One result of this avoidable confrontation was the explosive demoralization of the Police Department, a demoralization that Lindsay and his aide Jay Kriegel would later invoke as the reason they could not move swiftly when Frank Serpico brought them evidence of widespread police corruption in April 1967.

Lindsay said he wanted to hire the best and brightest people in the country to manage New York City. He dispatched talent scouts to other cities; he talked to his friends in Congress and in the academic-foundation elite. And then he named a string of mediocrities to be his aides. Two of Lindsay's commissioners went to prison for bribery: James Marcus of Water Resources, and the late Theodore Gross of Youth Services. There were scandals in the Police Department and in the municipal loan program. Among the most obvious incompetents whom Lindsay appointed were: Arnold Fraiman as Investigations Commissioner; Howard Leary as Police Commissioner; Jason Nathan and then Albert Walsh as back-to-back Housing and Development administrators; Joseph English as president of the Health and Hospitals Corporation; George McGrath as Corrections Commissioner; and Norman Levy as Tax Commissioner.

What went wrong? A former Lindsay aide says: "John just got fooled by resumés with formal credentials. . . . Some of the people just didn't know New York City. Leary came from Philadelphia, Joe English from Washington, McGrath from Boston. Marcus had all these social connections with the Lodge family. Kriegel and Goldmark had the right schools on their resumés."

Lindsay wanted the bureaucracy to function better, a fine goal. So he turned to the technocrats, to the systems analysts and management experts at RAND and McKinsey and Company. Between 1968 and 1971, Lindsay spent $10 million of public funds on outside consultant contracts. Most of the studies were worthless, written in trendy jargon about minor problems.

Lindsay recruited a staff of forty-five program planners for the budget bureau, forty-one of them from Ivy League colleges. They tried to construct a rational system for an irrational environment, to quantify the unquantifiable. And Lindsay, because he saw the flow charts, thought what was on paper was reality. But it was no more the whole picture than the body counts and kill ratios were in Vietnam. The Program Planning Budgeting Systems approach created only a mirage of coherence and progress. Yet Lindsay swore by it, and preached the gospel of scientific management wherever he went. He became an admirer of McNamara and Bundy, despite his strong, early opposition to the Vietnam War.

This is what a former aide in Lindsay's budget bureau told us: "The mayor was just snowed, taken in. Lindsay was tired of hearing he was a lousy administrator. And then these bright Ivy League guys from RAND and McKinsey came to him and said they knew how to rationalize city government. Lindsay really believed they were *supermen*. Their use of statistics and charts just dazzled him. The statistics made him feel the city was controllable with expertise. So the mayor was converted without really understanding what it was all about. He was convinced that RAND had a skill that was really a *science*. I remember that I once wrote a speech for Lindsay and he made me use the phrase 'new budget science' three times in it. And I'm convinced he didn't know what the words actually meant."

John Lindsay was a mass transit man, a critic of the automobile. His first good intention as mayor was that he wanted to remove Robert Moses as chairman of the Triborough Authority.

Between Lindsay's election and inauguration he met privately with Moses at the Hotel Roosevelt. If Lindsay was naive as an assessor of men, Moses was profound. After the first meeting, Moses, then seventy-seven, prophetically told his staff: "If you elect a matinee idol mayor, you're going to get a musical comedy administration."

During his second week in office, Lindsay announced legislation creating a new, centralized transportation authority that would merge the Triborough Authority with the Transit Authority, and empower the mayor to name the chairman of the new agency.* This would also allow Lindsay to use Triborough's existing cash surplus on behalf of New York's subways, which were badly in need of renovation. Thus the young Mayor thought he would cleverly and quickly end Robert Moses's public career. Lindsay told reporters he was confident that his merger plan would be approved by the legislature in Albany, and that Moses himself appeared to be amenable to his own political execution.

A week later, the resourceful Moses blocked Lindsay's thrust with one deft maneuver. He released a "memorandum of opposition," citing his binding legal covenant, his "independent contractual obligations" with the holders of the Triborough Authority's bonds. Moses (and his lawyer Sam Rosenman) asserted that any attempt to alter the lawful covenant with the bondholders "would contravene" the New York State Constitution, and Article I, Section 10 of the United States Constitution, which forbids any state to "pass any . . . law impairing the obligation of contracts." None of Lindsay's Harvard and Yale staff, fresh from Law Review honors and clerking for the right federal judges, had anticipated this argument. When the issue came

*Again, we acknowledge our debt to Robert Caro, *The Power Broker*, the source of many of these facts.

before the state legislature, Lindsay and his young aides thought they were actually winning the confrontation, although all the real decision-makers were laughing at them behind their backs.

At a joint public hearing of the state Senate and Assembly rules committees on March 11, 1966, Lindsay's envoy to the legislature, Richard Rosen, arranged for only one speaker (besides Lindsay) for his side—the city's assistant corporation counsel, Norman Redlich, just hired from the faculty of the NYU Law School. He didn't pay much attention to the line-up of men speaking on behalf of Moses until a few minutes before the public hearing began. Then he saw the list. Two former governors headed it: Thomas E. Dewey and Charles Poletti. It included: former Mayor Wagner; Peter Brennan, the leader of New York's construction unions; a representative of the Chase Manhattan Bank; several investment bankers; a spokesman for the city's biggest stock brokerage firm; several respected bond lawyers; and Moses himself.

Two days after the hearing, the Chase Bank announced that if the legislature should happen to adopt the Lindsay merger plan, then Chase, as trustee of $379.3 million's worth of Triborough bonds, would file a law suit to invalidate the legislation. And Assembly Speaker Anthony Travia told a few reporters that the Lindsay plan should never have been sent up to Albany in the first place, since it did not even have the legally required home-rule message from the City Council, without which the legislature could not even consider it.

On his first day as mayor, Lindsay, with Puritan rectitude, had denounced the "power brokers" who rule the city. "They know who they are," Lindsay had said in ominous tones. But his inept losing fight to remove Moses showed that Lindsay himself had no understanding of who they were or how they operated.

Two years later Robert Moses was finally removed from power. Four able and ruthless men ganged up on the old man and forced him to accept a merger with the Metropolitan Transportation Authority and resign as chairman of the Triborough Authority. The four men whose combined guile and leverage it took to topple the unelected Moses were: Governor Nelson Rockefeller; David Rockefeller, chairman of the bank that was trustee of the Triborough Authority's bonds; former Governor Dewey, lawyer for the Chase bank; and William Ronan, Nelson Rockefeller's trusted advisor and retainer. The Rockefellers installed their own man, Ronan, as chairman of the MTA, and then the governor broke his promise to Moses—that if he went along quietly with the merger, he would be appointed as a full voting member of the new MTA—and instead Moses became a "consultant" to the now subsidiary Triborough Authority, an honorary position of no power.

The MTA members were the next generation of power brokers: lawyer Bill

Shea; Eben Pyne of Citibank; William Butcher of the County Trust Company of White Plains; and Leonard Braun, president of Newport Petroleum.

At one golden moment in recent history the spiral of disintegration might have been stopped. That came with John Lindsay's reelection as mayor in November 1969. Lindsay was re-elected without the support of either major political party. He was re-elected as the Liberal Party candidate with 42 per cent of the vote, defeating Democrat Mario Procaccino and Republican John Marchi.

Lindsay began his second term liberated from many of the city's vested interests, particularly the Democratic clubhouse system. He owed his election to Alex Rose, the benign boss of the Liberal Party; to blacks, who gave him 80 per cent of all their votes; to David Garth, his brilliant media consultant; and to the fat cats who contributed more than $2 million to his campaign. He owed no other obligations.

Lindsay could have begun to make the unpopular changes that were necessary. He could have begun to annul the sweetheart deals and special favors every organized group had at the expense of the public interest. He could have pared the budget of waste. He could have reduced the city's short-term debt.

Instead of using the gift of liberation to make difficult decisions, Lindsay's staff, and then Lindsay himself, became seized with the ambition to run him for president in 1972. This ambition propelled Lindsay into voluntary dependency on the power brokers he had once derided. He needed to consolidate his local base to run nationally. So he used the lines in the capital budget and the expense budget as bribes to this group or that group to stop criticizing and let him run for president as the man who prevented riots, or as the man who had no strikes. He made deals with Democratic Party bosses for jobs and contracts, even though they had supported Procaccino against him. Boondoggles—like the twenty-year, no-bid day-care leases to landlords, the $101-million renovation of Yankee Stadium, and the 99-year lease to one landlord of the Bronx Terminal Market—were foisted upon the taxpayers, because the pols would get the gravy. Short-term borrowing from banks was increased to finance quick-fix programs designed to inflate the mayor's popularity quickly. Excessive pension settlements were made with municipal unions to improve his image as a negotiator—by averting strikes. Bunny Lindenbaum had as much mysterious influence over zoning variances during Lindsay's second term as he had during Wagner's third.

The golden moment passed. Re-elected as an independent, Lindsay had become a volunteer cuckold of the permanent government. And in the end, Lindsay was screwed by the political bosses he tried to sell out to. Meade Esposito of Brooklyn struck the crucial, disloyal blow against Lindsay's presidential campaign in 1972, suggesting, after Lindsay lost the early Florida primary: "Come home, little Sheba." This remark made the front page of *The New York Times*, and it finished Lindsay's presidential campaign.

Lindsay had violated one of the most sensible axioms in politics: Do your job well and the future will take care of itself. Plain, cold ambition ruined Lindsay's second chance.

One failure of Lindsay's administration in New York City deserves special notice. It had nothing to do with the hidden power of some elite interest. It was not an area where Lindsay's intentions were of high purpose. It was a failure that Lindsay chose of his own free will, because of his own human frailties. And it had a terrible consequence for the city. It was the failure, for three years, to do anything about police corruption, and to respond only when it became a PR problem.

Over the last fifteen years there have been few genuine heroes in the history of government in New York. Two of them are named Frank Serpico and David Durk. They were honest cops.

On the last Sunday in April 1967 Serpico and Durk came on a confidential mission to the City Hall basement office of Jay Kriegel, to tell him about police corruption. Kriegel was Lindsay's staff man assigned to liaison with the Police Department. Sergeant Durk was Kriegel's friend, and he had helped draft Lindsay's White Paper on crime during the 1965 campaign. Serpico was a plainclothes cop who had refused to go on the pad.

Serpico had already tried, through the byzantine, military channels of the Police Department, to report corruption, but he had not been successful. He had come to the mayor's office—outside normal channels—at the urging of his friend Durk, who himself was not a witness of corruption.

Serpico talked for two hours. "I poured out my guts," he later said. Serpico told Kriegel that every plainclothesman in the South Bronx 7th Division, except himself, was taking graft. He said he had reason to believe that men at the level of the borough command were corrupt. He asked Kriegel to organize a full-scale investigation, using undercover men, cameras, electronic surveillance, all the technology the Police Department had in its aresenal. Kriegel said he would tell the mayor about the whole problem.

A few weeks later Durk realized nothing would come of the meeting with Kriegel. Durk told us: "Jay fucked us. He decided that if he started a real investigation into police corruption, it would disrupt the department, and that might lead to riots. Lindsay's political image depended on [having] no riots in the ghettoes. . . . They told us they would investigate as soon as Lindsay was re-elected in 1969. They always had some new date in the future. In October 1969 I even took Kriegel up to Pleasant Avenue in East Harlem to show him police corruption involving heroin. Not gambling, or vice, but heroin. It had no effect.

After Kriegel, Serpico and Durk went to the city's Investigations Commissioner, Arnold Fraiman, also during 1967. Kriegel was merely a staff man, a twenty-six-year-old with many other responsibilities besides police corruption. But Fraiman's only job was to investigate official misconduct. Serpico told his story to Fraiman—the story of refusing to accept $300 from a crooked cop, of his frustrating attempts to tell his superior officers about the organized pad, of the threats and pressure he felt to join it, of his growing paranoia that no one in the whole city was honest.

Fraiman suggested that Serpico wear a concealed recorder to collect evidence, but Serpico protested that this would only catch men at "the patrolman level," and that a massive investigation was required to expose the higher-ups—the sergeants, captains, and inspectors—"where the real problem was." Later Durk saw Fraiman alone and asked whether he would now begin such an investigation, but Fraiman told him that Serpico struck him as sort of a "psycho." As Durk kept pleading, the Investigations Commissioner of the City of New York turned his back on him, picked up a pair of binoculars, and stared at the ships in the harbor below his window. It was the perfect symbolic gesture of the city's attitude toward police corruption.

Desperation led Serpico and Durk to the press. On February 12, 1970, they met with reporters and editors of *The New York Times*. Accompanying Serpico and Durk, backing up their allegations, giving them credibility, was Paul Delise, a full inspector, who risked his police career of twenty years to do it. Serpico and Durk then gave the *Times* a week of secret interviews.

As soon as Lindsay learned that a *Times* story was in the works, he decided to respond, to pre-empt the criticism, to beat the *Times* to the punch, to treat the whole problem as one of the aggressive public relations. On April 23, 1970, almost three years to the day since Serpico and Durk had first gone to Kriegel's office, Lindsay announced the appointment of a "special committee" to investigate police corruption. The committee included Lindsay's corporation counsel, J. Lee Rankin; district attorneys Frank Hogan and Burton Roberts; Robert Ruskin, whom Lindsay appointed to succeed Fraiman as Investigations Commissioner; and, incredibly, Police Commissioner Howard Leary, the man who had been presiding over the Police Department since 1966. It was if Richard Nixon had appointed John Mitchell and Richard Kleindienst to investigate Watergate.

In announcing the formation of the committee, Lindsay said with a stern, straight face: "This government must root out corruption and wrong-doing with every means at its command."

Two days later, on April 25, 1970, the *Times* published its exposé on police corruption on the front page under the headline:

GRAFT PAID TO POLICE HERE
SAID TO RUN INTO MILLIONS

Four days later Police Commissioner Leary was claiming that it was all part of an irresponsible smear campaign. "McCarthyism all over again," he said, alleging that the *Times* story had been based on the word of "prostitutes, narcotics addicts and gamblers, and disgruntled policemen."

The rest is history. The firestorm reaction to the *Times* story, and the backlash against Leary's comments, forced Lindsay to scrap his PR defense and appoint a commission to conduct the long-delayed probe of police corruption in New York City. Wall Street lawyer Whitman Knapp was named chairman, and its members were independent of the Lindsay administration. On July 21, the City Council appropriated $325,000 to the Knapp Commission for six months. In November the Commission received a grant of $215,000 from the federal government's Law Enforcement Assistance Administration. On Christmas Eve the Commission's life was extended for six months by the City Council (over the bitter opposition of Matthew Troy).

The final 264-page report of the Knapp Commission, released on December 27, 1972, concluded that corruption was "an extensive, department-wide phenomenon," and that the Lindsay administration had failed to respond appropriately to the evidence brought to its attention by Serpico and Durk. But, the Commission said, it was unable to pinpoint the culpability of Lindsay personally because of unresolved contradictions in the public and private testimony of Jay Kriegel.

In his original executive session testimony, Kriegel said that he had told Lindsay about Serpico's and Durk's allegations of corruption and had reported to his boss that the two cops were dissatisfied with the way the allegations were being handled by their superiors in the department. But in his later public testimony, Kriegel claimed that Serpico and Durk had complained only about the existence of graft, not about the conduct of their superiors in the department or about the lack of departmental investigations. Then the Knapp Commission's chief counsel, Michael Armstrong—at the public hearing— asked Kriegel: "And did you also report to him [Lindsay] that the police officers [Serpico and Durk] were dissatisfied with the pace of the investigation?"

"No, I did not," Kriegel responded.

Armstrong then confronted Kriegel with his private testimony under oath that he had indeed told the mayor that both Serpico and Durk were "not satisfied" with the Police Department's response to Serpico's charges. Kriegel replied, after studying the transcript of his executive session testimony, that he "talked at some length to the mayor about that incident. And I am now clear that following the meeting with Frank and David, I did not report to him that allegation."

Lindsay was never subpoenaed to testify at a public hearing about Kriegel's two conflicting versions of what happened. At a panel discussion at the New School in 1974, Jack Newfield asked Whitman Knapp why this had never been done. "How can you investigate the man who appointed you?" Knapp replied, by then a federal judge.

The Knapp Commission report also passed this final judgment: "Although Walsh [John Walsh, first deputy police commissioner], Kriegel, and Fraiman all acknowledged the extreme seriousness of the charges, and the unique opportunity provided by the fact that a police officer was making them, none of them took any action. . . . No serious investigation was undertaken. . . ." About Arnold Fraiman, who by then was a state Supreme Court justice thanks to Lindsay, it said, "Fraiman failed to take the action that was clearly called for in a situation which seemed to involve one of the most serious kinds of corruption ever to come to the attention of his office, and which seemed to be precisely the sort of case his office was set up to handle."

Police conduct which the Knapp Commission report described as "typical" and "numerous" included:

—cops selling heroin;

—cops selling information to dealers and accepting heroin in payment;

—cops protecting heroin dealers by registering them as informants;

—cops financing heroin transactions;

—cops selling the identity of police informants to the Mafia;

—cops kidnapping important witnesses to prevent them from testifying at the trials of heroin dealers;

—cops providing protection (riding-shotgun) for heroin dealers;

—cops providing "hit men" to kill potential witnesses.

Five weeks after the Knapp report was released, before most of us could digest its mass of narrative details, the news broke that $73 million worth of pure heroin and cocaine (398 pounds) had been stolen by cops from the Police Department's own property clerk's office, between March 1969 and late 1972. The biggest single supplier of heroin in New York City turned out to be the Police Department itself.

During the last five years, city, state, and federal prosecutors have indicted more than 300 police officers in New York City on criminal charges of corruption. More than 120 have been convicted, with many cases still pending. An additional 60 crooked cops have been forced to resign from the department as a result of disciplinary proceedings.

The Knapp Commission report had one moral hole. It did not make a connection between the failure of Fraiman, Kriegel, and Walsh, and the heroin tide that became an epidemic between 1967 and 1970, the years when the Lindsay administration looked away from police corruption. It was left to Adam Walinsky, a lawyer and a former aide to Robert Kennedy, to draw this connecting thread in a moving article in the March 1, 1973, issue of *The Village Voice:*

The issue, the unspoken story of the [Knapp] report, is the slow destruction of a generation in the ghettoes of Harlem and Bedford-Stuyvesant and the South Bronx, their minds and bodies ravaged by heroin, everything that makes a life thrown back at them from a perverted funhouse mirror. Junkies for fathers, whores for mothers, a daily fix the only routine of their days, and how many thousands cut down in the indiscribable shooting galleries of the ghetto. The Mayor, the Police Commissioner and the Attorney General, the District Attorneys and Judges pursued their routines, their ambitions, and their careers, made speeches and accepted human-relations awards. Under their blind benevolent gaze, the children died, and they continue to die today.

All this the Commission does not mention. Nor does it draw the final conclusion: We have, in fact, no laws against the selling of heroin. We have a system whereby, for the appropriate license fees to the proper authorities, certain people obtain a protected monopoly franchise to sell heroin, at least to certain classes of people. Not for nothing did the police refer to Harlem, so poor in everything else, as the "Gold Coast" where the real money was to be made. . . .

A few months ago, long after the facts of this report were known, John Lindsay intones that the murder of Professor Wolfgang Friedman was "the worst outrage" to afflict the city in all his term as Mayor. Not a word for the cab drivers, the little shopkeepers, the eighty-five-year-old grandmothers killed for the price of a fix. Not a word of all the years his police force sold heroin to the children of the city, while we slipped into our daily hell, our triple-locked doors and empty night streets, our life-in-death.

There was one other realm where Lindsay's motives were not good—his manipulations of the budget, his dramatic increase of the city's short-term debt, and his concealment of deficits.

During his first month as mayor, Lindsay went on television to inform the public that his predecessor had spent the city "into very serious difficulty," and he criticized Wagner for balancing the budget by borrowing. This new mayor, Lindsay promised, would not repeat the mistake.

It was not until his 1971 budget that Lindsay borrowed $360 million to balance the budget. But during his eight years as mayor, New York City's short-term debt multiplied by almost five times. This is how the short-term debt expanded, year by year:

1965-66	$1.6 billion	1970-71	$6.5
1966-67	$2.0	1971-72	$5.2
1967-68	$2.4	1972-73	$4.0
1968-69	$3.2	1973-74	$7.3
1969-70	$4.4		

And most of the increase after 1971 was the selling of Revenue Anticipation Notes and Tax Anticipation Notes to finance existing debt service. It was as if the city was an individual going to a garment-center loanshark to pay off a waterfront loanshark, at even higher interest rates.

In the October 27, 1975, issue of *New York* magazine, Ken Auletta compiled a list of twenty key decisions taken between June 1944 and February 1975 "that broke New York City," and he sensibly included Lindsay's 1973-74 expense budget. Lindsay and Controller Beame both called the document a "balanced budget," but it was balanced with gimmicks and fictions. Among the gimmicks were: listing $564 million in expense items in the city's capital budget; a rollover of $308 million in budget notes issued to cover the 1970-71 budget deficit; the inclusion of a $211 deficit and an invitation to the state to close it; the arbitrary postponing of the statutory repayment of $96 million to the "rainy day" fund. And it all papered over the biggest one-year increase in short-term debt in the city's history.

The cost of Lindsay's deceptions and promiscuous short-term borrowing was a glutted market and higher interest rates, thus more borrowing, thus more reliance on accounting tricks. In June 1975, Steven Clifford, an aide to Controller Harrison Goldin, completed a memorandum for him analyzing the recent history of budget gimmicks. Clifford estimated that *$1.5 billion* of the city's current short-term debt had been caused by "gimmicks" to create an illusion of a balanced budget. (One such gimmick was the change in the date of the city's billings. To gain additional revenue in 1973, Lindsay altered the date for water billings so that eighteen months of billings were credited to the 1973-74 fiscal year ending June 30, 1974. The immediate benefit was a quick $56 million in revenue. But because the receipt of water charges was subsequently delayed until July and August, the city had to borrow an average of $60 million to cover the delay—a borrowing that will recur every year. And the taxpayers must pay the interest on a paper illusion.)

The fiscal philosophy of the Lindsay years was inadvertently summed up in two comments that his last budget director, David Grossman, made to journalists. "You get a million dollars here and a million dollars there," Grossman once told a reporter, "and before you know it you've got some real money." On another occasion he observed that "a reasonably honest" budget was one that was really only $50 million out of balance.

When Lindsay left office he claimed that all his budgets had been balanced as mandated by law. When a thorough audit was conducted by the state and MAC accountants in August 1975, it was verified that Lindsay had left behind him a concealed deficit of about *$1.5 billion*.

Abraham Beame was Controller of New York City from 1961 to 1965 and again from 1969 to 1973. That was like being the look-out on the *Titanic*.

He was the city's chief fiscal officer when all the budget tricks started, all the estimates of revenues that did not exist, all the rollovers, all the hidden deficits, all the raids on "rainy-days" funds, and all the trips to the money market for short-term fixes of RANs and TANs. Beame knew the truth. He sold the notes and bonds to the investments syndicates. He saw the books and ledgers. He had all the private meetings with the bankers and securities brokers. He was a CPA. He had to know.

Yet on November 1, 1970, Controller Beame released his 587-page annual report for fiscal 1969-70. New York City's debt, Beame certified, was "well within its debt-incurring power" and the city's fiscal condition was "sound and healthy." On November 1, 1973, he issued another optimistic annual report, this one 556 pages long. In it, he said the city's fiscal health was continuing to improve and again praised the city's debt-incurring power and credit rating.

Beame ran for mayor in 1973 as the quiet, prudent man who "knew the buck." He knew the real facts, the real numbers, and he promised the voters a new world. But he did not level, he did not tell us the truth—that the money was running out, that cash flow was becoming a problem, that the debt was breaking our backs. Beame promised to hire 3000 new cops and put them "back on the beat." He promised to hire "Envirmaids" to "enforce the city's antipollution program and keep the streets clean." He promised expanded methadone-treatment programs. He promised to keep the City University "tuition-free." He promised on May 30, the week before the Democratic primary, not only to save the thirty-five-cent fare "but to reduce it." He promised to build industrial parks and a new convention center. He promised to freeze rents. And he promised to remove expense items from the capital budget.

He broke every promise. On June 5, the day before the primary, his campaign took out a full-page advertisement in the *Daily News*. The ad ended with this summation:

> There's going to be a 10 billion dollar budget sitting on the next Mayor's desk, and he'd better know what to do with it—fast.
>
> Believe me, I won't have to wait five seconds to know what to do with it. And you won't have to wait either. For more police protection. Better transportation. Education. To help hospital services. To fill up a few thousand potholes.
>
> Vision and leadership are beautiful words. But a city in trouble needs one thing more. Competence. A Mayor who doesn't know where the money is coming from, where it's going, and who has to rely on other people to tell him can never be his own man.
>
> That won't happen with Abe Beame.

If these words were in a stock prospectus for a public corporation, the author would be convicted of stock fraud.

June 26, 1973: a watershed day in New York City history. It is the day of the Democratic primary run-off for mayor between Abe Beame and the South Bronx Congressman Herman Badillo. The victor will certainly be the next mayor. The Republican, Liberal, and Conservative candidates have no chance to win the general election in November. And the two political forces propelling the Beame candidacy—the real-estate industry and the clubhouse system—are determined to win.

There are differences between Beame and Badillo. Badillo, remote, proud, rigid, "difficult"—is committed to the poor, especially to New York City's million Hispanic citizens. (Like Lindsay, he is a snob about white lower-middle-class problems.) He is independent of the party bosses like Esposito and Cunningham. He will not use the public payroll to subsidize the clubhouse system with patronage jobs. He will resist higher rents and zoning bonanzas for developers. He is against using taxpayers money to build a convention center. His priorities are hospitals and schools. And he is Puerto Rican.

In the frenetic last few days, money, big money, has been pouring into Beame's campaign headquarters at the Barclay Hotel. Beame has raised $857,000 for the primary, and he will get another $800,000 for the general election. Charles Bassine, the chairman of Arlen Realty, has contributed $85,000; Harry Helmsley and his partner, Irving Schneider, each donated $5000; Irving Goldman of the Shubert Theatre organization gave $5000 and made a $25,000 loan. (Goldman was later to be indicted for bribery, perjury, and tax evasion.) Albert Schwartzberg, the nursing-home builder, gave $25,000. Landlord Samuel Rudin gave $5000. Banker Abraham Feinberg loaned $25,000 and contributed $5000 under the name of "Elsmere Associates," a family trust. Bill Shea gave the campaign $30,000 and three full-time political operatives from his law firm—Bernard Ruggieri, Kevin McGrath, and Peter Smith. Nursing-home operator and slumlord Charles Sigety kicked in $1250. Anthony Scotto's longshoremen's union turned over $7500. Real-estate developers Sigmund Sommer and Sheldon Solow each wrote checks for $5000. Arnold Kagan, a stockbroker, gave $25,000 that later turned out to have been laundered through a dummy corporation in Canada and a Lichtenstein trust. And in the final week David Rockefeller, no Democrat, has contributed $5000 to stop Badillo. In the last twenty-one days, $206,312 has rolled into Beame's treasury.

We spent the day of the run-off election driving around the city, listening to John Dean testify on the car radio, watching the vote being pulled, and learning how the Democratic machine can still win an election in New York City when it feels its survival is at stake.

In Harlem clubhouse captains were distributing a flyer that said: "BADILLO IS NOT BRADLEY. BRADLEY IS HONEST." (Thomas Bradley was the newly elected black mayor of Los Angeles.) (After the election, Manhattan Borough President Percy Sutton acknowledged that *he* had ordered the 150,000 flyers printed and distributed.) In the Parkchester housing development in the Bronx, teenagers were giving out leaflets that said Badillo was a partner in the law firm of Strook, Strook and Levan. This was damaging because the law firm was at that time representing Parkchester's owner, Harry Helmsley, in an unpopular plan to convert Parkchester into a condominium. Beame had made this allegation on June 16, and Alan Strook had immediately responded that Badillo did not share in the firm's fees and had resigned as a partner three years earlier. Beame had not raised the issue again. But there was no way, no time, to refute the literature on election day in Parkchester. And the cynicism of it was that Harry Helmsley was actually a financial contributor to Beame's campaign. The chairman of the committee that circulated the leaflet was Stanley Friedman; after the election Beame appointed him deputy mayor.

In the Jewish middle-class Flatbush section of Brooklyn clubhouse workers were giving out copies of a purported newspaper called the *Brooklyn News*. This sheet contained inflammatory and false statements about Badillo, among others that he "wants Forest Hills type projects throughout the city except where he lives"—a reference to a low-income housing project which the city was building a Jewish middle-class Forest Hills, and the subject of passionate controversy at the time. It also contained an apparent reprint from the *Daily News* that implied that this paper—the one with the largest circulation in the country—endorsed Beame in the run-off. This was also false. The *Daily News* did not endorse anyone in the election, and the reprint was a fake. All this material was, moreover, unsigned, in violation of the state election law. A few days after the election, Sheldon Katz admitted responsibility for the literature. He is vice-president of CHIP, a landlord association that lobbies to end rent control, and the brother of the Flatbush city councilman, Leon Katz, who also happens to be a landlord.

Finally we visited the Bensonhurst, Canarsie, and Bay Ridge district of Brooklyn—conservative, ethnic, and regular. Here we found thousands of copies of yet another leaflet, written half in Italian, half in English. It was wholly anonymous. It had no identification, no committee, no address. Section 457 of the election law says that all campaign literature must contain the name of the "person or committee at whose instance or request such handbill, pamphlet, circular, post card, placard or letter is so printed, published, or distributed."

The anonymous appeal to fear and prejudice said:

ABE BEAME'S opponent is in favor of quotas in hiring and education.
ABE BEAME'S opponent is supported by the Black Panthers and Young Lords.

We traced the leaflet to the Ropp Press, at 4509 New Utrecht Avenue. The owner of the shop, Alan Silver, admitted he had printed the leaflet and delivered it to a Beame campaign storefront at 1722 Kings Highway. Later, campaign finance statements filed with the Board of Elections showed that Ropp Press received two payments for printing totaling $4841.75 during the week of the run-off. The treasurer of the Beame committee that made the payments was Joseph Slavin. Slavin is now a judge in Brooklyn.

At Beame's storefront headquarters at 1722 Kings Highway, we found Arthur Brasco in charge. Arthur Brasco is the brother of Meade Esposito's chauffeur and the cousin of Brooklyn Congressman Frank Brasco (since convicted of conspiring to take a bribe from a mobster). He told us that the particular piece of literature we asked about had been shipped into the "Italian districts" where kids were giving them out "for a few bucks."

Abe Beame, on this day, received 548,125 votes. Herman Badillo received 354,105 votes.

Abe Beame's life, his values, and his way of looking at the world were shaped by the two institutions that nourished his career: the Brooklyn Democratic organization and the civil service. They made him cautious, suspicious of new ideas, reactive, a believer in patronage to the party, a believer in the old ways of doing things.

He had been a methodical doorbell ringer in the Madison Club, a Democratic party stronghold in Brooklyn, and a civil servant since 1929. In 1946, Mayor O'Dwyer appointed him to be assistant budget director, a job he got through the Brooklyn organization, where by then he was an election captain for one block and knew all 900 voters on it. In 1952, Mayor Impellitteri asked the Brooklyn organization to suggest a budget director. The name that came back was Abe Beame.

From his first days in the budget bureau in 1946, Beame surrounded himself with four advisers, known among the clerks and budget examiners as "the four bishops" because they were all austere Irish Catholics: John Carty, William S. Shea, James Carroll, and James Cavanagh. When Beame became the city's 104th mayor, he made James Cavanagh his first deputy; he named John Carty's son to run the Office of Neighborhood Services; and he appointed Jim Carroll's brother John to be Municipal Services Administrator.

The civil service mentality was once summed up perfectly by Mildred Perlman, a thirty-eight-year veteran whose job is to classify New York's 3600 civil-service job titles. She explained her philosophy to a *New York Times* reporter: "You start by saying 'no' to all requests. Then if you have to go to 'yes,' that's okay. But if you start with 'yes,' you can't go to 'no.' "

As for the clubhouse mentality, that was summed up for us by Meade Esposito, the boss of Brooklyn: "Yeah, I pick every fuckin' law secretary in Brooklyn Supreme Court. I say there's nothing a matter with that. If any guy I send over to a judge turns out to be a rotten apple, I tell the judge it's okay to fire him. Only I get to pick the replacement. I keep pickin' 'em until one guy works out. That way the party keeps the job. The judge is happy. And I get the credit."

When it came time for Mayor Beame to staff the government of New York City, he relied most heavily on the civil service and the political back rooms. But he was not smart. Governor Hugh Carey would give the back rooms the harmless second- and third-level jobs, and make quality appointments for the top jobs. But Beame appointed unqualified hacks for his own staff and as commissioners.

Beame made Irving Goldman the Commissioner for Cultural Affairs. He made Michael Lazar, a councilman from Queens, the Transportation Administrator. He made Paul Screvane, a former City Council president, chairman of Off-Track Betting. He made Moses Kove, an old DeSapio crony, the chairman of the Taxi and Limousine Commission. He made Queens district leader Ralph DeMarco deputy sanitation commissioner. He made Bronx district leader Gerald Esposito deputy commissioner of Marine and Aviation. He made Stanley Friedman, the cigar-smoking caricature Bronx hack, his Albany lobbyist and then deputy mayor. He made Sam Berman the lobbyist for OTB because he was the most effective captain in the Madison Club. Beame named Cyril Regan, an ex-cop, to be the $37,500-a-year vice-president of OTB, when his only apparent qualification was that he made two separate $25,000 loans to Beame's campaign. (OTB was the only city agency to increase the number of its employees during the crisis months between December 1974, and October 1975. While 4125 policemen and 1,549 fire fighters were dismissed or lost through attrition, OTB increased the size of its payroll by 115.)

Beame appointed Abe Goodman, whose benefactor and sponsor, or "rabbi," was Stanley Steingut, to be first deputy administrator of the Economic Development Administration—at $41,541 a year. And he chose Arthur Levine, a former Bronx district leader, to be an EDA administrative manager, at $30,967. Salvatore Grieco was appointed executive director of the Council on Port Development, at $29,253; Grieco was an assemblyman from Brooklyn who had been ousted, a Democrat who had given his name to Richard Nixon's campaign committee in 1972.

So it is no miracle that jobs and businesses continued to flee New York during the Beame years. The people hired to attract and keep business in New York City were unqualified politicians with no expertise for the jobs they were given.

Even some of the civil-service veterans whom Beame appointed had unpublicized political connections. John O'Hagan, the Fire Commissioner, was sponsored by Steingut and Esposito. Ira Duchan, the Real Estate Commissioner, had good relations with the Queens organization. As Director of Labor Relations, Beame appointed John Burnell, a sixty-three-year-old incompetent, because Harry Van Arsdale asked him to. And as Budget

Director he named the inept Melvin Lechner, because Lechner was a nephew of Beame's oldest friend, Bernard Greidinger.*

And as first deputy mayor, Beame named his bishop, James Cavanagh. This is the team that would face the gravest crisis in New York City's history:

Beame lost his credibility during the first six months of the city's fiscal crisis—between November 1974 and May 1975. After that he could not lead, and could not govern, because no one believed any number he uttered. He destroyed himself. He announced lay-offs that never happened. He could never find out what the three basic numbers were: the size of New York City's total deficit, the total number of full-time city employees, or the total number of lay-offs actually made at any point in time. He relied on Cavanagh, who first treated the crisis as a game and then overcompensated and switched to advocating default. Budget Director Lechner was a comical figure whom no one took seriously, not Governor Carey, the press, the bankers, or Beame himself. And week after week, with perverse loyalty, Beame refused to fire the 5000 to 7000 clubhouse hacks on the city payroll, choosing to lay off cops, and firemen, and nurses, and teachers, rather than the dreck from the backrooms.

Why didn't Beame function better? He could have used the fiscal crisis as a personal liberation to do what had to be done. He could have acted with integrity and independence: At the age of sixty-nine, he should have been beyond blackmail or reprisal.

But he didn't. For months Mayor Beame refused to take New York City's crisis seriously. He had cried wolf so many times that he could not believe the real monster had appeared. He refused to admit the debt, because he took all criticism personally—and Beame's ego is more tender than most politicians'. He reacted in almost Nixonesque ways; he became bitter, stubborn, resentful, determined to survive while repressing the cause of his problem, covering up his past mistakes with public relations.

Beame could not do what had to be done because he believed in the system, the same system that had created both him and the crisis. Like Mrs. Perlman, Beame was conditioned to say no first, and then wait, and delay, and hope the problems would solve themselves or go away. But New York's new problems, building up for almost fifteen years, could not be solved by the automatic no. The historical moment required a heroic leader—a young Al Smith, a La Guardia, a Lehman, a leader of imagination and political independence, a

---

*Lechner's incompetence was so powerfully apparent that he became a semipublic joke during the city's fiscal crisis, and he was forced to quit as Budget Director in January 1976. In August he was awarded $57,360 in city pension-fund consulting contracts. The job was pure patronage since almost all of the pension-fund money was being invested in city bonds. And Controller Goldin, who opposed the contract, said that an established pension consulting company, Dreher, Rogers & Associates, had offered to perform the same services for less than one-fourth the fee.

leader who was tough and smart and truthful, and who had a sense of justice and reality. This was not Abe Beame.

The tragedy was that Beame's abdication was the justification for the bankers' taking over. The bankers did not exactly seize power; there was a vacuum, and they rushed to fill it. Wriston and Rockefeller and Rohatyn used New York City's fiscal crisis as a cover to do what the bankers wanted—kill free tuition, freeze wages, raise the subway fare, end self-government in New York City. If Beame had been competent and credible, the usurpation of power could have been averted.

But it was difficult for reasonable people to oppose the creation of MAC, and later EFCB, because Beame was not functioning. His personal default of leadership allowed the permanent government to arrange a coup that looked like salvation. The banks and investment houses and securities brokers acted out of self-interest. Beame did not.

On July 1, 1974, the Beame administration implemented its budget for the 1974-75 fiscal year. More than $700 million's worth of expense items like textbooks and salaries were smuggled into the capital budget. A new agency, the Reserve Stabilization Corporation, was created to borrow $520 million. Another $280 million was raised by borrowing from union pension funds and changing the dates of collection of sewer taxes. The budget was balanced by predicting a decrease in the number of welfare recipients—pure fantasy, given the rising rate of unemployment.

Then, in October, Controller Goldin warned that unless the city reduced its short-term borrowing, its real-estate tax would have to be increased by 45 per cent over the next six years. But at that point, Beame was at the peak of his authority. He had just purged Matthew Troy as Democratic leader of Queens and replaced him with Donald Manes. Newspapers were printing generally favorable assessments of his first nine months in office. So Beame mocked Goldin's math, and said: "There is absolutely no question about the city's ability to repay all of its debts on time."

On November 30, Goldin sent a letter to Beame saying that the deficit accumulating in shortfalls and spending overruns in the current year's expense budget was $650 million. The mayor was in Florida when this hit the front page of *The New York Times*, so Deputy Mayor Cavanagh put out a rejoinder that rejected Goldin's figures as "inaccurate." Beame had said three weeks earlier that the deficit was $430 million. Goldin, however, when asked by reporters, refused to designate a single specific area where he thought spending cuts could be made. In a public relations thrust, Beame's budget bureau said that the city had made dramatic gains in productivity, including the repair of 862,000 potholes and the collection of 9.95 tons of refuse for each sanitation-truck shift. The data seemed dubious to anyone who had to drive over the city's streets or who saw the garbage on the sidewalks of the Lower East Side.

By January 1975, the sense of crisis was strong, and Mayor Beame had announced, at various times, that 5000 city employees had been dismissed. But each time reporters checked, the number of layoffs was inflated. Beame was firing ghosts who had already resigned, or retired, or died, or were only part-time or seasonal employees. At the time, one of Beame's close advisers told us: "It's not Abe's fault. The commissioners and the budget bureau are sending him rubber numbers. How can he go out and check every name personally?"

By February 12,000 city employees were supposed to have been dismissed. But a check by *The New York Times* revealed that only 1700 real, full-time bodies had been let go. The city was switching people from one budget line to another, and counting each move as a layoff. Commissioners would add up all the unfilled budget lines in their agency and count them all as layoffs. Five months later, on July 23, Beame acknowledged that he could not tell, even then, exactly how many full-time city employees had actually been purged from the payroll. Budget Director Lechner said he thought it might be 13,500 but he could not be sure. It was probably about 6000.

Meanwhile the City Club of New York was saying that Beame had at least 5000 useless "clubhouse patronage" employees on the payroll at a cost of $100 million a year. But Beame said there were none who were not necessary. Joel Hartnett, chairman of the City Club, claimed at least 5000 3-by-5 index cards with the names of all the city's patronage appointees could be found in the desk of Beame's assistant, Thomas Roche. But Roche said no such file existed. Most reporters knew, though, that the backroom dreck *was* buried in the Office of Neighborhood Services, in EPA, in the Taxi and Limousine Commission, in OTB, in the Transporation Administration, in the Economic Development Administration (where sixteen of the twenty highest-paid people got their jobs through politicians), and in the Parks Department.

By June default was a fearsome specter. The city's paper was unmarketable. Investors confidence was long gone. Beame kept insisting that the budget deficit was now only $641 million, when it was actually $3.3 billion. One night, continuing to dwell in his cocoon of fantasy, he attended the annual Catholic Interracial Council Dinner at the Americana Hotel, with 2000 people filling the grand ballroom, where he paid tribute to the guest of honor, former Mayor Wagner calling him "one of the greatest Mayors the city of New York ever had." Wagner then got up, looked at Abe Beame, and said, "I'm sure *he's* going to be the best Mayor the city ever had."

One night also in June, Peter Grace, president of W. R. Grace & Co. and an old friend of the mayor's, came to see him. Grace was also a member of the board of directors of Citibank. Grace came armed with a long confidential report about the city's fiscal crisis prepared for Citibank's directors.

Grace told the mayor precisely how grave the crisis was and said that *he* must act decisively to admit a specific deficit, make a plan to reduce it, and stick to it.

On Thursday, July 10, Beame involved the regular City Hall reporters into his office to tell them the city's fiscal agony was "reasonably behind us now. . . . I think we've gotten over the major problem." He told the cluster of incredulous journalists that the only problem the city ever had "was cash flow. . . . There wasn't a crisis, only a problem."

Then why had the mayor called his budget a "crisis budget?"

"You got me on that," the mayor replied with a giggle. "We couldn't think of a better word."

During July, members of the governor's staff and members of MAC were telling reporters off the record that, based on their observations in closed meetings, they thought Beame was "cracking up," that he was a "basket case," a "zombie." The money men from Citibank, Chase, Morgan, and Lazard Frères began talking about a method actually to remove Beame from office. But they eventually realized that Beame's legal successor would be Council President O'Dwyer, and O'Dwyer did not understand the most primitive economics and had almost no one's confidence as a substitute leader for the city. So the bankers decided their strategy would be to take Beame's bishop—James Cavanagh*—and then impose a management structure that would remove Beame from all control over the city's finances. At the time, a member of MAC said to us: "We were close to trying to remove Beame. We backed off because we were afraid it would be perceived as anti-democratic. And because O'Dwyer is so bad. This city has no elected leader worth a damn."

By this point, July 1975, large forces, inexorable forces, were exerting the accumulated pressures of history.

The flow of jobs and capital to the Southwest, to the Sunbelt, had drained the economic strength of all the old cities of the Northeast. Years of Richard Nixon's anticity policies had cut New York off from a vital source of funds. The national problems of unemployment and inflation had hit New York especially hard; the city was suffering an inflationary rate of 15 per cent per year. The state government was broke and could not help. And the city, in the minds of Arthur Burns and William Simon, had to be punished. Burns and Simon saw New York City as a guinea pig, whose death in an ideological test tube would

---

*On Friday, September 13, 1975, Kenneth Axelson, the sixty-three-year-old vice-president of J. C. Penney, was appointed to replace Cavanagh as deputy mayor in control of the budget. On Friday, November 15, Cavanagh was forced to resign completely. He had worked with Beame for thirty-seven years.

prove, scientifically, that liberalism is a failure. And even the vice-president of the nation, Nelson Rockefeller, was trying to plunge the knife in. Rockefeller was telling anyone who would listen that free tuition and the thirty-five-cent subway fare were luxuries the citizens of New York could no longer afford.

New York was defenseless, ganged up on, at the mercy of external policies and people. It was too late for Beame to do anything. The game was up. The years of mistakes and waste had placed the powerless city at the disposal of Burns and Simon, who thought, for a while, they would fatten their reputations by making New York an example of profligacy, of excess humanism, to the rest of the country. Beame, overwhelmed by history, could do nothing.

Finally, on Friday night, August 29, Governor Carey, Controller Goldin, state Comptroller Levitt, and Felix Rohatyn forced Beame to admit that New York City's deficit was, in fact, not $430 million as Beame had said in November, not $641 million as he had insisted in June, but *$3.3 billion*. The man who was elected on the slogan, "If you don't know the buck, you don't know the job," was no longer the real mayor of New York City.

A campaign ad for Beame had said: "A Mayor who doesn't know where the money is coming from, where it's going, and who has to rely on other people to tell him, can never be his own man. That won't happen with Abe Beame." This language would seem a good description of Beame's relationship to the new Emergency Financial Control Board imposed on the city in September 1975.

There is a temptation to feel sorry for Abe Beame. He has an impossible job. He's small. He's shy. He's inarticulate. He's old. It's not all his fault. He has suffered humiliation.

But we resist the temptation. Beame made conscious decisions, and like all of us he is responsible for his actions. His campaign promises had no relation to reality. He misled us, all those years, when he said that New York City's fiscal health was excellent. He refused to fire the clubhouse hacks and continued to service the backrooms all through the fiscal crisis. He faked layoffs. He falsely certified to investors that the city's revenues matched expenditures. These things cost New Yorkers their self-government.

The Bankers Take

Over

7

> Power always thinks it has a great soul and vast views beyond the comprehension of the weak, and that it is doing God's service when it is violating all His Laws.
>
> —JOHN ADAMS

In June 1975 the Municipal Assistance Corporation was created, and in September the Emergency Financial Control Board was put in place, and between them was a revolution in the governance of New York City.

Democracy has been a fragile membrane in New York. Boss Tweed, Robert Moses, and the Rockefellers always had more say than the rest of us. But throughout the history of the city and state, there had been occasional elected politicans of serious egalitarian views, and they served as a countervailing weight on the side of democracy: John Purroy Mitchell, mayor from 1914 to 1917; Fiorello La Guardia, mayor from 1933 to 1945; Governors Alfred E. Smith, Franklin D. Roosevelt, and Herbert Lehman; Senators Robert Wagner and Robert Kennedy; and the gadfly Republican City Councilman Stanley Isaacs.

And throughout the history of New York, there had been moral catalysts for change who worked outside the structure of government. The journalist Jacob Riis, who described the immigrant poverty of the Lower East Side in the 1880s. The Reverend Charles Parkhurst, who preached against Tammany's Boss Croker in the 1890s. C. C. Burlingham, a lawyer, and Lincoln Steffens, a muckraker who inspired reform groups early in this century. And Rabbi Stephen Wise of the Free Synagogue, and John Haynes Holmes of the Community Church, who were activists for equality during the 1920s. And Judge Samuel Seabury, who harnessed his great legal mind to a sense of outrage, to conduct the investigations that ended the corrupt reign of Mayor James Walker in 1932. And then, for a time, during the late 1950s and early 1960s, two elderly private citizens—Eleanor Roosevelt and Herbert Lehman—were generally respected as custodians of democracy and honesty.

But in the summer of 1975, there was no citizen in New York City who could fill this role: No Steffens wrote, no Rabbi Wise spoke, no Seabury thought to say that self-government was threatened. In retrospect, perhaps this vacancy should have been recognized as a symptom of the city's decline, of what was missing from the chemistry of democracy.

The coup that looked like salvation transformed New York City's representative form of government. The theoretical repositories of the people's will—the mayor, the Board of Estimate, the elected legislators—lost much of their authority, which shifted decisively away from the elected mayor and the Board of Estimate, to the bankers and businessmen who dominated MAC and EFCB. Decision-making shifted from the semi-public forum of the Board of Estimate to an endless round of private meetings in boardrooms, summer homes, and law offices.

The concept, structure, and powers of the Municipal Assistance Corporation was worked out, according to most accounts, in a meeting held on May 26 (Memorial Day), 1975, at the Greenwich, Connecticut, home of Richard Shinn, president of the $33-billion Metropolitan Life Insurance Company. The participants included investment banker Felix Rohatyn, and several commercial bankers, including Frank Smeal, the municipal bond expert at Morgan Guaranty Trust. There is no transcript, no minutes are available of this informal meeting that changed the history of New York City.

The concept, structure, and powers of the EFCB were worked out, according to most accounts, over a breakfast of sausage, eggs, and pastry, on August 20, 1975, in the office of William Ellinghaus, the president of the New York Telephone Company and at that point chairman of MAC. Those attending this private breakfast meeting, besides Ellinghaus, included: commercial bankers William Butcher of Chase Manhattan; Walter Page of Morgan Guaranty Trust; and Edward Palmer of Citibank; Lazard's Felix Rohatyn; and Governor Hugh Carey, the only elected official in the room.*

Of the nine original members of MAC, five were picked by the governor, four by the mayor. MAC's responsibility was to convert $3 billion in short-term debt to long-term bonds. It was also empowered to audit New York City's budget for ten years, and had access to all the city's ledgers and records. It failed of its main original purpose—to market the city's bonds—and thus the creation of the EFCB was required after only three months. The much greater powers of the Control Board included: eliminating the debt, balancing the

---

*The creation of both MAC and EFCB were approved by the City Council and state legislature. Only one of forty-three council members voted against the creation of MAC—conservative Bronx Democrat Michael DeMarco, who said, "This bill will come back to haunt us." On September 5, Councilwoman Miriam Friedlander of the Lower East Side cast the lone negative vote against the creation of the EFCB. She said: "With each new plan we become a city more concerned with figures and less and less with people. . . ."

budget by 1978, the authority to review all city revenue and expenditure estimates and to monitor the budget, and authority to overrule municipal union contracts freely negotiated at the bargaining table.†

Of the nine original members of MAC, eight had banking or brokerage connections. The nine were:

- Felix Rohatyn: 47, a partner in the global investment banking firm of Lazard Frères, and a director of six corporations, including ITT, Engelhard Minerals, and Pfizer. He later became the chairman of MAC and at the same time a member of the Emergency Financial Control Board. As an investment banker, Rohatyn had arranged mergers or acquisitions for Gulf & Western and Loew's Corporation, had married Kinney to Warner Brothers and Lockheed to Textron, and had received underwriting fees for ten corporate take-overs by ITT. In 1970, he had been chairman of the special crisis committee of the New York Stock Exchange to prevent bankruptcies by brokerage companies. Rohatyn's nickname, "Felix the Fixer," awarded him by the columnist Nicholas Von Hoffman, was given him when it was revealed that he had met privately several times with John Mitchell and Richard Kleindienst in 1971 and argued, successfully, that the Justice Department reverse itself and drop its antitrust suits against ITT. Later the Senate Judiciary Committee asked Rohatyn what he was doing, going over the head of the antitrust division and having private meetings about ITT with two attorney generals of the United States. "I was trying to make an economic case, sir, of hardship," Rohatyn told Senator Philip Hart, about a conglomerate with $12 billion in annual sales; 400,000 employees; and operations in ninety separate nations.

- Simon Rifkind: This brilliant corporate lawyer was born in Russia and came to New York at the age of nine as part of the great immigrant stream of 1910. A former federal judge, Rifkind was also a director of the Sterling National Bank.

- Robert Weaver: Lyndon Johnson's Secretary of Housing and Urban Development, a director of the Bowery Savings Bank and Metropolitan Life Insurance, he proved to be a passive, acquiescing member of the new governing agency.

- Donna Shalala: A professor of political science at Teachers College of Columbia, she emerged as the most independent-minded and skeptical member of MAC and the only original member without a personal banking or brokerage interest.

†On October 7, 1975, the Control Board rejected the contract which the city's 55,000-member teachers union had negotiated with the Board of Education, arguing that it was too costly. The contract had ended a five-day teachers' strike. The contract was finally approved in December of 1976.

- Thomas Flynn: A partner (now retired) in Arthur Young and Company, the accounting firm; director of the Household Finance Corporation; trustee of the American Savings Bank, he was MAC's first chairman but was purged after five weeks. Flynn's fall offers an early example of Rohatyn's influence on MAC and his great gifts at palace-guard manipulation. Flynn annoyed Rohatyn at the July 14 meeting of the MAC board by warning the group that it should not usurp the democratic prerogatives of the elected city administration. Rohatyn made no direct response (although later during the meeting he chided Flynn about being indiscreet in his conversations with Mayor Beame's people, telling them of plans not approved by the MAC board or staff), but within a few days, he had used his unlimited access to Governor Carey to suggest that Flynn was a nice fellow but just not up to the tough task of being MAC's chairman. Rohatyn proposed the harder, blunter Ellinghaus as a substitute.

Rumors immediately began to circulate around town that Flynn was being eased out, and they were printed in the July 20 editions of the *Times* and *News*. But nobody had bothered to inform Flynn. Flynn told inquiring reporters on July 20: "I am still chairman. The stories come as a complete surprise to me. . . . I have been assured that there is no present change in the MAC board chairmanship being contemplated."

Flynn was allowed to twist slowly in the wind for forty-eight hours. On Tuesday, July 22, Governor Carey finally announced that Ellinghaus would replace him as chairman of MAC. From that point on the insiders respected—and slightly feared—Rohatyn.

- William Ellinghaus: In addition to being president of New York Telephone and chairman of MAC for six months, he was also a director of the Bankers Trust Corporation, a trustee of the Union Dime Savings Bank, chairman of the Regional Plan Association, a trustee of the New York Racing Association, and a director of J. C. Penney. Ellinghaus was a powerful force until January 1976, when he was named vice-chairman and director of the national American Telephone and Telegraph, possible apprenticeship for the board chairmanship held by John D. deButts. After that he was still influential, but his attention was divided.
- John Coleman: senior partner in Adler, Coleman & Company, a stock brokerage house; former board chairman of the New York Stock Exchange, and for many years a significant influence, behind the scenes, in the New York Archiocese of the Roman Catholic Church. Coleman, seventy-three years old, was not in the best of health and did not become a full participant in the new structures of government. In January of 1977, Coleman would be replaced by his son, Thomas, also a partner in the brokerage firm of Alder, Coleman & Company.

- Francis Barry: the likeable president of Circle Line Sightseeing Boats; president of Campbell & Gardiner, a brokerage firm; chairman of the city's Council on Port Promotion and Development; and a valued fund raiser for the Bronx Democratic organization. He hardly spoke at MAC meetings.
- George Gould: chairman of Donaldson, Lufkin, Jenerette Securities, who in June 1976 had become president of the Madison Fund, a closed-end investment trust; in a disclosure statement filed in August, he listed: "working interests in some twenty oil and gas wells"; an "unsecured note" with Citibank; a "revolving letter of credit" with Citibank; and common stock in sixty-three companies.

Later, when Rifkind and Ellinghaus resigned from MAC, two new members were appointed: Richard Netzer, dean of the Graduate School of Public Administration at NYU; and George Brooker, principle stockholder of Webb & Brooker, a real-estate management and consultant company. Brooker, who is black, is also a trustee of the New York Bank for Savings and a director of the Real Estate Board of New York.

The members of New York City's Emergency Finance Control Board included Governor Carey, Mayor Beame, state Comptroller Levitt, city Controller Goldin, and three business members—Rohatyn, Ellinghaus, and David Margolis, the $364,000-a-year president of Colt Industries. Margolis is a former assistant to the president of ITT, where he met Rohatyn, and he says that Rohatyn was "instrumental" in getting him onto the Control Board.

Not on any of the public boards, but powerful factors in private, were the top executives of the three largest commercial banks—Citibank, Chase, and Morgan; and the chief officers of investment banking houses like Salomon Brothers and Lehman Brothers, and of securities brokerage houses like Merrill Lynch. And Metropolitan Life's Richard Shinn, who helped Rohatyn devise this new super structure and is chairman of the Mayor's Management Advisory Board, acts as a bridge to the commercial bankers and the more conservative elements of the business community. (Shinn is also a director of Chase Manhattan.)

The most striking deficiency of this whole structure is that it is so unrepresentative. The memberships were negotiated and screened by bankers, whose primary concern was the bond market. At an early point, the labor lawyer and mediator Theodore Kheel, a man of moderate liberal views, was blackballed from membership on MAC by the bankers, because of his years of perfectly sound criticism of the Port Authority. There is no labor-union representative on either board; Jack Bigel attends EFCB meetings with booming voice but no vote. There is no Hispanic representative on either board. The blacks who are present do not speak for, and are not in contact with, the propertyless black masses of New York City. There is no participant who clearly identifies with the point of view of the small homeowner, who has mortgage payments to make, and is worried about his job at the plant, and how he is ever going to finance three kids through college. There is no resident of either Brooklyn or Queens, the city's most populous boroughs, where most of the city's ethnic lower middle class eke out an alienated existence. There is no neighborhood activist on either new agency, no one who feels the importance of neighborhoods to the fabric of the city and to the psychology of its people. There is no one on either board who is an advocate for the city's badly organized 1.5 million tenants living under rent control. There is no one so poor as to need the use of a day-care center, or a municipal hospital. These new decision-makers are psychologically removed from the way ordinary people live in New York.

New York City's sovereignty, home rule, was lost, not to a pluralistic coalition government, which might have been acceptable under the emergency circumstances of possible default and unremitting federal hostility, but to a group dominated by one economic interest, one economic class, with scarce comprehension of common life in the city beyond Manhattan.

The banks, and those with banking connections, were parties at interest. Even after they had dumped city paper, the banks together held $1.2 billion of New York's paper debt and an additional $1.1 billion in MAC securities. They held billions more in the securities of other wounded cities. They were not about to consider a twenty-five-year or thirty-year debt repayment plan to save New York (although this is exactly what they were considering for the shaky loans they had made to foreign governments). They were not about even to place such an idea on an agenda they controlled.

At the time, a few voices were heard in dissent, raising questions about constitutionality, about democratic process, about priorities. Notable among the dissenters were New York members of Congress, Bella Abzug, Edward Koch, and Herman Badillo. But they were merely elected officials—and thus were patronized as outsiders in the crisis rush to judgment.

It is difficult now to reconstruct the exact decision-making process as it evolved during the summer and fall of 1975. It was meant to be secret. Much of the basic conceptual and strategic work was done ad hoc, on Long Island, where Carey owned a summer home on Shelter Island and Rohatyn rented a summer residence twenty minutes away in Wainscott. Having more information about a subject than anyone else is one form of power, and Rohatyn knew more and had more ideas than anyone else about how to finance a rescue of New York City. So Rohatyn and Carey were at the center of the wheel.

Separate spokes extended out to the banks; to Jack Bigel and the municipal labor unions; to Warren Anderson, the fair-minded but conservative Republican leader in the state Senate; to sympathetic reporters and editors whom Rohatyn briefed privately; and to the hostile forces in Washington—Treasury Secretary William Simon, and Arthur Burns, chairman of the Federal Reserve Board. The mayor of New York was kept informed as a diplomatic courtesy. The only person Rohatyn seemed to consult at all was his legendary seventy-seven-year-old mentor, André Meyer, chairman of Lazard Frères and one of the international finance masters of merger, acquisition, and arbitrage.

The formal meetings of MAC—there would be eleven in one thirty-one-day period—were closed to the media and to the general public. But minutes were taken, and after the participants had an opportunity to edit or modify any indiscretions, they were approved and are now available for inspection in bound volumes in the MAC offices on the 45th floor of the World Trade Center.

The minutes of one MAC board meeting are especially instructive to a student of the new power arrangements, that of Thursday, July 17, 1975, held at 345 Park Avenue, where Simon Rifkind has his law office. The minutes show that the entire leadership of the banking and bond-underwriting community were invited to this meeting: David Rockefeller, chairman of Chase, and his 39-year-old executive vice-president and bond expert Thomas Labrecque; Ellmore Patterson, the chairman of Morgan, and his bond advisor, Frank Smeal; William Spencer, president of Citibank and vice-regent of the boss banker, Walter Wriston; Donald Regan, chairman of the nation's biggest brokerage house, Merrill Lynch, and William Salomon of Salomon Brothers.

While these bankers met with MAC directors and staff, including the new executive director, Herbert Elish, three people were waiting, impatiently, uncomfortably, in a reception room in another part of Rifkind's law office. Waiting their turn, like petitioners, were Mayor Beame, Deputy Mayor Cavanagh, and Controller Goldin. Governor Carey sent his budget director, but did not attend himself, because at this point, for the political appearance of things, he did not want to be perceived as a responsible participant in the high-risk situation. Carey's undercover phase was to end a month later, when the bankers, who respected his intelligence and political adroitness, insisted he become a full, open participant, to help restore "investor confidence."

At the July 17 MAC meeting the bankers applied their muscle. According to the official minutes:

Mr. Rockefeller, acting as spokesman for the group . . . said that there exists a perception on the part of the investors that the city is continuing on a "business as usual" basis. He said that the investors do not feel that the state is helping to develop a total plan, but rather is approaching the problem on a piecemeal basis. There is a crying need for a credible fiscal plan in order to support any further financing. . . . He stated that in the judgment of the underwriters there are two basic requirements that are needed. First, there should be an immediate, dramatic, credible, highly visible program of fiscal control supported and backed by the governor, the state legislature, and the city administration. In addition, he said that a visible monitoring program by the corporation is also required.

The minutes show that Ellmore Patterson then emphasized that it was "vitally important that the corporation [MAC] take the leadership with the full backing of the legislature."

Rohatyn asked the assembled group whether "any action by the Mayor at this time would have a positive effect." The minutes read at this point, "They all expressed an opinion that any such action would be viewed as having no credibility."

So here were David Rockefeller, William Ellinghaus, William Spencer and the rest saying there was nothing—no act, no gesture—that the elected mayor of the city, sitting then just outside the room, could do; that he was totally irrelevant.

The bankers left, and then Beame, Cavanagh, and Goldin joined the meeting. At this point Beame did not have it in him to stand up to the demands of the bankers. For a few weeks he had blamed the banks for all of New York's troubles, just as at various other times he had blamed Lindsay, Goldin, the media, the state, and the president. He never made a coherent analysis in his own mind of what went wrong and when, although to his credit he never tried to make the welfare population a scapegoat. And just as Beame was essentially a party hack rather than a party boss, he was, in self-image and temperament, a bank employee rather than an important elected official who could talk to bankers as social equals. (Beame, had, in fact, worked for American Bank and Trust for three years, after he lost the campaign for mayor in 1965.) So he was not about to look David Rockefeller in the eye and tell him his historic and moral obligation to the city he had helped to bankrupt.

After Beame came into the room, Thomas Flynn began to summarize what the bankers had said a few minutes before. Beame said he agreed that "dramatic action should be taken." According to the minutes, "Mayor Beame said he was willing to consider a wage freeze and across-the-board service cuts." This, remember, was just seven days after Beame had invited the regular City Hall reporters into his office to tell them that the fiscal crisis was "behind us."

But a wage freeze for the city's workers and service cuts for the city's residents was not enough. Rohatyn, then, for the first time, raised the idea of ending free tuition at the City University and put on the table an increase in the transit fare. He said, according to the minutes: "An over-kill was required, if for no other reason than the shock impact. . . . The possibility of revenue increases such as fare increases and tuition increases should be examined. . . . It was apparent from what the banking community had said that the city's way of life is disliked nation-wide."

Rohatyn had graduated from Middlebury College in Vermont, but Beame had graduated from City College. The minutes read: "Mayor Beame pointed out that a doubling of fees at the City University would only produce $34 million . . . and that 71 per cent of the students come from families with an income of less than $14,000."

Everything the commercial bankers and Rohatyn discussed at this meeting happened within a year. The austerity agenda was set by the unelected men of privilege and property: a wage freeze for city workers, service cuts, more layoffs, a higher transit fare, and the end of free tuition at the City University of New York.

The minutes show no discussion of alternative ways of bringing the budget closer to balance, ways that would not fall so disproportionately upon poor and middle-class families. MAC never discussed the possibility of asking the banks, which had made pushers' profits all those years while New York became addicted to borrowing, to forgive the interest or accept a restructuring of the debt (a stretch-out of the debt payments to twenty-five or thirty years, say). No one argued that Beame must fire all the clubhouse hacks on the city payroll. No one suggested breaking the twenty-year leases that the Lindsay administration had given, without competitive bidding, to a few favored landlords. There was no mention of the unpaid real-estate taxes which landlords like Irving Maidman and Sol Goldman owed the city. No one suggested raising the taxes on Consolidated Edison, a monopoly that had nowhere to move and had been bailed out by the state with a $500-million sale and leaseback deal in 1974. No one urged de-politicizing the Tax Commission so that reduced real-estate assessments for "hardship" were no longer awarded to Prudential Insurance, Con Edison, Chemical Bank, Rockefeller Center, and New York Telephone. No one asked for an audit of all the Medicaid mills that were ripping off millions of dollars every year.

Yes, the pressures for symbolic, gross economies originated with Ford, Simon, Rockefeller and Burns in Washington. Yes, the senators and congressmen of the Sunbelt did not care much about New York City. Yes, most of the economic indices showed that New York City was anemic: Unemployment was high, retail sales were down, housing starts were down, the city was still hemorrhaging jobs and capital. And yes, a wage freeze and some layoffs were necessary.

But "across-the-board service cuts" were not. Thoughtful, selective, pinpointed layoffs could have preserved the life-support services of fire, health, and police. The thirty-five-cent subway fare and free tuition could have been saved—if there had been just two or three informed advocates for alternative ways to increase revenues (for instance, collecting unpaid taxes) or to reduce expenditures (for instance, stretching out debt-service payments to the banks, which were 17 per cent of New York's total budget). And if equivalent sacrifices had been made by the banks and bond underwriters, the budget reductions that so deeply affected ordinary New Yorkers might have seemed fair.

But the great financial institutions would make no sacrifice during the crisis at all. They gave up nothing, not one per cent on their interest. They designed and controlled the new machinery of government, and their only function was to maximize profits. David Rockefeller has given a thousand high-minded speeches about the social responsibility of banks, about how Chase was "a good corporate citizen." But on July 17, 1975, all he cared about was his bank's bond portfolio, his bank's balance sheet, his bank's real-estate investment trusts.

Rohatyn's "over-kill," and the "service cuts" insisted upon at this meeting by bankers who did not know the city or have need of its services, in a few months had devastating consequences upon other people's lives. People bled to death in the emergency room of Lincoln Hospital in the Bronx for want of plasma, a nurse, an empty bed. Wood-frame houses burned to the ground because eight firehouses were closed. Twenty-eight day-care centers closed, displacing 1800 children of working parents. A new school—I.S. 390 in Crown Heights—was 80 per cent completed, but construction stopped. Eleven eye clinics treating 10,000 children closed down. Coney Island Hospital closed four of its seven operating rooms. Garbage collection on the Lower East Side dropped from six times a week to three. The Child Health Station on DeKalb Avenue, in the Fort Greene neighborhood of Brooklyn, shut its doors. The 70th police precinct in Brooklyn lost one-quarter of its force. Honest cops, cops young enough to run up four flights of stairs and catch a mugger or a purse snatcher, were the ones to lose their jobs. And because the budget cuts were simplisticly conceived to be made across the board, they ensured the layoffs of unskilled hospital workers, day-care counselors, school para-professionals— the last hired, the lowest paid.

The minutes indicate that the MAC meeting of July 17 ended with a short seminar on open government.

Some discussion took place regarding what should be said to the press upon adjournment of the meeting. Mr. Rohatyn strongly expressed his view that there should be no expression of optimism in the light of the gravity of the situation. Mr. Goldmark [state Budget Director Peter Goldmark] felt that the two points that should be made with the press would be a recognition on the part of all parties of the gravity of the situation and that everyone is going to work for a satisfactory solution. He advised that there should be no attempt to answer questions from the press.

Let us examine two specific decisions made by the city's newly appointed managers—to raise the transit fare to fifty cents, and to eliminate free tuition at the City University.

Formally, the decision to raise the fare on busses and subways by 43 per cent, without even a public hearing, was made by the eleven appointed members of the Metropolitan Transportation Authority in August 1975. These loyal captains of the permanent government included: chairman David Yunich; Eben Pyne; Harold Fisher; and Donald Elliot.

But the MTA was merely the visible vehicle, and scapegoat, for a decision reached at an even higher and less accountable level. The Four Horsemen of Hostility—Ford, Rockefeller, Simon, and Burns—were certainly pressuring the city very hard to raise the fare. Walter Wriston and David Rockefeller also advocated an increase. And, as we have seen, at the July 17 MAC meeting Rohatyn had suggested it. By the next day, the MAC staff and state Budget Director Goldmark had prepared a lengthy memorandum reporting that a 5-cent fare increase would produce $54 million in new revenue; a 10-cent increase would yield $102 million; and a 15-cent increase would generate $147 million. Within three weeks the decision was officially made by the MTA that a fifteen-cent fare increase would go into effect on September 1.

Immediately, many of the elected leaders of New York City objected—and demonstrated their futility by holding rallies, press conferences, and making speeches. A press conference at Grand Central Station was called by twelve legislators to demand passage of a "broad-based regional payroll tax" to raise the revenue necessary to freeze the fare at 35 cents. Wandering around Grand Central, trying to get interviewed by television news crews, Congresswoman Abzug, Congressman Koch, Borough President Abrams, Assemblyman Oliver Kopell, and state Senator Franz Leichter resembled frustrated student protestors of the 1960s trying to get attention for a cause, more than elected lawmakers in a democracy.

On August 19, City Councilman Henry Stern, the only elected Liberal Party legislator in the city, had summarized the reasons against raising the fare in a generally ignored press release.

> Even if the MTA were committed to a policy of soaking the poor and making transit pay for itself at the fare box, this increase would be unproductive, because it will simply lead to reduced use. The only people who should applaud this increase are the taxi industry, because only they will gain from it. . . .
> This 43 per cent increase is an imposition on the working poor and middle class. It will lead to increased traffic congestion and air pollution, it will weaken the central business district, and discourage shopping, theatres, and social visiting. . . . The MTA policy seems to be simply the futile pursuit of spiraling expenditures. . . .
> Another factor to consider is the relative lack of success of the MTA's cost-cutting efforts. There is an air of futility and unreality that surrounds the Authority in these matters. The MTA was created, in part, to avoid waste and bureaucracy said to characterize city agencies. Yet it has grown in size and expenditures, and is now immune from the constraints which necessity has imposed on city agencies.

It rather quickly became apparent that the disenfranchised critics were right. Ridership declined and the taxi industry flourished. Midtown retail merchants complained that business was off. The MTA's bloated budget and bureaucracy remained uncut. And after a year, the fare increase had produced "about $50 million in revenue," according to MAC's executive director Herbert Elish, not the $147 million projected in the staff memorandum of July 18, 1975. Elish acknowledged to us that raising the fare to 50 cents, "with hindsight, on balance, was probably a mistake."

In August 1975 we interviewed Donna Shalala, a member of MAC. She candidly agreed that the decision to increase the fare by 15 cents "was a mistake," and she characterized the decision-making process as "irrational and uninformed."

There was tremendous pressure [Ms. Shalala recalled] to get the Mayor to do something. The people on MAC who kew the [money] market, told us that a symbolic act for investors was necessary. They thought raising the fare was the symbolic act that was necessary, and something we could get the Mayor to do. . . .

The process wasn't that rational. There was possibly a half hour of discussion about raising the fare, that's all. There was never a set of staff papers prepared, so we could study it. We did no background work. We had no hard facts. That's the horror of it. We were just throwing together a list of things that might be cut. There was no conspiracy to screw the people. Beame had his budget director, Melvin Lechner, in the meetings. It was just something decided in a half hour. . . .

We were told this decision would open up the market. Now we know there was nothing, nothing, we could have done to open the market. I should have stuck to my guns and opposed the fare increase. I'm sorry we misled the public that the money markets would open.

When pressed on who was at the center of the decision-making process, Ms. Shalala responded, "Even though I'm a member of MAC, I was only on the fringes of things. There were a lot of private meetings going on all the time, with Carey, Rohatyn, Ellinghaus, various bankers, and Shinn. You have to remember it was a crisis, and things were happening very fast, and Felix can be very intimidating. But I can't really say for sure who is most responsible. I'm not even clear on how it came to be a fifteen-cent increase, rather than five cents or ten cents."

When we asked Rohatyn about the paternity of the fifty-cent fare, he replied: "It was mostly Beame, as I recall." When we asked Beame, through his public-relations adviser Howard Rubenstein, the mayor's recollection in August 1976 was: "It was Washington's idea."*

Free tuition for public higher education is an almost sacred tradition in New York. The Free Academy was created by a referendum of the voters in 1847. One hundred and twenty-nine years later the City University consisted of

---

*On November 19, 1976, state Comptroller Arthur Levitt released an audit that disclosed that MTA had concealed $58 million that should have been used to keep mass transit fares down. The $58 million was earned as interest on the investment of tolls from the Triborough Bridge and Tunnel Authority, an MTA subsidiary. The Levitt audit said: "The MTA has not used these TBTA surplus funds for fare maintenance or operating equipments as appears to be required by law."

275,000 students, twenty-one colleges (including eight two-year community colleges) and a graduate center. It includes the apparently inevitable excesses of high faculty salaries, mansions for college presidents, luxuries for a few bureaucrats, a proliferation of administrators, middle management, and consultants, generous welfare and pension benefits, and an over-ambitious construction program. But the quality of education is superior (in contrast, say, to the low quality of health care in municipal hospitals). And free higher education for the "worthy poor" had been a visa into the middle class for the Irish, the Jews, the Italians, and every other immigrant group that came to "the land of opportunity."

The City College (now University) produced Jonas Salk, the man who developed the vaccine against polio. Nobel Laureates had come from City: Julius Axelrod, Arthur Kornberg, Robert Hofstadter, and Kenneth Arrow. CCNY educated Felix Frankfurter, Upton Sinclair, Senator Robert Wagner, and Lewis Mumford. And Ira Gershwin, and Bernard Malamud, and Zero Mostel, and Paul Goodman, and Bernard Baruch, and E. Y. Harburg, and Irving Howe. And hundreds of thousands of other productive citizens who would otherwise never have had a college education. Moreover, the two authors of this book could never have afforded to pay tuition if Hunter College had not been free in 1956 when we entered the freshman class.

Since before the Civil War, free tuition at New York's colleges has meant upward mobility, an essential part of the dream among the working class that their children might have a better life than their parents. The City University was the pure incarnation of the Jeffersonian ideal of an aristocracy of "virtue and talents," rather than "an artificial aristocracy, founded on wealth and birth." The City University system has also been one of the strongest reasons for middle-class families to stay in New York; as the president of one municipal college put it, "Free tuition is one of the best incentives for the middle class to live in New York. It is the single greatest financial attraction to middle-class taxpayers."

In July 1974, when Hugh Carey was running in the Democratic primary for governor, the CUNY students wanted their usual guarantee that free tuition would be preserved. Carey wrote a letter to Jay Hershenson, head of the City University Student Senate: "I have long supported free tuition at the City University of New York. I will do all in my power, whether I become Governor or not, to preserve free tuition at the City University."

But up-state and suburban Republicans in the state legislature, and most of New York City's bankers, have long resented CUNY's free tuition. Walter Wriston, in private, has been known to become irrational in his fury against free higher education, as well as against another of his pet peeves, bilingual education. And early in the fiscal crisis, in May 1975, Vice-President Rockefeller proposed the termination of free tuition at a White House meeting with Mayor Beame, Governor Carey, and President Ford. Rockefeller's attack—delivered in front of the president and widely reported—on a policy in his home state, where he was deferred to as an expert, what was the first wounding blow struck against free tuition. The second, although the public could not know it at the time, was inflicted by Rohatyn at the private MAC board meeting on July 17. Rohatyn's words were taken as a signal that Governor Carey would not fight to save New York's free tuition.

The next critical public assault upon free tuition came on Tuesday, September 16, when State Education Commissioner Ewald Nyquist released the text of a letter he had written to Alfred Giardino, chairman of the Board of Higher Education. Nyquist's letter urged the imposition of yearly tuition of $650 on freshmen and sophomores and $800 on juniors and seniors—the same fees as those charged at the State University of New York. Nyquist's letter claimed that because of various state and federal subsidies, only those students whose families earned more than $20,000 of net taxable income would actually have to pay the tuition money out of their own pockets. Carey had been governor for only eight months when his own education commissioner thus advocated tuition. When he asked to comment, Carey said: "I have not changed my position that applying tuition at the City University would solve very little. The numbers involved will not solve the city's fiscal problems. The Emergency Financial Control Board is not going to assume any decision-making powers over any aspects of city life. Mr. Beame has to make recommendations on matters within city jurisdiction. And if there should be a change in the tuition situation at the City University of New York, the initiative must come from that quarter." More appearances.

A survey by *The New York Times* made in September 1975 showed eight of the ten members of the Board of Higher Education steadfastly opposed to imposing tuition. Five of the eight eventually resigned in protest rather than be party to any change of policy.

By January 1976, the pressure to do away with free tuition was mounting in private from Washington and Wall Street. And the issue was becoming a political football between Beame and Carey. Again—the appearance of things. Who would bear the blame for annuling the last best hope of the dispossessed in New York City? In his "State of the City" address on January 22, Beame said: "The primary responsibility for higher education rests with the state. . . . The City cannot continue to finance the City University. We are exploring ways to achieve the necessary transition over the next few years." Beame did not say he would fight to save free tuition. And Carey was no longer making any promises. Two members of the BHE, Harold Jacobs and Dr. Gurstin Goldin, the psychiatrist brother of Controller Harrison Goldin, were already, in fact, maneuvering behind the scenes to prepare the transition to tuition.

On March 24, Stephen Berger, whom Governor Carey had appointed executive director of the Control Board two weeks before, came to lunch at the *Daily News* to meet with the paper's top editors and writers. Berger's self-image is that of a brutally frank tough guy. He had worked for the politically inspired Scott Commission, created in 1971 by Nelson ᴿockefeller to do a hatchet job on the Lindsay administration. Berger loved it and was very good at it, and Rockefeller still speaks admiringly of the job Berger did.

Earlier in his career, Berger had been a highly regarded campaign mechanic and technician for liberals who usually happened, like Rockefeller, to be millionaires, such as Congressmen Jonathan Bingham and Richard Ottinger. But by 1975, Berger was Hugh Carey's Commissioner for Social Services. In that position, Berger began a crusade against the "16,000 ineligible children" who he said were in city day-care centers. He did not begin any equivalent crusade against the day-care landlords who were getting paid inflated rents by the city on twenty-year leases.

So Stephen Berger, a graduate of Brandeis University, probably did not really mind being the hit man against free tuition when he came for lunch with the editors and writers of the *Daily News*. Berger was his usual factual, articulate, candid self. He said it, flatly, clearly: Free tuition must end. Berger, at least, did not calculate much about the appearance of things. The next morning, the *News* quoted him as saying: "You can't expect to have tuition in the state colleges, and expect the legislature to approve aid for the city system without some sort of a tuition program."

The crunch came in April. There was, by then, a $70-million deficit in the BHE's budget. The city was broke, and the state legislature was opposed to any state aid. In a desperate effort to stave off tuition, the BHE had voted to restrict admissions and to consolidate four of CUNY's branches. Franklin Williams quit the BHE on April 5, saying the board's new admissions policy was "racist" and would segregate the university into white senior colleges, and black and Hispanic community colleges. Henrik Dullea, an aide to Carey, was pressuring board members to vote for tuition. So was T. Edward Hollander, the deputy state education commissioner. When a reporter asked Dullea whether he had been "twisting arms" in behalf of tuition, Dullea replied, in bureaucratic off-English, "We've talked to a lot of people about all the issues confronting the university, but we haven't made any specific calls on tuition. I won't deny tuition has been discussed, because it's one of the principal options that have to be confronted."

By the end of April there were four firm votes in favor of tuition on the ten-member BHE: Harold Jacobs; Dr. Gurstin Goldin; James Murphy, the executive vice-president of the New York State Bankers Association; and Armand D'Angelo, who had been appointed by Carey in October at the urging of Robert Wagner, in whose administration D'Angelo had served from 1957 to

1965 without distinction. (In fact, D'Angelo had been marginally tainted by scandal during the Wagner administration. A 1961 report by the State Commission of Investigation charged D'Angelo, then the city's water commissioner, with "impropriety" in his dealings with Sydney Baron, Carmine De Sapio's PR man. And at the bribery trial, James Marcus testified that D'Angelo was friendly with the man who bribed him, the Mafia boss Tony "Ducks" Corallo.) On April 27, the board asked for a face-to-face meeting with Governor Carey, so that Carey could directly request the imposition of tuition. Several wavering members said they might vote for tuition if the governor was at least willing to accept the ultimate responsibility for the decision and not have it reside with an appointed board. They also wanted a commitment from Carey on the exact dollar amount of aid which the state would provide CUNY if tuition were imposed. Carey refused to attend the meeting. BHE member Rita Hauser said, "Mr. Carey's representatives have offered every possible kind of number [of state aid to CUNY] but they never commit the Governor. And if we ask them frontally—'Does the Governor want tuition?'—they back off," Again, the politician's concern with the appearance of things, nor their actuality.

Also on April 27, Carey named Francis Kilcoyne, the former president of Brooklyn College, to take Franklin Williams's seat on the BHE.

In the middle of May Carey finally went public and said he reluctantly favored that City University students be charged tuition. Tuition, Carey said, would raise $135.5 million in operating revenues. The way the tuition formula was structured, those hardest hit would be part-time students who had to work, and students from families whose gross annual income is above $10,000. The poorest students would receive assistance and reimbursement grants from state and federal programs.

In the end, the victims of tuition would be lower-middle-class students and, perhaps, women in hard-pressed families that had to choose one child to send to college and chose the brothers. By September the combination of tuition and fewer admissions had cut CUNY's population by 38,000 students. And almost 1000 untenured faculty were dismissed. Some of the luxuries, managerial sinecures, and departmental duplication were uncut, according to the usual ass-backward priorities of the bureaucrats who controlled the budget axe.

On May 25, five members of the Board of Higher Education resigned rather than vote for tuition. They were led by the BHE's chairman, Alfred Giardino, who had graduated from Brooklyn College in 1934 and was the first member of his family ever to attend college. Vincent Fitzpatrick, Sandra Lopez de Bird, and Rita Hauser also quit. And so did Francis Kilcoyne, whom Carey had appointed only the month before.

On May 28, Mayor Beame promoted his old close friend the businessman and clubhouse Democratic Harold Jacobs to the chairmanship of the BHE, and appointed three new members, all quietly felt out in advance, as to their views on tuition: Albert Maniscalco, former Staten Island borough president and director of the Community National Bank & Trust Company; Nicholas Figueroa, a lawyer; and Loretta Conway, a lawyer active in the Fordham University Alumni Association. (The private colleges favored tuition at CUNY.) The appointments were made without the official screening-panel interviews. Howard Squadron, a member of the mayor's screening panel, said Beame circumvented the screening process "because our members have considered it our function to be sure that candidates are committed to free tuition. . . . I think the Mayor is making a terrible mistake."

The struggle was over. For longer than a century, from the Land Grant College Act of 1862 to the GI Bill of Rights, our national policy had been to expand access to higher education. But in New York City, one month before the national bicentennial, this policy was reversed. An economic barrier rose against higher education.

The City University was closed and broke when the Board of Higher Education met at its headquarters, at 535 East 80th Street in Manhattan, at 7:30 P.M. on June 1. Six members had quit rather than violate their consciences: Giardino, Williams, Hauser, Fitzpatrick, Lopez de Bird, and Kilcoyne. The climactic meeting was dull and passionless, according to the participants. The three new members asked almost no questions, though they had less than seventy-two hours to become familiar with the complex issues. The meeting lasted a little more than two hours. The vote was seven to one. Voting "yes," for tuition, were the new chairman, Harold Jacobs; the three instant appointees—Maniscalco, Figueroa, and Conway; Carey's appointee, Armand D'Angelo; Dr. Gurstin Goldin, the brother of the controller; and James Murphy, the banker. The formal resolution to impose tuition was offered by D'Angelo. The solitary "no" vote was cast by Vinia Quinones, an administrator at Arthur Logan Memorial Hospital in Harlem and the only black member remaining on the board. Two months later, Beame, the first graduate of the City University ever to become mayor of New York, refused to reappoint Quinones to the BHE.

In June Congresswoman Elizabeth Holtzman of Brooklyn delivered the commencement address to the graduating class of Queens College. Holtzman, who was one of the independent and intelligent elected leaders in the city, spoke an honest epitaph for New York's 129 years of free higher education. She told the Queens College senior class, "Tuition is being imposed at CUNY not because there is no other way to raise enough money for New York's survival, but because the city's managers want to appease a hostile federal government and an envious country . . . not to mention some bankers who graduated from Princeton or Fordham."

The Clubhouse System

8

To grasp the essence of the clubhouse system, to feel its power, to understand its values, come with us to the annual dinner of the Kings County Democrats. See the long black limos, and the Brooklyn cars with license plates that display the owners' initials, doubleparked outside the Waldorf-Astoria on Park Avenue. See five judges sitting at Bill Shea's table. Watch the judges approach Carmine DeSapio's table and pay respect. See the landlord with his arm around the deputy commissioner of real estate.

Come with us to the May 16, 1974, annual dinner of the Brooklyn Democracy. At table 23 is Congressman Frank Brasco, who will go to federal prison for conspiring to accept a bribe from a Mafia trucker. At table 16 is Congressman Bertram Podell, who will go to federal prison for taking a $41,350 bribe to influence the Civil Aeronautic Board's decision on an airline route. At table 92 is Eugene Hollander, who will plead guilty to stealing $1.1 million in Medicaid funds from four nursing homes he owns. At table 55 is Queens County leader Matthew Troy, who will plead guilty to income-tax evasion on money taken from the estates of his law clients. And at table 50 is Carmine DeSapio. DeSapio has served almost two years in prison for bribery. Manhattan public administrator Thomas Fitzgerald, who will be indicted with his friend, sits at table 53.

At table 5 is the immaculately dressed, war hero Congressman, John Murphy of Staten Island. In December of 1980, Murphy will be convicted of conspiracy and conflict-of-interest in the FBI's Abscam undercover sting. At table 20 is Councilman Sam Wright, czar of an anti-poverty empire in Brownsville that controls millions of dollars in federal funds. In April of 1978, Wright will be found guilty of accepting a $5,000 pay-off from a textbook company that wanted to increase its sale to the Brownsville community school board that was part of Wright's machine.

Sitting at table 11 is Anthony Scotto, the president of ILA Local 1814. In

175

November of 1979, Scotto will be convicted on 33 counts of racketerring, conspiracy, bribe-taking, and tax evasion. Scotto would be found guilty after Governor Carey, former Mayor Wagner, and Judge Willie Thompson all testified to his honest character. Congressman Mario Biaggi is at table 4. A year ago he was caught lying to the voters about his refusal to testify fully before a federal grand jury.

Joe Pape is at table 14. Pape, a former party district leader in Manhattan and a business associate of Stanley Steingut, will be named in an eighty-count indictment claiming he falsified records of the Computer Specifics Corporation to conceal bribes paid to a Board of Education official. Speaker Stanley Steingut himself is at table 47, and his son, Councilman Robert, is at table 18. Their indictment for a scheme to get a $2500 contribution for Robert's campaign in exchange for getting the contributor an honorary position with the city will be dismissed on a jurisdictional technicality.

State Assemblyman Harvey Strelzin is at table 108. In 1957 Strelzin was forced to resign as chairman of the city's Board of Assessors after it was disclosed that he was a partner in a garbage-disposal business with a mobster named Anthony Ricci. Milton Kessler, also seated at table 108, was until March 1972 both the managing agent for a Crown Heights slum building that had been cited with 130 violations and an aide to Councilman Howard Golden. When Kessler's activities were exposed by *New York Post* reporter Joe Kahn, Kessler quit his job with Golden (but remained the agent for the slum building). When Kahn was working on his story, Kessler had said to him, "It's none of your business. All the other reporters know about it, and they aren't writing anything, so you better forget it."

Twenty-two city marshals have bought tickets to this dinner, including Kenneth Brand (table 101), who earned $181,000 in 1973; Herbert Klein (table 312), who earned $163,000; and Alex Chapin (table 101), who made $189,000. Frank Vaccaro, seated at table 110, will become a judge and then be suspended from the bench by the Commission on Judicial Conduct for accepting gifts from a lawyer who appeared before him. Roy Cohn is at table 35. He has been indicted and acquitted three times.

District leader George Meissner is at table 23; he is a convicted slumlord. And with him is Bernard Deutsch, who will be convicted of stock fraud. Irving Polk, seated at table 308, is president of Esposito's political club and a city pothole inspector who gets $666 a month for his work—a task notorious for requiring no work. Judge Jerome Steinberg is at table 116. In January of 1977, Steinberg will be indicted for perjury and contempt for lying to a grand jury probing his alleged "participation in a money-lending scheme" involving more than $250,000.

Frankie Folan, at table 88, contributed $13,125 to Beame's mayoralty campaign and a few months later became Democratic Party district leader in

Bay Ridge. He was later caught selling 2500 tickets on a charter flight that never existed.

Seated at table 37 are Arthur Vare, Stanley Kreitman, and Saul Kagan, all directors of the American Bank and Trust Company. Mayor Beame once was a director of the bank himself, and the bank's president, Abraham Feinberg, was Beame's most important campaign fund raiser in 1973. On September 15, 1976, the charter for the American Bank and Trust Company will be taken away, and State Banking Superintendent John Heimann will accuse the bank of "practices in violation of law" and of being in an "unsafe and unsound condition." The Federal Reserve Bank will discover that one-third of the American Bank and Trust Company's $152 million loan portfolio is "sub-standard, doubtful, or lost."

Larry Gurino, at table 74, is a part-owner of the Queens Terrace Catering Corporation, which was denied a liquor license by the State Liquor Authority because Gurino had "business connections with various individuals who have close connections with organized crime." Among Gurino's partners in the ownership of the catering company were the son and the nephew of former Mafia boss Joseph Columbo. Gurino's brother John has at various times held six day-care-center leases from the city. These day-care centers received $590,000 in construction loans from the pension fund of Local 355, an independent trucking union which was started by the convicted labor racketeer Johnny Dio.

Builder and bank director Vincent Caristo is at table 104. In 1961, Caristo was banned from submitting construction bids to the Board of Education because of past rigged bids, a ban that was upheld by the courts but rescinded in April 1962. And now the Caristo Construction Company is the single biggest recipient of construction contracts from the Board of Education. (In 1969 it was disclosed that the file dealing with the decision to reinstate the Caristo company was missing from Board of Education archives.)

Sidney Lipkins, chairman of Broadway Maintenance Corporation, is at table 43. In 1961, the State Investigation Commission accused his company of "extensive irregularities" and "excessive profits" in its contracts with the city to service traffic lights and parking meters, and in 1976 Broadway Maintenance will once again be accused, in an audit by Controller Goldin, of over-billing the bankrupt city by $195,000.

Fortune Pope is seated at table 59. Pope is president of Colonial Sand & Stone Company and owner of *Il Progresso*, New York City's Italian-language newspaper. In 1961, Pope was fined $25,000 and received a suspended prison sentence after pleading guilty to filing false proxy statements with the American Stock Exchange. A few years later, he caused the dismissal of a city purchase commissioner after it was disclosed that he had made too much profit selling the city rock salt from the Dominican Republic.

Builder Fred DeMatteis, a registered Republican, is at table 9. His giant construction company had been accused of pouring weak cement on a Nassau County project—until DeMatteis hired away the diligent engineer who discovered his shoddy work. And builders Donald and Fred Trump (father and son), at table 10, have been accused by the Justice Department of violating the Fair Housing Act by discriminating against blacks in their rental policies. The Trump family owns and rents 14,000 apartments. The Trumps, and their lawyer, Roy Cohn, eventually signed a consent decree.

Louis Friedman, at table 81, was removed from the State Supreme Court in 1963 for abusing his office and obstructing an investigation into an ambulance-chasing racket. Norman Levy, at table 73, was once chairman of the City Tax Commission, but he was convicted of fixing parking tickets, a conviction that will later be reversed. Dr. Mario Tagliagambe is at table 211. The Waterfront Commission would secretly film Dr. Tags, as he is known entering an organized-crime clubhouse on the Lower East Side. Joseph Parisi, at table 30, clerk of Brooklyn Supreme Court, is under indictment for illegally using union pension funds.

George Kerner, at table 38, and Frank Gilligan. at table 39, are law secretaries in Brooklyn Supreme Court. Gilligan has been the treasurer for twenty-five years of the Kings County Democratic organization. On June 18, 1976, Gilligan and Kerner will plead guilty to stealing the receipts of this dinner and of three previous Brooklyn dinners, thefts totaling $100,000 in party funds.

The guest speaker at this embezzled 1974 Waldorf-Astoria dinner is Abraham D. Beame, who was sworn in as mayor of New York City only four months ago. Beame is speaking with uncommon passion to the 2000 assembled guests—Podell, Brasco, Troy, Hollander, DeSapio, Goldman, Pope, Lipkins, Kessler, Gilligan, and all the other honorable men and women of the Brooklyn Democracy. The new mayor is saying:

We are sometimes accused of running a strong county organization. Critics call it a machine. But Brooklyn has demonstrated that effective party organization need not be synonymous with smoke-filled rooms. Rather, it is a vital force in the American party system. . . . I have been a member of the Brooklyn Democratic organization the last forty years. I've always been proud of my membership, and my pride has increased. No one, no one need apologize for being part of this kind of party organization.

Our favorite insight into the mentality of a machine politician was given us inadvertently one night in September 1974. We ran into Brooklyn district leader and City Councilman Howard Golden one night during a Democratic primary for a congressional seat. We asked the recklessly extroverted Golden why he and his political club were working so hard to re-elect Bertram Podell, when Podell was under indictment for bribery.

"We're for Bert only because we have inside information that he's guilty and will be convicted," Golden explained in a confidential whisper.

We confessed we did not follow his reasoning.

"Schmuck," the councilman said. "If we help Podell win the primary and *then* he is convicted, that way we get to pick his replacement, and stop that kid Steve Solarz. We want to save this seat in Congress for our guy, Leonard Silverman."

Now Leonard Silverman, chairman of the state Assembly's Insurance Committee, happens to be even more mindless than is normal for Brooklyn hacks. He was briefly notorious in June 1976 when he sponsored a bill to raise the annual salaries for members of the legislature to $44,600, and to allow both parties' legislative leaders to collect $65,600 for their six months' work a year. The *Daily News* observed, "On the basis of performance, Silverman and colleagues should be down on their knees begging the public's forgiveness, instead of brazenly attempting to gouge the taxpayers further."

But the logic of I'm-for-him-because-I-know-he-is-corrupt remains the terminal absurdity of the clubhouse ethos. Howard Golden, philosopher of the Brooklyn Democracy, has since risen to become Brooklyn borough president. He has the potential of becoming an unconscious Plunkett.

In his definitive early history of Tammany, M. R. Werner quoted from an article that appeared in the *North American Review* of October 1866: "We have undertaken to write something about the government of the City of New York, and yet we have fallen into a discourse on stealing. The reason is, that, after having spent several weeks investigating our subject, we find we have been employed in nothing else but discovering in how many ways, and under what a variety of names and pretexts, immature and greedy men steal from that fruitful and ill-fenced orchard, the city treasury."

By the time of his death in 1878, William Marcy (Boss) Tweed, the leader of Tammany, had stolen at least $30 million from the ill-fenced orchard. The Tweed courthouse still stands just north of City Hall, at 52 Chambers Street, as a gray monument to Tweed's imagination. The courthouse, which was originally supposed to cost $250,000, ended up costing the taxpayers $13 million. A bill for three tables and forty chairs was $179,729, and Andrew Garvey, the "prince of plasterers," billed the city for "repairs" before the courthouse was completed. Tweed named the prizefighter Jim "Maneater" Cusick the court clerk, upon his release from Sing Sing Prison, and made Pudding Long, who could neither read nor write, the courthouse interpreter. In a final act of creative generosity, he placed three dead men on the courthouse payroll.

Since Tweed's day, political bosses all over the country have occasionally been portrayed as charming rogues, colorful Robin Hoods, who distribute turkey baskets to the immigrant poor at Christmastime. A mixture of nostalgia, amnesia, and romanticism has begun to sugarcoat the reputations of Hague of Jersey City, Pendergast of Kansas City, Curley of Boston, and Jimmy Walker of New York. Daniel Patrick Moynihan and others have rationalized that at least the clubhouse Democrats represented the working class, while reformers have represented the middle class. And, starting about a decade ago, a new conventional wisdom began to emerge among sociologists, journalists, and "urbanists," that the ega of big-city political machines was over—except for Mayor Daley's in Chicago—and that television had changed everything, that the tube had replaced the old precinct captain in the voter's trust and loyalty.

It is our contention that the romanticization of the party boss is naive, that the theory of the vanishing machine is not supported by the evidence, and that the premise of the theory is based on an out-dated stereotype of the party boss and an overly narrow definition of the clubhouse system.

Some observers introduce as evidence of the machine's demise in New York City the defeat of organization-backed candidates for the Democratic Senate nominations in 1974 and 1980. And it is true that both Lee Alexander in 1974 and Bess Myerson in 1980 lost statewide primaries. But the Democratic machine in New York doesn't care that much about a Senate primary: Senators don't control leases on contracts; no patronage, no favors for clubhouse hangers-on are at stake. What the machine does care about is who is mayor and who are surrogate judges. And the machine continues to win primaries to nominate men for those positions because that is where it invests its money and manpower.

As for the party structure, resilient as ever, it has adapted to modern times and become more modern itself, more subtle and, at its highest levels, more like a corporation than a gang of pirates. This is true all over America. Except for Daley in Chicago and Frank Rizzo in Philadelphia, there are few modern stereotypical boss personalities in the tradition of Tweed, Hague, or Curley. The more successful backroom type, as we find it in New York City, is the publicity-shy, affable private manipulator with a couple of corporate directorships—like Bill Shea, or Harold Fisher, or Eugene Keogh. In fact, the Democratic machine should be viewed as a corporate enterprise that is run to produce a steady profit for its Class A shareholders. Some of its well-publicized leaders, like Meade Esposito or Matthew Troy, may cultivate an earthy image of *macho* populism, but it is only an assumed persona. The clubhouse system is, today, what it was more than seventy years ago when Lincoln Steffens described it as "government of the people, by the rascals, for the rich." The only difference is that it is now much more sophisticated.

The New York Democratic machine, which was thought moribund when Lindsay was re-elected in 1969, now controls the whole machinery of the city government through Abe Beame, from pothole inspectors on up. It controls the courthouses in Brooklyn, Queens, the Bronx, and Staten Island, with more than 200 judgeships and several thousand courthouse patronage jobs. In the Bronx alone, six party district leaders have jobs as clerks on judicial budget lines.

The machine controls the patronage-rich Surrogates Court in every county including Manhattan. Each year the Surrogates award at their discretion millions of dollars in legal fees and guardianships for probate estates to lawyers from the clubhouses. In Brooklyn, judges we have interviewed have even seen a typed list of approved lawyers that the party headquarters delivers to the Surrogate. In addition, the Surrogates give out thousands of dollars in agate-type legal advertising to small, community newspapers—that is, to those weeklies that are willing to puff the clubhouse pols and ignore the local reformers.

Through Assembly Speaker Stanley Fink, the machine controls $6 million's worth of jobs in the state Assembly—plus about $1 million in "lulus" (cash in lieu of unitemized expenses) for those lawmakers who vote the way they are instructed. The machine also controls the City Council payroll through majority leader Tom Cuite and the public administrator's offices in four boroughs.

Despite the fiscal crisis, despite scandals and indictments, the clubhouse system is still strong because it is based on an infrastructure of institutions. Personalities are transient, but institutions are permanent. The machine's power rests upon the county organizations: banks; law firms; insurance companies; unions and union pension funds (especially Local 1814 of the ILA, run by Anthony Scotto even after his conviction for bribery). Its power rests upon antipoverty corporations; community newspapers subsidized by the Surrogates Court; and the agencies of government itself. These institutions are unaffected, even when a strong personality like Troy goes to prison. The only consequence is that the power and the profits shift to a different law firm, a different insurance company.

The Democratic clubhouse system, in this one-party city, bears its share of the historic responsibility for the city's fall. It is not as responsible as the great banks, or Nelson Rockefeller, or the managers of the national economy, or the anonymous, shadow government of public authorities—but it is responsible enough.

The clubhouse system made Abraham Beame the major of New York. It is responsible for rotten judges on the bench. Through its subservience to the real-estate developers and savings banks it has played a negative role in the decay of neighborhoods all over the city.* It has done favors for corrupt

*For the full account of what happened to Columbia Street, for example, read Denis Hamill, "Nobody Gets Indicted for Killing a Neighborhood," in *The Village Voice*, September 20, 1976. Hamill explains how politicians like Abe Stark and Tom Cuite were instrumental in the decline of a once-thriving shopping area in South Brooklyn.

businessmen like Bernard Bergman and Eugene Hollander—at the taxpayers' expense. It has used the phrase "merit system" as a racial codeword to win votes, and then ignored merit and filled the city government with unqualified club members, in jobs that pay a lot for very little work. And it has put up for public office serfs who are not free to vote the way they think.

There was a great moment in the City Council ten years ago, when Dominick Corso of Brooklyn got so frustrated in a debate with a reformer that he blurted out an existential truth: "You think it takes guts to stand up for what is right?" he asked. "That doesn't take guts. What takes guts is to stand up for what you know is wrong, day after day, year after year. That takes guts!" Despite this confession, Corso went on to his reward for services rendered, and is now a Civil Court judge in Brooklyn.

The party apparatus not only fills the legislature and City Council with rubberstamps and future felons but aggressively tries to purge lawmakers, no matter how able, who exhibit independent judgment. For example, in September 1976, four hard-working, community-oriented members of the state legislature were punished with primary fights by the regular organization: Frank Barbero, Major Owens, and Joe Ferris in Brooklyn, and Vincent Marchiselli in the northeast Bronx, whose challenger was a realtor. All four incumbents, however, won their primaries.

The various forms of legal graft we have discussed, which have cost the taxpayers so many millions of dollars, are dependent upon the complicity of the clubhouse system. Stanley Steingut and Anthony Scotto put in a good word for Christopher Boomis to get his no-bid contract and tax abatement. Pat Cunningham and all the Bronx councilmen pushed for the public funds to renovate Yankee Stadium. Steingut did many favors for convicted nursing-home czar Bernard Bergman, including arranging a private meeting with Mayor Beame, and intervening in Bergman's behalf with state health officials, and in return he received campaign donations and insurance premiums. The beneficiaries of the padded, no-bid, twenty-year day-care leases included clubhouse politicians like Sam Wright, Leonard Simon, clients of Shea's law firm, and friends of Donald Manes. Cunningham was in the middle of the Bronx Terminal Market rip-off, as the high-priced lawyer for the landlord. Bunny Lindenbaum's clients got the highest proportion of reduced real estate tax assessments from the City Tax Commission. Democratic Party lawyers like Joseph Slavin (now a judge), Kevin McGrath of Bill Shea's firm, and Mario Biaggi were the ones chosen to be closing attorneys on mortgages from the city employee pension fund.

Because they are Democrats, and because they need the votes of New Yorkers, the clubhouse politicians say the words of economic liberalism, when they are required to speak on issues. But in practice—and this is perhaps the key to seeing the machine for what it really is—in practice the clubhouse Democrats usually vote in the interest of the banks and property owners. In his wonderful book *Boss*, about Richard Daley's Chicago, Mike Royko made this same point again and again: the Chicago Democratic machine fronts for, and favors, the real-estate developers, insurance companies, construction unions, banks, and city contractors, rather than the neighborhoods and families who vote for the Chicago Democratic machine.

And in *The Power Broker*, Robert Caro explains how clubhouse politicians supported all of the public works of Robert Moses, including his costly blunders, like slum clearance and the World's Fair. Moses used his control over bonds, legal fees, public-relations retainers, and, especially, insurance premiums, to purchase their support. And he had it. Despite the destruction of wonderful neighborhoods, and the waste of millions of dollars, the pols went along with him. One of the reasons, Caro shows, was that three of the five Democratic county leaders had insurance companies that derived profits from the patronage of Moses's Triborough Authority.

A recent example of collusion between the clubhouses and special interests occurred in June 1970, when New York's City Council voted on a complicated piece of legislation that permitted landlords to charge higher rents to about one million families. This first revision of the rent-control law, then twenty-seven years old, raised rents for some families by 15 per cent, and for others by 8 per cent. The bill also included a provision for the computerized calculation of rents, which proved to be an administrative nightmare and failure. At the last minute an amendment that would have protected low-income families from rent increases was deleted from the draft bill; it contained no protection for tenants against harassment by landlords, no machinery to compel landlords to provide heat and hot water, to repair violations of the housing code, or to pay their unpaid real-estate taxes before being allowed to increase rents. The bill had nothing for tenants.

The rent bill needed twenty-five votes to pass in the Council. After a nasty marathon meeting that adjourned at 3:30 A.M. the final version of the bill was approved 27-10. The three Republicans on the Council voted for the bill, which was no surprise, and two Liberal Party members as well, which was. And the remaining twenty-two votes were provided by clubhouse Democrats.

The rent-increase legislation has been sponsored by the Queens clubhouse Councilman Donald Manes (who has since risen to become, simultaneously, Queens county leader and borough president). Reform Democrats, led by Theodore Weiss, tried and failed three times to liberalize the bill through amendments.

Voting consistently against the interest of tenants were the two clubhouse councilmen from Staten Island, Edward Curry and Robert Lindsay; the last unreconstructed Tammany Democrat from Manhattan, Saul Sharison, who represented the rapidly decaying Lower East Side; and the late David Friedland, of Washington Heights, another regular. Every clubhouse Democrat from Cunningham's disciplined Bronx machine, voted with the landlords: Michael DeMarco, Aileen Ryan, Mario Merola, Bertram Gelfand, Muriel Stromberg, and Barry Salman. So did every clubhouse councilman from Queens: Manes, Matthew Troy, Edward Sadowsky, Mike Lazar, Tom Manton, and Walter Ward. Queen's one reform Democrat, Arthur Katzman, voted against it. Similarly, six of the seven regulars from Esposito's Brooklyn organization stood with the real estate industry: Majority Leader Tom Cuite (who is a licensed real-estate broker); Rudy DiBlasi; Monroe Cohen; Leonard Scholnick; Ted Silverman; and Willie Thompson (who owned buildings in Bedford Stuyvesant, and is now a judge, as is Scholnick).

Five years later, in the spring of 1975, the City Council debated another rent bill, this one allowing landlords to raise rents by $2 per room per month for 900,000 tenants living in rent-controlled apartments, to cover the rising costs of fuel. According to the bill, landlords would be allowed to do this without an audit of their financial records by any city agency to determine the actual margins of profit on their buildings. There was no allowance for the effect of escalating inflation upon tenants. And again no remedy for harassment or tax arrears by property owners.

On April 28, the Council's General Welfare Committee convened to vote on what was known as the fuel pass-along bill. Majority Leader Cuite had worked out a subtle deal to have the committee approve the bill by getting its one Republican, Jack Muratori, to support it—so long as his was the seventh vote, and not the decisive *sixth* vote, so that responsibility would appear to rest with the Democrats.

But there was a surprise. Freshman Councilman Luis Olmedo from the Williamsburg-Bushwick area of Brooklyn voted no, the roll call was tied 4-4, and Harlem Councilman Fred Samuel was explaining why he too would vote against the rent increase. As Samuel was speaking Cuite's aides began whispering to Councilman Ted Silverman, and Silverman jumped up to make a sudden motion to lay the matter aside—a quick maneuver to save the bill from formal defeat—and the lay-over motion passed, 6 to 3, with two abstentions. (In 1974, Silverman had voted against an equal rights bill for homosexuals, two weeks after he had voted *for* the same bill in committee.)

The next day the agenda called for the full Council to convene at 1:30 P.M.. But for six hours the councilmen milled around City Hall corridors while Cuite, Mayor Beame (in Albany that day, and working by remote control), and the Democratic county leaders tried to line up six votes on the committee and twenty-nine votes in the full Council to pass the bill. One by one reluctant councilmen were escorted into Cuite's office for "private talks." Three wavering members received personal phone calls from the major. Esposito called Councilmen Robert Steingut and Sam Horwitz and asked them to vote for the rent bill. Then he called young Luis Olmedo and told him that if he voted no, he would face an expensive primary for renomination, and if he voted yes, funds could be found in the budget for a senior citizens center in his district, which Olmedo has been trying to get for a year. Donald Manes phoned Councilman Eugene Mastropieri, who had voted against the bill in committee. But the numbers did not add up, and at 7:30, the full Council meeting finally began, with the rent hike off the agenda.

On Friday, May 9, the bill that Beame and the landlords wanted was finally passed by the General Welfare Committee 8-3. Remember, Beame had gotten more than $600,000 in contributions from landlords in 1973. Mastropieri voted yes, after voting no two weeks before. Samuel from Harlem voted yes, even though he had been in the midst of explaining his no vote two weeks before. (As a reward, he became the one Manhattan councilman invited to private budget meetings with the major.) The other clubhouse Democrats who voted for the rent increase were Aileen Ryan, Ted Silverman, Robert Steingut, Anthony Geata, Stephen Kaufman, and the Republican, Muratori. The pro-tenant votes were cast by Olmedo, Tom Manton, and, as ever, Ted Weiss.

A half hour later, Cuite had the full Council considering the bill. About seventy-five tenants, from the Metropolitan Council on Housing, were in the balcony, cheering and booing, when the roll call began. Mastropieri of Queens voted yes, and the balcony chanted "Shame, shame, shame." They began the chant again when Robert Steingut of Brooklyn voted yes. In explaining his yes vote, Ted Silverman said, "It may not be right, but at least we're trying to do something." The tenants cheered as the usual Manhattan heroes of the Council voted no: Weiss, Greitzer, Wagner Jr., Stern, Burden, Friedlander. And cheered again when Katzman and Manton of Queens voted no. Olmedo said, "When oil was cheap, landlords did not give heat to my people in Wiliamsburg and Bushwick." He voted no.

But the $2 per-room per-month rent increase passed, 30 to 13. Five months later, Councilman Howard Golden from Brooklyn, who had voted in favor of it, announced that he was preparing legislation to repeal the new law. He said the landlords were cheating on the law by submitting fraudulent claims. But Golden's repeal bill never got out of committee.

In April of 1980, Mayor Ed Koch pressured a reluctant City Council into approving a new fuel pass-along rent increase for tenants living in about 350,000 rent controlled apartments. The increase was an average of $3.50 per room, and was made retroactive to 1979.

The opposition was led by reformers Stanley Michaels and Ruth Messinger.

And the margin of victory for the landlords was provided by what Claude Rains called "the usual suspects" in Casablanca: Eugene Mastropieri,* Robert Steingut, Tom Cuite, Edward Sandowsky, Aileen Ryan, abetted by black hacks Enoch Williams and Archie Spigner. And sadly, the tenant hero of 1975—Louis Olmedo—voted for the landlords in 1980. Although his people in Bushwick and Williamsburg remain without heat, and are now afflicted by the new plague of arson-for-profit by landlords.

There are other examples of clubhouse Democrats siding with special economic interests and against the larger public interest.

● For two years Manhattan Councilman Carter Burden has been trying to pass a bill that would abolish private, profit-making methadone-mainte-nance clinics, and strictly regulate the non-profit ones. The owners of the profit-making clinics make windfall medicaid profits—Dr. Allen Hausknect, in testimony before Burden's City Council health commit-tee, admitted making $100,000 in one year, in one clinic. A city health department report disclosed "serious violations" at many of the clinics—charging for services never performed, inadequate medical attention, excessive dosages of methadone, and a lack of job or psychiatric counseling for the addicts, or any serious rehabilitative services.

When he was running for mayor, Abe Beame held a press conference outside a notorious methadone clinic—the Ithaca, on East 84th Street—and promised strict regulation of such clinics after he was elected. But Burden's bill has never gotten out of the Council's health committee, for Beame and Majority Leader Cuite are against it. And very quietly, so are some of the city's giant private hospitals, like Beth Israel, which controls thirty-eight methadone-maintenance clinics, and is not eager to see stricter regulation.

● On June 25, 1976, the state Senate passed a bill that mandated an audit and review by the EFCB of all 171 day-care center leases. By then almost everyone had agreed that they were scandalous. The idea behind the bill was to allow the EFCB to renegotiate, or cancel, any lease that was exorbitant, and Franz Leichter, who had co-sponsored it, predicted it would "save the city $10 million a year." But three days later, the bill, opposed only by the handful of day-care landlords and lawyers, was killed in the Assembly by Speaker Stanley Steingut. State Senator Major Owens, another co-sponsor, told us, "Our bill wasn't supposed to pass the Senate. When it did, Beame called Senator Conklin at 2 A.M. to complain about it. Then he phoned Steingut, and Steingut ordered the bill killed in

---

*Mastropieri cast his vote an hour after his arraignment on a federal indictment. He was convicted a few months later.

committee on the last day of the session. It was a typical example of how the system works in Albany."

- For years the Citizens Union, the Legal Aid Society, and the Bar Association have been trying to abolish the system of using city marshals. The marshals are technically part of the city's Civil Court, although they are appointed by the mayor, on the recommendation of political party leaders, for six-year terms. There are no qualifications for the job, and no civil service test is required. They are under no day-to-day scrutiny by any judicial, executive, or legislative authority. The marshals are private entrepreneurs working with the authority—gun and badge—of government. Marshals execute evictions for landlords. They garnishee salaries and welfare checks for creditors. They collect judgments for banks, loan companies, credit companies. They repossess merchandise for department stores. They pull out gas and electric meters for utilities. They are the scavengers of the system. A Citizens Union pamphlet on the marshal system is called "A Puddle of Patronage."

Now the interesting thing is that the marshals receive no salary, but take 5 per cent off the top of all judgments they collect. Last year 14 of New York's 73 marshals grossed more than $100,000. They make such large incomes by refusing to collect the small claims of individual citizens and by working only for large institutions like Household Finance, Brooklyn Union Gas, landlords like Goldman and DiLorenzo, and stores like Korvette's. In theory, they are supposed impartially to execute the mandate of the Civil Court, including the Small Claims Court. But in September 1976, the Public Interest Research Group's three-year analysis of the Small Claims Court showed that more than 40 percent of the indivdual claimants who actually won judgments were unable to collect their money because the city marshals would not exert themselves on their behalf against the landlords, or TV repair shops, or department stores.

A Legal Services lawyer told us this story of how the marshals can affect the lives of powerless people: The lawyer's client—a Puerto Rican dishwasher—owed a department store $200. The dishwasher offered to pay installments of $10 a week. The marshal illegally demanded a $75 down payment before accepting the installment arrangement. The dishwasher had to borrow $75 from a loan company to satisfy the marshal. Two weeks later, the dishwasher's child fell out of a tenement window. There was a doctor's bill. So he borrowed another $300 from the loan company. The marshal, suspecting he would not get paid, then went directly to the dishwasher's employer to garnishee his small salary. The employer, not wanting any trouble or extra paperwork, fired the dishwasher.

In 1975, an all-out effort to abolish the marshals was made in the state legislature, organized by Stephen Shestakofsky, the legislative representative of the Citizens Union. City Investigations Comissioner Nicholas Scoppetta wrote a strong letter to several legislators supporting the bill to outlaw marshals and replace them with salaried, less political people. The *New York Post* published an editorial urging abolition. And the abolition bill, sponsored by Republican Roy Goodman, passed the state Senate on May 7, 46 to 10.

Then it came under the jurisdiction of Stanley Steingut, the Democratic Speaker of the Assembly. In the past, bills relating to marshals had been assigned to the Judiciary Committee, but Steingut did not fully trust the membership of that committee—too many free-thinkers—so he ignored tradition and sent the bill to the Committee on Cities, chaired by Anthony DiFalco, a loyal clubhouse man and the son of the powerful Surrogate Judge Samuel DiFalco. (Josh Friedman of the *New York Post*, the only Albany reporter who paid any notice to this legislation, wrote a story pointing out a certain conflict of interest: Two district leaders in DiFalco's Lower East Side Assembly district happened to be city marshals themselves. The honorable DiFalco quickly called Friedman to say there were actually *three* Democratic district leaders in his area who were marshals.) In committee, a Steingut acolyte from Brooklyn, Assemblyman Howard Lasher, helped DiFalco defend the marshals, and the Committee on Cities voted not to let the bill come to the floor for a vote, a necessary strategy, since no assemblyman would have wanted to get caught in public having to choose between good government and Stanley Steingut.

And there are the two cases we described in detail in chapter 4, where we told how Speaker Steingut, Assemblyman Cincotta, and other clubhouse Democrats refused to support a mortgage pool to end redlining by savings banks. Until there was intense lobbying from the savings banks, Steingut had been telling urban liberals and members of the Black Caucus that he favored the mortgage-pool concept; then he told them he had made a deal with the Republicans. And we told the story of how Arlen Realty and the Museum of Modern Art got a tax-exemption deal to build a $40-million luxury high-rise condominium, how on June 28, 1976, the deal was voted down in the Assembly, 72 to 53, how then the party bosses like Manes, Cunningham, and Esposito, along with other power brokers like William Paley and various Rockefeller viceroys, got on the phone to the legislators, and how thirty-three assemblymen changed their minds. As with the fuel pass-along rent increase, the politicians knew what was right on the merits, but they could not stand up to pressure; they believed they owed their elective offices not to the people, but to the political machine.

One reason for all this economic illiberalism might just be that so many elders of the clubhouse system have vested banking and real-estate interests that are a source of personal income.

Council Majority Leader Tom Cuite, a registered real-estate broker, is also vice-president of the Brooklyn Federal Savings and Loan Association. Alfred Lama, the former Brooklyn Assemblyman and still a quiet power, is a director of the Central State Bank, and a partner in Lama & Vassalotti, an architectural firm that does a lot of business on state-funded housing developments.

Counterfeit common man Meade Esposito is in the banking and insurance business. He owns a large interest in Grand Brokerage, is a director of a mortgage company called Mortgage Affiliates, and was a vice-president of the Kings Layfayette Bank—until former federal prosecutor Robert Morgenthau accused him of arranging an unsecured $225,000 loan for a company Anthony Scotto had an interest in, right after Scotto moved his union's pension fund account into Esposito's bank. Esposito was also on the payroll of the American Bank and Trust Company before it collapsed in September 1976.

Stanley Steingut is a director of the City Title Insurance Company, and of Modular Cities, which owns a tract of land on Staten Island.

Eugene Keogh, important power broker, was a congressman from Brooklyn for twenty years. He is a director of the East River Savings Bank; a director with Meade Esposito of Mortgage Affiliates; a partner in the stock brokerage firm of Hardy & Company; and a director of City Title Insurance with Steingut.

James Mangano, Brooklyn district leader for thirty-four years, was chief clerk of Brooklyn Supreme Court, where he controlled about 500 patronage jobs, until his retirement in 1976. Mangano is still a director of the Atlantic Liberty Savings & Loan Association. The chairman of the bank is George Clark, Sr., the father of the Republican county leader of Brooklyn.

Bill Shea, the clubhouse fund raiser and thinker, is a trustee of the Metropolitan Savings Bank; his law firm represents hundreds of clients ranging from the Catholic Archdiocese to landlord Harry Helmsley, to several banks, to Yonkers Raceway and Madison Square Garden, where Shea's partner Milton Gould is on the board of directors. Shea is also a director of four corporations. He is a counsel to, and a director of, the Colonial Sand & Stone; chairman of the General Battery Corporation, which pays him $82,000 a year, plus expenses; a director of the Fidelity (insurance) Corporation and of Diamond International (with annual sales of $610 million). Shea is also a registered lobbyist for the American Stock Exchange and the Securities Industry Association. Lawyer Harold Fisher also has banking and insurance directorships. He is the chairman of the Dime Savings Bank of Williamsburgh. And he is a director of the American Plan Corporation, the holding company for American Fidelity Fire Insurance, and American Consumer Insurance.

Our focus on Democrats should not suggest that the Republicans are disinterested full-time servants of the public good. We are focusing this chapter on Democrats because they hold elected power in New York City. But clubhouse Republican politicans have a similar personal interests in real estate and banking. Vincent Albano, the Republican county leader in Manhattan, was chairman of the Century National Bank and receives an average of $25,000 a year in "consulting fees" from the National Kinney Corporation. George Clark, the Republican county leader in Brooklyn, is the vice-president of George L. Clark Realtors, Inc. State Senator John Marchi, the Republican Party candidate for mayor in 1969 and 1973, is not only a lawyer but also a licensed real-estate broker. Joe Mangiotta, the boss of Nassau, runs a law firm and has an insurance brokers license.

This selection of judges and court personnel in New York is, as it is in most cities, under the control of the clubhouse system. And of all the failing, unworkable institutions in New York City, there is none closer to toal breakdown than the courts.

The Kerner Commission told us exactly what was wrong with America's cities. The McKay Commission did an excellent job documenting what went wrong at Attica. The Knapp Commission told us all we needed to know about police corruption. So we have a shelf full of documents that prove the New York City court system is a failure. The social cost of politicized, slothful, mediocre, a possibly venal judiciary can be substantial. It can undercut respect for the rule of law. It can lead to favoritism and unequal justice in cases involving landlords, insurance companies, and others with political influence. It can demoralize the legal profession. And it can contribute to the city-killing tide of street crime, by giving lenient treatment to narcotics dealers and mobsters in the junk trade.

In October 1972, the New York State Legislative Committee on Crime published an analysis of 1762 dispositions of organized crime cases in state courts in New York City between 1960 and 1969. The report observed that 44.7 per cent of all the indictments against Mafiosi were dismissed by state judges, while only 11.5 per cent of the indictments against all other defendants were dismissed.

During 1971 and 1972, one Brooklyn Supreme Court justice alone—Joseph Corso—dismissed criminal indictments against five different Mafia defendants, and all five indictments were later *unanimously* reinstated by the Appellate Division. Perhaps it is pertinent to add that before reaching the State Supreme Court bench, Joseph Corso had been chairman of the Assembly Ethics Committee.

In June 1973, the Economic Development Council released a study of productivity among judges. The study disclosed that Supreme Court justices handling criminal cases in Manhattan were on the bench an average of 3 hours and 21 minutes a day. And, the *Daily News* reported about a secret Bar

Association document that accused five State Supreme Court justices of misconduct ranging from "improper" relations with lawyers, to laziness, to "screaming at lawyers and witnesses from the bench," to the imposition of "unduly harsh sentences." At the same time the State Investigation Commission concluded that the judiciary of New York City had "failed to fulfill its obligation to properly discipline judges . . . . The present practice of allowing the judiciary to police itself has not worked. In certain cases where serious allegations were made involving corruption, ulterior motives for decisions, and the failure to accord litigants basic rights, the responsible persons in the judicial system either took little action . . . or, at best, investigated them in the most cursory and unprofessional manner."

Five months later, the State Select Committee on Crime released a study that documented how fifteen different Manhattan Supreme Court justices had granted sixty-seven illegal discharges in narcotics cases. An illegal sentence under the state's old penal law was a conditional or unconditional discharge to anyone convicted of a narcotics felony. The report pointed out that of the sixty-seven defendants who were freed illegally, "41 were re-arrested, some within weeks, for crimes which often increased in magnitude and violence." The committee attributed 20 of the illegal sentences to Justice Harry Frank, 16 to Justice Gerald Culkin, and eight to former Justice Mitchell Schweitzer, who was forced off the bench in 1971, accused of conspiracy and of having private business activities inconsistent with his duties as a judge.

The same legislative committee, a few months earlier, had discovered nineteen illegal felony discharges in Queens drug cases; of the nineteen, eight were granted by one judge, Albert Bosch.

But no one need not depend on lawyerlike reports to know the court system does not work. Just sit for a week in a chaotic courtroom, where justice comes to look like a meatgrinder gone berserk.

You will see arraignment proceedings in which bails are set in forty-second conferences at the bench. You will see judges with unmistakable prejudices against blacks and Hispanics. Judges too stupid to follow subtle legal argument. Judges who coerce guilty pleas and civil settlements, who malinger and manipulate the calendars, who will do anything to escape the mental labor of conducting a jury trail. You will see judges who are rambling and incoherent from too many martinis at lunch. Judges who are abusive, insulting, and sarcastic.

You will see judges who open court at 11 A.M.., break for lunch at 1 P.M., and reconvene court at 2:30 P.M. for 45 minutes, and then leave to catch the last two races at Belmont Racetrack. One Friday at 4:30 P.M., in the summer of 1975, we were present when a rape defendant jumped bail in Manhattan Supreme Court, and court attendants urgently needed a judge to sign a bench warrant. *One* jurist out of the twenty-five who were supposed to be working at the time was actually in the building—Justice Peter McQuillan. He signed the bench warrant.

You will see judges bend the law to favor the clients of clubhouse lawyers. You will see judges in the landlord-and-tenant parts go out to lunch with the landlord's lawyer.

To be fair, you will also see perhaps thirty superb judges*—out of about 350 members of the bench. These thirty judges have a strong sense of justice and integrity, are impartial, hard-working, wise in the law, and independent. And some of them do come out of political clubs. But the considered generalization stands: The overwhelming majority of judges are unqualified for the job. They were chosen because of their influence with a district leader, or a relative's cash donation to the political party, and not for the brilliance of their legal minds. In Brooklyn, Queens, or the Bronx, a defeated candidate for Assembly has a better chance for judicial nomination than a law school dean. Merit is an alien factor—an accidental bonus—in the selection of judges.

And beyond the daily, grinding absence of justice for the average defendant, the average crime victim, and the average lawyer, there is another consequence of clubhouse control over the courthouse: corruption. As we completed this book, seven judges in New York City are under criminal indictment, and awaiting trial.

The method for selecting State Supreme Court justices in New York is cynical and manipulative. In 1932, the Association of the Bar said in a report recommending the merit appointment of justices of the State Supreme Court: "The elective system . . . . has merely permitted the electorate to vote for candidates selected by leaders or bosses of the various political parties, with no control by the electorate over the choice of candidates so selected, with the result that the elective system usually has resulted in the dominant party in every locality merely ratifying by election the candidate of such party so selected."

Today the Democratic and Republican Party leaders will meet in private to choose judges in bi-partisan deals that makes elections a farce. Judicial delegates, usually party functionaries or patronage jobholders, run in party primaries, and then vote as instructed in judicial nominating conventions. The public never has a chance to vote directly for a judicial candidate in a primary, and then in the general election it usually can only rubberstamp a candidate who already has the nomination of both parties.

Of the last 150 State Supreme Court justices "elected" in New York, 126 ran with such a pre-arranged endorsement of both major political parties. And ten of these bi-partisan brokered judges were found to be "unqualified" or "not

*Among the fine judges in New York are Milton Mollen, Peter McQuillan, Samuel Silverman, Ernst Rosenberger, Eve Preminger, James Leff, Leonard Sandler, John Carro, Mel Glass, Leon Polsky, and Israel Rubin.

approved" by the Association of the Bar, although the public, by then, could do nothing to prevent the knighting of these incompetents.

In 1968, the Bar Association found four judges with cross-party nominations to be unqualified: Isidore Dollinger, the Bronx district attorney; Criminal Court Judge Manual Gomez; Bronx State Senator Ivan Warner; and Paul Fino, the Bronx Republican Party boss.

In 1971, Frederick Hammer, endorsed by all four political parties, was "not approved" by the Bar Association, "because of his lack of judicial temperament."

In 1972, the Bar Association rejected Leonard Scholnick and Edward Lentol for the State Supreme Court in Brooklyn. Scholnick was a city councilman, and Lentol a state senator.

In 1973, the Bar Association found "not qualified" two bi-partisan Supreme Court nominees in Queen county—Ann Dufficy and Joan Marie Durante. The Association said Mrs. Dufficy was rejected because of a "lack of experience and professional ability."

In 1975, the Bar Association disapproved Irwin Silbowitz, a two-party nominee for Bronx Supreme Court, because he "lacked qualifications." Silbowitz had been "not qualified" before—he ran successfully for the Civil Court in 1972 with the backing of the Cunningham machine.

Here are a few examples of how the bi-partisan backroom manipulation of the judiciary has worked. In 1970, there were six vacancies for Supreme Court in Brooklyn. Instead of having an election, Democratic boss Meade Esposito, a former bail bondsman, sat down with several Republican district leaders and made a deal for cross endorsements of five Democrats and one Republican. The Republican party gave their line on the ballot to five Democrats: Frank Composto, John Monteleone, Abraham Kalina, Irvin Kartell, and Charles Rubin, a party fund raiser. In exchange, the Democrats gave their line on the ballot to a Republican—Joseph Soviero.

On May 17, 1971, when Matthew Troy was the Democratic boss in Queens, and the late Sidney Hein was the Republican boss, the two men met in a diner on Queens Boulevard and, in Troy's words, "divided up the county for the next couple of years." An agreement was made on the division of spoils, to avoid elections. "The Package," as Troy called it, was actually written up, and Troy carried the folded copy in his wallet for several years. He showed it to us one night, and later he allowed Richard Reeves to quote most of it in the March 5, 1973, issue of *New York* magazine. The Troy-Hein pact read in part:

Five new Supreme Court judgeships. Repubs to get three-Dems to get two (plus Dems to get replacement for Tony Livoti)—all on a bi-partisanship basis. . . . If legislators go to Civil Court vacancies, then the special election for legis. vacancy will have no Repub.

opponent. . . . Repubs agree to give bi-partisan endorsement to Boro Pres . . . District Attorney and Surrogate. . . . Repubs and Dems will split (half-each) Counsel to Public Administrator replacement for Lou Laurino. . . . Repub to permit MJT [Troy himself] to appoint reapportionment head, once Repub seats are protected. . . . MJT to receive bi-partisan Councilman endorsement in 1973.

It all came to pass, and the registered voters of Queens County had no voice in any of it.

In 1973 Troy worked out another package with the Republicans to share eight Supreme Court judgeships with cross-party endorsements. Troy's Democrats endorsed two infamously inept Republicans—Harold Hyman, counsel to the county clerk; and Bar Association reject Joan Marie Durante, the daughter of the county clerk, John Durante. And the Republicans gave their line on the voting machine to six Democrats: Seymour Boyers, Kenneth Browne, Edwin Kasoff, Leonard Finz, George Balbach, and Bar Association reject Ann Dufficy.

The same year, the Democrats in the First Judicial Department (Manhattan and the Bronx) made a deal with the Republicans to carve up four Supreme Court judgeships. The Democrats endorsed one Republican, Irvin Kirschenbaum, the former GOP party treasurer in Manhattan. And the Republicans endorsed three Democrats: Joseph Marro, a former state senator; Alexander Chananau, a Bronx assemblyman of no distinction; and Alfred Callahan, a Civil Court judge of poor reputation. Once again, the voters were given no choice.

And then in 1976, the patronage-rich fourteen-year job of Surrogate of Brooklyn came vacant and was up for election. So the Democratic party boss, Meade Esposito, and the Republican party boss, George Clark, both decided to support the same candidate Bernard Bloom. It was a marriage made in hack heaven. Bloom was a Democratic party district leader in Flatbush, and for years had held a seldom-show, $27,000-a-year state job as director of servicemen's voting. Bloom, an outspoken defender of clubhouses and patronage who called reformers "garbage," wasn't much of a lawyer and had no judicial experience, but it didn't matter. He had the endorsement of both the Democratic and the Republican organizations. When a lawyer of our acquaintance asked Clark why he had given his party's endorsement to a Democrat, Clark explained that Bloom had promised the Republicans 20 per cent of the patronage. We can't elect a Republican in Kings County, so why not take him? The reformers will give us zero patronage, and Bloom has promised us a regular slice.

Bloom, opposed by every good-government group, had a Democratic primary challenge from a respected attorney, Daniel Eisenberg. So to divide the "reform-Jewish vote" Esposito contrived the entry of a lower court judge, Abraham Schulman, into the race, and Schulman siphoned off enough votes to allow Bloom to win, and to go on to win the general election with dual party endorsement. This machine trick of covertly helping spoiler candidates is a tactic that the resourceful Esposito has used before. In 1973, he encouraged one Ruth Lerner to enter the race for Brooklyn borough president. The lady took enough "reform-Jewish votes" away from Stephen Solarz so that the clubhouse-backed Sebastian Leone won. She was then compensated with a $31,758-a-year-job in the Beame administration.

This, then is the clubhouse system. Corrupt politicians—like Matthew Troy, Carmine DeSapio, Frank Gilligan, John Murphy, and Bert Podell. Corrupt entrepreneurs—like Bernard Bergman and Eugene Hollander. Intellectual serfs—like City Councilmen Eugene Mastropieri and Dominick Corso—who are not free to vote their own beliefs. Terminal cynics—like Howard Golden. Unqualified, incompetent judges—like Irwin Silbowitz, Gerald Held, and Joan Durante. Lawyers with shady reputations—like Roy Cohn. Businessman who have been caught cheating or breaking the rules—like Vincent Caristo, Sidney Lipkins, and Fortune Pope.

This system has not been challenged or disturbed by Mayor Ed Koch. The secret to understanding Koch is that he is a bully to the weak, and a toady to the strong. Koch has always accommodated to power. When he was in Congress he cultivated and then defended the autocratic chairman of the administration committee, Wayne Hays. To prove he was "one of the boys," Koch appeared as a character witness for his two corrupt colleagues, Frank Brasco and Bert Podell.

Koch won the Democratic primary run-off for Mayor in September of 1977 over Mario Cuomo mostly because the clubhouse bosses of Brooklyn and the Bronx supported him. Stanley Friedman, Meade Esposito, Harold Fisher, and Abe Beame somehow understood they could trust Koch and work with him, despite his image as a reformer.

As Mayor Koch has not disappointed the clubhouse system. Friedman and Esposito have gotten what they want. As soon as he won, Koch switched his position and gave in to the money interests on Westway. Businessmen allied with the county leaders still get their franchises, parking lots, express bus routes, vendor contracts, and tax abatements. The clubhouse drones are still on the payroll at city agencies. Koch deals with the county leaders on judgeships and reapportionment.

As Mayor Ed Koch has become part of the same system he used to so eloquently denounce when he was a young reformer campaigning against Carmine DeSapio.

LABOR PAINS | 9

New York City's unions have been the big losers in the new power game that has been played since the city's fiscal crisis began. The public employee unions have been the most visible casualties, but almost every segment of organized labor is weaker today than at any time since the end of the 1940s.

In the winter of 1975-76 unemployment in the city's giant construction locals averaged 60-70 per cent, and for the first time in memory, highly skilled workers were applying for "traveling cards" to work in states like Louisiana and Texas or on the Alaskan pipeline. Some locals even had trouble meeting the payments on medical bills for members and families from their seriously depleted welfare funds. The powerful Communications Workers of America failed to stop the Bell system's New York Telephone from imposing a charge for information service, and this meant layoffs for hundreds of operators. (Thousands more are scheduled for the slag heap as Bell pushes ahead with its Draconian automation program. Nationally, 50,000 operators will be displaced in less than four years.)

Under the dual impact of permanent recession and continuing loss of jobs, powerful labor leaders saw their memberships and treasuries shrink, and they knew that their political power—national as well as local—was ebbing away with the decline in bodies and dollars. This will, of course, hasten the transition to a new generation of leaders and, perhaps a new style of leadership in New York City's unions.

Perhaps the biggest loser is Harry Van Arsdale, who for decades was the city's top labor power broker. Although superficially his power stemmed from his presidency of the New York Central Labor Council, his real power base has always been the numerically small but politically and financially potent building trades. Van Arsdale controls New York's skilled electricians who wire new buildings and keep the city's heavy electrical equipment running; his son Thomas is the nominal head of the union, Local 3 of the International Brotherhood of Electrical Workers. And, after years of bloody organizing wars, Van Arsdale also controls New York's 11,000 fleet taxi drivers, who belong to a special "federal local" union, affiliated directly to the AFL-CIO in Washington. Both of these unions have fallen on bad days. Local 3, while not so badly hit as some other construction unions, has plummeted with the rest of the industry, and as for the taxi industry, it is coming apart at the seams. Most of the large fleets whose drivers Van Arsdale controlled grew up during Prohibition when bootleggers used them to deliver their goods. When Repeal was passed, the thugs who owned the fleets found they still had a lucrative business potential. By seeing to it that the number of cabs allowed on the streets was restricted, they retained a stranglehold on the only profitable element of New York's transportation business. This state of affairs persisted until the last years of the Lindsay administration, when blacks and Puerto Ricans effectively took control of the cab business in their own neighborhoods after white drivers refused to service the ghetto areas—so that today a fleet of "gypsy" cabs equal in size to the fleet that carries the official licenced medallions, plies the city's streets. The fleet owners had no stomach for the all-out war that would have resulted from any effort to drive the "gypsies" off the streets, and they began selling off their medallions to individual drivers. In 1980, the fleet owners received permission from the Taxi and Limousine Commission to "lease" cabs directly to drivers, effectively putting the union out of business.

Perhaps the high point of Van Arsdale's power came in 1970, when he virtually stole the endorsement of organized labor in that year's gubernatorial election for Nelson Rockefeller. The incident is expressive of the state of democracy within America's most "liberal" labor bastion.

As we have earlier noted, Nelson Rockefeller "bought" large segments of the traditionally Democratic labor movement—not with his own sumptuous purse but with great gobs of gravy from the public treasury, especially his massive building projects and lavish pension settlements. In 1970, his Democratic opponent was Arthur Goldberg, a lifelong labor lawyer and former general counsel of the AFL-CIO, a former Secretary of Labor, a former Supreme Court justice. Goldberg turned out to be one of the most boring, inept candidates in American political history, but there was little doubt that he was also one of the most prominent members of the labor movement ever to have run for office, anywhere in the nation. He deserved labor's support in New York, and everyone expected him to get it.

Trouble started as soon as the State Federation convened at the Concord Hotel in the Catskills late in September. Ray Corbett, head of the tiny Sheet Metal Workers union and permanent factotum of the State Fed, refused to give Goldberg's forces a list of the delegates accredited to the convention. Without it, there could be no valid rollcall votes. While Corbett stalled, Van Arsdale was rushing busloads of his electrical workers from New York City to the convention site. On the night of the vote, a reporter from the Buffalo

Courier-Express wrote that a box of delegate badges, "slightly smaller than a shoe box," suddenly materialized and the badges were distributed to the newcomers. There were only 1303 delegates registered for the convention, but reporters who were present said that at least 2500 bodies packed the convention floor.

As soon as Nelson Rockefeller was nominated, Victor Gotbaum, a Goldberg partisan, demanded a rollcall vote. But Corbett called for a standing vote instead and ruled that Rockefeller—clearly the favorite of the newly arrived "delegates"—had won. Gotbaum continued to scream for a rollcall from the floor, but Corbett had Gotbaum's microphone turned off and then quickly recognized a Rockefeller delegate who called for adjournment. Without further ado the convention was adjourned and the lights in the hall were turned out. At this point, outraged delegates began scaling large glass ashtrays at the dais. Lights were visible only around the CBS-TV film crew; they silhouetted Gotbaum and Van Arsdale as the following conversation took place.

"What are you getting so excited about?" Van Arsdale asked.

"You stole it from us, Harry!" the hulking Gotbaum answered.

Despite the ensuing public outcry, the labor vote stayed stolen for Rockefeller. The governor spent the rest of the campaign claiming that he had "the backing of organized labor," effectively undercutting one of the few strong issues that the bumbling Goldberg might have used to win.

No single labor leader in New York City can be expected to exercise the degree of power until recently held by Van Arsdale. Albert Shanker, the man who Woody Allen said was most likely to instigate a nuclear World War III, was everybody's bet as Van Arsdale's eventual successor, but Shanker has become a surprising loser in the new arrangements of power since the onset of the fiscal crisis.

Shanker has a visceral understanding of how to accumulate power. We remember seeing him late at night in a small print shop on the Lower East Side in the late 1950s, editing proof of the then fledgling teachers union paper. In those days, Shanker was a quiet, efficient bureaucrat who stood in the shadow of David Selden, his close friend, the dynamic leader of the teachers' efforts to win recognition from a hidebound oligarchy that ruled the city's schools from the fortress headquarters of the Board of Education at 110 Livingston Street. After the teachers' organization drive took fire, Selden ascended to the presidency of the national union, the American Federation of Teachers, in Washington, and left the crucial New York local, the United Federation of Teachers, in the hands of his trusted aide. Shanker quickly consolidated his power by dealing with the volatile and complex issue of race in New York City's schools as if nothing more were involved than bread-and-butter trade-union issues. He protected inept and insensitive teachers from parents' demands for change by strictly enforcing seniority regulations in the contract. His union members were frightened by the parents' growing demands to be involved in educational decision-making, by the racially charged atmosphere in the schools and the demands for more black teachers and administrators, by the growing debate over how New York's inadequate educational resources would be allocated between teachers' salaries and educational programs. Instead of building an effective coalition with the parents, Shanker consistently took the narrow view that the educational system would improve as teachers' salaries and fringe benefits were improved, period.

The incredible insensitivity with which Lindsay's administration introduced "decentralization" into New York's school system played right into Shanker's hands. Three trial districts for decentralization were chosen, not one of them in a white area. As a result, the flareups that occurred during the disastrous school strike of 1968 were easily portrayed as conflicts between "radical" blacks and embattled white professionals. It became a political strike over the issue of who would control the schools, and Lindsay dealt Shanker all the winning cards.

Since then, Shanker has been able to beat back any challenges to his leadership of the UFT. He has built alliances with corrupt political machines in the ghettoes, like Sam Wright's in Brownsville, which try to control the popularly elected, decentralized school boards and their juicy patronage pies. Shanker can now pick up the phone and have a "militant" black teacher fired in Brownsville or a dozen other localities whenever he chooses. He has convinced his membership that its security lies in politics, and through alliances with the building trades and other right-wing elements in state labor, he has become a king-maker in New York politics. (At the same time, Shanker has used his New York power base to axe his old friend Selden and succeed him as president of the AFT. Until Lane Kirkland succeeded to the presidency when Meany resigned, Shanker appeared to be the "great white hope" of labor's right wing to succeed George Meany as president of the AFL-CIO. If nothing else, he is a man of limitless ambition.)

But despite Shanker's considerable local and national political power, the UFT and Shanker himself have fared poorly since the onset of the fiscal crisis.

As Stephanie Harrington reported in the November 17, 1976, *Village Voice*, 13,000 out of 56,000 full-time teachers have been laid-off, as well as 600 out of 3000 paraprofessionals, 3000 out of 8000 aides, and 1000 of 2000 school guards. The firings and vacant positions in the schools have resulted in up to 45 students in a class, the disappearance of guidance teachers, of music, art and library. New York City's schools are in even greater chaos than they were during the troubled years of the 1960s.

Of all areas of city life, the schools have been among the hardest hit in the layoffs for a variety of reasons. First, the parent constituency remains unorganized. As middle-class whites withdrew from the city's public-education system, the schools became yet another minority service that elicits little consideration from New York's new decision-makers. More and more they are seen on a par with the municipal hospitals, which also serve a predominantly minority population. Secondly, considerable savings can be made by laying off well-paid teachers, rather than larger numbers of other civil servants, so this naturally is particularly appealing to the politicians. Teacher salaries and benefits have been a key component in the rising costs of local government all over the nation, and there is also a clear desire among the corporate decision-makers to hamstring the teachers where they have been most successful. Finally, and ironically, Shanker is universally feared and hated, even by his political allies, and they have seized this opportunity to savage him and perhaps pull his fangs. Some people have that kind of effect on others.

Van Arsdale and Shanker typify the traditional "business unionism" of the old AFL, which has predominated over the "social unionists" of the CIO since the merger of organized labor in the early 1950s. But if these right-wing "bread and butter" unionists have now fallen on bad days, their traditional enemies in the "progressive" unions have hardly fared better. The entire labor movement is drifting without goals or direction, and many of the old rallying cries are obsolete. The unions seem to be suffering from a potentially fatal lack of ideas and leadership at a time when the hammer blows of change are falling with brutal regularity.

Typical of this drift are the public-employee unions, nationwide still the fastest growing segment of organized labor despite massive layoffs. Until quite recently the business press was always warning that the public-employee unions represented a radical new force in the house of labor, the modern equivalent of the CIO in the 1930s. Victor Gotbaum, head of New York City's polyglot District Council 37 of the American Federation of State, County and Municipal Employees, was the paradigm of the kind of sophisticated, hungry public-employee leadership which the editorial writers feared. But when we interviewed Gotbaum and asked what his program was for the new period of stringency facing public workers, he gave us a one-word answer: "Survive."

Yet in the wake of the fiscal compromises worked out by MAC and the EFCB, Gotbaum is in the unenviable position of being not only New York City's major labor leader but its biggest creditor as well. And public-employee pension funds are likely to go on being the city's fiscal crutch for at least a decade. To protect his billions in city paper, Gotbaum will continue to be asked to sacrifice his members. He walks a narrow line: a misstep in one direction means endangering the pensions; a wrong step in the other direction means new layoffs. In the event, Gotbaum has become frozen, a captive of the business elite running New York City and now effectively running his union.

Gotbaum recognizes his position—and he hates it. The constant tensions show in his craggy face, and he seems physically diminished, the husky body hunched lower, the roaring voice now an exhausted grumble. He admits that he did not foresee the crisis, that he never knew the banks were destroying the city's credit until he was told about it by a high-placed friend in Albany—six months after the fact. He is uncomfortable with the phalanx of fiscal experts with whom he now bargains ("I've got fiscal advisers up the ass," he told us), but at the same time he has no alternative approaches, no analysis of the larger crisis besetting the national economy. A young staff aide of his told us, "It's pitiful. There isn't anyone around Victor with any ideas. There's no one to counter what the banks tell him. He just stumbles from one crisis to the next."

What troubles Gotbaum most is the inherent impotence of public-employee unionism. He recognizes that the power to strike, the only ultimately meaningful power that any union possesses, is worthless in the current situation. His workers struck the city hospitals—and no one cared. Gotbaum's members serve the poor of the city, and the power brokers couldn't care less if the poor are victimized. Only half jokingly, he told us that about the only group of workers in his union who could inconvenience the rich are the sewer laborers. "Maybe we should just open up all the treatment plants and let all that shit float around the city for a few weeks," he growled.

More than anything else, Gotbaum really believes that New York "is dying." Felix Rohatyn has put together a coalition of midtown real-estate speculators and right-wing union leaders that advocated the construction of a $1.1-billion superhighway on Manhattan's West Side and a convention center which would require a permanent subsidy from the city treasury. Under changes in the Federal Highway Act, the funds for the highway could, on the other hand, be transferred to mass transit construction, benefiting the many city workers who use the subways as opposed to the three per cent of travelers, mostly Wall Street executives, who would use the new highway. Gotbaum endorses the construction plans for the superhighway and the convention center: "I guess that makes me a reactionary too. We need these symbols of movement to show that New York is still alive."

Victor Gotbaum will be New York's most important union leader for at least another few years. The other public-employee unions are small and their leaders are inept or aging. John DeLury, former head of the Sanitationmen, which is loosely affiliated to the Teamsters, had always exercised power far greater than the size of his membership would warrant, because of his well-oiled political apparatus, but Gotbaum has long since eclipsed him in the scope of his political operation, and DeLury has died. The Transport Workers Union, the leading public-employee union while the inimitable Michael Quill was alive, is now isolated and poorly directed. (Blacks and Hispanics make up three-quarters of the membership but have been excluded from leadership in a bitter internal civil war with Quill's remaining heirs. But this situation can't continue much longer.) The other uniformed services, police and fire, have been riven by factionalism and opportunism; they will be forced to accept the patterns established by Gotbaum whether they like it or not, and cannot much longer be the tail that wags the dog in municipal bargaining.

From the members' point of view, the best thing that could happen would be for most of these small fiefdoms to merge into Gotbaum's District Council 37. But this is unlikely, given the lush salaries and other benefits enjoyed by the legion of union officials that has proliferated under the current fragmented system. The only conclusion we can make is that city workers face a bleak future. After generations of being at the bottom of the employment ladder, they began radically to alter their situation in the late 1960s and early 1970s. But that progress has now been frozen, and it will take a drastic shift in the entire structure of the national economy before any thaw sets in.

This might be a good place to say a word about pensions, a subject that has generated a great deal of controversy in the public debate over New York City's indebtedness. Traditionally, ample pensions were one of the few attractions of public employment. The other significant benefit was security. The civil service didn't expand or contract with the sudden gyrations of the general economy, and once you had gotten a job, you were likely to keep it. Governments didn't suddenly go out of business. When you reached the end of your productive years, the pension was waiting. As his part of the tradeoff, the public worker was expected to forego high wages and decent working conditions—until the sudden upsurge of public unionism in the 1960s, that is.

For the elected officials who ran the system, at least, it was an ideal arrangement. The average worker lived only two or three years after his retirement at sixty-five, so pensions were no great drain on the public treasury and there were no sudden wage raises and attendant tax increases to deal with. Government was subsidized by its workers. Then, the rules changed. The increasing demand for government services required an expanded work force. The new workers were not the docile civil servants of the past. Very shortly, they attempted to "catch up" for the lost benefits of a generation.

At the same time, the public perception of government workers remained hostile. Civil servants didn't create things, they delivered services, and therefore they were "unproductive." Everybody wants policemen and firemen to appear when called, they want their garbage picked up, they want dozens of other necessities—sewers, schools, hospitals—to function well. But the people who peform these jobs are largely invisible, and their salary demands are, by definition, "excessive" since we pay for them directly with our tax dollars. When auto workers strike Ford, no one really gets upset. But when hospital workers walk out, the general public is alarmed—and outraged.

After all, we all may *need* a hospital, but we may only *want* a new car. Public employees are therefore often perceived as public enemies.

As public employees achieved parity with, and in some areas actually surpassed, their counterparts in the private sector, attention focused on their lavish pension schemes. For New Yorkers in the early 1970s, it soon became apparent that the rivalry between Nelson Rockefeller and John Lindsay as to who could give away more of the public's money had created a monster that was costing the city $1 billion a year. Here are just some of the abuses:

- Retirement at half pay after twenty years' service had spread rapidly from the police and firemen to sanitation, correction, and transit workers. Other groups were demanding the same benefit. State legislators, the source of all these goodies, had also extended the twenty-year retirement scheme to themselves, undoubtedly because of the "arduous" nature of the work they put in as part-time playboys in Albany. Length of service before retirement has been under general attack. A New York City teacher, for instance, can retire at full pension at 55 with only 25 years of service.
- In an open bid to buy the support of the uniformed services in the 1969 election, Lindsay had granted dollar-a-day annuity payments to the police, fire, correction, and sanitationmen and all their officers. These amounted to "supplementary pensions" on top of regular pension and Social Security payments. This "sweetener" cost the city $16.7 million a year. In 1976, the New York Public Interest Research Group charged that these payments were "illegal" under the state constitution and brought suit to force the unions that were managing the money to return it to the city treasury. They lost the suit and the payments continue.
- The time span on which pensions were computed was constantly reduced until a worker's earnings in his final year became the common basis for pension payments, as opposed to average earnings over the last five years of employment. To add insult to injury, overtime pay was included in this final year's salary, the *Daily News* revealed, and supervisors, themselves the beneficiaries of this system, were allowing retirees to work excessive amounts of overtime to drive up their pension base.

While all of these things were going on, the true cost of public-employee pensions was systematically hidden from the public. This was accomplished by allowing the costs to be computed on the basis of outdated mortality tables, some dating back to 1918. Even though this outrageous gimmick reduced city pension contributions in the present, it left a vast gap to be made up by future taxpayers. As a matter of fact, the pensions were systematically underfunded by at least $1 billion a year. The underfunding also resulted from an incredibly poor investment return provided by the banks and professional money managers in charge of the funds. When the stock and bond markets were near their all-time peaks New York City pension funds earned as little as 1 per cent a year.

Then, in the midst of the fiscal crisis, the pension funds were forced to accept most of the burden of forestalling bankruptcy by investing in MAC securities. By the end of 1976, the pension funds were holders of $3.8 billion in city debt, a little less than 40 per cent of their total assets. (A federal law had to be passed to allow the unions to invest more than 10 per cent of their pension assets in any one security.) This figure declined to 27 per cent of assets by late 1980.

A great deal of attention has been focused on the public pension mess in New York City, but it should be noted that the mess is endemic throughout urban America. For instance, a survey of forty-four cities in Pennsylvania showed that more than three-quarters of them lacked adequately funded pension accounts. Nor is New York the most generous employer, by far. The State of Louisiana provides pensions equal to 75 per cent of take-home pay plus $300 for its retirees. And many public pension plans include automatic cost-of-living increases, something New York's does not.

Congressman Les Aspin has revealed that U.S. military retirement plans are easily the most lavish of all. As he wrote in the December 1976 issue of *Harper's* magazine, "The average officer retiring this year is a forty-six-year-old lieutenant colonel receiving a pension of $15,400 a year; his opposite number in the enlisted ranks is a forty-one-year-old Army platoon sergeant getting $6,400 a year. These retirees continue to enjoy, among other benefits, subsidized medical care, military commissaries with cheaper food, and free aircraft flights." Aspin observes that military pensions absorb 8.5 per cent of America's military budget ($8.4 billion in 1976), and warns that by the year 2000, we will be paying $34 billion a year in military pensions. Total federal pension commitments amount to $300 billion, a "secret debt" half the size of the official $600-billion national debt."

These massive federal, state, and local pension obligations raise a basic question of equity. While public employees frequently retire on salaries higher than those earned while working, 70 per cent of all U.S. citizens 65 and older are forced to live on Social Security and savings. Only half of the current work force is covered by any pension plan at all, and most of those are inadequate by any standard. And these computations don't even begin to consider the pension plans, such as the Teamster's, which have been systematically looted by corrupt union officials and employers, often in collusion with the mob.

The time has clearly come to ask how we shall provide a decent retirement income for *all* Americans, instead of perpetuating the vicious two-tiered system we have now, which creates a tiny privileged elite while the rest must subsist at the margin of starvation. The current system simply doesn't work—in New York or anyplace else.

The Labor Day boast of politicians and labor leaders that New York City is a "union town" has a hollow ring. Among white-collar workers, who are a larger and larger majority of the labor force, union organization is almost nonexistent outside the civil service. Repeated efforts to sign up the clerks, typists, and general office workers who move thousands of tons of paper each day in the teeming office towers of midtown and Wall Street have foundered on the inverse class consciousness of a generation that considers it a privilege to wear clean clothes at work. It is ironic that college and school teachers have flocked to organize while bank tellers and computer clerks disdain a union card. Part of the problem involves the high proportion of young women in these latter jobs. Despite increased feminist consciousness, these women still see marriage and raising a family as their primary route of escape from the low wages and drudgery of their jobs—although the lower-middle-class family is less and less able to survive unless both parents work full time. The unions had hoped that the increasing proportion of young blacks and Hispanics in this work force might infuse some militancy into the white-collar group, but so far this seems not to have been the case, perhaps because these workers have little reason to feel any identity with organized labor; they know about their parents' experiences in factory jobs, where more often than not the union was as much an enemy as the employer was.

Despite the false image projected by the press and by the employers, New York remains what it has always been—a sweatshop city. Average wage figures in New York are misleading, because of the minority of relatively high-paid construction, printing, and uniformed civil service jobs. Most unskilled and semiskilled workers struggle at jobs that pay far less than the minimum budget of $12,949 prescribed by the Bureau of Labor Statistics in late 1979 for a "lower than intermediate" standard of living for a family of four in New York City. Moonlighting is common, and is one significant reason why young workers find it impossible to gain even entry-level jobs in the shrinking economy. Inflation rapidly consumes whatever benefits legitimate unions manage to win. This problem is hardly limited to New York, however; for several years now, the real wages of American workers—and their standard of living—have been falling steadily. The average worker today makes less than he did in real terms in 1971.

This general trend is exacerbated in New York City by two special problems: The first is the recrudesence of gangster-dominated locals, either "independent" or affiliated with the cancerous Teamsters Union, which dominate many marginal industries in the city. Despite recurrent declarations of war against these racket unions by the AFL-CIO Central Labor Council, little has been done to curb their growth since the late 1950s. Larger, legitimate unions in the same industries ignore their parasitic neighbors, refusing to commit the money and manpower necessary for an all-out drive against corruption. Government at all levels has ignored this problem since Robert Kennedy left the Justice Department. Since this outrage affects minority workers almost exclusively, even the press ignores the hegemony of the mob over a large segment of low-wage workers. Very few papers any longer cover labor as a regular beat, and then only when major strikes or negotiations are in progress. But the mob's thumb is on the scale every time a housewife buys a pound of meat or a bag of fruit; they add a few cents to the cost of every garment purchased, every manufactured item that any American buys. Racket unions are the dirty little secret of our economic life, and they will remain so until another Kennedy or Kefauver comes along who believes that the Constitution doesn't become "inoperative" at the factory door.

The second problem is the slow rot that has infected New York's largest industry and the union that controls it—the International Ladies' Garment Workers Union, AFL-CIO. The ILGWU has a special niche in American labor history. Plays, movies, and dozens of books have been written about it. It is the only American union that had its own political party—the Liberal Party.

No one can deny the seminal influence of the ILG on American labor. For decades its only peer in the fight for better wages and working conditions was the United Mine Workers.

But the bright myth of the progressive ILG has a dark underside that is rarely examined. After a bitter struggle between Socialists and Communists for control of the union in the mid-1920s when pitched battles raged on the streets of the garment center, the victorious Socialists instituted an authoritarian regime that banned opposition caucuses in the union and concentrated power in the hands of a few hereditary bureaucrats. (ILG locals are famous for being passed from father to son or son-in-law. Dubinsky created Local 23A as a wedding present for his son-in-law, Shelley Appleton. As Herbert Hill, former national labor secretary of the NAACP, says: "They call it a union, but in fact it's just a large family business."

And long after any threat of a Stalinist takeover had disappeared, the rigid controls on democratic opposition, within the union continued. Until the early 1970s, no member who was not a delegate to the national convention and a paid member of the union staff could run for either of the two highest international offices, president and general secretary treasurer. This reduced competition for the leading posts to perhaps 200 members in a 450,000 member union. Only 300 members could run for a post on the General

Executive Board. Power was, and is, restricted to a small club that excludes the working rank-and-file.

Right after World War II, two profound changes began to take place within the garment industry. The Jewish and Italian immigrants who had made up most of the work force in New York's garment shops were replaced by blacks and Puerto Ricans. And the manufacturers began to leave New York in search of low-wage havens in the South or in gangster-protected runaway shops in northern Pennsylvania. New garment products, especially leisure wear and bathing suits, developed mini-industries near their resort markets, primarily in California. The union had a basic choice to make. It had a huge treasury (it still does; union assets in 1976 were $147 million), and it could have followed the runaways and organized the nonunion shops or enforced a boycott of their products in the big Eastern cities. Instead it chose what at the time seemed an easier alternative. It began to cut wages and working conditions in New York and its neighboring states to make local manufacture "competitive." It also began making loans to garment manufacturers from the union treasury. This in turn led to "soft enforcement" of union contracts in favored shops.

This is how Herbert Hill explains the union's waning militancy. "They were never old-fashioned racists; they never said 'nigger.' But in fact they were afraid of these new workers, they had nothing in common with them. They had more in common with the bosses in the industry, many of whom were former members of the union who had scraped together enough capital to open a shop. The union and the bosses sat down and negotiated sweetheart contracts over the heads of the workers, and they even refused to show the workers the contract."

When the workers began setting up caucuses to seek power within the ILG, or even when they protested speed-up and declining piece rates, the union identified these "trouble-makers" to the bosses and had them fired. Hill tells of hundreds of meetings with minority workers over the years. "It was like being a member of the Resistance in occupied Paris. These workers lived in terror of being exposed by the union, because they would never be allowed to work in the industry again." As a result of these conditions, he says, garment workers as a whole were reduced to a "condition of poverty." *The Wall Street Journal* recently reported, "Average hourly earnings of apparel workers are still only two-thirds of the average for all manufacturing employees, and the union's $100-a-month-pension after twenty years is among the lowest in the nation."

In weighing these charges, it is interesting to contrast the newly merged Amalgamated Clothing and Textile Workers Union with the ILG. The Amalgamated is the dominant union in men's clothing, and it faces many of the same problems found throughout the garment industry in general. It has had a markedly different history from the ILG and is not only one of the most democratic of American trade unions, but the most innovative and crusading. The Amalgamated never crushed the Communists; it allowed them democratic rights even during their most destructive phase. When in the 1930s the ILG flirted only momentarily with the CIO and then scampered back to the AFL, the Amalgamated became a bastion of the CIO, and Sidney Hillman, its long-term president, became a major architect of labor's crucial activities during World War II. In the years thereafter the union fought the runaway shops and never gave up the difficult, demanding task of organizing the antiunion clothing factories in the South. (It was an Amalgamated local in Georgia that gave Jimmy Carter his first crucial labor support in his second, and successful, attempt at winning the governorship.) It waged a $6-million national boycott against the Southwest border sweatshops of the Farah pants company, and it conducted the first mass organizing drive among Chicano workers. In 1976, the union merged with the always embattled Textile Workers Union in order to mount a massive new effort to bring union wages and benefits to the infamously anti-union textile industry. As the first stage, they launched a $1-million boycott against the $1.4 billion J. P. Stevens textile empire, which has consistently broken the law and kept unions out of its plants. And through all of this it has successfully maintained wages and working conditions in its organized shops in New York City. (The Amalgamated, by the way, was one of the most outspoken opponents of the war in Vietnam, while the ILG stayed in the trenches with George Meany and his septuagenarian band of Cold War bitter-enders in the right wing of the AFL-CIO. There is no record that the white, male leadership of the ILG polled the black, Puerto Rican, and Chicano mothers who make up the membership, and whose sons provided such a high proportion of the cannon fodder in Southeast Asia, on their views about continuing the struggle.)

The Amalgamated has continued to grow, surpassing the ILG, while the latter has lost 75,000 members in only eight years. Both unions face an increasing challenge from foreign imports. One out of four garments sold in the United States in 1975 was imported, compared with one in twenty only a decade ago. Much of this competition comes from the police states of ILG's beloved "free world" like South Korea, Taiwan, and Haiti, but there is also a flow of men's garments from sweatshops in Eastern Europe, especially Rumania and Hungary. The large banks and multinational corporations are financing this flood of imports—and exportation of American jobs. It will demand a drastically altered stance on the part of the entire labor movement if national policies favoring these forces are to be overturned.

There are some slight glimmerings that the ILG may be awakening to the need for a change in internal structure and external policy. Sol C. Chaikin, the first American-born president in the union's history, has taken the helm. (Chaikin also received a chauffeur-driven limousine and $52,000 salary with the job.) There are rumblings that he is easing out some of the *alte cockers* who were cronies of Dubinsky and Stulberg and who have been getting fat salaries for running dying locals. He has hired a handful of new organizers, and plans to add more. But *The Wall Street Journal* in 1976 reported on a pep rally for employers led by Chaikin in New York at which he preached the need to increase assembly-line pressures in order to improve the workers' ability to compete with Southern and foreign competitors.

The crucial question is how far Chaikin is willing to go in allowing the rank-and-file to compete for union office. As Hill has pointed out, the irony of the ILG is that its "hysterical anti-communism actually recreated the model of Stalinist totalitarianism within the union in the name of a free labor movement." Chaikin and the restless minority members of the ILG must effectively break with that ossified past and establish a transition to full democratic participation for the membership without rending the union apart. A healthier course would probably be to merge the ILG into the new ACTWU, but this seems unlikely. Very few labor leaders can be found today who will sacrifice their limousines in the name of class solidarity.

In a very real sense, the economics of the Northeast region will determine the fate of organized labor not only in New York City but throughout the country. Union organization in the South still faces a long and bitter struggle, forty years after the CIO began the first mass unionization drives in Dixie. Today less than 20 per cent of the American work force is organized, and the unionized workers are still concentrated in the heavy-industry states of Pennsylvania, New York, Ohio, Michigan, New Jersey, Illinois, Indiana, and Wisconsin. Unless labor hangs on to jobs and members in these states, it will wither into impotence.

To succeed, labor must rise to a number of fundamental challenges. The first is to create a new leadership that can replace the "country club" pork-choppers who control so many large unions. This process began when the Mineworkers overthrew the murderous Tony Boyle and his henchmen. Now tough young reformers like Ed Sadlowski have dug in for the long fight to win back the Steelworkers. Other insurgents at the local and district level are succeeding by the hundreds, although the victories go largely unreported in the press. Many of the old progressive unions, like the United Auto Workers, the International Union of Electrical and Radio and Machine Workers, and the Machinists, are undergoing evolution from within. Younger unions, like the Oil, Chemical and Atomic Workers, seem to have healthy internal democratic structures and are in the forefront of the crucial struggle for the worker's health and safety. But the building trades, with their obdurate resistance to integration, remain a bastion of the status quo. Recent attempts to reform New York's scandal-tainted District Council 9 of the Painters Union have been stamped out. Many of the building-trade baronies make the ILG look like a model of democracy. And the same can be said for the Longshoremen, the Seamen's unions, and of course, Shanker's AFT.

In New York City, the question of black ascendancy haunts the left as well as the right of the labor movement. In the Hospital Workers union and in District 65, a generation of white radicals who worked openly and valiantly to improve the lot of black workers is approaching the point where it must turn its cherished institutions over to the workers it liberated. It will be a difficult parting. Many militant black workers have grown old waiting for their benefactors to retire. In unions like the Transport Workers, the struggle will be bitter, but black hegemony is inevitable. In others, the new black leaders may lack the tactical skills or ideological fervor that allowed some marginal unions to persevere, but this is a risk of democracy well worth taking.

The ideological crisis facing labor in American cities is far more serious than racial turmoil alone. When Samuel Gompers was asked what labor wanted, he could answer simply, "More." It was a formula that worked for half a century as America became the world's dominant power. Now every American must learn to live with "less," and the crucial question is how the "less" will be apportioned. Living standards of the lower and middle classes are already being sacrificed to maintain the hierarchy of privilege that grew up when social tensions were minimized because everyone—no matter how poor—was doing at least "a little bit better" than the preceding generation. That time has ended. The banks, and the clever manipulators like Felix Rohatyn and Stephen Berger who do their bidding in the councils of government, have decided that New York's workers and its millions of average citizens will bear the principal burdens in the bleak new age. The banks have moved quickly to secure their radically decreased investment in New York City by gaining sequestered tax revenues to back MAC securities. They have accelerated their disinvestment in New York's housing and neighborhoods. No matter how much others lose, the banks will win under these rules. After all, they invented the game.

If the unions, and New York City itself, really want to "survive," then the game itself must be changed. Banks are not immune to democratic control. The simple fact is that no social force, except perhaps the ill-fated prairie Populists of the late nineteenth century, has ever even tried to bring them to heel. Banking giants like Citibank and Chase can be required to invest specific percentages of their assets in social spending. State-chartered savings banks can be forced to invest in viable city mortgages. Their rates of profit can be regulated. They can be forced to pay full federal and state taxes.

A successful publicly owned bank can be established, as it was in North Dakota. We have no illusions that these reforms will be easy. Right now, the banks, the giant insurance companies, and other financial powers own the New York State legislature and control the majority of votes in both houses of

Congress. This stranglehold can be broken by concerted political action, and political action can be helped significantly by tough prosecution of laws, already on the books, against fraud and collusion. Labor lacks not an alternative program, but the will to break with its comfortable past and get on with the tough, bitter job of making America a political *and* economic democracy. We think that one is impossible without the other.

The Political
Economy of
Organized Crime

First it was the Irish gangsters, coming out of the Five Points and the Bowery, stealing and stabbing, killing and bribing their way into what America called respectability. They were followed by the Jews, by Arnold Rothstein and Herman Rosenthal, by Lepke Buchalter, and Gurrah Shapiro and the other boys from Brownsville who organized murder along the lines of the American corporation. And it was the Italians who perfected it, creating the Mafia as the first multi-national corporation, with help from Meyer Lansky and a lot of lawyers and respectable people in a lot of high places. Now, in this town, it is the turn of the blacks, the Puerto Ricans, and the Cubans.

— PETE HAMILL, 1974

The gangster is the man of the city, with the city's language and knowledge, with its queer and dishonest skills and its terrible daring, carrying his life in his hands, like a placard, like a club. . . . For the gangster there is only the city; he must inhabit it in order to personify it; not the real city, but that dangerous and sad city of the imagination which is so much more important, which is the modern world.

— ROBERT WARSHOW
The Gangster as Tragic Hero, 1948

Most people get their image of the gangster from the movies. They get it from Edward G. Robinson, James Cagney, George Raft, Richard Widmark, Humphrey Bogart, John Garfield, and Marlon Brando playing public enemies and syndicate bosses. This film fantasy of what a gangster is really like exerts its power over even the originals. A friend of ours grew up with the Brooklyn gangster Joe Gallo. He remembers the young Gallo going to the movies to see Richard Widmark playing Tommy Udo in *Kiss of Death* "at least ten times." Gallo, an aspiring hoodlum, began to imitate Widmark's slang, body language, and style of dress. Years later, when Hollywood was preparing to make another gangster movie and Gallo was by then a chic Mafia symbol, an actor asked Gallo if he could hang out with him, to observe and learn some *macho* mannerisms, those Gallo had originally borrowed from another actor.

This story suggests some of the difficulty in separating myth from reality, legend and lore from fact, in attempting a serious, sober perspective on organized crime. The problem is complicated by the fact that relatively little reliable material on organized crime is available that is untainted by hype or melodrama.*

The actual power of organized crime in New York City has generally been underestimated by historians, economists, political scientists, and other academics.* But it has also been fantasized about and exaggerated by some reporters and other media faddists trying to cash in on the Godfather market. Also, the values and life-styles of gangsters have occasionally been severely romanticized. They are not immigrant populists, or street-corner philosophers with benevolent dignity, or tragic, half-ethical Godfathers who draw some moral line at pushing white powder.

Low-level Mafia men walk out of restaurants on Mulberry Street without paying the bill—because they are so cheap. Most mobsters would rather stick an icepick in someone's ear than work. Powerful mob bosses like Carmine Galente were as bestial as the most vicious elevator mugger you will ever read about. Talk to the federal agents who knew Carmine Persico, the Snake. Talk to now broke and broken former boxing champions who were owned by Frankie Carbo, and then were tossed aside like pieces of contaminated meat when their eyesight was damaged. Talk to Herman Goldfarb, who worked undercover for seventeen months in the garment center, infiltrating the mob. Talk to respected prosecutors like Joe Hynes and Thomas Puccio. Read the trial record of Louis Cirillio, a heroin dealer who had one million dollars buried in his Bronx backyard. Read the transcripts of the tapes made secretly by the Brooklyn district attorney inside Paul Vario's junkyard trailer in Canarsie. These men, and these pieces of evidence, will tell you that Mafisoi are not Bogarts and Brandos. They are mean, greedy, small-minded men. "Mutts," as Joe Hynes likes to call them.

---

*Law enforcement agencies have a near monopoly on the raw data about organized crime. But prosecutors have the incentive of publicity and funding, which occasionally incites them to self-serving exaggerations, especially when estimating the "street value" of confiscated narcotics. Probably the best sources of dependable information about the mob are the bound volumes of the Kefauver and the McClellan Senate committee hearings of the 1950s. More recently, a valuable resource has been the work of scholars like Harold Lasswell and Thomas Schelling. Several books have offered realistic insights into organized crime, including: *The Valachi Papers* by Peter Maas; *The Fall and Rise of Jimmy Hoffa* by Walter Sheridan; *Black Mafia* by Francis A. J. Ianni; *The Crime Confederation* by Ralph Salerno; *Lansky* and *The Silent Syndicate* by Hank Messick; *The Politics of Heroin in Southeast Asia* by Alfred McCoy; and *The Grim Reapers* by Ed Reid. There has also been excellent journalism by Nicholas Pileggi, Jeff Gerth, Jim Drinkhall, Tom Renner, and by *Wall Street Journal* reporters Stanley Penn and Jonathan Kwitny.

*In *Governing New York City*, Sayre and Kaufman devote only 2 out of 699 pages to a discussion of organized crime.

It is instructive to recall this dialogue from tapes released by the FBI in New Jersey after a long period of electronic surveillance of the Mafia there. The colloquy is between one Angelo DeCarlo (called Ray) and Tony "Boy" Boiardo:

TONY: How about the time we hit the little Jew?
RAY: As little as they are, they struggle.
TONY: The Boot hit him with a hammer. The guy goes down and he comes up. So I got a crowbar this big, Ray. Eight shots in the head. What do you think he finally did to me? He spit at me and said [obscenity].

We hold the view that organized crime is a separate permanent government in New York City. It is dangerous, corrupting, and virtually all-powerful in specialized areas like the waterfront, the garment center, and the private carting industry. It holds, through the threat of force, cartel franchises on illegal services like narcotics, loansharking, gambling, pornography, and prostitution. Its dominant role in the international heroin traffic makes the mob one of the central villains of this book. But, ultimately, organized crime has less economic and political power than the biggest banks, insurance companies, corporations, and utilities. For example, the mob's leading loanshark, Fat Tony Salerno was reported to have about $80 million out on the street in loans at any given time, but that—though Salerno charged 156 per cent annual interest and had the muscular helpers to make default quite risky—should be measured against Citibank's assets of $106 billion and Citicorp with $62 *billion* out in loans at the close of 1980.

There is also a problem of definition. Organized crime, to us, is not limited to Italians who shoot other Italians. There is a level at which corrupt businessmen and lawyers and politicians, crooked union leaders, and traditional gangsters meet and become indistinguishable, where businessmen begin to act like racketeers, and racketeers begin to act like businessmen. In this gray area crime and capitalism converge and become almost identical in their values, methods, and influence. This is where Bebe Rebozo, Frank Fitzsimmons, C. Arnholt Smith, Richard Nixon, Alvin Malnik, convicted congressman John Murphy, Morris Shenker, Allen Dorfman, Teamster union vice president Jackie Presser, Meyer Lansky, Robert Vesco, Sidney Korshak, Richard Kleindienst, Roy Cohn, Michele Sindona, Robert Dorsey, and other power brokers operate in a twilight realm.* Bernard Bergman's stealing of $2.5 million from Medicaid perhaps should be considered as a form of organized crime. And what is Gulf Oil chairman Bob Dorsey's disbursing of millions of dollars of corporate funds in secret payments to domestic

*The most original and sophisticated account of this twilight world can be found in the four-part series on lawyer, "fixer," "mob intermediary," and labor consultant Sidney Korshak written by Seymour Hersh and Jeff Gerth, and published by *The New York Times*, June 27-30, 1976.

politicians and foreign governments? The bilking of various Teamster Union pension funds has certainly been crime that is planned and systematic. And so was C. Arnholt Smith's complex bank frauds in San Diego.

So our definition for the purposes of this book must remain somewhat open-ended. Unlike a bank or a public authority, organized crime has no one definition that is universally acceptable.

Organized crime's domination of New York City's politics and judges began during Prohibition, when bootlegging was the source of illegal wealth. It reached a peak during the 1940s and 1950s, when Frank Costello, Thomas Luchese, and Joe Adonis cemented the alliance for mutual profit between the clubhouses and the underworld. But today the influence of organized crime upon the governance of the city seems diminished.

Under Frank Costello's Mafia reign, Tammany district leaders were asked to resign at gunpoint. Costello had the power to make a man a judge with one phone call. Costello is even credited with arranging Tammany's backing for William O'Dwyer in the 1945 election for mayor. O'Dwyer did come to Costello's apartment for a meeting in 1942, and the graft and corruption that flourished under O'Dwyer represented a golden era for the mob.

The man who interrupted the mob's hold on New York politics was Senator Estes Kefauver, whose televised committee hearings during 1950 and 1951 exposed the Mafia's deep, systemic influence on the Democratic Party in New York and other major cities. The mob's withdrawal from politics continued when the sophisticated Costello was replaced by more primitive, Old World Mafia bosses like Vito Genovese and Carlo Gambino, men with little appreciation of the value of political power.

Since the Costello period, organized crime's influence on New York City's government has been more *ad hoc*, more personalistic. It is not systemic the way it is in Philadelphia, or South Jersey. Individual mobsters have had access to individual politicians and judges. City Commissioner James Marcus and Brooklyn Congressman Frank Barsco went to prison for corruption involving Mafia leaders. Queens city councilman Eugene Mastropieri was convicted of helping mobsters evade paying taxes on more than $500,000 of illicit income. State Supreme Court Justice Andrew Tyler was convicted for lying to a grand jury about his meeting with "Spanish Raymond," a convicted gambler who is believed to be the mob's biggest policy banker in Harlem. (The conviction was later overturned.) But these seem to have been particular circumstances, not the structured graft of the 1930-1950 era. And some judges appear to display generosity toward organized-crime defendants. Supreme Court Justice Joseph Corso has dismissed five separate indictments against Mafia members, indictments that were all subsequently reinstated by appellate courts. The great fear of the crime-clubhouse connection is that a prosecutor will win election who has no ties to the machine and is willing to look below the enveloping foliage of street crime to dig up the roots of official corruption. This seems to us to account for the bitter resistance put up by the Brooklyn organization when Liz Holtzman mounted her campaign for District Attorney. Her independence makes her a dangerous woman for people with something to hide. The secret connections between Mafia dons and politicians and judges are raw meat for gossip and television drama. But the element of legal proof seems lacking, although we would not be surprised if it were discovered tomorrow by an enterprising prosecutor.

The gossip and drama, however, may be distractions from the real, concrete, and devastating impact organized crime does have, in many areas, upon New York City and its people.

The juice of a plant is destroying New York. The cultivation, processing, importation, distribution, and sale of heroin is probably the most organized crime in all history. What the fine white powder has done to America as a whole is beyond mathematical calculation. It has created an army of muggers who cause more than half of all the violent crime in our large cities. It is responsible for the overloading of our courts and prisons. It has cost billions and billions of dollars in public funds to combat, treat, and prevent the plague of crime and addiction. The federal government estimates that 15,000 deaths—murders and overdoses—last year were related to heroin use. Heroin corrupted the police departments of many big cities during the 1960s, including New York.* And there is no possible way to measure the personal pain of the addicted, and the fear of the nonaddicted, caused by *Papaver somniferum*, the beautiful opium poppy.

Heroin is New York's tumor. Heroin is causing the crime that is chasing the white middle class to the suburbs, thereby eating away the city's revenue base. Street crime equals organized crime because of heroin.

The Police Department says that heroin is a $1-billion-a-year industry in New York City. The number of addicts is estimated at 150,000–300,000, and is now increasing again, after leveling off between 1972 and 1974.

The Mafia is the ITT of heroin. One needs computers, processing laboratories powered by electric generators, and private planes with radar to transport heroin from Asia, Turkey, Mexico, and France to the Pit in Harlem, and to all the young men without veins in their arms. And despite the mythology to the contrary, the traditional Italian Mafia has always been in the heroin business. Court records show that important Mafia members and associates have been indicted, tried, and convicted in narcotics cases for twenty years. Among those who have gone to prison for violations of the narcotics laws have been: Vito Genovese, Carmine Galante, Carmine

---

*A good summary of police corruption and narcotics can be found in the Knapp Commission Report, pp. 91-112. For a longer account, read *Serpico*, by Peter Maas (New York, 1972).

Trumunti, Joseph DiPalermo, Angelo Melo, Virgin Aessi, Vincent Papa, John Ormento, Louis Cirillio, and Frank Cotroni, one of the leaders of the Montreal syndicate that smuggles heroin into the United States.

Thomas Puccio, the prosecutor who conceived and directed Abscam, earlier in his career set up the narcotics unit in his office and has supervised the prosecution of more than a dozen major narcotics cases. He told us: "The Mafia has the cash to bankroll the heroin traffic. They use the cash from policy banks as the front money to start an international shipment of 25 kilos coming to New York. Italian Mafia people may deal through a Cuban or Latin, who has the direct contact with the overseas supplier, but I would say that the Mafia causes the heroin importation to happen, because they are the financiers of the traffic.

"I've worked for the Justice Department since 1969, and there has never been a time when organized crime wasn't involved in the heroin business. I have never seen any evidence to support the newspaper publicity that Gambino kept them out of it. Heroin is just too lucrative for those guys to stay out of it."

What has happened, it seems, is that blacks and Latins have taken over a piece of the narcotics market at certain levels and on certain routes of distribution. Spanish-speaking Latins obviously find it easier than Italians do to deal with Mexican cocaine suppliers. Most law-enforcement authorities regard the Latin and black gangs as simply a part of the organic structure of organized crime, and as examples of the historic continuum of ethnic succession in crime.

In December 1975, the New York Police Department released the names of the thirteen biggest narcotics importers, financiers, and dealers in the city. The list consisted of five blacks, four Latins and four Italians.

At the start of 1981, we interviewed FBI agents, Customs officials, federal prosecutors, and drug experts who all agreed that a new tidal wave of pure heroin was reaching the streets of New York, and other large cities. These enforcement officials agreed that the remnants of the old Carmine Trumunti crime family, once based on Pleasant Avenue in East Harlem, was flooding the market with tons of heroin refined in Sicilian laboratories from opium cultivated in "the Golden Crescent"—Afghanistan, Iran, and Pakistan.

FBI organized crime experts believe that mob-built heroin factories, hidden in the mountains of Sicily, have replaced the drug labs of Marseilles, memorialized in the film, "The French Connection."

During the federal fiscal year that ended on September 30, 1980, Customs agents confiscated a total of 98.2 pounds of Southwest Asian heroin. In the previous fiscal year, they only seized 49.6 pounds from "the Golden Crescent." New York City narcotics detectives estimate that the flow of heroin into city streets has probably tripled between 1978 and 1980.

Federal agents now speak of "The Italian Connection," and the Trumunti family's elaborate new smuggling route from Pakistan, to Sicily, to the slums of New York.

But while law enforcement is able to track the new heroin routes, it has not been able to prosecute the biggest traffikers. In all of 1979, only 45 persons were convicted of A-1 drug felonies in New York City. Between 1976 and 1979 in New York City, 1,330 persons were indicted for A-1 narcotics crimes. Only 134 were convicted, and only 107 went to prison. A-1 felonies involve heroin worth more than $30,000 in street value.

Heroin is far from being the only contribution organized crime is making to the problematic fate of the city. New York's district attorneys and Police Commissioner estimate organized crime's gross annual income from illegal gambling at between $1.75 million and $2 billion. What is so hurtful to the city is that none of this revenue is taxed. The experts all agree that sports betting and the numbers game—the ghetto lottery—are the biggest sources of income for the mob, and this money is used to finance other rackets like narcotics, loansharking, pornography, and the infiltration of legitimate businesses and unions. Mafioso-turned-government-witness Vincent Teresa told a Congressional committee in July 1971: "If you could crush gambling, you could put the mob out of business."

A useful insight into the city's biggest illegal gambling operation was afforded by the eight-week trial of Jimmy Napoli and eight associates during the summer of 1976 before Federal Judge Jacob Mishler. Tapes made by the FBI and played during the trial told of bets being placed at the HiWay Lounge on Metropolitan Avenue in Brooklyn. The tapes also indicated that cops from the Public Morals Division were being paid off to protect Napoli's phone banks, runners, and comptrollers. FBI agents testified that Napoli and his employees took between $120 million and $150 million a year in bets, mostly on horse racing, that between 1969 and 1975, Napoli personally took home more than $1 million a year, and that he lived in a $150,000 Manhattan townhouse. Napoli also paid (in addition to his bribes to police) the salaries of about twenty assistants; the three closest to him (including his son) each took home about $500,000 a year in untaxed illicit income.

Napoli was convicted, and in October 1976 he was sentenced to five years in prison by Judge Mishler.

Several years earlier, the final report of the Knapp Commission in December 1972 had made two important points about organized bookmaking and the numbers racket in New York City. Organized "pads" created by gamblers to pay off plainclothes police, the report said,

serve as an important breeding ground for large-scale corruption in other areas of the Department. . . . Policemen, especially those in plainclothes units, were found to shake down gambling operations throughout the City on a regular, highly systematic basis. . . .

But perhaps the most important effect of corruption in the so-called gambling control units [of the Police Department] is the incredible damage their performance wreaks on public confidence in the law and the police. Youngsters raised in New York ghettoes, where gambling abounds, regard the law as a joke when all their lives they have seen police officers coming and going from gambling establishments and taking payments from gamblers.

In dozens of areas of city life racketeers have infiltrated, or completely taken over, legitimate businesses and unions. Wherever this happens, the cost of extortion, padded payrolls, bribes, shakedowns, or kickbacks, is inevitably passed along to the consumer. The extra cost of private garbage collection, of linen supply, of construction, of vending machines or jukeboxes, of labor "consultants," of truckers, of security, of liquor licenses, of cargo thefts at airports and on the waterfront—all of it is paid by each of us in higher prices. This is the mob surcharge exacted unwittingly from virtually every citizen of New York City.

A few years ago, for example, Moe Steinman, the former vice president of labor relations for the Daitch-Shopwell supermarket chain, which has shops throughout the city, pleaded guilty to a bribery and kickback scheme that involved union racketeers in the meat business. At Steinman's sentencing, Manhattan Assistant District Attorney Frank Snitow said that the racket cost New York City housewives 1 to 3 cents for each pound of meat they bought at several supermarket chains. "The sole victim has been the consumer," he said.

In April 1975, the New York-New Jersey Waterfront Commission, a watchdog agency, accused the major airlines of concealing vast amounts in cargo thefts at Newark, Kennedy, and La Guardia airports. Its report said that in 1973 all airlines combined had reported a total of only $805,118 in cargo thefts, but that in reality there had been "close to $16 million" in cargo thefts at the three metropolitan airports. The conclusion was gloomy:

The incontrovertible fact is that the airlines are helpless to deal with the problem of organized crime at the airports. The dominant air freight trucking union, for example, remains under the control of criminal elements. The problem of cargo security is simply a facet of the larger problem of organized crime; and conditions at the airports cannot improve until a government body, vested with sufficient powers to break the grip of organized crime over the airports, intervenes to regulate the airports.

The airlines intentionally underreported the cargo heists by $15 million in one year to avoid such regulation and to keep labor peace with Harry Davidoff's Teamster Local 295, which is the union involved in air freight trucking. The airlines chose rather to pass the cost of the mob's thefts along to their own innocent customers.*

*The original scoop on the airport ripoffs was by Nicholas Pileggi in "New Hustles on the Waterfront," in New York, May 21, 1973. As usual, Pileggi was two years ahead of the government in recognizing a problem—one that is still unattended and unremedied. Local 295 still runs the airports.

The oral history of New York has always maintained that the mob controlled the private carting industry. In 1972, the Brooklyn district attorney, Eugene Gold, and the head of his rackets bureau, Joe Hynes, set out to test the thesis by buying a used garbage truck for $3800 and setting up their own undercover private carting company.

The undercover project lasted for sixteen months. According to Hynes, the detective who ran the business knocked on doors, distributed flyers, and even took newspaper ads offering restaurants, supermarkets, and shopkeepers prices *30 per cent* below all other competitors, but still only got 19 clients of 2000 directly solicited. The reason was that the small businessmen in the Coney Island and Bay Ridge sections of Brooklyn were afraid to change their carter. Those who tried to were threatened with bombing and arson, and others who attempted to remove their own trash found it returned to their doorstep the next morning, with a menacing note attached.

The undercover cops found that honest shopkeepers and restaurant owners had to pay for carting even on days they were closed; that they had to pay large, sudden rate hikes; and that they had one carter assigned to them by the borough-wide Trade Waste Association "for life." This Trade Waste Association was controlled by hoodlums from three different Mafia families, and they cooperated with each other no matter what gang wars raged elsewhere. Hynes recalled for us how the association assigned "territories" to cartmen, and that the cartmen had to pay exorbitant dues to the association to keep their routes. In Brooklyn it eventually became apparent that the Trade Waste Association was a mob monopoly when the undercover company was denied membership in the association.

In March 1974, the Brooklyn DA's office announced the indictment of fifty-four private carting companies and the officers of the Trade Waste Association for conspiracy, restraint of trade, and perjury before the grand jury. In November 1975, the carting companies and two association officials pleaded guilty, and Brooklyn Supreme Court Justice Milton Mollen ordered that the association be dissolved. The grand jury that heard the evidence and voted the indictments also released a presentment proposing that the city take over the entire $300-million-a-year private refuse collection business as "the only way to break organized crime's stranglehold on the private carting industry." The grand jury observed that shopkeepers and retail businessmen in Brooklyn were paying private carters twice as much per cubic yard as they should be, and that this inflated rate became the mob surcharge that the "mom and pop" storekeepers of Brooklyn had to pay.

But the Beame administration ignored the grand jury's proposal, and the city has not even taken away the convicted companies' carting licenses. The city's silly Consumer Affairs Commissioner, Elinor Guggenheimer, who has the authority to revoke, was quoted in the December 11, 1975, *New York Times* as saying: "We have no evidence now that the [carting] industry is ridden with crime."

And so, despite sixteen months of hazardous undercover work, despite indictments and convictions, nothing has changed, and organized crime continues to run the private carting industry in Brooklyn.

In the spring of 1973, two much larger and much more ambitious undercover operations were set up in Manhattan, and these concerned not garbage but one of New York City's central industries—the garment industry. One was a coat company, given the code name of Operation Detroit, which was financed by the federal Law Enforcement Assistance Administration (LEAA), and the other was an undercover trucking company, known as Operation Cleveland and financed by the New York City Police Department. The two projects together led to 34 indictments and 21 convictions (several cases are still pending); mobsters and union officers have been convicted of extortion, illegal receipt of money by a union official, bribery of an IRS agent, conspiracy, and tax evasion. (However, because of inept federal prosecutors, Matty Ianiello and four other defendants were acquitted in November 1976.)

We spent about twenty hours interviewing the principals in the undercover trucking company, at the conclusion of the investigation. The principal undercover agent was Herman Goldfarb, a dapper fast-talking civilian ex-convict with a 159 I.Q. and an adding-machine brain; also involved were Lieutenant David Durk, who helped expose police corruption with Frank Serpico, and three members of Durk's squad, including a blonde policewoman who posed as the secretary of the company. (Goldfarb has been awarded the highest honor the Police Department can confer on a private citizen, and has been given a new identity and relocated outside of New York by the Department of Justice.) The story they told us was educational:

On March 28, 1973, Gerro Trucking started business at 1441 Broadway under new management, for it had been purchased by the Police Department for $60,000. Hidden cameras and microphones were installed in the third-floor offices; four legitimate drivers and three undercover agents carrying hidden microphones were employed. Goldfarb ran the company while secretly reporting back to a task force consisting of the FBI, the organized crime strike force, the IRS, and the Police Department. Every day, as he met with street-level gangsters, crooked union business agents, and Mafia bosses, Goldfarb wore a Nagra tape recorder and a Kel transmitter concealed in his crotch. Although he was Jewish, Goldfarb was trusted by the Mafia bosses because of his ability to earn money and think up legitimate business ventures, and also because of his prison record for grand larceny and forgery.

As soon as Gerro Trucking opened for business in the garment district, mobsters started coming through the front door with their hands out. Over seventeen months, Goldfarb paid out $20,000 of the Police Department's money in bribes and "commissions." For organized crime siphons millions of dollars annually out of the ten square blocks of dress houses, cutting rooms, trimming rooms, clothes racks, and triple-parked trucks which New York knows as the garment district. The garment industry is a declining, under-capitalized, seasonal business, regulated by no agency except organized crime. The mob controls dress houses, union locals, building cleaning services, private carters, even parking places. (If a businessman doesn't pay the mob, his trucks get sand in their gas tanks and slashed tires.) And most significantly, the mob has a monopoly on trucking—the lifeline of the fragile industry.

The tapes make it clear that a businessman cannot fire his trucker, even if the trucker suddenly wants to charge him twenty cents more for hauling each dress. Every garment-center businessman needs a trucker to move his "goods," and every trucker belongs to a mob-dominated association. So, the businessman must pay, and pass the cost along to the retail customer. This has been going on ever since Johnny Dio took over garment-center trucking in 1935.

The mob has bookmakers all over the garment industry, in delis, in cafeterias, on street corners. If a manufacturer falls into debt to his bookmaker, he quickly gets a visit from a mob loanshark. If the manufacturer can't pay the "Vig" (the interest) to the loanshark to pay off his gambling debts, then the mob moves in as an undisclosed partner in his company, and starts placing its own people on the payroll in phantom jobs. Moreover, union "consultants" will take payoffs not to unionize a shop or a trimming room. This is called "controlling labor costs."

The cost of all this untaxed tribute to the mob is passed along to the general public in the retail price of dresses, coats, and other apparel. The August 1975 issue of the trade publication *Chain Store Age* quoted a "retail executive" as estimating that the cost of corruption adds "an easy five per cent" to the pricetag of every garment. The same article quoted a second apparel-industry figure as saying that the mob surcharge "could be as much as ten per cent of the retail price tag."

The 2000 undercover tapes recorded by Goldfarb showed, for example, that he had to pay an extra ten per cent "commission" to the trucking association in order to join it and have labor peace. And that he paid $10,000 in cash to one official when he sold Gerro Trucking at the end of the investigation. Goldfarb also had to hire a mob "enforcer" named Larry Paladino for $200 a week, for which price Paladino became Gerro's expeditor—he was known to have "respect" on the street. Paladino made sure Gerro had no union problems, made sure Gerro's trucks had curb space, and allowed his name to be used at Kennedy Airport, where it guaranteed friendly cooperation from Teamster Local 295. The weekly payments also insured that no rival trucking company raided Gerro's accounts, or "jumped" its routes.

In a mob-dominated subculture like the garment center, the psychology is that everyone pays, so why not me? It is the conditioning of history, reinforced by the fear of violence—a beating, a fire. The corruption is so ingrained that it is easy for the average businessman not to notice it, really, and view it as merely another tax or licensing fee.

During Operation Cleveland, Lieutenant Durk asked a well-known garment-center manufacturer, whose company grosses $110 million a year, to help in the investigation. The manufacturer took off his shirt and showed Durk the ugly scar tracks of his back, inflicted by gangsters in the 1930s. He explained that he was now, thank God, successful enough to hire an accountant who knew how to write off all the "commissions" and "labor costs" as deductions on his corporate income tax.

Today, the Mafia controls fragments of geography—the airports, the docks, the garment district. And it still controls fragments of the economy: the sex industry, large chunks of the private carting, trucking, and waste disposal industries. It controls many bars and discos, with their useful cash economy. It controls construction companies, dozens of Teamster Union locals, part of the cheese and pizza industry. And the Atlantic City experience strongly suggests that the mob would control any casino gambling industry that developed in New York.

Federal prosecutor Tom Puccio placed all this in the appropriate economic and historic perspective when he told us: "No question, the Mafia is real. But I think the Fortune Five Hundred corporations are responsible for more lawbreaking than the five Mafia families." Puccio thinks—and we agree—that the future of organized crime is in the national white collar, twilight world of the mega-Mafia. This is the realm of vast Teamster pension funds; laundered Las Vegas money; off-shore banks in the Bahamas; mob lawyers who function as deal makers like Alvin Malnik, Morris Shenker, and Sidney Korshak; shady real estate entrepenurs like Alan Glick and Hyman Green; and Teamster bosses like Jackie Presser and John Cody, who are tied to the traditional goons and gangsters.

This is the semi-legal, super-mob of the 1980s. Abscam came to the cusp of this twilight world with John Murphy and the Atlantic City casino corporations. But it did not penetrate to its secret, essentially corporate heart, where racketeers act like businessmen, and businessmen act like racketeers.

While the mob still can be found, then, in many of New York's major industries or areas of activity, the illegal services that organized crime sells—gambling, heroin, cash at high interest—find most of their consumers in the city's slums. The poor, as ever, suffer most from organized crime. The junkies, craving their daily high, will rob, mug, and slash other poor people for the price of their $5 bag. Welfare checks sometimes go directly to pay loansharks, because slum dwellers are so often denied credit by "legitimate" sources. In 1970, the late State Senator John Hughes, chairman of the Joint Legislative Committee on Crime, said: "The flow of money from the ghetto to organized crime is so great that there can be little meaningful economic improvement in New York City's ghettoes until it is stopped."

In September 1972, a pioneering study, "The Impact of Organized Crime on an Inner City Community" by Harold Lasswell and Jeremiah McKenna, was released by the Policy Sciences Center in Manhattan. The study analyzed the economic consequences of organized crime upon the Brooklyn ghetto of Bedford Stuyvesant, one of the city's six main slum neighborhoods. It covered the geographic area of the 77th and 79th police precincts, in which 280,000 people reside.

Lasswell and McKenna concluded,

> Organized crime was the single most powerful force in the community. It grossed more revenue from its gambling and narcotics operations than the federal government collected in income taxes; it was the single largest employer of community residents; it had effectively nullified whatever counterattack had been mounted against it by government; and no present program, public or private, appears capable of controlling or reducing its major illegal operations. . . .
>
> This analysis demonstrates the important position of organized crime in the social process of Bedford Stuyvesant. The policy and narcotics operations are continuous and stable, so that increased income for the community will result in the transfer of a larger amount of community wealth to organized crime; a larger demand for narcotics; and further deterioration of the whole area.

One of the most interesting data sections of the report was the research on the disposition of persons arrested in the course of various police raids on policy banks that controlled the numbers gambling. Lasswell and McKenna found that out of 356 persons arrested, 198 had their cases dismissed by judges; 63 were acquitted; 77 were fined (the average was $113); five were convicted and sentenced to jail (the average term was 17 days); 12 had their sentences suspended; and only one of the 356 received a sentence of more than a year in prison. Their conclusion was that the best thing for the economy of the ghetto, and the best thing for the integrity and productivity of the Police Department, would be the legalization of gambling, particularly of numbers betting.

Organized criminals violate law and decency in many more ways than those we have recounted here—from laundering money in order to legalize criminal wealth, to shooting each other in public places. But the mob's heroin cartel is the most direct means by which organized crime has become a factor in New York City's pain.

Arrogant Power   11

On November 9, 1965, an electric relay device malfunctioned in Queenston, Ontario, and northeastern United States and eastern Canada were plunged into darkness by a cascading power failure. The effects of this Great Blackout touched everyone in the region, sometimes tragically but generally without serious effect. (A study published a few years later showed that the birth rate in the area had taken a mysterious jump nine months after the Blackout; perhaps this suggested what television-watching has done to our mating habits.)

New York City was different, however. In one wrenching moment, the metropolis simply stopped functioning. At the height of the evening rush hours powerless subways coughed and expired in airless tunnels far below the city streets. Packed elevators lurched to a halt twenty stories above the ground. Streams of homebound autos turned into churning rivers of metal as traffic lights blinked out. Tenants huddled in apartment-house lobbies before starting the exhausting climb to their apartments twenty and thirty stories above. Tons of foodstuffs slowly spoiled in refrigerators and supermarket freezers.

Some hospitals were lucky enough to have auxiliary power, but others did not, and nurses flitted from patient to frightened patient in true Florence Nightingale fashion—candles aloft. In many ghetto neighborhoods, over-flowing trash baskets were ignited to provide at least momentary protection from muggers and rats.

There was a lighter side to the crisis. Movies and theaters were closed, but Broadway was far from deserted and midtown restaurants thrived under candlelight as a Blitz mentality infected secretaries from Brooklyn and junior executives from Larchmont stranded together.

Few who experienced that night in New York can't recall it vividly after more than a decade. They remember that it was warm for November, how frustrating it was to be unable to get information about loved ones (the phone system collapsed for several hours under the sudden overwhelming demand for circuits), the sense of fear and impotence because the machines on which New York depends could no longer do their bidding at the flick of a switch. In those long hours of darkness, New Yorkers came to realize as they never had before just *how* dependent they were on the invisible electric network running beneath their streets.

Or rather, how dependent they were on the Consolidated Edison Company. A subsequent study of the Blackout by the Federal Power Commission demonstrated that Con Ed lacked the automatic load-shedding devices that could cut off customers selectively and avoid a total blackout (these were standard for other utility systems). The engineer in charge of the company's power control center had ten minutes between the beginning of the breakdown and the total collapse of the system, but he lacked instructions on cutting ties with the other systems in the region that had already blacked out. Far more serious was the fact that Con Ed lacked auxiliary generators and had to rely on slow-starting steam turbines for reserve power. Boston's subways continued to run through the entire blackout period, but New York's were disabled for fourteen hours.

In the years following 1965, New Yorkers were to become increasingly familiar with localized blackouts and brownouts (voltage reductions) as the utility's aging capital plant broke down. But whenever anything went wrong, and especially when it was applying for a rate increase or approvals to build unnecessary new plants, Con Ed would continuously invoke the specter of the "Big Blackout."

Con Ed, the nation's second largest utility, which supplies electricity to three million customers in New York City and Westchester County as well as natural gas to 1.2 million consumers, and the steam that heats the spires of midtown Manhattan, was rapidly falling apart after generations of corruption, bad management and almost nonexistent "regulation" by state officials. In response to a growing chorus of criticism from small consumers, the New York business community, and city government, the company and the state Public Service Commission gave essentially the same answer: The problems could be solved only by money, and consumers would have to pay a whopping bill to put the old girl back together again. In the intervening years they *have* paid (New Yorkers consistently pay the highest electric rates in the nation, and the average bill tripled in the decade 1965-75), and although service has taken a sharp turn for the better—partially because many consumers simply can't afford to use as much electricity as before—most Con Ed customers are still wondering whether the price has been worth it.

By 1967 the company's board of trustees was convinced that a new image, if not a new policy, was necessary to allay public anger. Charles Eble, chairman of the board and chief executive officer, the quintessence of Con Ed's "up from the ranks" management (he started as an office boy forty years earlier and worked his way up through the accounting department without benefit of higher education) announced his retirement, and the search for a successor began.

The choice fell upon Charles Franklin Luce, an austere lawyer-bureaucrat who once worked as a meter reader in his native Wisconsin and subsequently rose, through political connections with Senators Henry Jackson and Warren Magnuson in his adopted state of Washington, to become administrator of the giant Bonneville Power Administration, one of the nation's largest public power agencies, and then Assistant Secretary of the Interior in the Johnson administration. (In a 1970 profile of Luce, Susan Brownmiller wrote that he had been hired by two Con Ed board members representing Citibank, "the heavy bank in Con Ed's financial relationships." This description best fits Richard S. Perkins, now retired but at the same time chairman of the executive committee of the bank and its holding company, and Frederick M. Eaton, a partner in the prestigious law firm of Shearman and Sterling, which represents both the bank and the utility.)

Luce's introduction to his new employer was harsh but revelatory. Only four months after he assumed his new job, Con Ed and Mayor Lindsay's new city administration were rocked by the disclosure of an attempt to shake down the company for granting an important construction permit. The conspirators included a city commissioner, the former behind-the-scenes leader of the state Democratic Party, a major contractor, a bizarre double agent, and assorted Mafiosi. Before the dust had settled the public had been given a rare view of the inside workings of the giant utility, and it disclosed that business-as-usual at Con Ed was a network of political deals and payoffs between contractors and top corporate officials which resulted in untold millions of dollars in padded construction costs systematically passed along to consumers in the company's rate base. New Yorkers are still paying the bill for those decades of corruption.

A brief history of the Marcus scandal is important to a basic understanding of the milieu in which privately owned utilities operate in a major city. The conspirators have long since served their time; only one, Carmine DeSapio, has re-emerged into the limelight. But Con Ed remains immersed in the political life of the city and the state, a major generator of profit and power, a permanent member of the permanent government.

James Marcus, a charming ne'er-do-well who had married into the Lodge family and used his ties with the first family of Republicanism to ingratiate himself with the GOP mayoral candidate John Lindsay, seems to have had an irrepressible attraction for other people's money and for stocks with a propensity to sink—a fatal combination. John Lindsay had a similar attraction for impressive but flimsy resumés. He made Marcus his Commissioner of Water Supply, Gas and Electricity.

Somewhere along the way, Marcus had acquired a not-so-silent partner named Herbert Itkin, one of the legion of bright hungry young lawyers in New York and every other big city who see their diplomas as licenses to steal. Itkin would have thrived at the court of the Borgias but managed to do well enough in America of the 1960s, working simultaneously for the CIA, FBI, various DAs, and his own account at the same time. When Itkin met Marcus, he thought he had finally found El Dorado.

Itkin was already deeply immersed in the dank netherworld where mobsters, larcenous "legitimate" businessmen, and corrupt union officials hunt together to share the benefits of pension-fund mortgages, government contracts, and deals within deals. He quickly introduced his friend "the Commissioner" to some of these acquaintances and the two were already negotiating their first corrupt deal on the day Marcus was sworn into office. That afternoon, Marcus and Itkin met with Tony "Ducks" Corallo, a top Mafioso, to learn how much a favored contractor (Henry Fried of S. T. Grand Co.) would kick back for being granted an "emergency" noncompetitive contract to clean one of the city's aging water reservoirs. It is instructive that as Marcus joined Corallo at a restaurant, he later testified, his predecessor as Water Commissioner (in the previous Wagner administration), Armand D'Angelo, was just leaving the great man and heartily shook Marcus's hand and wished him well. A changing-of-the-guard ceremony.

It is impossible to tell exactly how much Marcus-Itkin reaped from their hegemony over this one small section of the city bureaucracy. (Itkin claims he personally made $120,000 in one year.) What is clear is that all other deals were seen as merely an appetizer for the main course: Con Ed.

Con Ed is "regulated" by the state Public Service Commission, which establishes utility rates and sometimes presses the giant companies under its purview to improve service. But on a day-to-day basis, Con Ed performs most of its functions within New York City and enters the jurisdiction of several city departments concerning such matters as street repairs, air pollution, taxation, etc. City decisions are rarely decisive for the company, although there are enough legally binding relationships between the two to make it desirable that Con Ed remain on friendly terms with leading public and party officials.

Charles Eble, Luce's predecessor as chairman, explained the relationship to a writer for *Fortune:* "Over the years I struck up friendships with many politicians. It was not something that I set out objectively to do at the beginning. But, as time passed, I found that many of my friends had moved into positions of authority in government. I could talk to them. It was as simple as that."

Well, not quite that simple. What Eble failed to mention was that many of these friendships were undoubtedly struck at the numerous political dinners he attended to further the fortunes of various individuals and both parties, dinners for which the utility never failed to buy a table at about $1000 a throw. While this excessive largesse has now ceased, officials of the utility are still to be found as paying guests at important political functions, and a staff of county coordinators and PR men make it a point to jump when elected officials bring them some constituent complaint about the shortcomings of the company. Con Ed is also extremely charitable with its rate-payers' money, passing out free baseball tickets and donating to the favorite causes of the powerful without regard to race, religion, national origin, or expense.

What Marcus-Itkin had in mind was somewhat more direct. New York City has the best and most extensive system of water supply in the world, with millions of acres of land outside the city in the Catskill Mountains watershed. This massive aqueduct system alone is as large as some of the world's smaller nations. For many years, it had been an abiding dream of Con Ed to build a large pumped storage plant on Storm King mountain above the major tunnel carrying water to the city. Marcus, protector of the city's water supply, would have to supervise the construction carefully. In 1967, the price tag on this job was $200 million—enough to set the mouths of Marcus-Itkin and their legion of co-conspirators watering.

Before tackling Con Ed on this "big one," however, they cut their teeth on something smaller. Con Ed also had a high-tension transmission line built on some of the aqueduct lands. Now, in the midst of the "power shortage" that had resulted from inducing consumers to buy more appliances than Con Ed could comfortably service, the company decided to break with tradition and expand modestly its ability to buy power from other utilities with surpluses to sell. They also planned to build a number of new plants upstate in the future. Increased transmission capability was the key to these projects.

As an aside, it should be noted that monopoly electric companies can remain profitable only by constantly building more and more expensive plants since their rate base is determined on a "cost-plus" basis, i.e., the more they spend, the more the regulators allow them to collect from consumers. Companies therefore try to produce by themselves every kilowatt that they sell, and religiously avoid buying surplus power from one another, although that would be much cheaper for their customers. Con Ed had lagged behind other firms in this regard and had purposely kept its transmission capacity to an absolute minimum over the years.

In 1958, the company had turned down a chance to buy cheap hydropower (1.5 million kilowatts every hour) from Niagara Falls. In 1964, they rejected a similar offer from the Churchill Falls power project across the border in Canada. Together these water-powered sources would have supplied half of Con Ed's peak load needs. Instead they plunged into the incredibly expensive construction of nuclear plants and polluting, oil-fired plants to maximize expenses—and profits.

Marcus would have to give his permission for the new transmission line. Instead of demanding a direct bribe from the company, the conspirators were told that they should work through the utility's independent contractors. The logic was that in return for getting the permission to build, the grateful company would reward the contractor who had had the initiative to "take care" of the sticky palms at the Department of Water Supply by granting to that contractor the lucrative construction contract for the high-line, on a noncompetitive and highly lucrative basis.

Henry Fried, the beneficiary of the reservoir contract, decided that he would be the one to help his old friends at Con Ed. It subsequently came to light that he already had Con Ed's vice-president for construction on his own payroll at $1000 a month ($2500 at Christmas) and, along with a number of other contractors for the utility, maintained good relations by distributing smoked turkeys and cases of whiskey to various key Con Ed employees at the festive season.

Fried had become wary of the ability of Marcus-Itkin to carry off so complex a deal, and he decided that the suavity of a master fixer, not the blunt-edged style of their earlier Mafia intermediaries, was needed. He introduced Itkin to Carmine DeSapio.

DeSapio, who had been the dominant figure in Democratic politics in both the city and the state throughout the 1950s, had backed Robert Wagner in successful bids for the mayoralty in 1953 and 1957 and was an architect of Averell Harriman's victory in the gubernatorial race in 1954. He subsequently became Harriman's Secretary of State, a position from which he nominated Henry Fried as an unpaid Commissioner of Corrections. (Had he been prescient, Fried would undoubtedly have done much more to improve life in the state's prisons than he apparently did.) As we have seen, DeSapio's fall from formal power came in 1961, when Wagner suddenly dumped the "bosses" and ran successfully against his own record on a "reform" ticket, and when the liberal Village Independent Democrats unseated DeSapio as district leader in the Greenwich Village fiefdom he had controlled for so long. But although "out of politics," DeSapio was still considered the man to see in certain circles.

His counsel to Marcus was simple: Do nothing on the transmission line contract until Con Ed was desperate and confused. Then he would make the proper representations to the proper people showing he had the ability to "deliver," and the deal would be struck. As it turned out, this was exactly the correct strategy. The only problem was that Marcus was neither a good bureaucrat nor a strong personality. Although he was being bled white to cover loans on a bad stock investment and desperately needed money, he wavered under the pressure being applied by Con Ed. In a bungled attempt to delay sending the utility a letter of commitment on the project, he alerted honest city officials that a new franchise for the line should be negotiated, since Con Ed was actually increasing its transmission capacity ninefold without increasing its rental payments to the city treasury.

The collapse of the conspiracy soon after is a tangled tale with an ironic twist. Both Marcus and Itkin came under separate investigations for misappropriating monies a businessman had entrusted to them for private business investment. Itkin had long since been "turned" by the FBI and in a desperate attempt to stay out of prison was telling everything he knew about everybody. At the end, he threw in the hapless Marcus, who had already resigned after disclosure of his stock mess. Marcus spilled everything, including the reservoir deal, which led to Fried's indictment. When Fried was removed from Con Ed's list of accepted bidders, he attempted to blackmail the company into continuing his services, and blurted out the details of his dealings with Con Ed officials to a member of the company's brass. This led to the forced retirement of Gerald Hadden, the vice-president for construction, and the demotion of Max Ulrich from vice-president for public relations to director of Brooklyn operations. (Within the company, the Ulrich move was actually seen by some as a promotion.)

Marcus ultimately served eleven months of a fifteen-month sentence in a minimum-security federal prison. DeSapio was sentenced to two years. Corallo received three years, to run concurrently with an earlier sentence. Fried got two years, and so did Daniel Motta, involved in the early stages of the plot.

Itkin's federal friends kept him out of jail, but he has emerged since in a characteristically convoluted child-custody case, and his most recent utterance to the press was that he was spending his days waiting for the Mafia finally to mark "paid in full" to his indiscretion at having kissed—and then told and told and told.

A crucial question emerges from this tangled skein. Where were the "regulators"? The New York State Public Service Commission is mandated to audit the books of utilities in order to protect the public from overcharges, yet it never questioned the company's unorthodox contracting procedures. Luce himself ordered competitive bidding as a result of the scandal, but the beneficial impact of that order remains doubtful.*

*As Walter Goodman points out in *A Percentage of the Take* (New York, 1971), a study of the Marcus scandal:

"As it happens, Henry Fried was master of another method of beating the nuisance of competitive bidding—an arrangement among contractors to rig their bids for paving and trenching contracts with Con Edison, with the Brooklyn Union Gas Company, and with the Empire City Subway Company, a subsidiary of the New York Telephone Company. In October 1969, Fried was sentenced to four months in jail and fined $25,000 for his role in this accommodation; Mackay Construction was fined $50,000; and S. T. Grand was fined $10,000.

If this system of kickbacks and bid-rigging was common on Con Ed's smaller contracts, what had gone on in the building of hundreds of millions of dollars' worth of generating plants—by the same group of contractors? The simple answer is that we will probably never know. But we pay dearly for that ignorance with each new electric bill.

Even more urgently we must ask whether the system of public regulation of natural monopolies such as the utilities, or even unnatural monopolies like the giant oil companies or defense contractors, can ever truly protect the best interests of the public. Monopolies are inherently inefficient; there are no market forces to punish either greed or poor judgment. Con Ed has no incentive to keep its costs low if its profits rise along with those costs.

Regulators, such as the Public Service Commission, live in a world dominated by the regulated. They require highly specialized skills, skills that can often be acquired only in the service of the utilities. There is no moral judgment automatically implied in noting that two recent chairmen of the Public Service Commission had both served as consultants to the utilities they ultimately came to supervise. (Joseph Swidler had been a consultant for Con Ed, and Alfred Kahn did a major pricing survey for AT&T.) The conflicts are inherent in the system.

From its very inception, the electric power industry has been deeply enmeshed in politics—an inevitability where vast fortunes could be made in the exploitation of a new technology, as it rapidly progressed from being an interesting novelty to being a basic necessity of life. A fundamental understanding of how and why the industry developed as it did and of the imperatives of the technology it pioneered is necessary to see how Con Ed has grown and the reasons why it, and its counterparts across the nation, face such a questionable and costly future.

It was probably inevitable that the first large-scale applications of electric power should have been tried in New York City. Thomas Edison established his company in a four-story brownstone at 65 Fifth Avenue in 1881. Then, as now, New York was the financial capital of the nation, and electricity has always required massive capital to build the gigantic generating plants and

---

"Henry Fried's fellow conspirators, a list of the city's contractor nobility, included: Vincent P. Di Napoli, chairman of Tully and Di Napoli; Francis Jordan, board chairman of Poirier and McLane; Alfred Korsen, vice-president of Slattery Contracting; Theodore Galucci, Jr., president of Samuel Galucci and Sons; Joseph J. Haggerty, Sr., board chairman of Sicilian Asphalt Paving; Samuel Aviron, superintendent of Lipsett, Inc.; Robert Crimmins, president of Thomas Crimmins Contracting; Arthur Cipolla, vice-president of Yonkers Contracting; Robert E. Lee, secretary of DeLee General Contracting; and Ernest Muccini, Sr., president of Oakhill Contracting. Two other companies were in on the bid-rigging: Gull Contracting of Queens and Casper Hellock of the Bronx. The price-fixing companies are still handling the bulk of Con Edison's $30 million a year worth of trenching, paving and foundation work. Explains Chairman Luce, "These firms are among the largest in the city and there simply are not enough other qualified contractors staffed and equipped to do the job.' "

distribution networks that have been the hallmark of its spread. Electricity remains the largest industrial investment in the history of the nation.

Two men, Thomas Edison and Samuel Insull, can be fairly credited with developing the modern power company, although neither actually created any of the technical components of the electric generating system. Edison, however, was the first to understand that electricity could be sold as a commercial product. Insull, his young British secretary, made an even more fundamental contribution: He "invented" the electric monopoly corporation.

Until Edison established his central-station generating plant at Pearl Street in the heart of New York's financial district in 1882, the nascent electric industry confined itself to selling the electric components necessary to establish individual, limited-purpose generating plants to supply street lighting in downtown neighborhoods of a few blocks, or to drive single-purpose motors such as elevators or pumps in large office buildings. J. P. Morgan and Henry Villard, already famous as "robber barons" in the nation's monopolized rail industry, controlled the development of this new industry.

Edison was the first to grasp the logic of creating a generating network that would provide a pre-existing system, or electrical infrastructure, into which individual customers could be wired without the cost of each establishing his own generating plant. He put together the components of such a system—generators, switches, underground cable, et cetera—and patented it. In essence this gave him ownership of an entire new industry. The only flaw in his system was that it used low-voltage direct current (D.C.) and therefore could be used only over a fairly limited distance—about a one-mile radius from the central generating station. This meant that hundreds of generating stations would have to be built to serve a city the size of New York, but since Edison owned the patents he was perfectly willing to see hundreds of small companies spring up as his licensees to meet the power needs of the metropolis. In fact, dozens of companies were formed in New York and Brooklyn, and these were ultimately merged, under the financial pressures of the Great Depression, into today's Consolidated Edison Company.

Samuel Insull immediately began barnstorming the nation selling the Edison system to municipalities, the most logical customers for the new technology. The irony in this was that Insull ultimately would spend much of his later life fighting to destroy the municipally owned electric systems he helped to spawn and attempting to replace them with privately owned electric companies.

The Edison system, as was so common in the early days of technological innovation in America, soon had unwanted competition. George Westinghouse had overcome the limitations of direct current by developing alternating current (A.C.), which made it possible to produce electricity at much higher voltage for transmission over much longer distances. This current could then be reduced or "stepped down" by the use of transformers to make it usable in low-voltage appliances such as light bulbs.

The rivalry between the two systems became bitter, and if the technical merits didn't win the day with municipal buyers across the country, bribery often took its place. Technology ultimately had little to do with the outcome of the struggle, however. The Thomson-Huston Company, controlled by J. P. Morgan, stole many of Westinghouse's patents and ultimately bought out both competitors. In 1889, Edison received $1.75 million for his patent rights, and distributed about $1 million to his early associates, including Insull, who received $75,000. Thomson-Huston then emerged as the General Electric Company. Westinghouse left nothing except his name to the only other competing company, Westinghouse Electric, and the two are still the only makers of heavy electrical equipment—as well as the predominant forces in the nuclear power industry—to this day.

(One gruesome reminder of the Edison-Westinghouse rivalry persists to the present. Edison had attacked alternating current as the "killing current" because of its high voltage, and in 1888 he managed to induce the legislature of New York and its governor to adopt the "electric chair," using A.C., as its legal means of execution.)

Insull emerged from the wreckage of Edison Electric to become president of the fledgling Chicago Edison Company, later to become the mammoth Commonwealth Edison. Still only twenty-nine years old, Insull devoted the next thirty years of his life to fulfilling Thomas Edison's dream: the creation of a single national monopoly over the electric power industry. He almost succeeded. By the time the Depression destroyed his vast electrical empire in 1932, he was president of eleven power companies, chairman of sixty-five others and a director of eighty-five more.

The construction of this empire was no easy task. Despite their intense rivalry, Edison and Westinghouse had failed to convert the country to central station generation, and the spread of electricity into homes and offices was very slow to progress until the boom of the 1920s. Large companies still preferred to build individual power plants for each building or factory they owned. The largest users of electric were the traction companies that ran the street railways or trolley cars that dominated urban transit by the turn of the century. Most traction companies had their own single-purpose generating plants, larger than anything ever constructed by Edison or Westinghouse.

In his masterful history of the American power industry, *The Electric War*, from which much of the foregoing information has been drawn, Sheldon Novick notes: "We are so used to the monopolies held by the electric power companies that we forget how recent they are and how bitterly they were opposed by the progressives and reformers of their early days. The power company which has a monopoly of power supply was an invention, not an inevitable development, and by and large it was Samuel Insull's invention."

When he took the helm at Chicago Edison, Insull immediately began absorbing the competing companies in the Chicago area with the assistance of General Electric. In 1907, the city of Chicago designated him as power supplier for the streetcar companies, which doubled his sales at a single stroke.

Insull not only created the model for the consolidation of electric-power generation in the hands of one regional company but developed and tirelessly proselytized the ideology of monopoly. Much of his case rested on the technology of electric production. Insull's argument is still the foundation for the industry's rationale for high rates and for most forms of government regulation of electrical utilities. The basic point he emphasized was that electricity, unlike competing fuels such as natural gas, cannot be stored. This means that since demand for electricity varies with the time of day, generating capacity has to be built to meet maximum demand but might stand idle for significant parts of the day or even week. A power company can use its generation more efficiently to supply all possible demands around the daily cycle than can a number of single-purpose generators that might, for instance, operate only during the rush hours for streetcars, or during the production day for a factory. Since power plants are expensive to build, and bigger plants are more efficient than small, he argued, there is a significant saving in providing one system to meet all demands. (Despite this efficiency, power companies consistently overbuild. Con Ed last year, for instance, had installed capacity to generate 75 billion kilowatts but actually sold only 32 billion—less than half.)

As long as there was no way to store electricity, Insull's argument made economic sense. What he carefully ignored, however, was that a way *had* been found to store electricity. In 1881, Lord Kelvin had traveled from Paris to Glasgow with "a box of electricity," the original storage battery, invented by a Frenchman named Fauré. If electricity could be stored on a large scale—that is, produced at a steady rate around the clock and then released during peak demand periods—there would be no need for either massive generating complexes or monopoly control. It is hardly an accident that the storage battery and other means of electrical storage have been ignored over the years by the utilities or that Insull's basic case for monopoly went unchallenged until the advent of the environmental movement in the mid-60s with its emphasis on decentralized, alternate power sources such as wind, solar, and thermal power.

Insull didn't content himself with making a successful case for monopoly. He recognized two other areas crucial for the survival of private power companies: regulation and perpetual growth. He had carefully observed the ferment occasioned by the growth of the railroad monopolies and recognized, long before the public or reformers, that only two alternatives could emerge to deal with the utilities' unlimited powers to establish rates and terms of service: some form of public regulation, like the railroad commissions which had grown up in almost every state, or public ownership and socialism. As early as 1898, when he launched his crusade for monopoly utilities, he combined it with a call for state regulation. As Novick notes: "Insull, therefore, became the first public advocate of regulation of the power companies, at a time when they were not even recognized as utilities in need of regulation. . . . In 1898, as in modern days, regulation was seen as a means of preserving the private ownership of power companies."

Soon the reformers were echoing Insull's arguments for regulation, and, despite Socialist demands for outright public ownership and the persistence of numerous municipal electric companies, state regulation became the dominant form of public control over monopoly utilities. Many states simply added the electric companies to the responsibilities of the railroad commissions, although today every state has a separate public utilities commission.

This early history has had a profound effect in shaping the pattern of regulation. The fundamental court decisions relating to railroads became the basis of the commissions' attempts to control utility prices, especially the basic regulatory law which required that the companies be allowed a "fair rate of return" on investment. In effect, this "cost-plus" mechanism of rate determination, which has subsequently been epitomized by the Pentagon in its relationship with defense contractors, was the driving force behind the industry. A monopoly company's rates were based on how much money it needed not only to provide existing service but to attract new investment funds for additional plant construction. This meant that a company would make more money if it spent more money, a fantastic incentive for waste which persists into the present.

Utility commissions never felt it was their place to tell the industry how or when to spend money for new plants. They were relegated to the bookkeeping tasks of determining that the company had spent the money and deciding how the cost of that spending was to be allocated to different classes of customers. If consumers rebelled over rising rates, the regulators and the elected officials who appointed them simply pointed to the companies' balance sheets to show that the new rates were justified by expenses. Again, it wasn't until environmentalists in the late 1960s questioned the doctrine of perpetual growth and pointed to the pollution and destruction that constant growth was causing, that state commissions even began to compare real demand with the companies' construction plans.

The only difficulty in this self-perpetuating cycle of expansion from the companies' point of view, of course, was the need for a constantly expanding market: Someone had to buy all the new electricity that could be produced by the new plants. This was no problem while vast numbers of homes were without electricity, although the companies dumped the expensive task of bringing electricity to isolated farm homes and the poverty-stricken areas of the South onto the government, in the Rural Electrification Administration and the Tennessee Valley Authority. But once America had been electrified, stagnation could be avoided only by creating new, and unperceived, demands for power. Thus the industry supported the development of electric appliances from the washing machine to the electric toothbrush. Most importantly, it stimulated the conversion of home heating from coal and gas to electricity by offering incentives to builders to install its products in new homes and subsidizing homeowners for converting their existing heating systems to electricity. The utilities spent billions to make the "All-Electric Home" the new American dream. Today that dream has turned into a nightmare.

For instance, tens of thousands of New York-area homeowners discovered the true economics of electricity only after the 1973 oil crisis. Con Ed, having already terrified the state government with tales of its impending bankruptcy, managed to win a fuel-pass-along clause from the compliant Public Service Commission. (Like most regulatory ripoffs, this one spread rapidly from state to state because no commission wanted to be left holding the bag when angry consumers asked, "But how come they don't do this in _____?" The pack instinct for survival is as great among regulators as it is among wolves, perhaps even greater.) Suddenly, homeowners found that their electric bills were greater than their mortgage bills, and all of Con Ed's customers found that electric rates were rising twice as fast as everything else combined during the worst peace time inflation in the history of the country.

One of the reasons why electric heat is so expensive is that it is incredibly inefficient. Utilities today make electricity much the same way that Thomas Alva Edison did when he opened the Pearl Street plant in 1882. Fuel—oil, coal, natural gas or uranium—creates heat which turns water into steam. The steam is released, as it is from the spout of a boiling teakettle, and directed at high pressure to turn a rotary turbine. The shaft of the turbine rotates a giant magnet within a coil of copper wire—a dynamo—and electricity flows through the wires and into the distribution system.

Most of the heat used to make electricity is wasted, i.e., is not converted into electricity. The waste heat gets pumped into the air or into a neighboring body of water, where of course it doesn't belong and where it does generally harmful things such as ruin our lungs, kill fish, alter the weather. Even after the electricity is produced, however, about ten per cent of it gets used up in transmission to the point of use. In the case of electric heating, it is then used to heat wires: The heat comes from the friction caused by the resistance of the wire to the passage of the current. About 27 per cent of the original fuel is converted into useful electricity in our home radiators. A well-maintained gas furnace, in contrast, is 60-70 per cent efficient. (European furnaces are more efficient than American furnaces because they have flues that keep down fuel consumption, but the flue had been forbidden here until recently by the collusion of the electric and gas industries.)

As Novick again points out: "All other things being equal, two or three times as much fuel must therefore be burned to provide electric space heating as would be needed for gas or oil heat. This means, roughly, three times as much pollution and three times the rapid depletion of natural resources." And for those once-proud possessors of all-electric homes, three times the cost.

Now let's resume the story of that controversial transmission line, because it leads inexorably to the next stage of Con Ed's crisis.

For four years the issue was dead; neither Con Ed nor the Lindsay administration wanted to summon up the Marcus scandal. In early 1971, however, a new contract was brought quietly before New York City's Board of Estimate and a new controversy was born. Con Ed agreed to pay the city for an enlarged franchise, but this time it was dealing with a far more enlightened cast of participants. Bronx Borough President Robert Abrams led a one-man crusade against any new contract unless Con Ed agreed to carry low-cost public power generated by the Power Authority of the State of New York over the proposed 345-kilovolt line. Abrams even questioned whether the transmission line shouldn't be twice the proposed size, equal to the 700-kv. lines then in operation in the Northwest. Con Ed balked, and for good reason.

Abrams had reopened the public power debate, which had blown hot and cold for thirty-five years ever since Mayor Fiorello La Guardia had proposed that New York buy up Depression-plagued electric companies and operate its own public electric system. For many years the city had actually owned the beginnings of a power network—the electric plants that ran the subways. These had originally been acquired when the private subway lines, the IRT and BMT, went bankrupt. In 1959, during one of the city's perennial cash squeezes, Robert Wagner had sold the plants to Con Ed. They were old, inefficient, and highly polluting, but the chairman of Con Ed's board told a stockholders' meeting that the purchase had been made to remove "a temptation for the city to expand its own power system in other fields."

E. F. Hutton, the brokerage house, concurred with the decision, stating: "Considering that it finally stilled the threat of public power, purchase was by far the wisest course." These reports of the death of public power were premature, to say the least.

As a matter of fact, the public power issue had re-emerged briefly in 1968 when a consultant hired by the Lindsay administration had written a scathing report on Con Ed operations and suggested that the city might find it necessary to "nationalize" the company and run it as a municipal power system. This report, uncovered by Lucy Komisar and discussed at length in *New York* magazine, had been buried by Lindsay staffers. When confronted by Komisar, Deputy Mayor Timothy Costello said: "Public power is not something that can be instituted lightly. A city power system would require a huge investment of capital funds. The city has no means of distribution." Costello noted that the city was negotiating with Con Ed to use its distribution system in return for granting the company a right-of-way over a municipal aqueduct. "They have been resisting," he told Komisar.

Lindsay offered a different view of the report, which had been written by C. Gerard Davidson, like Luce a former Assistant Secretary of the Interior and, ironically, Luce's former boss as general counsel at the Bonneville Power Administration. (Recalling Luce, Davidson told Komisar: "He was very competent, but you never had the feeling about Chuck that he was ever dedicated to the philosophy of public power.") Lindsay shied away from the idea of public ownership but said the city *might* intervene to gain low-cost power from PASNY or public agencies in Canada, or buy the power itself and resell it to Con Edison. This possibility was never pursued, however, and Davidson angrily charged that Lindsay had been influenced by his close personal ties to Luce. (Chairman Luce, who seemed genuinely appalled by the more tawdry side of his predecessors' political methods, quickly proved to be a master of political log-rolling of a more sophisticated sort. In 1968, he was already chairman of Lindsay's Business Advisory Committee.)

When Abrams demanded that the contract terms reportedly under negotiation in 1968 be implemented in 1971, Lindsay staffers said the plan was "unworkable"—and proceeded to make the same arguments in opposition that Luce had announced three years before. Let's pursue those arguments for a moment because they show how even the state's massive public power agency has been converted for the use of the private power companies.

The State Power Authority has a long and interesting history. It was inaugurated in the late 1920s under the governorship of Franklin Delano Roosevelt and subsequently served as the model for the creation of TVA. Its fortunes flourished under Democratic governors and waned under Republicans. Since its basic source of power was the waters of the St. Lawrence, an international river, it was subject to federal as well as state law, and New Yorkers were protected in the use of the power by clear provisions in the statutes of both levels of government. Under these statutes, the output of the St. Lawrence River generators was to be allocated first to municipal power systems, and half of the power was irrevocably reserved for this purpose. Localities in the state's depressed North Country used the cheap power to attract industry, but since transmission technology was in its infancy, that is where the St. Lawrence power stayed. (The huge aluminum smelter complex at Massena was built specifically to benefit from the cheap power.)

Under Governor Harriman's administration, large expansions in the PASNY system were undertaken. As fate would have it, however, the new power became operable under his successor, Nelson Rockefeller, a man with an instinctive commitment to using public investment for private profit. Rockefeller simply took this new public power and sold it on long-term contracts to upstate private utilities. The irony of this was that several public power systems, including two on Long Island, were unable to benefit from their "preference" for the new public power because private utilities like Con Ed and Long Island Lighting refused to "wheel" or transmit the public power through their transmission systems.

This battle over "wheeling" rights, the basic method used by the private companies to quarantine public power, raged for decades in Congress. And it was why Abrams demanded that the Con Ed contract be based on a willingness to use its ties with other utilities to bring power to the city. (Electricity from different sources is as indistinguishable as one gallon of water from another once it enters a transmission network.)

The company's answer, and subsequently the city government's answer, was that no power was available since it had all been sold by Rockefeller. Abrams rejoined that these sales were specifically barred by both federal and state law and that the city could break the existing contracts and bump the illegal users. This would not mean that lights would blink out upstate, however, since PASNY had also begun building nuclear plants, and the million-kilowatt Fitzpatrick plant at Nine Mile Point was due to open soon. This power could be used to make up the difference. (The Fitzpatrick power had been committed already to upstate companies, but since no one was using it, it could easily be re-allocated.) The city therefore could benefit from a minimum of one million kilowatts (about 12 per cent of Con Ed's capacity) of cheap hydropower and at the same time reducing Con Ed's need to borrow for expensive new generating plants. This transfer would substantially reduce the average consumer's electric bill and end Con Ed's perpetual growth cycle.

The debate went on throughout the spring and summer of 1971. The contract was scheduled twice for a final vote and twice postponed. Finally, in the dog days of August, Abrams announced a victory. The city had agreed to sue for its fair share of PASNY power and Con Ed had agreed to deliver the new power over its transmission network. Like so many consumer victories, this one proved to be illusory. The city simply refused to implement its part of the bargain, and as subsequent court decisions ruled, Abrams, although a major elected city official, could not bring suit on behalf of the city. (Lindsay, then contemplating a run for the presidency and keeping his options open for other statewide offices, had the added incentive for inaction of not wanting a protracted legal battle that seemed to pit the city's interests against the desire for unlimited industrial growth upstate. While this wasn't the actual case,

Lindsay had learned one lesson as mayor, and that was that the appearance frequently becomes the reality in political dogfights.) A compromise of sorts was struck when the state legislature in 1972 mandated PASNY to build two new plants to service New York City, but this solution was outrun by events, in the form of the Mideast oil crisis in 1973 and the controversial Con Ed flirtation with bankruptcy in 1974.

While high rates and lousy service were undoubtedly the major irritants in Con Ed's relations with its customers, air pollution ran a close third. Because of Con Ed's desire to produce all of the power it sold as near as possible to the center of its service area (the only exception being its complex of nuclear plants twenty-five miles north of the city line), the company accounted for half of the city's sulfur dioxide pollution by burning vast amounts of oil each day. Subsequently, by burning "sweet" (lower sulfur content) but more expensive oil, the company was able to cut this pollution in half, and naturally, this additional cost was borne by the consumers. But Con Ed remained heavily was on the verge of bankruptcy. It was the first of a three-part series by David Andleman, and by the time Andleman had finished recounting the dire prophecies of Luce and other company officials, Wall Street analysts, and PSC Chairman Joseph Swidler, most New Yorkers were surprised that their lights were still burning.

The Arab oil boycott in 1973 and the subsequent escalation in oil prices hit the utility, or rather its customers, very hard. Once the extent of the crisis was clear, Con Ed got busy and made sure that its increased prices were passed along to customers, already reeling under the highest electric bills in the nation. Finally, the Con Ed consumers struck back: Many stopped paying their bills on time. At the same time, electric consumption also began to fall (actual consumption in 1974 and 1975 was two billion kilowatt-hours less than the record year of 1973 and still lags several hundred million kilowatt-hours behind 1971 consumption.) As a result, Con Ed experienced a cash squeeze.

In what can only be called a brilliant political power-play, Chairman Luce proceeded to seize opportunity from the jaws of adversity. On March 31, 1974, a front-page story in *The New York Times* hinted that Con Ed was on the verge of bankruptcy.

Three days after the *Times* series concluded, Luce was in Albany for a public meeting with Governor Malcolm Wilson. The "solution" he proposed for the crisis was surprising in the light of Con Ed's past history, but quite in keeping with government bailouts of troubled corporations, which have become commonplace in this age of corporate welfare. Luce urged that the state, through the Power Authority, purchase two plants under construction for $500 million. The plants would ultimately be run by Con Ed and the power they produced would become part of its baseload generating system but would be completed and owned by PASNY. This would see the company through its cash-flow crisis and ultimately provide some relief for consumers.

As Judith Bender revealed in *Newsday*, the "emergency" meeting was simply the culmination of a bailout campaign that Luce had been conducting since January. He had decided to turn up the flame in order to force the governor, currently running for reelection, and a legislature that was in no mood for seeming to aggrandize the most hated utility in the state to capitulate.

Luce got the furor he expected. What the public didn't get was the careful analysis by the press and public regulators that would have thrown cold water on the whole thing. As David Kusnet, an energy specialist and consumer advocate, wrote in the December 7, 1974, issue of *The Nation:* ". . . consumers would have been ready to pull out their electric cords, turn off the lights, and vote out every seat-warmer in Albany if their daily newspapers had told the full story of the Con Ed bailout."

On April 23, Luce played his hole card. The company's board of trustees voted to suspend the utility's 45-cent quarterly dividend. The action sent a tremor through the nation's financial markets and Con Ed's stock plummeted from a high of $18 to $6 in a few weeks. Con Ed was front-page news everywhere. Editorialists jumped into the fray; typical of the unquestioning support they gave the company's tale of woe is the following specimen from the May 10 *New York Times:* "There are abundant grounds on which to fault Con Edison, but legislators will be making no useful contribution to protection of the company's hapless customers in this city and Westchester County if they adjourn without authorizing the issuance of self-liquidating bonds for purchase of the two plants. Such a default would merely invite a collapse as devastating in its way as that of the Penn Central."

The legislature got the message, and on May 16 it passed a bailout bill authorizing $500 million to be paid to Con Ed for the unfinished plants and an additional $300 million to cover the costs of completing construction. (Subsequent studies have shown that the actual cost of this undertaking may rise to more than $500 million.)

But what was the real story? Well, for one thing, Con Ed was making money while it was threatening bankruptcy in May. When *this* information surfaced months later, only the *Times* reported it—on an inside page. And it wasn't until the September issue of *Fortune* that anyone bothered to report that the missed dividend payment amounted to only $28 million, an amount the utility could have scraped together in its petty cash accounts or taken from a $130-million line of credit it had with New York banks at the time. If the company was feeling a genuine pinch, why not just halve the dividend ($14 million) instead of throwing the financial markets into a tailspin? This question was asked by angry executives at other utilities whose stocks felt a serious spillover from the Con Ed "collapse."

Even more interesting was the irrational behavior of the state legislature. With Con Ed's stock plummeting, the state could have purchased the *entire company* outright for little more than the $500 million it paid for the two uncompleted plants. The issue was actually raised at the time, but New York state legislators are not known for their "socialistic" or foresighted tendencies. The simple reality was that in the midst of the carefully orchestrated bankruptcy campaign, no one dared ask some very fundamental questions.

Con Ed's recovery after the bailout has been nothing short of astounding. Token 5- or 10-per cent pay cuts issued to corporate executives during the crisis were quietly restored the following October. The dividend was restored to 20 cents per quarter in the second half of 1974, rose to 30 cents quarterly in 1975, and was further increased to 40 cents in the first quarter of 1976. In January 1977, the dividend was again increased by 25 per cent to 50 cents per share—its highest rate in history. In January, 1981, it stood at 67 cents quarterly.

Yet even in the light of this "miraculous" recovery and a radically altered economic climate, the bailout had gone on like clockwork. With New York State itself teetering on the edge of bankruptcy, Governor Carey rejected pleas from Abrams and then Representative Bella Abzug to rescind it. The legislature has been silent on the issue, apparently unwilling to sift the ashes of its earlier mistake in public. (Some apologists argue that since PASNY is an independent agency, its borrowing $800 million in the credit market has no relation to the plight of the city and state in those same markets. This is nonsense. The PASNY borrowing simply means that there will be $800 million less seeking an investment vehicle and helps to assure that the nation's financiers can continue to do without the credit demands of New York city and state, two of their biggest previous customers.)

The largest question remaining is why Charles Luce opened the door to public power, and brought Con Ed's greatest nightmare to life? The answer is simple: He didn't. As we have already suggested, PASNY was coming to the New York market as a result of the protracted transmission-line controversy, and it was scheduled to build two new plants for the city by 1980. Luce saw a way to make the inevitable serve his company's purposes. By selling the two existing plants, Luce not only removed Con Ed from the capital markets at a time when costs for borrowers were soaring, but also forestalled the building of additional capacity in the New York region by PASNY that would have cramped Con Ed's long-range plans. Con Ed gave the game away when it entered into a longterm contract with six other private companies in the state to build seventeen additional plants, mostly nuclear, at a conservatively estimated $3.5 billion during the 1980s. The contract was announced at exactly the same time that Luce was in Albany pleading bankruptcy—another crucial fact ignored by the New York press.

In addition, technical reports by PASNY auditors show that the two plants that were sold will require $130 million more in repairs than first estimated, for such reasons as "inadequate storage practices, lack of cleanliness during assembly, and unsatisfactory construction processes." It also turns out that one of the plants, a nuclear reactor known as Indian Point 3, was built near a geological fault and its safety devices are being challenged by environmentalists. Mr. Luce sold New York State two of the most expensive "lemons" in history.

In September 1976, PASNY power began flowing to New York City and Westchester governmental agencies. The city alone expects to reduce its electric bill by $25 million a year because of PASNY's lower rates. But in the "heads I win, tails you lose," world of Con Ed, the PSC has already granted the utility a "transfer adjustment" that will increase the bills of consumers and small businesses by $57 million to make up the revenue it is losing by no longer having these government agencies as captive customers. A similar situation arose when Con Ed launched its highly successful "Save a Watt" campaign. Consumers cut their consumption but subsequently found themselves paying more per kilowatt hour to sustain Con Ed's guaranteed minimum rate of profit, which is now officially 13½ per cent.

How does such a universally despised utility manage, year after year, to work its will on a hostile public? Part of the answer emerges from a look at Con Ed's board of directors, a sort of snapshot of the permanent government in action.

- William S. Beinecke is the chairman of the board and chief executive officer of Sperry and Hutchinson Company, a conglomerate best known for its "green stamps" but also a major supplier of business services and interior furnishings. Beinecke is also Felix Rohatyn's partner in a real-estate venture in the Bronx called Lambert Houses. (The third partner is Jane Englehardt, the widow of the owner of Englehardt Minerals of South Africa, an infamous employer of black indentured labor. Mrs. Englehardt is best known, at least in certain circles, for her stable of thoroughbreds.) Beinecke is also a director of Manufacturers of Hanover and of Bigelow-Sanford, the giant carpet company. He is a trustee of the Pingry School and Yale University.
- Edmund Virgil Conway is chairman of the board and president of Seamen's Bank for Savings. He is a board member of J. P. Stevens, the giant Southern anti-union textile concern that is currently the object of a nationwide boycott by the Amalgamated Clothing and Textile Workers Union. He is also on the boards of National Securities and Research, Atlantic Mutual Insurance, and Centennial Insurance. Conway, a longtime critic of New York City's social spending, is on the boards of the city's Chamber of Commerce and Industry, Economic Development

Council, and Citizens Budget Commission, a business front group. Mayor Beame appointed him to the Mayor's Management Advisory Board. He is also a trustee of Colgate University.

- Mrs. Andrew Heiskell is better known as Marian Sulzberger, one of the heirs to America's most powerful publishing empire. She is director of special activities at *The New York Times; her present husband is chairman of the board at Time.* She is New York's reigning lady bountiful, serving simultaneously as a member of the board of the Community Service Society; co-chairman (with the mayor) of the city's Council on the Environment; and board member of Rockefeller University, New York Botanical Garden, and the Polytechnic Institute of New York (formerly Brooklyn Poly). She is also a member of the advisory councils for the National Parks, Historical Sites, Buildings and Monuments Committee and for the Dartmouth Medical School; a board member of the Inter-American Press Association, the National Planning Association, and the drug-manufacturing company Merck.

- William W. Lapsley was briefly president of Con Ed until he was replaced by Arthur Hauspurg in 1975. Prior to joining Con Ed in 1969, he had spent thirty-two years in the U.S. Army, retiring with the rank of major general—an unspectacular achievement. He also served as program manager for Kaiser Jeep Corporation on Taiwan.

- Charles F. Luce sits on a number of boards, befitting his rank as Con Ed's ex-chief executive. Luce is a board member of U.A.L. Inc., and United Airlines. He also sits on the board of Metropolitan Life Insurance, which did $10.2 million's worth of business with Con Ed in 1973. He is a trustee of Columbia University; the Conference Board, a major business forecasting group; GAB Business Services Inc.; the New York Chamber of Commerce and Industry; the Economic Development Council; the National Association for Mental Health; the Fresh Air Fund (which sends poor kids away from the Con-Ed-polluted streets of New York each summer); and the New York Botanical Garden.

- Milton C. Mumford is a director and former chairman of the board of Lever Brothers. He is also a director of Atco Industries, Crown Zellerbach, Equitable Life Assurance, Thomas J. Lipton, the Presbyterian Hospital, the Stamford Hospital, and Educational Facilities Laboratories.

- Peter S. Paine is chairman of the executive committee of Great Northern Nekoosa, a giant paper manufacturer. He is on the boards of the Continental Corporation, Continental Insurance, and Irving Trust, and is chairman of the Essex County-Champlain National Bank. He is also a board member of the Vincent Astor Foundation, the Juilliard School of Music, and the Bodman Foundation.

- Richard S. Perkins is Con Ed's friend at Citibank, former chairman of the executive committee of both the bank and its holding company. He is also a director of Allied Chemical, Hospital Corporation of America, International Telephone and Telegraph (ITT), New York Life Insurance, Southern Pacific, the Carnegie Institution of Washington, the Metropolitan Museum of Art, and the Vincent Astor Foundation.
- Donald C. Platten is chairman of the Board of Chemical Bank.
- Luis Quero-Chiesa, the board's token Puerto Rican, is senior vice-president of Roy Blumenthal International Associates, a public relations and advertising firm. He is also on the boards of Blue Cross and Blue Shield of Greater New York, Inter-American University, the New York Philharmonic, the Academy of Arts and Sciences of Puerto Rico, and the city's Committee on Cultural Affairs.
- William S. Renchard is chairman of the executive committee of Chemical Bank and a director of the bank's holding company. He also sits on the board of the oil firm Amerada Hess, which received $53 million from Con Ed in 1973, as well as Armstrong Rubber, Baker Industries, Borden, New York Life Insurance, C.I. Realty Investors, Cleveland-Cliffs Iron, and the International Executive Service Corps. He is chairman of the Citizens Budget Commission and president and director of the Manhattan Eye, Ear, and Throat Hospital.
- Frederick P. Rose is the leading realtor and president of Rose Associates, Inc.
- Donald K. Ross is vice-chairman and director of the New York Life Insurance Company.
- Myles V. Whalen is a partner in the Wall Street law firm of Shearman and Sterling.
- Franklin H. Williams is the board's token black. An attorney, he is president of the Phelps-Stokes Fund. He is also a director of Chemical Bank and of its holding company, U.R.S. Inc., Lincoln University, the New York state advisory committee to the U.S. Civil Rights Commission, and the New York City Center of Music and Drama.

On July 13, 1977, the lights went out again when lightning from a severe summer storm knocked out two lines of Con Ed's flimsy transmission network. There was to be no love fest of civic virtue this time. Within moments after the lights flickered out, a perceptible roar went up from the city's poverty neighborhoods and the smashing of glass and the wail of police sirens which was to continue for the next twenty-four hours marked the beginnings of the worst looting and rioting in New York history since the Irish anti-draft riots of 1863.

It is important to note that this was almost exclusively an attack on property. The worst hit merchants were those furniture and appliance dealers who exist in the shopping district of every ghetto. Whites walking the streets went unmolested and many poorer whites joined in the looting, there were surprisingly few injuries overall and no deaths. But the middle class emerged from the prolonged Blackout of July 13-14 thoroughly terrified. The Police had been shown incapable of stopping the widespread looting, and while hundreds had been arrested, many had to be freed. With a brilliant sense of timing, Ed Koch stepped into the leadership vacuum and called for the dispatch of the National Guard. Sensing the public's lust for blood to slake their fear, he soon after began his incessant calls for the resumption of capital punishment and his long climb from the bottom of the polls had begun.

A year later, the Federal Energy Regulatory Commission issued a report which placed full blame for the blackout on Con Ed, saying that its staff was poorly trained for the job, that the transmission grid was inadequate and that the automatic load-shedding system, the lack of which caused the '65 Blackout, still wasn't in adequate working order. But no one in top management was fired as a result of this unbelievable incompetence, and Con Ed has been rewarded with higher and higher rate increases.

Far more serious than the Blackout, although so far without significant political fallout, was a nuclear accident at the Indian Point 2 nuclear plant on October 3, 1980. Cooling water began leaking into the reactor's containment vessel, and while a warning light flashed, automatic pumps which should have been triggered failed to operate and the water continued to rise. Incredibly, another set of safety devices shut down the reactor on October 17, but Con Ed workers started it again without discovering the leak. Hours later the reactor shut down again and was again restarted. Finally, on October 20 the plant was shut down for an extended period.

Several anti-nuclear scientists we talked to warned that had the water risen another *nine* feet in the containment room, and overflowed into the reactor vessel, the 50 degree Hudson River water could have cracked the 550 degree reactor vessel and a cloud of radioactive steam 1,000 times the size of the radioactive cloud released by the Hiroshima bomb blast would have been released. Indian Point is just 25 miles from Manhattan.

Of course, Con Ed denies these charges. But they are given serious weight by a scathing report released by the Nuclear Regulatory Commission which blasts the company for its incompetence in ignoring rudimentary safety measures. Meantime Con Ed has been allowed to pass along the costs of this near-catastrophe to its customers at a cost of $850,000 a day, although this has been challenged by State Attorney-General Bob Abrams, Con Ed's old foe.

Through the years, Con Ed has failed every test of operating an essential public service. We simply can't afford any more nuclear "mistakes," fantastic rate hikes or the latest threat, burning high-pollution coal in its generators. Con Ed cries out for public takeover.

The Koch Years

12

Edward Irving Koch has been the most popular mayor of New York since Fiorello La Guardia, yet no two men could be more dissimilar in their use of the office. La Guardia was the hero of the immigrant poor and the scourge of their exploiters; Koch has been the opposite. La Guardia was a populist; Koch is a bully to the weak and a toady to the strong.

There are a few parallels between them, however. Koch, like La Guardia, is an obsessive hard-worker, and personally honest. And he has the little Flower's flair for self-dramatization, managing to stay on the city's front pages even when on a trip to Egypt.

While waiting half an hour for an overcrowded subway train that arrives with most of its interior lights broken, or huddling on a garbage-crusted street corner hoping to catch a 20 year old bus, we have had ample time to meditate about Ed Koch's popularity. The paradox of deteriorating public services and a 60 per cent approval rating for the mayor requires a major effort at explanation.

There is no mystery about the popularity among white voters of Koch's punitive policies toward blacks and Hispanics. The more he calls responsible black leaders "demagogues," the more he rants against "quotas," the more speeches he makes urging the death penalty, the more he closes ghetto hospitals and calls them "welfare programs"—all these things increase Koch's esteem among white ethnics and the white middle class.

This is hard to accept, but it is easy to understand. It is the poison politics of polarization. It is Koch appealing to the worst in people during a selfish epoch of shrinking opportunity and insecure status.

What is hard to comprehend is why these mean mouthings are sufficient to make the tax-paying middle class exonerate Koch for the daily diminishing quality of life in their own communities. The same homeowners who never forgave Lindsay for failing to clean up after one snow storm in Queens, seem willing to forgive Koch almost anything. Koch has tickled the middle class into ignoring its own self-interest.

If Ronald Reagan's simple, unoriginal question—"Are you better off today than you were four years ago?"—is asked of the lives of most New Yorkers, the answer would have to be, no. But, for over three years, Koch has remained the most popular elected official in New York, even though essential services like police protection, the subways, education, sanitation and health—services which he is more responsible for delivering than Governor Carey or Senator Moynihan—have seriously declined.

The crime rate is getting worse. Homicides reached 1,814 in 1980, an all-time record, topping 1979's peak of 1733. New York City, in 1980, ranked **first** among the nation's 25 largest cities in robberies. There were 210,000 burglaries—another all time record. A study released in February of 1981 showed that the odds a burglar will be arrested, convicted, and sent to state prison are 263 to 1.

Crime is spreading, even to so-called "quiet" neighborhoods. In 1979, 60 of the city's 73 precincts experienced increases in serious crimes. The 123rd precinct on Staten Island, New York's internal suburb, had a 33 per cent increase in reported felonies. The 102nd precinct in Queens was up 50 per cent. The 20th precinct in Manhattan was up 26.3 per cent. The 62nd precinct in Bay Ridge in Brooklyn was up 9.5 per cent.

Overall, the felony crime rate in 1980 was 16 per cent ahead of the previous year, although felony arrests dropped by 5.5 per cent. Gold chains have been ripped off the throats of women at high noon on Fifth Avenue, and loaded pistols have been confiscated from grammar school students.

The crime rate in the city's 267 public-housing developments, which have their own separate police force, is out of control. Murder is up 24 per cent; rape is up 43 per cent; and assault is up 89 per cent.

One obvious reason for this fear-inducing crime rate is New York's seriously shrunken police force. In 1972, there were 31,000 cops on the force. Today there are 22,000. Faced with a court order that he hire more minority cops, Koch dragged his feet for 18 months and then announced a budget allotment for 1,000 new recruits in 1981, an election year. But the heralded 1,000 new cops won't even make for one year's attrition rate. Individual cops, aging and embattled, tend to react with maximum force in every situation, and further embitter the minority communities whose residents face the highest crime rates. Blacks and Hispanics increasingly demand protection from criminals—and the police. Yet on the midnight to 8 a.m. tour of duty, there are now just 1,066 cops on patrol across the city.

Adding to the cynicism and lack of confidence toward the police is the thriving drug trade throughout the city. A new wave of pure heroin is flooding into the city from Pakistan and Southwest Asia, through Sicily, where it is refined in Mafia-constructed laboratories. But most of the good, young narcotics detectives were let go in 1975.

A study by the Senate Select Committee on Crime has disclosed that during all of 1979 in New York City, only 45 persons were convicted of an A-1 narcotics offense—which is possession with intent to sell of a quantity of heroin worth at least $30,000 on the street. For the years 1977, 1978, and 1979, 1,330 persons were indicted for A-1 drug crimes, but only 107 went to prison. The executives of the heroin cartel are at small risk doing business in New York today—and they know it.

Even street criminals know the odds are heavily in their favor. In 1979, there were 539,102 felonies committed in the five boroughs but police made arrests in only 63,000 cases. But 84 per cent of those arrested in these cases had their charges reduced to misdemeanors or dismissed. **Only 1 per cent served time in a state prison.**

The subway and bus system is in a state of chaos and collapse despite yet another fare increase to 60 cents. This is the direct effect of shortfalls in capital investment as well as severe attrition in personnel.

There were 30,000 train breakdowns in 1977; 43,000 in 1979; and 71,700 during 1980. Delays caused by broken doors have increased from 6,000 in 1978, to 9,000 in 1980. The number of track fires increased by 40 per cent in 1980.

The independent Permanent Citizens' Advisory Committee to the MTA has revealed that the number of trains which had to be taken out of service almost doubled from 5100 in October, 1979 to 9,773 in October, 1980. The number of disabled trains jumped 22 per cent in one month alone between September and October, 1980. And the miles between breakdowns in the subway car fleet has fallen from 8400 to 6500 in less than a year.

A broad survey by the Straphangers' Campaign, a project of the New York Public Interest Research Group, found that 30 per cent of the subway car doors don't open, 17 per cent of the cars are dimly lit or entirely dark, and in 70 per cent of the cars the maps are missing or unreadable because of graffitti.

One reason for this state of affairs is the cosmetic priorities in budget cutting. The deepest cuts have been made in preventive maintenance, because that is least immediately visible to voters. Between 1971 and 1980, the maintenance staff for the city's subways has declined from 5800 workers to 3800.

Koch can hardly insulate himself from this management breakdown; he has appointed four of the 14-member MTA board, including Deputy Mayor Robert Wagner, Jr., and MTA chairman Richard Ravitch was named with Koch's support. He decides the size of the Transit Police force, and he played a critical role in provoking the 1980 transit strike, and then prolonged it with his anti-union posturing for television cameras. The MTA, like the original Transit Authority, was designed to avoid accountability by the Governor and the Mayor. But the constant pushing and shoving between Koch and Carey over the fare, and Koch's Hamlet routine over the Westway boondoggle, have allowed the veil to slip.

Slowly, but with increasing anger, the harried straphangers are awakening to the fact that behind the largely faceless MTA board stand those masked puppeteers—Ed Koch and Hugh Carey.

It is in the area of public health, however, where Ed Koch has been most bitterly determined to reduce the public sector, and where he has met the most determined opposition from the black and Hispanic communities. From the beginning of his administration, Koch sided with right-wing idealogues like William Simon and Steve Berger that the city should not be in the hospital "business." To accomplish this, a central strategy was devised to "shrink" the municipal hospital system and the world-renowned Health Department.

To oversee this strategy, Koch brought into his administration Dr. Martin Cherkasky, head of private Montefiore Hospital in the Bronx, and long the city medical establishment's leading cheerleader for dismantling the municipal system and parceling its hospitals out among the private medical empires which tended to dominate the various boroughs. Cherkasky's greatest victory, won under the Lindsay and Beame administrations, had been the closing of Morrisania hospital in the South Bronx and its replacement with a brand new "Cadillac" of a hospital, North Central Bronx, five miles away in the North Bronx and directly adjacent to Montefiore (actually linked to it by a series of bridges and tunnels).

There was nothing new about the Cherkasky plan, except the overt support it was receiving for the first time from a mayor of New York. Many of the older and smaller city hospitals, such as Greenpoint and Cumberland in Brooklyn and Sydenham in Manhattan, and those which competed directly for patients with neighboring voluntaries such as Metropolitan in Manhattan, would be closed. Several large, modern hospitals constructed or completed by the Lindsay Administration, such as North Central Bronx or Bellevue, would be taken over by neighboring voluntaries. At the plans completion all that would be left of the 18-hospital municipal system would be five or six hospitals, probably two in Manhattan and one each in Brooklyn, Queens and the Bronx, to handle the 1.4 million medically indigent residents of the city who lack Medicaid or private health insurance and are therefore undesirable patients for the voluntaries.

When Koch announced the planned closing of four hospitals in the summer of 1979 and budget cuts of $30 million to be spread throughout a system, a firestorm erupted in the affected communities. Sit-ins, court challenges, demonstrations, mass marches—the struggle to save the hospitals finally galvanized the community resistance which had failed to materialize throughout the entire "fiscal crisis" since 1975.

To anyone unfamiliar with health care, Koch appears to be losing the battle to dismantle the municipal health system. Only one hospital on his hit list, the small, 119-bed Sydenham has been closed. But in reality, he is winning the war. The city hospitals are dying. Clinics have closed, doctors often lack critical supplies, staff quit threatened hospitals, it has become almost impossible to hire trained nurses because the traditional parity of wages with the voluntary hospitals has been destroyed, American medical graduates refuse to sign on as house staff. Despite inflation, the city has effectively frozen its tax-levy expenditures on the municipal system for the past three years. The result, according to a staff member of City Council President Carol Bellamy, is that sick people are turned away: inpatient days are down 10 per cent, emergency room visits are down 10 per cent and outpatient visits are down 15 per cent. Those with Medicaid may find care at a voluntary; those with no insurance will avoid rising fees, long lines and chaotic disorganization until they feel much sicker.

While the hospitals have been condemned to a slow death, most observers feel that the Health Department has already passed the point of no return. Even before Koch took office the Department had lost 25 per cent of its budget and one-third of its staff. In the four years between 1974-78, the city's extensive system of community clinics were gutted. Child health stations were closed, dental visits (Health Department dentists were the only dentists for the children of the poor) were slashed by 80 per cent, school health examinations feel by 41 per cent, chest examinations by 19 per cent and eye exams by 45 per cent. In a city with a burgeoning population from the Caribbean, Latin America and other tropical locals, tropical disease services were cut 41 per cent.

Koch continued the assault with a vengeance. His disastrous Health Commissioner, Reinaldo Ferrer, closed two of the three remaining tropical disease clinics. The waiting list at the remaining clinics is six weeks long for the hundreds of patients seeking assistance, many of whom work in the city's restaurants and other food handling occupations. The Health Department sought to abolish completely the school dental clinics bought astounded when a tough constituency arose to fight off these cutbacks.

The best index of what has happened to the quality of health care is the increased rate of disease. For the first time in 16 years, tuberculosis is re-emerging as a major health threat in New York City. In the first quarter of 1979 alone, there was a 38 per cent increase in new cases; there was an overall increase of 17 per cent for the entire year of 1980. The New York Lung Association reports that 1800 new cases a year are being discovered and that a quarter of these are highly contagious and likely to infect people they contact. In ghetto areas like the Lower East Side and Central Harlem, the TB rate is four times the national average for new cases, And these areas, despite

Medicaid and the advances in medical care of recent years, still have diseases and death rates on a par with Third World countries.

Public education has been another major victim of Koch's preoccupation with balancing the budget to impress the bankers at the expense of basic services. Average class sizes have grown to thirty-eight or forty pupils, violence and disruption are a daily reality in many schools because security guards have been laid off. 100,000 pupils are truant each day, and middle class parents continue to remove their kids from a system which fails to compete on an educational basis with suburban schools. Despite a disputed increase in official reading scores, employers continue to complain that public school graduates simply lack the basic skills necessary to make it in today's job market.

The decline of sanitation services has been documented by Operation Scorecard, the Koch administration's own management report. Only 51 per cent of all the city streets are acceptably clean, compared to 74 per cent in May of 1976. In Brooklyn, only 38 per cent of the streets are clean. Broadway has always gotten noticeably filthier as it slopes down from Columbia University into Harlem, but white middle-class communities are also dirtier than ever. Flatbush, Coney Island, Bensonhurst, Canarsie, Manhattan's West Side, and Greenwich Village are not acceptably clean. Koch's management report said that not a single sanitation district in the city showed an improvement in 1979 over 1978.

Again, a basic explanation goes back to excessive, counter-productive budget cuts. Over the last five years, the Sanitation Department has reduced its street-cleaning force from 2700 to 500 workers. Again, the streets are filthier despite a declining population.

The decay and decline of other public services is evident to anyone who lives or works in the city. The city's parks are dying because all of the technical personnel has been laid off and a sharply reduced work force has an average age of 55 years. Libraries are only open 19 hours a week. The Roosevelt Island Tramway has been broken for months. Ambulances cannot reach a victim of cardiac arrest or gunshot or automobile crashes in less than 20 minutes and frequently much longer. In other cities, the response time is six minutes—the maximum margin for someone dying of cardiac arrest. Water mains burst with almost daily regularity as the city faces a prolonged drought because they haven't been replaced in forty years. Bridges rust away, streets crumble, boilers and elevators go uninspected. No public service or amenity seems better today than when Koch was first elected with the probable exception of fire protection.

Ed Koch is not merely a virtuoso performer, but a consummate politician.

He has bartered his popularity to assure his tenancy in Gracie Mansion for 12 years, offering himself as the Mayor of all the parties, if not of all the people. In the 1980 elections, the Democrats were making a desperate bid to unseat incumbent Republican State Senators and gain control of the upper House in order to pass redistricting legislation based on a census which seriously undercounts the population of New York City and other urban areas.

At the same time, Koch was jockeying to get the Republican nomination, and possibly the Conservative nod as well, for his re-election bid. Even a brief interruption in the usually symbiotic relationships between the two major parties in New York State gave him a golden opportunity. He immediately began openly endorsing Republican State Senators like John Marchi and the abominable John Calandra, who control the votes of their county organizations, and all-but-endorsed other Republican candidates like the mediocre Congresssman Bill Green, who was facing a tough challenge from former Nader aid Mark Green. When Koch confidante Bess Myerson lost the Democratic U.S. Senate nomination to progressive Congresswoman Elizabeth Holtzman, the Mayor sulked and did everything possible to subvert Holtzman's campaign, finally giving press conference embrace to the scandal tainted Republican, Alphonse D'Amato. He also managed a last-minute mutual admiration session with Ronald Reagan, sawing the legs off the Carter candidacy in New York.

The Republican accession in Washington saddens Democrat Koch not at all. His broad support on the Right strengthens his hand in fighting progressives and reformers within his own party who have consistently questioned his service cutbacks, race-baiting, and tax policies. The man who was given his start in politics as the candidate of the "anti-boss" faction now seeks to become the biggest boss in New York's recent political history.

On Election Night, 1980, Koch was at a private party at Rupert Murdoch's home. Those who saw him that night report he was "giddy" and "delighted" with the Republican landslide. One party guest asked Koch how he felt about a Democratic president and a Democratic senate going down to defeat. Koch smiled and said: "Publicly disconsolate."

In May of 1981, Senator D'Amato and Rep. Green voted for the Reagan budget that cut the heart out of New York City.

Ed Koch is very good at the theatrics of governing. He's a witty man, a master of the quick one-liner for radio and television. He has a sense for the symbolic act, like his anti-union cheerleading on the Brooklyn Bridge during the transit strike, or his photo-opportunity embrace with Republican Al D'Amato at City Hall late in the 1980 Senate campaign. He's smart and he has a lawyer's verbal facility. He's a fine actor, and seems spontaneous each time he calls a legitimate critic a "demagogue," each time he whines "I will not be intimidated." He knows all the latest racial code words. He knows how to stroke the publishers. He knows how to look tough by attacking less-powerful, less-popular people, like Judge Bruce Wright, or John Lindsay, or Herman Badillo.

But none of this has anything to do with successfully managing the government, with doing more with less, with delivering necessary services, with communicating a sense of fairness to the 45 per cent of the city population which is non-white. Koch is running the city with his mouth, articulating resentments as if he were still a Congressman.

Part of his popularity is his genius at articulating a scapegoat. And in any period of diminishing opportunity and insecure status, scapegoating is the key to gaining and holding power.

Crime? Koch blames the "soft judges," and invokes the image of the electric chair, while refusing to appropriate more money to expand the police or make the courts work.

Dirty streets? He blames the commissioner he appointed.

Name a problem and Koch will pass the buck—to Lindsay, to Beame, to the state, to Carter, whom he endorsed over Kennedy, to welfare cheats, to lazy city workers, to OPEC.

The transit breakdown? Koch will blame the MTA, as if he had no power over its appointed members; or that he never broke his campaign promise to trade in Westway's $1.7 billion for mass-transit funds.

This is how Koch has bamboozled the middle class. He has a scapegoat for every failure. Koch has actually brainwashed most of the city to think of blacks and municipal workers as "special interests," but to think realtors and developers as avatars of the "public interest."

Koch's secret is that he has made us resigned to decay. He wants us to feel guilty for expecting adequate services from the government we pay our taxes to.

Koch the entertainer, Koch the cheerleader, frequently speaks of New York's Renaissance, of a new spirit of optimism in the city. And there obviously is a renaissance going on in New York. Only it is limited to the wealthy, white fragment of Manhattan between Wall Street and 96th Street. In this golden fragment there is a booming real estate market, an influx of foreign investment, co-op conversions for those with equity, wonderful opportunities for leisure and pleasure. This is one New York, the New York that Koch in his inaugural speech described as a place of "heightened reality and splendor."

But the story of New York today is a tale of two cities. The four other boroughs are being starved. They have little heightened reality or splendor. A wildly disproportionate amount of development money is being invested in Manhattan.

The Urban Development Corporation (UDC) was created by an act of the State legislature in April, 1968 as a "memorial" to Martin Luther King. Its founding purpose was to build affordable rental housing for the poor. In 1980, the UDC did not build a single unit of housing for the poor. It is, however, helping to finance the Theatre Row development on 42nd Street ($1 million); Donald Trump's Grand Hyatt Hotel ($80 million); the new Convention Center at 34th Street ($375 million); the South Street Seaport renovation ($119 million); and the luxury Portman Hotel at 45th Street ($241 million). Koch supported all of these projects at the Board of Estimate. In addition, Manhattan has the gigantic Battery Park City development, the wasteful Westway, and large tax benefits for the new corporate headquarters of AT&T.

Herman Badillo has said that Koch is converting Manhattan into a "fantasyland" while neglecting the 'family-based, homeowner neighborhoods."

A disproportionate amount of the tax incentives in the J-51 program have been given to Manhattan landlords south of 96th Street. Manhattan, with 19 per cent of the city's population, has more J-51 conversions to residential use than any other borough. The J-51 program was created in 1955 to help finance the installation of heating and hot water systems in coldwater flats. In 1979, the city exempted or abated $42 million in real estate taxes under the J-51 program—most of it to finance luxury housing in white Manhattan, where the real estate market is strong and the vacancy rate is less than 1 per cent.

The real estate tax favors handed out by the Industrial and Commercial Incentives Board (ICIB) have also benefitted Manhattan disproportionately. Councilwoman Ruth Messinger has pointed out that only one of 27 applications submitted to the ICIB by Manhattan office buildings and hotels was turned down. These Manhattan projects account for $150 of the $200 million in abatements granted. They include the new headquarters for the Goldman Sachs securities firm ($9 million); the Hilton Hotel ($15 million); AT&T's new corporate headquarters ($20 million); and the telephone company's new home at 1166 Sixth Avenue ($10.5 million).

Fantasyland is thriving. The fortress behind the moat is prospering because it is subsidized. But the rest of the city is not. Those bedrock residential neighborhoods that still love Koch are being hurt by his priorities—his Manhattan fixation, his support of higher rents, his cutting services to the point where the quality of life becomes intolerable in small ways. Coney Island and East Tremont and Flatbush and Williamsbridge and Astoria and South Jamaica and Sunset Park and Williamsburg and Borough Park are not better off today than they were four years ago. They are not getting a fair share of the UDC's bonding authority, or of the ICIB's tax incentives.

The tourists and media opinion-makers don't see this other New York. They see Lincoln Center, Elaine's Restaurant, the Palace Hotel, the sumptuous

Park Avenue co-ops. They don't leave Manhattan to visit the alternative reality that Dickens called the worst of times, the winter of despair.

And they surely don't see the city's permanent underclass, the minority slums, the 900,000 (two-thirds of them children) without a welfare grant increase since 1974, the illegal aliens working in sweatshops for $5 a day, the Charlotte Streets and Sutter Avenues where hope is a memory.

At the close of 1980, Ed Koch said in several year-end interviews that race relations in New York City, "have never been better." He cited as proof the fact there had been no riots during his administration, and that there had been riots under mayors Beame and Lindsay.

The truth is that race relations are more dangerously polarized today in New York than ever before, because of Koch. By every statistical measurement, from unemployment, to health care, to housing abandonment, to welfare dependency, to school segregation, to crime, drug addiction and alcoholism—life in New York's non-white communities is worse off today than it was ten years ago. At the start of 1981, in New York City, with 45 per cent of its population non-white, there was not a single black or Hispanic on the Board of Estimate. There was no black or Hispanic Deputy Mayor, in violation of a Koch campaign promise. Today minorities are less represented than at any time since 1953.

Koch's basic priorities and policies have been punitive towards the poor. He has, behind-the-scenes, undercut efforts to raise the basic welfare grant in the state legislature. He has closed Sydenham Hospital in Harlem, and threatened to close Metropolitan Hospital in East Harlem so many times that some of the best staff has quit and applied for other jobs. The service crisis in police, transit, and sanitation has hit the poor the hardest. But in a way, it has been Koch's words as much as his policies, that have made the minorities of New York feel that the Mayor does not care about them as individuals. Through code words, symbolism, and rhetoric, Koch communicates an attitude of hostility to blacks, and this is a dirty little secret of his vast popularity with the white majority that votes. But it is also the source of a bitter poison spreading silently through the city. The bill for Koch's race politics may not come due for 10 or 15 years, but our children will have to pay it.

Koch says repeatedly that "blacks like me," that only **black leaders** don't like him because he has dismantled their corrupt anti-poverty empires.

But polling data reveals an extraordinary dislike of Koch among average blacks in New York City. In July of 1979 Penn and Schoen Associates polled 750 registered voters. Asked what they thought about Koch, 70 per cent of the whites gave him a favorable rating, but 55 per cent of the blacks gave Koch an unfavorable rating and almost 40 per cent of the blacks said they thought Koch was a racist.

In August of 1980, *The New York Times* took another poll and discovered even deeper racial polarization. Among whites, 69 per cent approved of the job Koch was doing as Mayor, while 60 per cent of the blacks disapproved.

Senator Daniel Moynihan is usually thought to be unpopular among blacks, but only 11 per cent of the blacks polled said they "strongly disapproved" of Moynihan. An incredible 46 per cent of blacks said they "strongly disapproved" of Koch.

There has been a pattern of behavior by Koch that polarized New York by speech and symbolism. We will mention just six of these divisive episodes.

● In September of 1979, Ken Auletta published a two-part profile of Koch in the *New Yorker* magazine. In the profile Auletta quoted a comment Koch dictated into a taping machine a few years earlier as part of an oral history project. Koch had said:

"I find the black community very anti-Semitic. . . . My experience with blacks is that they're basically anti-Semitic. . . . Now, I want to be fair about it. I think whites are basically anti-black. . . . but the difference is: it is recognized as morally reprehensible, something you have to control."

First, this inflammatory stereotype reflects Koch's pure, gut attitude. In the secrecy of his mind, he thinks of blacks as an anti-Jewish, special interest group.

Second, Koch curiously confuses religion and race. He says blacks are biased against **Jews**, but that whites are biased against **blacks**. His hate equation is unbalanced.

Third, Koch speaks of "my experience with blacks. . . ." We have known Koch personally for 20 years, and during these 20 years he has not had a close personal friend who is black. His closest friends have almost all been white, middle class clones of himself: David Margolis, Daniel Wolf, Henry Stern, Bess Myerson, David Garth, Allen Schwartz, and Robert Wagner, Jr. Koch has almost no intimate, autobiographical knowledge of what blacks actually think and feel.

Fourth, it is certainly not our observation that whites more than blacks recognize hate and discrimination as something "morally reprehensible." In the last few years white racism seems to have become more open, more legitimized and not something whites feel particularly guilty about.

There is no question that black anti-Semitism exists in New York. Black nationalist writer Amiri Baraka published an anti-Semitic article on the front page of *The Village Voice* in December of 1980, but it is inaccurate and irresponsible for a Mayor to say that blacks are "basically" anti-Semitic. A poll taken in 1979 showed that blacks felt more sympathetic to Jews than to any other ethnic group. However, more recent polling data among black New Yorkers is beginning to suggest that Koch himself is giving rise to feelings of resentment against Jews because of his own conduct in office. His prejudice might become a self-fulfilling prophesy.

Most black leaders are sympathetic to Jews, not antagonistic. Assemblyman Denny Farrell, Secretary of State Basil Patterson, most black clergy, the leaders of the NAACP and the Urban League, are models of decency and brotherhood. But Koch has almost no contact with them. He will not even meet with Dr. Clark because Clark published a letter in *The New York Times* criticizing him. But Koch thinks of the black community as "very anti-Semitic." Such a moral blindness is itself an insurmountable obstacle to governing a multi-racial community with fairness, equality, and racial harmony.

Koch's *New Yorker* remark was widely reprinted and created a firestorm of criticism among blacks. A few days after the quote first appeared, Koch invited Harlem Congressman Charles Rangel to Gracie Mansion for coffee, danish, and a carefully scripted press conference that sent the message out that all should be forgiven and forgotten.

Koch actually seemed to expect that blacks would easily erase his observation from their memory. Yet, in that same *New Yorker* profile, Auletta described Koch as "unforgiving" of the smallest rejection, and quoted Koch as saying of himself: "I always like to tweak people if I can, especially if I don't like them. This is something that is really vicious in me."

In July of 1980, the United States Supreme Court issued its decision in a case known as Fullilove v. Klutznick. The Court ruled that Congress had a right to establish quotas for minority employment in circumstances where that was the only remedy to systemic discrimination. In October of 1979, New York City's Corporation Counsel submitted a 36-page brief in the same case in support of a minority set-aside as "the effective remedy for an entrenched system of discrimination in the construction industry. . . . In light of the documented history of race discrimination in the construction industry, there can be no question that Congress' action in enactng the MBE (minority business enterprise) was justified by a compelling government interest."

A few days after the Court's opinion in Fullilove v. Klutznick was announced, Ed Koch denounced it as an "abomination." Ignoring the reasoned brief written by his own Corporation Counsel, Koch said of minority set-asides: "I don't happen to think its unconstitutional. I just happen to think it's wrong." Koch made these inflammatory remarks to a meeting of the National Association of Jewish Legislators.

Koch also said in the same speech that he was opposed to minority set-asides **even in circumstances where there was a provable pattern of entrenched racial discrimination.** Koch called all quotas "reverse discrimination"—the code word that most satisfied his audience and his constituency.

And in an echo of George Wallace, Koch said, "I will never give in," referring to a pending court order signed by Federal Judge Robert Carter that the New York City Police Department hire a quota of qualified blacks from among those who scored above 94 on the last police civil service exam. Yet, a month later, Koch quietly agreed to the court-mandated formula that required one black cop be hired for every two white cops. But Koch's rhetoric had already further inflamed race relations in New York. It had implied defiance of laws and court decisions he did not agree with.

In March of 1980, Koch was aggressively campaigning for Jimmy Carter against Edward Kennedy in the New York presidential primary. When the tilt of Carter's policies against Israel became a local political problem, Koch blurted out that the fault resided not with the President himself, but with his four anti-Israel advisers. Koch named them: Secretary of State Cyrus Vance, UN Ambassador Donald McHenry, Former UN Ambassador Andrew Young, National Security Adviser Zbigniew Brzezinski. While exonerating the chief policy-maker, Koch said that Young and McHenry were, "third world oriented and viciously anti-Israel."

When Koch suddenly discovered that 50 per cent of the subordinate plotters were black, Murray Kempton wrote the next day: "His (Koch's) distaste for affirmative action seems to keep a firm hold on him until he has to start blaming people, and then his quota system for the black share among candidates for public attention seems to turn out markedly out-sized just a bit too often."

In April of 1979, Criminal Court Judge Bruce Wright released without bail a man named Jerome Singleton who had been accused of slashing a policeman with a knife. The suspect was a college student with no prior criminal record. Mayor Koch immediately went before the television cameras to denounce Judge Wright's decision as "bizzare," and asked that his own committee on judicial appointments give him a report on Wright, who was up for re-appointment that year. Koch also issued a written statement saying that Wright's bail decision, "is personally distressing to me."

It was not the first time that Koch used his daily access to the media to ridicule Judge Wright, who is black. Koch had made Wright one of his black punching bags ever since his campaign for Mayor in 1977. Wright was an obvious target for a Mayor whose philosophy is to bully the vulnerable and toady to the strong. The *Daily News* had already frequently attacked Wright's liberal bail policies, and the police union had compared the jurist to Hitler on more than one occasion. Wright often responded in kind, and was already perceived as a symbol of black extremism by much of white New York.

A 22-member committee of the Bar Association of New York published a report that reached the conclusion that Koch's comments were "inappropriate and ill-advised." The Bar Association report said: "The Mayor's criticism of

Judge Wright will have a 'chilling effect' upon the exercise of discretion by judges in setting bail, since judges inclined to release a defendant on bail may think twice for fear of public criticism or denial of re-appointment." The Bar Association also concluded that Wright's original bail decision, "was certainly permissible and well within the exercise of his discretion." The report added: "It is not generally understood that the only proper purpose of bail is to assure the appearance of a defendant at trial. The Mayor has contributed to the public's misunderstanding of bail," and "failed to pay due deference to the presumption of innocence."

On December 9, 1980, Health and Hospitals Corporation Chairman Dr. Abraham Kauvar attended a meeting of about 40 community health activists in Brooklyn. During the meeting, Kauvar used the word "niggers." In response to a question, he said: "I can assure you there are no niggers in the woodpile."

The largely Hispanic audience was dumbfounded, Robert Santiago, a leader of the advisory board to Cumberland-Greenpoint Hospital said: "I couldn't believe that Kauvar would say something like that. No one in a position of responsibility to the public should come out with such a statement."

The Queens Citizens Committee for Political Alternatives wrote Koch a letter saying: "It is unthinkable that a man who would use this sort of language is heading up the agency that wants to close hospitals in black and Hispanic communities."

Dozens of black leaders asked that Kauvar—who was paid $95,000 a year—be fired. Even Koch's friends and commissioners, conceded privately that if Kauvar had said "kike," or "cunt," or "faggot" he would have been dismissed immediately.

But Koch held a press conference to announce that he would not fire Kauvar over a "foolish" statement. Kauvar blamed his slur on the fact he had a 102 degree fever on the night he used the word. The episode could be taken as a sign its okay to say nigger in Koch's New York.

In the summer of 1977, New York City was in a fearful frenzy about crime. The Son of Sam was loose, killing women and writing notes to the press. There had been widespread looting, burning, and rioting during the July blackout. Several bombs had exploded in the City, set off by Puerto Rican terrorists. A *New York Times* poll in August of 1977 of just registered Democrats showed 75 per cent for capital punishment.

Into this tinderbox came candidate Edward Koch, making the death penalty the centerpiece of his campaign even though the Mayor had no legal authority to institute the death penalty. Only the state legislature can do that. Nevertheless, day after day, Koch visited senior citizen centers, where fear was understandably in the room, and talked about his commitment to bring back the electric chair. In the weekly Brooklyn newspaper *Flatbush Life*, reporter Sheryl Meccariello described Koch campaigning in the Borough Park neighborhood: "Ed Koch stopped a woman on the corner of 48th Street and 13th Avenue. 'I'm for capital punishment, are you?' he asked her. The woman's disinterested face became animated. She furowed her brows and nodded. . . 'Did you know that that Beame was against capital punishment until three weeks ago when he saw the polls?', Koch told her."

During his campaign Koch made his support for the death penalty one of "the five reasons all New Yorkers need Ed Koch" in all the literature his campaign workers handed out in Queens and Brooklyn. But all the Koch leaflets handed out in more liberal Manhattan omitted the death penalty as one of the five reasons New Yorkers needed Koch.

During the summer, Koch campaign workers distributed a "voter's scorecard" to baseball fans at Shea Stadium with a regular Mets' game scorecard on the reverse side. One of the five issues that Koch asked the voters to score a Mayor on was capital punishment.

Koch was, to a large measure, elected to office on an emotional issue over which the Mayor has no responsibility. Yet, when violent street crime and murders increased in 1979 and again in 1980, Koch claimed the rising crime rate was not his responsibility.

Lieutenant Governor Mario Cuomo, the man Koch defeated to become Mayor, has suggested a standard by which history could judge a contemporary mayor of New York. In a speech to a group of bankers in January of 1980, Cuomo said: "Fiscal soundness is essential, and balanced budgets to achieve it are legally mandated. But, the purpose of government is to make reasonably secure the condition of people's lives. If it fails to do that, it fails utterly, no matter how neatly symmetrical the columns of its ledgers. A Triple A bond rating for a state that has failed to meet its basic needs would be an emblem of hypocrisy."

So yes, Edward Koch is very popular. Yes, he is personally honest, amusing, and diligent. Yes, the columns of his ledgers are neatly symmetrical. But he has pitted race against race to win political advantage. He has governed this injured city according to whatever will look good on the six o'clock television news. He has governed with what John Lindsay has movingly described as "a meanness of spirit and a pettiness of heart." And he has failed to make reasonably secure the condition of people's lives.

Ed Koch's biggest accomplishment has been his reputation.

New York Can Revive Itself

13

At the outset of the Reagan years, things have never looked more bleak for New York or, for that matter, the entire Northeast-Midwest quadrant of the country. Here severe recession has become permanent during the Nixon-Ford-Carter years. And as a result of the latest census, the few remaining shreds of Eastern political power will be drained away along with billions in Federal aid based exclusively on population, and not on indices of real need.

Yet New York need not continue to waste and die. There is nothing inevitable about the life cycle of cities. No one is predicting the death of Paris, London, Athens, or Rome, and they are thriving long after the colonial empires which once supported them have ceased to exist. Of course, they—like most European cities—receive significant aid from their national governments, and are a focus of national pride. In America, unfortunately, there is a deep, pernicious current in our history which despises cities because they are the entry point of new immigrants and new ideas. We received a bitter taste of this nativism in 1975 from Jerry Ford and the Yahoos in Congress who left the city twisting in the wind for ten months. We are likely to see a lot more of it under Ronald Reagan and the Senate of the Apes.

We are realists. We know that New York desperately needs to continue many of the existing Federal aid programs just to keep stumbling from day to day. If food stamps are abolished, or Social Security benefits reduced, or community development and mass transit operating funds discontinued, then millions of New Yorkers will suffer and tens of thousands will be pushed beyond the margin of subsistence. Therefore, the political history of the next four years will undoubtedly consist of a series of bitter rear-guard skirmishes to salvage a portion of what seriously imperfect programs currently provide.

At the same time, we refuse to abandon as utopian these fundamental reforms which the Left has fought to implement for the last decade.

263

Democratic national planning, public control of investment, energy conservation, full employment, an equitable tax structure, and a Federalized welfare system which provides a decent standard of living for those who can not work and their families (two-thirds of welfare recipients are children) are still the requisites for an acceptably just society as we enter the last two decades of the 20th century. We have no sympathy for those frightened liberal officeholders who cut their principles to fit the latest polls or election returns. By the same token, truly committed progressives have got to stop announcing good ideas and then failing to do the hard, gritty and often frustrating job of working at the grass roots to convince people of the need for change. Fortunately, during the 70s several groups have grown up which are laying the foundation for an effective national progressive movement by working on gut economic issues in neighborhoods and focusing on state and local legislatures as the training ground for the next generation of national politicians. Among these groups are the Citizens Alliance, the Citizen-Labor Energy Coalition, Campaign for Economic Democracy in California, the National Tenants Association, the Clamshell anti-nuke groups and the Conference on Alternative State and Local Policy.

While we support a national resistance to Reagan's corporate economic priorities which will unite minorities, Senior Citizens, labor, tenants, environmentalists, small businesses, students, and family farmers, we recognize that for at least four years New York will have to depend increasingly for its survival on the resources, community strengths, and skills and ideas of our own people and institutions. New York still has incredible wealth and if we can harness it to serve the people who created it we will not only survive but prosper. The critical ingredient lacking so far has been the political will to confront the permanent government and tell them that the needs and priorities of New York's citizens will supplant the corporate plundering imposed in the name of "fiscal austerity."

Here then is our agenda for New York City in the early 1980s. Each item is not only do-able, but eight of the nine won't cost anything, and some will actually generate more revenue.

1. Elect the MTA; Trade-in Westway; Salvage the Railroads

Nothing is more urgent to the survival of the entire metropolitan New York region than an immediate and substantial improvement in subway, bus, and commuter rail service. Ironically, the existence in place of an extensive mass transit system is probably our single most important competitive edge in attracting new businesses to the city. But because of almost unbelievably poor administration the system has now reached the point of virtual collapse, and is driving existing businesses away instead of inducing new ones to locate here.

From 1904 to 1953, the subways, first as private companies, and after the Depression as public service, were regulated by the Mayor and City Council (until 1938 called the Board of Aldermen). When then-Mayor Impelletieri wanted to raise the fare from a nickel to 10 cents, he won the cooperation of the Republican Administration in Albany in creating the Transit Authority to insulate the politicians from the public protest that erupted. A great propaganda blitz was launched to convince the public that taking mass transit "out of politics" would enable a disinterested chairman and board of directors to provide "businesslike" service. When the commuter rail lines were taken over by a state buyout after the scandalous Penn-Central bankruptcy, the current MTA was formed to run the entire regional transit system in 1968.

The authority was never "out of politics," of course, only outside the reach of democratic control. A series of highly political chairmen have managed the MTA to insulate the Governor and Mayor who appoint them from criticism as the fare has skyrocketed and service has plummetted. (William Ronan was Rockefeller's secretary and chief henchman; David Yunich was the former head of Macy's; Harold Fisher is the deal-maker, banker, and clubhouse lawyer *par excellence;* Richard Ravitch is a politically connected builder who made his fortune constructing government-subsidized housing.) Most of the Board members over the years have been bankers, political favorites or campaign contributors.

The big losers in this arrangement have been the riders, and to a lesser degree, the transit workers. Things have finally reached an intolerable nadir under Ravitch and MTA Executive Director John Simpson, a West Pointer and former lieutenant-colonel of engineers in Vietnam. They have become the Laurel and Hardy of transit management. The wheels fall off their subway cars; the motors fall out of their newest buses. If the lives and safety of 3.5 million people each day weren't involved, it might almost be funny.

Al Smith once said: "The answer to the problems of democracy is more democracy." We agree, and urge the creation of a 15-member board elected from single member districts based on population. To assure maximum turnout, the board should be chosen in gubernatorial years. The chairman should be chosen by a majority of the members and should be a full-time salaried official.

An elected board is no panacea, and is subject to the same pressures and temptations as any elected body. But we feel there would be several salutory effects: a significantly higher sensitivity to service complaints; greater concern for dangerous working conditions; an unwillingness to kowtow to the technical mumbo-jumbo of the bloated MTA bureaucracy and a demand for real answers; much greater openness with the press; and enhanced credibility in

266 The Permanent Government

the Legislature and Congress. The MTA's biggest problem—entirely merited by its performance—is that nobody, anywhere, trusts it anymore.

In *The Hot Rock*, a very funny comedy from the early '70s starring Robert Redford, a haughty African diplomat hires a bunch of bumbling jewel thieves to recover a precious diamond. At one point, frustrated by their constant failures, he declares "I've heard of habitual criminals, but I've never before encountered the habitual crime." Westway has become the "habitual crime" of New York politics.

In 1974, Hugh Carey campaigned against the highway, then did an abrupt about-face under pressure from the city's establishment before he was even sworn in as Governor. In 1977, Ed Koch vacilated over his long-term opposition to Westway during the first primary, but then made his famous "Westway will never be built" proclamation in the runoff to stem a drift of liberal voters to Mario Cuomo over the capital punishment issue. He then reversed himself and supported the $1.8 billion highway in an elaborate deal with Carey that involved non-existent capital funds for transit and a worthless pledge to maintain the 50 cent fare until 1982. When the fare went up, Koch was free again to play election year politics with the issue.

Meantime, the subway system is dying because it needs $1.4 billion each year in capital investment, and currently gets only about one-seventh of that amount, mostly from Washington. A trade-in of Westway for federal mass transit funds, even if part of the money were used to build an imaginative replacement for the old West Side highway like the River Road proposal, would still leave $1 billion for subway repairs. If these funds are lost to the Reagan budget-burners, then Carey and Koch will be directly responsible for whatever catastrophe befalls our crumbling regional transit system and its beleagured riders.

One final word about transportation. New York remains the only major American city without a direct link to the national rail freight system. This deficiency leads to truck-clogged streets, a shrinkage of the port and higher prices for everything we need from fresh vegetables to electric generators. Since 1919, the Port Authority has been mandated to build a freight tunnel under the Hudson. It has refused to do so and instead uses its billions to subsidize the automobile and shift blue collar jobs from New York to New Jersey. In an age of energy shortage, effective rail freight service becomes a critical lifeline.

We propose that the Port Authority be compelled to meet its 1919 mandate: sell the World Trade Center and put it back on the tax rolls; earmark the $1 billion plus from the sale to build the freight tunnel, the key to a rejuvenated rail system serving the city, the region (especially Long Island), and New England.

2. Pass Commercial Rent Controls, Save Controls on Apartments, Regulate Co-ops

New York's economy has been generally misunderstood. Behind the facade of the world's financial capital and the headquarters center for international capitalism lies the reality that 90 per cent of the city's businesses employ fewer than 20 workers. Firms this size tend to be undercapitalized and particularly sensitive to price increases. That's why the sudden jump in commercial rents in the last two years has played such havoc with the local economy.

The city is suffering from what one analyst calls an "historic" shortage of commercial space. The vacancy rate in the prime midtown office market is less than 1.5 per cent. In the traditionally "soft" Wall Street office market, which was overshadowed for years by the giant, and largely vacant bulk, of the now fully-rented World Trade Center, the vacancy rate has fallen to 3.7 per cent. The reason for these figures is easy to uncover: between 1969 and 1975, 50 million square feet of office space was constructed in New York; from 1975 through 1980 only 3.5 million square feet were built. Less than 11 million square feet are currently planned or under construction which means that the shortage will continue well into the '80s unless there is a catastrophic, 1930s Depression.

That's why landlords are able to demand 300 or 500 percent increases for lease renewals from small stores, offices, service firms and manufacturers. Complicating the picture even further is the disappearance of thousands of lofts and older office spaces which are being converted to luxury housing under the city's disastrous J-51 tax abatement program.

No one denies that landlords' costs are also rising, but at a rate below the Consumer Price Index which has been running at about 12 per cent for the last several years. The astronomical increases imposed on commercial tenants stem not from need, but from old-fashioned greed—"what the market will bear." As a result, small businesses either fold up, or where they can, pass the increased costs along as higher prices, giving the inflationary spiral another nasty little twist.

New York need not tolerate this destructive rent-gouging so that a handful of large landowners can become mega-millionaires. The State Legislature should immediately pass enabling legislation giving the city and other localities the right to enact commercial rent control statutes as a key component in a local war on inflation. Then the City Council should pass legislation proposed by Ruth Messinger which guarantees landlords a fair profit but protects tenants from massive rent increases, guarantees minimum services and prohibits arbitrary evictions.

The commercial rent situation underlines a crucial point about the kind of economy we actually live in, not the Adam Smith dreamworld inhabited by Ronald Reagan, Milton Friedman and the young fogeys of the new Republican right. Each major segment of our economy—cars, energy, food processing, communications, or in this case office buildings—is dominated by a relatively small group of individuals and businesses which is able to set prices and control supplies in order to maximize their profits. Helmsley Enterprises, directed by Harry Helmsley, controls one-quarter to one third of all the commercial properties in Manhattan. A handful of others—the Rudins, the Fishers, Seymour Durst, Sylvan Lawrence and Seymour Cohn, the Tishmans—control a large portion of the remaining properties. These are the men who decide what rents will be, not some mythical "invisible hand" of an equally mythical "free market." The only force capable of dealing with this kind of raw power is government mandated controls. That's why price controls, especially rent controls, are so bitterly anathema to corporate apologists: they know they work and are the quickest and most effective way to scotch inflation.

It has been relatively easy thus far to deflect public anger at inflation onto government and taxes. And most politicians have been delighted to take the easy way out, slashing taxes and shrinking services especially for the poor or powerless group like mental patients. Where there was bureaucratic fat or significant budget surpluses as in California the job was that much easier. But now the true impact of service cuts is being widely felt by the middle class as well as the poor. This means that if people want to escape the stranglehold of inflation, they must begin to control its true source: corporate manipulation of prices. And the one item that can be effectively controlled at the local level is rent, commercial or residential.

That's why it is so ironic that as hundreds of communities across the country enact or restore rent controls on local apartments, New York State threatens to abolish controls completely and the Mayor appoints a transparently pro-landlord majority to the Rent Guidelines Board and the Conciliation and Appeals Board which administer the rent stabilization system for 800,000 apartments, and rams an onerous fuel-cost passalong through the City Council for 350,000 rent controlled tenants.

Citywide the vacancy ratio is about 2.5 per cent, and in Manhattan south of 96th Street it is literally impossible to find a rental apartment. The latest rental housing survey commissioned by the city showed that average rents were rising at 23 per cent while operating expenses were rising at 16 per cent per year. Given those realities, rent controls must not only be continued, they must be strengthened to further protect tenants. The landlords, and the Mayor, will argue that rent controls cause abandonment. This isn't true as every major study by disinterested parties has shown over the last ten years. But abandonment is being caused by the failure to raise both the basic welfare grant and the rent allowance since 1974. The freeze on welfare rents means that mothers must choose between paying the landlord and feeding their kids. They invariably choose their kids. As Horton and Brecher have pointed out in *Setting Municipal Priorities—1981* ". . . by 1980 shelter allowances were far below the cost of even minimally acceptable housing. The result: a $1 billion annual gap between what poor people can afford to pay and what housing costs." Inflation has absorbed 50 per cent of the welfare check since 1975. Poverty, not rent control, is destroying our housing stock.

Another urgent housing issue which must be dealt with by the Legislature is the rapid proliferation of co-op plans which remove thousands of units of rental housing from the market each year and seriously shrink the housing options of middle class and working class families. The worst thing about the current co-oping rules is that they allow a minority of tenants and the landlord to strike a deal which may lead to the eviction of the majority of tenants in any building.

There is nothing wrong with co-ops *per se*. But in the current housing shortage, tenants may be blinded to the real long term costs they must absorb in paying both rent and a mortgage. Also there are no guarantees that the claims made by a landlord in a prospectus are accurate or that the tenants aren't going to be hit with totally unexpected expenses for the replacement of major capital systems such as a boiler, or major plumbing and wiring repairs. Most co-ops being sold today will require substantial refinancing within five years, when no one can forecast either the availability or cost of money.

We urge two major reforms. First, the Attorney General should be empowered to compel landlords to prove the validity of claims they make in an offering prospectus and declare any conflicts of interest which may exist such as relations with mortgagees. Second, the State should ban all eviction plan co-ops and protect the rights of all existing tenants until they choose to move voluntarily. Other cities have been forced to institute co-op and condominium conversion moratoriums. We need not go that far if we act decisively now to correct the unfairness and potential for consumer fraud in the existing system.

3. A Real, Well-financed War on Crime, and not the Demagoguery of Koch or the Gimmick Press Releases of Carey.

The Present Danger is not Russia or Cuba. It is the criminal class, the feral youth, incapable of guilt or remorse, who are destroying urban civilization. We have been hawks on crime for 15 years. We favored tougher, swifter punishment even while Jerry Rubin and Tom Hayden were saying armed robbers were revolutionaries and cops were "pigs." Today, just about nobody is a liberal on the crime issue. But still the problem is spiraling out of control, and government seems to have given up.

We recently had a private conversation with a friend who is a respected law enforcement official in New York City. He conceded that the criminal justice system can do nothing to reduce the rate of violent felonies that have increased during each of the last four years. But he said the demographics show that the birth rate began to decline about 1965, and this historical trend will soon cause a decline in the crime rate by itself, without any action or intervention by government. This is what we call the Margaret Sanger School of Law Enforcement. It is a fatalistic cop-out, a confession of futility and cynicism, but it is the way our leaders think in private.

In the January 19, 1981 issue of *New York* magazine, Nicholas Pileggi published a remarkable piece that said—and proved—for the first time, that the emperor has no clothes. Pileggi wrote:

> The brutal truth about crime in New York is that the police, the courts, and the prison system have given up. . . . As flabbergasting as the city's crime statistics may appear, they don't mirror the real number of crimes being committed on the sidewalks of New York. First, many victims don't bother to report crimes out of fear, or a what's-the-use sense of futility. And, in a way, they're right: it takes an average of six months and 17 court appearances to dispose of a felony arrest in New York. . . .
> Indisputably, the authorities made little if any attempt to capture those responsible for committing 335,775 burglaries in the 21 months ending last September, nor did they try to return the stolen property. . . the city has given notice to its citizens that they are no longer to be protected from burglars. Today, only a tiny fraction of the burglaries in the city are even investigated. . . This unannounced but all too real retreat from enforcement of the law against many crimes is demonstrable. . . .
> . . . . it turns out that during the average midnight-to-eight a.m. tour, there are only about 1,000 men patrolling the city. . . . According to the president of the Detectives' Endowment Association, Dennis Brennan, the Police Department is trying to get by as best it can strictly on public relations.

Pileggi's article went on to document that the Criminal Courts have stopped functioning, and that there are no cells available in the state prison system for new inmates. The law enforcement professionals have given up, and seem to be waiting for the demographics to eventually solve the problem for them.

And at the same time, Mayor Koch waves the bloody vest of a wounded cop and demands a death penalty that will do nothing to reduce crime except ventilate vengeance. And Governor Carey, in a manic phase, issues press releases and makes speeches that change nothing because they are conceived as business-as-usual headline grabbers and gimmicks.

But concrete steps can be taken, by government, to try and deter violent crime.

Certainty of punishment is a key. Not severity, but **certainty.** Everyone accused of a violent felony, or a crime committed with a gun, should be tried within 90 days. This would mean that weaker cases and non-violent cases that clog the court calendars would have to be disposed of. But the army of career criminals must know they face sure, swift punishment—including mandatory minimum sentences—if convicted. It would take a super-human effort by court administrators and prosecutors to implement a 90-day rule, but we think it would make a difference by making the risk of going to jail greater than before.

Second, we need money to deal with the breakdown of law enforcement. This is the only one of our ten remedies that will cost the taxpayers, but it is the one that needs it. If we can finance convention centers, and sports stadiums, and luxury hotels with bonds, then let us have a criminal justice bond issue. It can finance the new cells that prison systems must have. We also need more money for police. The police force should be brought back to the 31,000 members it had in 1972. Today it is 22,200.

There is no reason why we can't have qualified, hard-working judges on the State Supreme Court. The federal courts are filled with gifted jurists appointed on a merit basis. But small-minded politics and patronage considerations still determine Supreme Court judgeships in the city. The result is a large number of lazy, stupid, intemperate, malingering judges unfit for a crisis battlefront. A strict merit selection appointment system for state supreme court—and for appellate and administrative judgeships—would improve a system that both criminals and victims know does not work.

Self-help, citizen action groups like the Guardian Angels seem, on balance, to act as a deterrent to subway crime, and to reassure the public. The Angels offer a valuable role model of volunteer service that should be duplicated and encouraged, instead of being scorned, as they have been by Mayor Koch, who refused to even meet with their founder, Curtis Sliwa. As Lt. Governor Mario Cuomo said in a speech to the Brooklyn Bar Association: "It is a dramatic embarassment that riders in our subways should pray for the appearance of a band of young, minority people in red berets and T-shirts, because there are so few men and women in blue, provided by our government."

Yes, we believe that the root cause of crime is poverty. Yes, in the long run, the cure to crime is jobs, schools that teach, and the end to racism. But as a city and as a civilization, we must survive today and tonight. And although they cut against the grain of liberal sentiment, the most immediate remedies to the present danger are more police, more jail cells, trials in 90 days, mandatory minimum sentences—and a philosophy of certainty of punishment.

4. Reduce City Interest Payments by Stretching the Debt

Today the city faces a service crisis far more ominous than the so-called "fiscal crisis" we faced in 1975. We need more cops, judges and prosecutors to stem the rising tide of crime. We need more building inspectors to keep people from freezing to death in their apartments. We need more health workers to replace the 15,000 workers in hospitals and health stations whose jobs were abolished in the last five years. (Tuberculosis is on the rise again, in a particular virulent and infectious form, after 16 years of decline). We need more young, dedicated teachers who believe that all children can learn so that a new generation will be prepared to perform the complex tasks of the 21st Century. We need ambulance drivers to save lives, and botanists to save our dying parks. The list could go on for pages. We haven't even begun to talk of the vast investments in construction and machinery necessary to keep this giant city functioning.

The critical question is: where will the money come from to meet the growing service gap? Ray Horton and Chuck Brecher are two professors who have produced a series of volumes dealing with the city's fiscal problems which have been praised by politicians and editorial writers. In their latest volume, *Setting Municipal Priorities-1981*, they propose that the banks and union pension funds which hold the bulk of the city's long-term debt be asked to renegotiate their holdings so that the city could pay less in interest costs each year while extending the life span of the bonds.

This approach was already applied successfully once, in 1977, and interest payments are reduced by $160 million in each fiscal year from 1978-1982. In spite of this, these bonds have been very profitable for the pension funds, and even more so for the banks since they are tax-free. Horton and Brecher suggest that a new restructuring could achieve similar savings well into the '80s and provide a sizable chunk for maintaining services. Some of this money might be necessary to sustain services destroyed by Reagan budget cuts.

So far the banks, the unions and the Koch administration have all rejected the idea. But, in fact, all three have much to gain. The unions could preserve jobs endangered by a new round of budget cuts. The banks are users of services, just like other businesses. At a time when rising interest rates and credit restrictions are making banks rich and everyone else poor, it might even be good corporate relations to come riding to the city's aid on a white charger. Stranger miracles have happened.

And even the Mayor must understand that yelling "Capital punishment!" at a mugger isn't a suitable substitute for the 9,000 cops we've lost since 1972.

5. Restore UDC to Its Original Purpose of Building Affordable Rental Housing for the Poor and the Middle Class

The Urban Development Corporation (UDC) was created by the state legislature in April of 1968 as a so-called "memorial" to the memory of Martin Luther King. It was given extraordinary powers to condemn private property, issue tax-exempt bonds—over-ride local zoning laws, and be exempt from local taxes. Its mandate was to rebuild the slums and finance new housing units.

But under its current chairman, Richard Kahan, the UDC in 1980 did not build one unit of housing for the poor. With $500 million in bonding authority, and $1 billion in construction projects, the UDC has become a secretive, unaccountable, self-prepetuating fourth branch of government. It has become almost a private bank that finances luxury and leisure projects for permanent government insiders.

The UDC is currently financing: the new Manhattan convention center, the luxury Portman Hotel; the luxury Grand Hyatt Hotel owned by Donald Trump; the new outdoor football stadium in Syracuse; a new corporate headquarters for the infamous poisoner of Love Canal—Hooker Chemical Company in Niagara Falls; the Albany Hilton Hotel; three suburban shopping malls; a convention center in Rochester; and about 100 other commercial projects.

UDC's chairman, 34 year-old Kahan freely conceedes that his authority has "clearly undergone a 180 degree shift" from providing a public benefit— housing at public cost—to "building large public works."

Before Kahan becomes a new Robert Moses, the elected state and city governments ought to give the UDC another 180 degree spin and return it to the noble purpose for which it was intended and originally created under its founding legislation in 1968.

UDC should use its vast wealth and powers to build housing—senior citizen housing, middle income housing, low-income housing. It should restore and rehabilitate existing housing, and the small commercial strips that are the heartbeat of urban neighborhoods. It should finance hotels for middle class tourists, instead of hotels for the mega-elite like the Grand Hyatt. It could begin to rebuild the South Bronx. It could even finance sweat equity projects, libraries, community health clinics—almost anything except what it is now being used for.

It is an obscenity that an agency that was created to honor Martin King is being used to subsidize an expansion of the Hooker Chemical Company, while it ignores the poor.

6. Require All Future Municipal Government Employees to Live in New York City

When Ed Koch was running for Mayor he claimed that 40 per cent of the city's police officers lived outside New York City. Some of the top management of the MTA currently lives in the suburbs. Present estimates are that anywhere from 10 to 30 per cent of the city's workforce live outside of the five boroughs. This means they spend the salary we taxpayers pay them in New Jersey, Long Island and in Westchester. Their children go to suburban schools. They develop suburban mentalities that either fear or loathe the citizens who employ them.

The time has come to revive the old Lyons Law for all **prospective** city employees. Residency laws adopted by Chicago and Philadelphia have been found to be legal by the courts. By most accounts they generate pride among city workers, and may even improve productivity.

In 1978, Mayor Koch asked the state legislature to pass a **retroactive** residency law that would have imposed unreasonable hardships and have been unfair. That rigid approach predictably failed to become law. But a prospective residency law makes sense psychologically and economically. And it would have the eventual affect of making the municipal union leadership more accurately reflect the city's actual population. It would hasten the day of black and Hispanic leadership in the transit workers union, in the correction officers union, and ultimately in the police and teachers unions. This democratic consequence of a residency law is, we suspect, the real reason that Koch and most of the city's establishment have ceased to fight for it, even though it would obviously benefit the city's economy.

7. Take the Profit Out of Arson

In 1979 there were 10,000 arson fires in New York buildings. Fifty people died in those fires, hundreds were injured. Property losses were almost $100 million. We've never heard a professional fire investigator say that less than 25 per cent of these fires are set for profit; the figure is probably closer to 50 per cent. But less than 2 per cent of these arson fires led to convictions.

Arson is one of the hardest crimes to solve. First you have to prove it was arson, and then you have to prove who set the fire after most of the evidence has gone up in the blaze. Professional arsonists, like big drug dealers, will often use teenagers to perform the actual crime.

The best way to reduce the arson plague is to remove the profit. Surprisingly, this could be done fairly easily. The State Legislature can require that landlords collecting fire claims use them exclusively to repair or replace the burned building, instead of just walking away with the money. Bronx DA Mario Merola has estimated that this one reform would reduce arson by 25 percent.

Another proposed law would require insurance companies to notify local tax authorities before paying fire claims, so that any liens against the building for unpaid property tax, emergency fuel deliveries, etc. could be collected. Since many landlords milk a building and let the tax arrears build up before they torch it, this would at least skim part of the profit from arson.

Ideally, of course, the insurance industry would carefully screen applicants and work closely with law enforcement officials to pinpoint potential arson sites. But the insurance companies have preferred to redline massive areas of the city, forcing everyone into the high risk pool known as the FAIR (Fair Access to Insurance Requirements) Plan, which is permitted to charge twice the normal insurance rates and higher, yet still suffers immense underwriting losses. The insurance industry talks tough, but does little to combat arson.

Senators Charles Percy and Sam Nunn are sponsoring S. 2992 which would make arson for profit a federal crime. The Percy-Nunn bill would give the FBI direct jurisdiction, and would enable prosecutors to attack arson rings and organized crime which plays a significant role in arson insurance scams across the nation. We think this is a good idea; *The New York Times* doesn't.

Finally, the city needs to spend more of its budget on hiring more fire marshals, Police, and the arson strike force to let the professional "torches" know it means business. As fires spread throughout the Lower East Side, Williamsburg, Bushwick, Morris Heights, the East New York section of Brooklyn and other communities, we have only approximately 165 fire marshals to investigate almost 115,000 fires. In 1979, when the City Council gave Koch additional funds for more marshals he refused to spend them.

A gifted new Fire Commissioner named Joe Hynes, appointed in November of 1980, has made arson his top priority, and has done more about it in three months than his two predecessors did in eight years.

8. Invest Municipal Pension Funds to Rebuild New York

Historically New York has been the nation's greatest exporter of capital. Money generated here built the first canals and railroads that opened the West and the South. Today our capital is being exported to construct housing in Florida and shopping centers in Texas. At the same time federal government siphons billions in excess taxes from our city and region to provide aerospace payrolls in California and giant water projects in the arid states of the Southwest.

New York is bleeding to death from this massive capital hemorrhage. Citizen movements have tried, and largely failed, to stop bank redlining. Jimmy Carter called the federal tax code "a national disgrace" but after his four years in the White House it is more unjust than ever. The Reagan Years promise only to make the banks less accountable and the tax loopholes wider. We must look elsewhere for survival.

Employee pension funds are the largest pool of capital in the nation. And the five pension funds covering most New York City employees, currently valued at $12 billion, are the third largest retirement system in the United States. (The city owes an additional $1.2 billion to the New York City Employee Retirement System, the largest of the plans, which it is paying gradually over the next several years).

When the city was on the verge of bankruptcy, the pension funds were dragged, kicking and screaming, into buying large chunks of MAC bonds. In retrospect, these were an excellent investment, and earned higher rates of return than many corporate bonds or stocks. They also were at least partly backed by federal guarantees. But aside from this profitable sacrifice, the pension funds, which are jointly administered by union trustees and city officials, have done very little investing in New York City. For instance, while 43 per cent of the assets are in taxable U.S. and corporate bonds, and 13 per cent in corporate stocks, only 3 per cent are in mortgages. Two mortgages, a $54 million mortgage on the Burlington Building and a $15 million mortgage on a new office building at 919 Third Avenue, make up 42 percent of the conventional mortgages granted by the NYCERS fund.

By the same token, an earlier study showed that 40 per cent of the common stocks owned by the pension funds were invested in companies that were non-union, occupational safety and health law violaters, equal employment opportunity violaters or major lenders or investors in South Africa.

Now a bright young budget analyst, Dan McCarthy, working as a consultant to Councilmember Ruth Messinger, has come up with an important new study that shows how the city employee pension funds could invest up to $100 million in rehabilitating housing and making loans to small businesses in the next two years. While the $100 million is less than 1 per cent of the funds' total assets, it would represent a significant increase in the severely limited monies available to aid development in these two critical areas.

These investments would be fully insured by existing government agencies. The housing loans would be underwritten by the State of New York Mortgage Agency and the city's Rehabilitation Mortgage Insurance Corporation. The small business loans would be insured by the Federal Small Business Administration. That way the funds and the pensioners wouldn't lose a penny if the loans defaulted. McCarthy has also worked out a clever scheme to provide the funds with competitve rates of return between these loans and competing investments using targeted rent subsidies and other existing Federal programs.

The Messinger-McCarthy plan is particularly enticing as an alternative to a plan offered by Controller Jay Goldin which would invest $250 million in pension fund monies in securities issued by the Government National Mortgage Association and backed by bank mortgages on one-family homes. These securities are already avidly sought by private investors and adding city pension monies to the market would just displace these private funds for more Sunbelt investment.

Capital is such a precious resource that we must carefully target the one major new source we have available to us. Clearly housing rehabilitation and small business development are two areas totally neglected by the banks and traditional sources of financing. The pension funds have an opportunity here to not only secure their members retirement, but to provide them with an improved quality of life right now.

9. Abolish Unjustified Real Estate Tax Exemptions

Because of tax exemptions about 40 per cent of New York City's property is untaxed. A decade ago it was only 33 per cent. The value of this tax-free real estate has risen from about $16 billion to $25 billion. Tax-exempt property includes land and buildings owned by religious organizations; charitable organizations, hospitals, universities, foundations, the state, the federal government, public authorities, and foreign governments. All these facilities receive city services—police and fire protection, sanitation collections, sewer and water services—paid for by the taxpayers.

In 1978, Mayor Koch and Council President Bellamy made a tentative, one-shot gesture towards closing some of these unjustified tax loopholes. They wrote letters to the owners of 2,300 tax-free parcels, and suggested they consider making "voluntary payments" in lieu of taxes. These 2,300 parcels were valued at more than $2 billion, and would yield about $180 million each year in tax revenues if they were fully taxable. The richest and most able to pay among these property owners are: Columbia University, NYU, Lincoln Center, Presbyterian Hospital, Mount Sinai Hospital, Rockefeller University, and New York Hospital. But not one of them agreed to make a voluntary payment in response to the polite 1978 letters. And now the issue of tax-exempt properties has vanished from the agenda of new revenue sources.

Some of these exemptions are justified. Some charitable organizations deserve their exemption because of the good works they do. Some smaller organizations clearly cannot afford to surrender their exemption.

But we believe that a portion of these exemptions are unwarranted in a time of budget cutbacks and general sacrifice. Income producing apartment buildings owned by universities and hospitals should be subject to taxation at the normal rate. Obviously affluent, elite institutions, like Lincoln Center, NYU and Columbia should be required to pay their fair share of taxes. So should the federal government and foreign governments. Foundations like Rockefeller, and Carnegie, with millions in assets, should pay taxes. Any swami or yogi who knows a tax lawyer has a religious exemption, and these should be rescinded. So, too, should the exemptions, enjoyed by Rev. Moon's Unification Church and by the Church of Scientology.

About 18 per cent of all the tax-free property is owned by public authorities like UDC, Battery Park City, and the Port Authority. Through political pressure and, if necessary, through planned shrinkage for the elite, these prosperous authorities should be compelled to pay real estate taxes. Currently not paying their fair share of revenue to the City are: the World Trade Center, JFK Airport, and La Guardia Airport. And the Port Authority has $4.5 billion in assets, and an annual profit of $500 million.

A conservative estimate is that perhaps $200 million a year could be recovered if all the unworthy, political, and frivolous tax exemptions were abolished.

If New York can freeze the wages of municipal workers, if it can shrink the police force by 9,000, if it can balance the budget a year early, if it can shut down schools and hospitals, then it surely can arrive at a method and summon the will, to abolish undeserving tax exemptions.

The future is unknowable. With Antonio Gramsci, we are pessimists of the intelligence, and optimists of the will.

They have done their worst to us—the banks; Nelson Rockefeller; Lindsay, Beame, Nixon, Carter, Koch, Reagan, Stockman, and lesser politicians; the Mafia; the Sunbelt; OPEC; the permanent government. Our services have been cut. Cops and firemen are unemployed. People are dying for want of a bed or a night nurse in municipal hospitals. Our children are not learning, fifty to a classroom. The upward mobility that came with a free college education is gone. Democracy is diminished. The subway system is collapsing. Crime is out of control.

But we are still standing. We are still here. We are survivors.

These ideas, these remedies offered, will not become law easily or quickly. We cannot trust our leaders to do all this just because it is logical, or necessary, or promised.

The most important lesson we have learned, as political citizens, is this:

Reform—change for the better—comes only when movements of common people rally around an idea and create new leaders from the bottom up. Movements of ordinary people, acting out of self-interest, can write law. The moral authority of exemplary action can change lives.

Leaders sell out. Leaders get tired. Leaders get killed. But movements of our countrymen stopped the Lower Manhattan Expressway, passed the Voting Rights Act of 1965, ended the Vietnam war.

From Rosa Parks starting the Montgomery bus boycott to Frank Serpico exposing police corruption, to Crystal Lee Sutton organizing workers against J. P. Stevens, common people saying *Enough!* have transformed consciousness, and altered history.

Index

)